THE GOLD OF THE BANDAS:
THE HISTORY OF THE NUTMEG

FSC
www.fsc.org
MIX
Papier aus ver-
antwortungsvollen
Quellen
Paper from
responsible sources
FSC® C105338

THE GOLD OF THE BANDAS:
THE HISTORY OF THE NUTMEG

The forgotten islands
that once made world history

by
Horst H. Geerken

Translated by
Bill McCann

A BukitCinta Book

Deutsche Bibliothek bibliographical information:
The Deutsche Bibliothek lists this publication in the
German National Bibliography; detailed bibliographical
data are available on the Internet at http://dnb.dbd.de.

© 2021 Horst H. Geerken, 53177 Bonn
2nd edition 2025
The first edition was published in German with the title 'Das Gold der Bandas:
Die Geschichte der Muskatnuss' in 2019

All photographs unless otherwise labelled © Horst H. Geerken
Layout & Design: Arthur Bartl
Editing: Michaela Mattern and Barbara Bode
Cover Design: Barbara Bode using a photograph by Abba Rizal Bahalwan
Set in Adobe Garamond Pro
Publisher: BoD · Books on Demand GmbH, Überseering 33,
22297 Hamburg, bod@bod.de
Print: Libri Plureos GmbH, Friedensallee 273, 22763 Hamburg
ISBN: 978-3-8192-9728-1

Contents

Thanks

My thanks first of all to Abba Rizal Bahalwan, the proprietor of the Cilu Bintang Estate and chairman of the Banda Neira Foundation, an organisation devoted to conserving the history of the Banda Islands. He is an inexhaustible source of information about this little archipelago in the Banda Sea and its painful history. I was pampered for three weeks in his hotel and Abba was always there with help and advice. He lent me picture material and other documentary material to help in my investigations.

My thanks to countless people, from simple fishermen, officials, market women, teachers and children on all the Banda Islands to the minister at the church in Banda Neira, who are too many to name individually. I had long conversations with many of them. Each of them had a different story about their family history: pieces of a puzzle which eventually came together to form a whole.

My special thanks also to Pastor Cornelis J. Böhm MSC of Ambon, an expert on Rumphius' history. He is the last Dutch minister living in the Moluccas. He has provided me with documents about Georg Eberhard Rumpf, also called Rumphius, which have found their place in this book.

Extra thanks to Michaela Mattern and Barbara Bode for proofreading and many helpful suggestions and to Arthur Bartl for the layout of the book.

Thanks, too, to my translator, Bill McCann, for working on languages from Middle High German to Portuguese and Dutch as well as early modern and contemporary German.

Then I would like to thank my brother Hartmut, who frequently managed to contribute new information about the subject of the book from his collection of antique encyclopaedias.

Thanks, too, to Margareta Krapf-Mlosch, who gave me a useful lead in finding a title for the book.

Thanks to Professor Meinolf Schumacher of the University of Bielefeld, who produced one of the translations from Middle High German used in the German version of the book, and to Cornelia Biegler-König and Marieke Weiß for making the introduction.

Last but not least I am very grateful to my friend Torsten, who was always ready to help me with computer problems.

I am also grateful to the staff of all the archives listed in Chapter 26. They were always ready to grant me access to old documents.

Horst H. Geerken, April 2021

Translator's Foreword

Little did I think, when I first started translating Horst's work over ten years ago, that I would still be at it over ten years and five books later. And here is the sixth. As always with Horst's books, new and fascinating challenges arose, this time mainly with early modern documents in a variety of languages, with botanical terminology, numismatics, and with Dutch. It was also a delight to encounter an old friend, Wolfram von Eschenbach, whose work I loved as an undergraduate, and which has formed a major part of my teaching and research over more than forty years. And I am grateful to Horst for giving me new insights into the book's cultural background. The extract printed in Chapter 10 comes towards the end of the romance of *Parzival*, and in the past I simply looked at the list of spices found there as a touch of exotic colour. Now the significance of spices for medieval society has come into much sharper focus.

Some details of presentation to help the reader:

Italics are used for foreign words and phrases, the titles of books, the names of ships and, most frequently, for quotations.

Square brackets [ ] are used for the translation of words and phrases that are given in the original language in the text, for author's notes, and for interpolations by the translator.

In the original German edition, many of the footnotes explain English terms that might not be familiar to a German reader. I have done the reverse with terms as diverse as *Maultaschen* and pudding (which means something completely different in German). Any errors in this respect are entirely my responsibility.

Bill McCann, Advent 2020

1. Prologue

Stefan Zweig begins his biography of the early explorer Ferdinand Magellan[1] with the words: 'In the beginning was the spice'. As he explicitly points out, this applies not only to Magellan, but also to all the early explorers, like Christopher Columbus, Bartolomeu Dias[2] and Vasco da Gama, who all set sail into uncharted waters in a frenzied hunt for precious spices, which in those days were more profitable than gold or silver.

This, of course, brought fakes into the picture. The 'forgers' produced nutmeg made of flour, clay, dyes and nutmeg powder, using cheap worm-eaten nutmegs, a ploy that constantly deceived their unsuspecting customers. Even experts sometimes fell for the deception. In 1860 a whole cargo of fake nutmeg arrived in England from Canton in China. The 'nuts' were all made of wood.[3] The holes that had been made in rejects by insects and worms were often filled with fat, flour and chalk – the nuts were then sold as top-class quality.

Powdered nutmeg is adulterated even now: they don't just grind worm-eaten rejects and poor-quality nuts with very little aroma – the powder is often cut with cheap turmeric.

Today is Boxing Day 2018. I'm sitting on the terrace outside my room on the Cilu Bintang Estate on the island of Banda Neira[4], one of the Banda Islands in the southern Moluccas in modern Indonesia. This was once one of the Spice Islands the Europeans were so madly keen to find. They form the most distant and at the same time the most fascinating group of islands in the Indonesian Archipelago. In front of me are the ruins of the old Dutch Fort Nassau and behind them, separated from us only by a narrow strip of water, the conical shape of the mighty volcano Gunung Api[5], the fire mountain, thrusts skywards like a pyramid from the deep azure blue waters of the Banda Sea. This volcano has in the past brought many a disaster on the Bandas. If I direct my gaze to the right of Gunung Api, I can see the massive second fort on the island, the restored Fort Belgica[6] on its hill.

---

1   Stefan Zweig, *Magellan: Der Mann und seine Tat* [Magellan: the man and his achievements]

2   Also Diaz

3   Elsner, *Die Praxis des Chemikers* [Practical Chemistry], 1895, S. 496

4   Also Bandanaira

5   Also Banda Api

6   The word Belgica goes back to the '17 Provinces of the Burgundian Netherlands', which once encompassed Belgium and Luxemburg as well as the modern Netherlands.

Exceptionally, the sea is not azure blue today, because it's been raining all day. It's the rainy season, the western monsoon. The hotel employees – all Muslims – have done their very best to conjure up a Christmas tree out of a native cedar decked with paper stars. This, together with the gloomy weather, makes for a degree of Christmas spirit even this close to the Equator. Apart from me the only other guests are a nice married couple from Stuttgart, Gunter and Karin. We get on very well. Three Swabians on these forgotten islands at once, we certainly have to drink to that! Gunter Haug is a bestselling author[7] and journalist, and has written an article about me and the Bandas in the *Stuttgarter Zeitung*.[8]

In recent days I have managed to collect a great deal of information about the Banda Islands, and a rainy day like today is a good opportunity to start on a new book – this one about the Banda Islands and the nutmeg. Boat trips to the other islands would be impossible today because of the heavy swell. I've been at my base on the Cilu Bintang Estate a good two weeks now. From here on Banda Neira I've made day trips to the other blissfully solitary islands in weather that has been mostly fabulous. I collected information and conducted lots of interviews. Now I need to get my notes down on paper. Abba, the proprietor here, has set up a little corner with a bright light in my spacious room for me to write in, and has provided me with books from his library.

But who is aware of the Banda Islands these days, eleven tiny islands, over 2,500 kilometres and two time zones to the east of the capital Jakarta, so tiny that they are shown on hardly any maps? Only six of them are inhabited, with a total population of about 14,000. I have never yet met an Indonesian who knows these forgotten islands and where they are located, even though Banda Neira with Fort Belgica and the Gunung Api volcano appear on the Indonesian 1,000 rupiah banknote.

It was all too much even for the post office in Ubud on Bali when I tried to hand in a parcel of some of my books for Abba in Banda Neira, even though there is a post office with a postcode in Banda Neira. The little Banda Archipelago is even less known abroad. Even in Indonesian terms they are at the end of the world. And yet 350 years ago they made world history. At that time they were – as we will see – on everyone's lips! A little nut, the nutmeg, once changed the world.

Illustrations next side:
Ill. 1-1, My room in the Cilu Bintang Estate
Ill. 1-2, My 'writing corner'

---

7   www.gunter-haug.de
8   See Chapter 25, Appendix I

Ill. 1-3
View of the Gunung Api
volcano from the terrace
of my room in the Cilu
Bintang Estate

Ill. 1-4
There was even a degree of
Christmas spirit

Ill. 1-5, 1,000 rupiah banknote⁹ with Fort Belgica in Banda Neira and the Gunung Api volcano

These days we can buy spices of all kinds for a couple of euros in the supermarket. But who of us is aware that several hundred years ago a number of European states embarked on a race to find the Spice Islands? Spices were the reason for wars, conquests and ruthless murder. Does anyone know that for a long time the Banda Islands were the only place on earth where nutmeg[10] grew and that nutmeg was worth more than gold; that out of pure greed the Dutch perpetrated the first genocide in modern history; that the only inhabitants of the Bandas are now the descendants of the slaves shipped there by the Dutch and Arabian merchants; that one of the islands, Pulau Run, was once exchanged for Manhattan in America, or that the Bandas were once the most expensive real estate in the world? There are many more stories about these little islands, all of them world-shaking events! As I said, a little nut changed the world, and there are exciting tales to be told!

Because of the precious nutmeg, things rarely happened on the Bandas without some kind of violence. The soil of the islands is drenched in blood, blood which stains the hands of the ruthless Dutch colonial power. They would use any means to establish and enforce their power with the thunder of the cannon. The inhabitants were mistreated and enslaved. But there have

---

9   The reverse of the banknote shows the Indonesian freedom fighter Tjut Meutia (aka Cut Nyak Meutia/Meuthia). She was arrested by the Dutch and executed in 1906. Today she is honoured as a national heroine.

10   Nutmeg is called *pala* in Bahasa Indonesia and *jebug garum* in Balinese; the Latin term is *myristica fragrans*.

been very few reports of this, as the Dutch to this very day have known very well how to sweep their past atrocities under the carpet. Here on the islands, however, these shameful deeds have not been forgotten. Every schoolchild is taught about the massacres committed by the Dutch. In every conversation I had here I was first asked what my nationality was. When I said that I was German, their expressions brightened. The Dutch are always treated with a degree of scepticism here.

Even in more recent times, in the 1930s, the Banda Islands had a role to play. It was to these remote, forgotten islands that the Dutch exiled influential Indonesian nationalists who advocated Indonesian independence.

The view of the volcano from my terrace in the Cilu Bintang Estate is stunning. I have seen this view in my dreams from my earliest childhood, but it is only now that I can be sure that it was this actual view that fascinated me as a child. When she was young, my mother spent several long periods staying with our relatives who lived in the Keizergracht in Amsterdam, and even learned to speak Dutch. She must have been fascinated by the Dutch East Indies, because every time she returned home – as she later told me – she brought books about the Dutch colony with her. These books filled a large proportion of the bookshelves in our home in Stuttgart. Until our home was destroyed in the Second World War, some of these books lay on a little table in what we called the study. As a little boy – I hadn't started school and couldn't read yet – I would leaf through those books and marvel at all the exotic pictures. One thing I found particularly impressive was old drawings of a fire-spewing volcano rising vertically out of the sea beside a narrow strait next to an island. I would browse through the books almost every day, always looking at that picture, which is why that landscape is etched in my memory even today.

And then, when my geography teacher in my first years at the secondary school in Schwäbisch Gmünd made the Malay Archipelago the focus of his teaching, that island world with its nutmeg cast its spell over me. I kept discovering interesting information which made my desire to visit the Banda Islands and write the history of the unassuming nutmeg ever more intense.

It is interesting to note that in all the old Dutch illustrations Gunung Api is active, spewing fire and ashes. An old tradition says that every time the Dutch fleet sailed into Banda there was a major eruption. Was this how the volcano showed that it was angry and disapproved of the actions of the Dutch and the way they ruled the islands? Because the Dutch would resort to any means to maintain their power and to enforce their monopoly.

Ill. 1-6, The Gunung Api Volcano, separated from the island Banda Neira (with Fort Belgica) by only a small strip of water.[11]

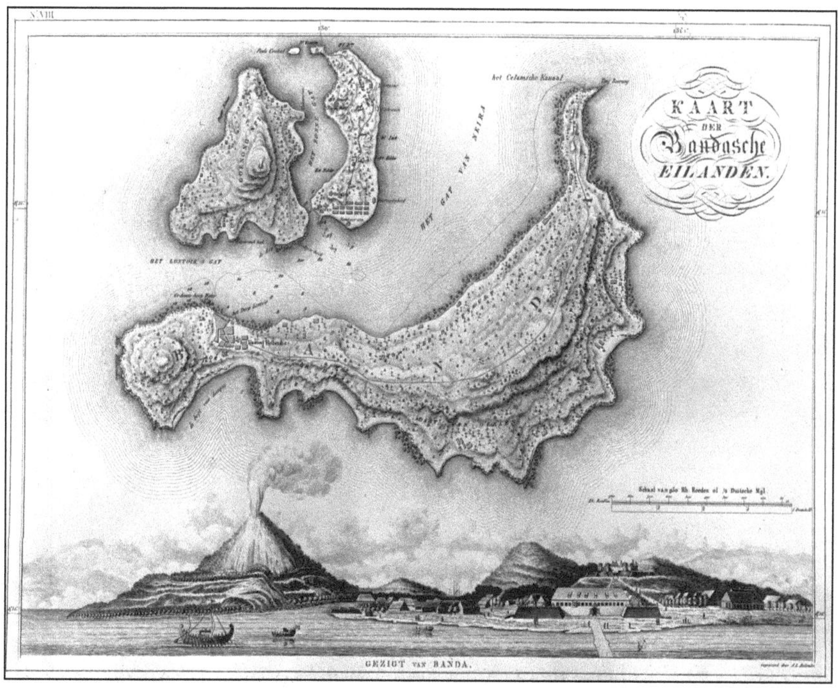

Ill. 1-7, 1820 map showing Banda Neira, Gunung Api and Banda Besar

---

11   Engraving from 1655

Ill. 1-8, The narrow strait between the Gunung Api volcano (left) and the main island Banda Neira[12]

Ill. 1-9, A 1724 etching of Banda Neira with Fort Belgica on its hill together with the Gunung Api Volcano

12 Lithograph based on a painting by Josias Cornelis Rappard, 1883-1889, Wikimedia Commons

Ill. 1-10, Sailing ships at anchor in the narrow strait between the Gunung Api Volcano and the island of Banda Neira.[13]

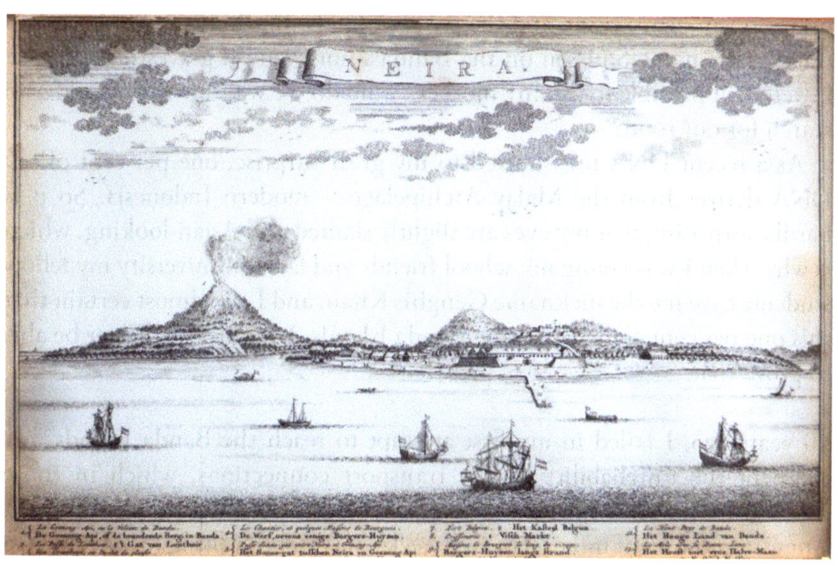

Ill. 1-11, Banda Neira with the Gunung Api volcano

---

13   Etching from *Atlas pittoresque*, 1699, Pl. 114

Now I'm sitting here, looking at the beautiful landscape, and I'm certain that the illustrations in the book I looked at as a child must have been of the Banda Islands. The landscape and the pictures in my memory are exactly the same. Were my Dutch relatives somehow connected with the Banda Islands? Had someone from the family worked here? Is this why my mother kept bringing books about this region from Holland? Was this the reason I had always felt drawn here? Unfortunately, I can no longer ask my mother about this, and our relations in Holland are all dead. I don't even know the name of our Dutch family. I only know that my mother's aunt, a Mannhardt by birth, lived in Amsterdam with her Dutch husband. If I had known more, I could have researched further here on the islands, as there were several Dutch families who lorded it over the Bandas until the Japanese occupation in the Second World War: families like the Decmaars, Van den Broeckes[14], Koks or Baadillas.

I do at least know that one of my maternal ancestors, Johann Wilhelm Mannhardt[15], married the daughter of a Dutch merchant who had business in the Netherlands East Indies: she was called Anna van der Smissen[16]. Her father, born around 1730, was persecuted in Holland because of his Mennonite beliefs. He fled to Germany and founded a lucrative trading business in Hamburg. Since he mainly traded in spices, I suspect that there was a link between van der Smissen and the Banda Islands. But I have so far found no trace of the name Smissen on the Bandas, not even on gravestones. I wish it were still possible to ask my mother. Why do we wait until we're older to search for our roots?

As a recent DNA test showed to my great surprise, one per cent of my DNA derives from the Malay Archipelago – modern Indonesia. So it is hardly surprising that my eyes are slightly slanted and Asian-looking, which is why when I was young my school friends and later at university my fellow students gave me the nickname Genghis Khan, and I am almost certain that this one per cent comes from the Banda Islands. I wonder if I'll ever be able to prove that.

20 years ago, I failed in my first attempt to reach the Banda Islands, because of the unreliability of the transport connections, which in those days were even more unreliable than they are today. My long-term partner Annette and I spent more than two weeks in Ambon waiting for a chance to

---

14 Pieter Van den Broecke (1585-1640), proprietor of nutmeg plantations on Pulau Ai and Banda Besar.
15 1760-1831
16 1771-1843

get to the Bandas. But unfortunately we had to return to Germany without any success.

Since the history of the Bandas is so interesting and varied, and also so terrible, I will concentrate in this book on this little group of eleven tiny islands. It provides quite enough material! The other spice islands, like Tidore or Ternate, where cloves are grown, have equally interesting histories, but to describe them as well would be beyond the scope of this book.

This is the history of the nutmeg! In centuries past the nutmeg was always of great significance, not only for the conserving and seasoning of dishes, but also and especially in medicine and as an aphrodisiac. And the only place in the world the nutmeg grew was here, on the tiny Banda Islands.

The Kingdom of the Netherlands has 12 provinces, two of which are Noord and Zuid Holland. From 1588 to 1795 the region was called the Republic of the Seven United Netherlands. After its conquest by French troops in 1795 what is today the Netherlands became the Batavian Republic. Since the Holland region made by far the greatest contribution to the colonising of the Netherlands East Indies and to the Dutch economy, as well as being the most influential, I will from now on – for the sake of simplicity – use the term Holland to refer to the whole Dutch kingdom.

The situation in Great Britain is much the same. England, Wales, Scotland and Northern Ireland are separate countries. England is only the southern part of the larger island. In 1707 the Kingdom of Great Britain was created out of England, Wales and Scotland, and in 1800 Ireland was added, after which the union was known as the United Kingdom. Following on the Irish independence struggle, the island of Ireland was divided into the Republic of Ireland and Northern Ireland in 1921. Since then[17] England, Wales, Scotland and Northern Ireland have formed the political unit known as the United Kingdom.

Since the expeditions to Southeast Asia mainly sailed from England and many of the most important personalities involved came from that part of the country I will once more for simplicity refer to England rather than Great Britain or the United Kingdom.

---

17 The situation in 2020, though this may change due to complications following Brexit.

2. How spices came to Europe

Spices have always possessed a magic of their own. Babylonian cuneiform tablets list more than 30 recipes including spices like coriander or caraway. Even in those days people wanted to have fine, tasty food. Hildegard von Bingen[18] also frequently mentions nutmeg, cloves and cinnamon in her medical recipes. In the Middle Ages the fragrance of nutmeg and mace[19] – like all the spices from the Moluccas – exuded its own special magic. For most of us, the scent of nutmeg, cloves and cinnamon still conjures up the oriental tales of the *Thousand and One Nights* and Sinbad the Sailor.

In France, a grocer's shop is still called an *épicerie* [spice shop]. In my younger days grocers' shops in Germany were called *Kolonialwarenladen* [colonial stores] and they always had a wonderful smell of oriental spices. But why were they still called *Kolonialwarenladen* as late as the 1960s? By then Germany had long ceased to have any colonies! The sago packaging had the Bismarck Archipelago as its country of origin and a colour picture of two dusky natives hollowing out a tree trunk. As a child, I was really impressed: there were places where you could even eat tree trunks! Today the island of Ceram in the Moluccas is one of the main regions where sago palms are cultivated.

Nutmeg and mace were not just used to spice up the rather monotonous cuisine of the time, but also in preserving food and as medication for digestive problems, colds and other illnesses. A whole cornucopia of diseases were treated with nutmeg in those days.

In ancient Rome cinnamon was a popular perfume, and as late as the 18th century wealthy women in Germany wore a silver pomander containing nutmeg and cloves around their necks if they wished to have a child and also as a protection against unpleasant smells and infectious diseases. Those who could afford the rare luxury of this spice also took it as an aphrodisiac: it was supposed to increase sexual pleasure. Young newly-weds were given a drink made of cream, wine, egg yolk, nutmeg, cinnamon and sugar to ensure a successful wedding night.

---

18 1098-1179

19 Mace is the reddish aril (covering) of the nutmeg. It is often erroneously said to be the flower of the nutmeg. It has an aromatic taste like that of the nutmeg, but is rather milder.

The nutmeg was the rarest of all spices. When London doctors recommended nutmeg, apart from its other medicinal uses, as the only remedy for the plague that was rife at the time, demand for it rocketed out of all proportion. The plague, which came to Europe from central Asia along the Silk Road, claimed over 30 per cent of the population of Europe as its victims between 1346 and 1353! Since nutmeg has a proven anti-bacterial effect, it may well have alleviated some of the suffering, but its effect on the plague was obviously nil. Because of the long and difficult trade route it was not possible to replenish supplies quickly, and so nutmeg became ever rarer and more expensive in Europe. At its high point nutmeg was worth more than its weight in gold! In Germany at the time the market price of two nutmegs was a full-grown cow.

Spice merchants from Arabia, China and eastern Asia managed to preserve the secret of the geographical location of the Spice Islands for centuries, thus maintaining their monopoly. No European had ever seen the mysterious islands, or even knew where to find them, as the Indian Ocean was as yet unexplored. They only knew that nutmeg came from far away in the east and took a very long time to reach Europe.

Fantastic tales were made up about the Spice Islands, and lies were spread to put off undesirable competition. There were terrible sea monsters where the nutmeg grew, horrendous beasts who would sink any ship, there were cannibals and headhunters who collected their victims' heads, and perilous reefs which no ship could survive. None of the Arabian or Malay sea captains who travelled the route to the Spice Islands wanted to reveal the source of their precious cargo. They spread the tale of the Pausengi tree[20]. It was said to spring directly from the depths of the ocean. The Garuda – a gryphon-like beast, half human, half bird – lived in its branches. A whirlpool around the base of the tree would drag any ship under – only a handful of sailors survived the whirlpool by hanging on to the Garuda's feathers.

It was the Arabians in particular who deliberately spread these gruesome rumours to deter Western explorers from travelling in the region, and thus the place the nutmeg originated from remained a mystery for ages.

But how did the spices get to Europe? There were several routes by which spices and other goods from Asia reached Europe. From very early on in the ancient world, spices were very appealing because they were always connected with the erotic. For centuries spices travelled west through the Chinese deserts and Arabia. Here they found many willing customers just panting for the next consignment. Archaeologists excavating in Syria found evidence

20 Rumphius (Chapter 20) also wrote about this mysterious tree

that cloves were used there as a spice before 1700 B.C.[21] Early evidence from China also shows that cloves were already being used around 300 B.C. to treat toothache and bad breath. The antibiotic properties of the clove were even said to be efficacious against athlete's foot.

It is only later that we find any mention of the nutmeg. Although Ptolemy mentions Malaya and Java as early as the middle of the second century, the first person to mention the nutmeg in his writings is Aaron of Alexandria, who wrote a Syrian compendium of medicine (*The Pandects*) in the 7th century: *est nux muskata et affertur ab India* [nutmeg is brought from India].

The first western writer to mention the nutmeg – in 1078 – was Symeon Seth. This Jewish-Byzantine doctor from Antioch combined Greek medicine with what was known about the medical traditions of Arabia, Persia and India. Among many others he wrote a book entitled *Syntagma de alimentorum facultatibus* [On the properties of foods] in which he mentions nutmeg several times.[22] After the 11th century there are an increasing number of mentions of the nutmeg.

However, the trade in spices must have begun about 4000 years ago – and it must have been a long-distance trade, since there is indisputable proof that at the time these spices can only have come from the Spice Islands in what is today Indonesia. It was only on the Banda Islands that nutmeg could be cultivated. And it was only on the Northern Molucca Islands – Ternate and Tidore – that the clove grew. It was the beginning of what is now so frequently called globalisation. But is it really so new? I don't think that there has ever been a world without globalisation.

The spices had a long way to travel before they reached Europe. The most important routes then met in Constantinople, which in the 4th century was an important Western commercial metropolis. It was presumably around then that spices from the Moluccas first reached the West. The Persian scholar and poet Ibn Sina (Avicenna) mentions the *Nut from Banda* around the year 1000.

Marco Polo's account of his travels[23] led to increased interest in spices. His account of the Indonesian archipelago, here particularly Java, written around 1290, tells us: *It is a very rich island, producing pepper, nutmegs, spikenard, galingale, cubebs, and cloves and all the precious spices that can be found in the world. It is visited by great numbers of ships and merchants who buy a great range of merchandise, reaping handsome profits and rich returns. The quantity of treasure in the island is beyond all computation.*[24]

---

21 Source: International Institute for Mesopotamian Studies
22 Hermes Othniel, *Simeon Seth*, 2013
23 Probably 1254-1324
24 Marco Polo, *The Travels*, trs. Ronald Latham, Harmondsworth, 1958, p. 251.

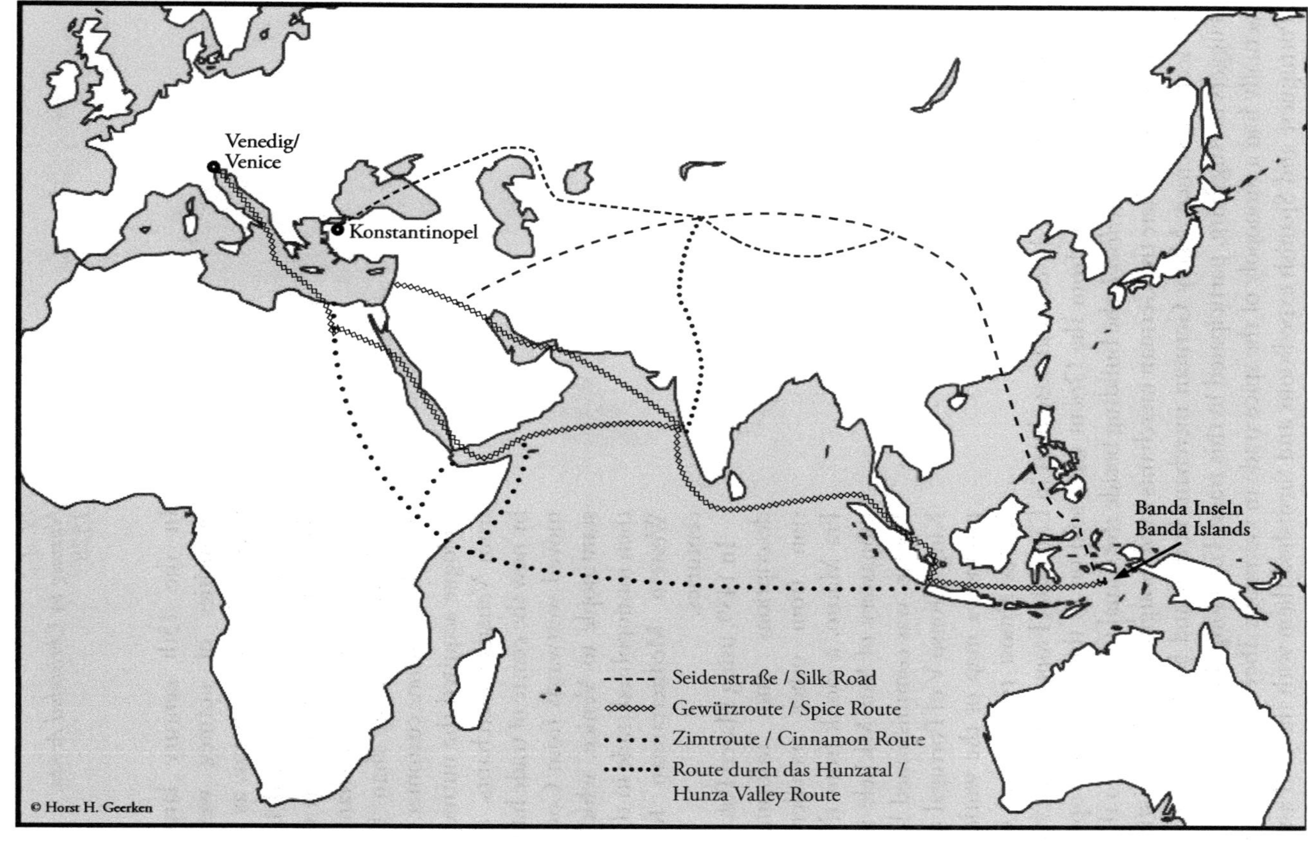

Ill. 2-1, There were several routes by which spices came to Europe

Ill. 2-2
Nutmeg by Christobal Acosta, 1578[25]

In the 13th century large quantities of nutmeg were imported into Germany, as is shown by a decree issued by the Archbishop of Cologne in 1259, stating that merchants could not sell more than 10 pounds to any one customer.[26] Cologne acquired the nutmeg from Venetian merchants, as by now the centre of trade had moved westwards from Constantinople to Venice, which then monopolised trade in the Western Mediterranean for centuries.

In 1459, using Marco Polo's descriptions and information from other travellers, Fra Mauro, a monk from the monastery of San Michele in Venice, was commissioned by King Alfonso V of Portugal to produce a map of the world. It was almost two metres in diameter and showed cities and coastlines in East Asia. From Venice spices, silk and other goods from the Orient were sold on to the rest of Europe. The *Fondaco dei Tedeschi*, the building beside the Canal Grande next to the Rialto Bridge, where the German merchants lived, bought and sold, can still be seen in Venice. Many German merchant houses and bankers, like the Fuggers in Augsburg, participated in this trade. For a long time the Fuggers actually had a monopoly of the spice trade in Germany. They also financed Portuguese and Spanish expeditions and furnished them with the gold and silver they needed for the spice trade.

25 Wikipedia, Public Domain
26 Ennen, *Geschichte der Stadt Köln (1863)*, II, S. 315

Ill. 2-3, Mappa mundi by Fra Mauro, Venice 1459[27]

Merchants and money changers from all over the world gathered in Venice. At least twice a year the Venetian fleet, protected by warships, sailed to Constantinople and ancient Antioch (in modern Turkey) to buy spices and other goods that had been transported there along the Silk Roads.

Arabian merchants and mariners from the Malay Archipelago used the Trade Winds and the Pacific Ocean currents to sail along the coasts from the Spice Islands to East Africa. They sailed to the Spice Islands with the North-East Monsoon from October to April, and then back again from June to September with the South-West Monsoon.

27 Wikipedia, Public Domain

Ill. 2-4, The Fondaco dei Tedeschi in Venice[28]

Recent DNA tests have shown that the population of Madagascar has the closest match to people from Kalimantan[29] in Indonesia. There must, therefore, have been very active long-term exchange between the two areas. It was the stars that guided the Arabians safely through the desert and across the seas. We have the Arab world to thank for the survival of much of the lore of antiquity: they rescued and translated the documents of the most famous library of the ancient world in Alexandria.

On the lowest level of the 8th-century Borobudur Temple near Yogyakarta on the island of Java you can see several relief carvings in stone which depict the merchant ships of the period.

In 2003 a replica of this ship set sail from the Moluccas: the Indonesian President of the time, Megawati Sukarnoputri[30] launched it under the name *Samudra Raksa*, Defender of the Oceans. In just 26 days the ship, crewed

28 Wikimedia Commons
29 Formerly Borneo
30 A daughter of Indonesia's first president, Sukarno

Ill. 2-5, Stone relief of a merchant vessel in the Borobudur Temple.

by 15 men and women, reached the Seychelles using only sail power. After another 15 days it was in Madagascar. This therefore proved that ships of the period could reach East Africa from the Spice Islands following the 'Cinnamon Route'.

In November 1980 the Sultan of Oman sent a replica of an ancient Arabian merchant ship to sea on the North-East Monsoon wind. After seven months the ship reached China. Another proof that trade between Arabian merchants and the Far East was possible from a very early period.

I have also seen murals dating back to 1493 B.C. in the temple of Queen Hatshepsut in southern Egypt: they show ships that were being unloaded after returning from a trading voyage. According to the inscription, the cargo included cinnamon and two other spices.[31]

In the early 1980s, when I visited the Ajanta rock caves in southern India, I also saw a rock drawing of a ship laden with spices. It was one of the ancient merchant ships that used to sail to India from Sumatra and Java.

31 Incense

The *lingua franca* along the long coastline from the Spice Islands to East Africa was Coastal Malay[32], a very much simplified form of Malay with little or no grammar. In Hadhramaut in southern Yemen in particular, the language has been in widespread use for generations because of their close contact with Java. When I was travelling out to Indonesia in 1963, I had the opportunity to visit the western part of Hadhramaut. I was astonished to discover that I was able to use the smattering of Bahasa Indonesia which I had learned before leaving Germany.

What we today call the Silk Road was actually a network of partly parallel caravan routes linking East Asia with the Mediterranean. Ferdinand von Richthofen, a geologist and geographer, was the first to name these trade routes through almost impassable deserts the Silk Road in a work published in 1877. He travelled to China in 1860 with a delegation of the Prussian Government to negotiate a trade agreement. He visited many Chinese provinces and only returned to Germany twelve years later.

Of course, it wasn't only silk that travelled to Europe along these routes; spices were also an important commodity. The best-known routes began in Xian – where in 1974 the famous 2000-year-old tomb containing the 8000 more than life-size terracotta soldiers was found. Here the spices were loaded on the caravans for their journey to the West. Some of the routes linked Xian with Constantinople solely overland, while others increasingly began to use the seaways. The caravanserai in Kashgar – in what is now the far west of China – was an important entrepot, as several of the routes connected there. Everything could be found in the market, and it was a good place for men and beasts to recover before setting out on the next stage of their journey.

Marco Polo also visited Kashgar. He described the oasis as a beautiful garden with plentiful fruit and vegetables. When I visited Kashgar in 1998, the Sunday market was still the most important market for miles around, just as it was in the old days.[33]

In Polo's time, a supplementary route went from the nodal point in Kashgar through the Hunza and Indus Valleys[34] to the Indian Ocean. Here it joined the Spice Route from the Spice Islands and continued, either directly over the Red Sea or through the desert to the Mediterranean. It was an occasion-

---

32 Sometimes also called Kitchen Malay
33 See Horst H. Geerken, *The Karakorum Highway and the Hunza Valley 1998*, ISBN 978-3-7448-1279-5
34 ibid.

Ill. 2-6, Spice market in Kashgar, 1998

ally hair-raising route, which at many places in the Hunza Valley could only be managed by using porters to carry the goods on narrow paths along the sheer cliffs over vertiginous heights. Today this has been replaced by the Karakorum Highway, financed by China, which is still under construction. It is intended to be a supplementary route for the New Silk Road.

Kublai Khan, the 'King of Kings'[35], took over a large part of the spice trade of the Malay Archipelago from the Arabs over the course of time. The Chinese had significantly bigger ships with a crew of 200, which could carry a cargo of 120 tonnes. In 1293 the first Chinese fleet sailed to Sumatra and through the Malacca Strait. When the Monsoon began, they sailed on to the Malabar coast in western India and then on to the Yemen. From here their wares were taken to Alexandria on the Mediterranean coast.

35   As he called himself

Ill. 2-7, Hair-raising tracks in the Hunza Valley[36]

The Cinnamon Route went directly over the Indian Ocean to East Africa, from where the route then headed north and joined up with the Spice Route just before the Red Sea. In the 14th and 15th centuries the Spice Route mostly followed the Nile downstream to Alexandria, and the goods were then shipped to Venice or Constantinople. When Alexandria drastically increased its customs charges, the route via Bagdad and Syria was mostly chosen instead.

36 Photograph by the author, 1998

This was an important trade route: it led through the Syrian Desert to Antioch, which is 30 kilometres from the sea and is the crossroads for several trade routes. As a result, the city experienced a boom, becoming next to Constantinople one of the most important cities in the eastern Mediterranean. It also had an important role to play in the history of Christianity: according to legend, the Apostle Paul is said to have preached in a rock church in the north-east of the city.

The Spanish and Portuguese were envious of the constantly increasing influence of the Venetians, and wished to find the Spice Islands for themselves. By 1444 the Portuguese had already discovered Madeira and the Azores in the Atlantic. The Canary Islands also wished to unite with Portugal, but the Pope granted them to the Spanish.

As the Turks advanced westwards in 1529 and again in 1683, the old trade routes fell into disuse and the western maritime powers now set out to search for the legendary Spice Islands.

Today, 350 years later, the Silk Road is once more on everyone's lips. But now we are talking about a 'New Silk Road' from China to Europe. And it is no longer spices that will be carried along it, but mass-produced products from the Middle Kingdom. It is a major Chinese foreign policy project, meant to orientate the global order more strongly towards China. China wants to expend hundreds of billions of dollars on conquering the world!

Ill. 2-8,
The ancient
rock church
in Antioch[37]

---

37 Photograph by the author, 1957

3. The Banda Islands

The Banda Islands were blessed, not only by the ancient myths that made them the centre of the world, but also because they were immensely rich. The islands were covered in nutmeg forests right up to the mountain tops; they were – and still are – surrounded by exceedingly rich fishing grounds which throng with tuna, mackerel, parrot fish, turtles and countless other marine creatures. But the most immediate things that strike the eye are the frequent earthquakes and tidal waves, and the eruptions of the Gunung Api volcano.

The 16th-century Portuguese historian de Barros was probably the first to describe the Banda Islands in his famous work *Del Asia*. He enthuses:

The Island of Banda is like a garden of nutmeg trees, and since they blossom at the same time as a multitude of pleasant-smelling herbs and flowers, the air at that season is filled with scents which are incomparably delightful. When the nutmeg fruits begin to ripen, hosts of parrots and other birds with the most varied plumage and song flock to eat them and delight the eyes and ears of mankind. In the middle of the island there is a mountain which is rather steep, but when you climb it, you find yourself on a plateau which is no less charming than the region at the foot of the mountain.[38]

In 1545, the Italian physician Antonius Musa Brassavola reported – based on Portuguese sources – that the Portuguese in their galleons could smell the scent of the islands on the air long before they move into view.

In the second half of the 17th and the beginning of the 18th century, the German naturalist, botanist and zoologist Georg Eberhard Rumpf, known as Rumphius, identified over 500 different species of fish in the waters of the Banda Sea, as well as even more plants.[39]

It was here, and only here, that the nutmeg so desired by the whole world was able to grow and flourish. And they were also able to harvest the bark of the *kayu manis* tree, cinnamon, which was also in great demand. There was no need for the roughly 15,000 original inhabitants of the Banda Islands to go without: they were well-off. They had everything in profusion! Whatever could not be grown on the islands, like rice and vegetables, was imported from Java or Ambon and exchanged for spices. Fabrics came from India or Arabia.

The first evidence of human habitation on the Bandas dates from 8,000 years ago: they lived under a rock overhang on the island of Ai. The first

---

38　Translated from Soltau's version in *Geschichte und Entdeckung der Portugiesen im Orient, 1415-1539*

39　See Chapter 20

written mention of the islands[40] was by the Portuguese apothecary Tomé Pires, who lived in Malaccca on the Malay Peninsula from 1512 to 1515 and visited the Bandas several times. He estimated that there were only about 3,000 inhabitants at the time. In 1516 he opened the first European embassy in China as ambassador.

The Bandas are just a small cluster of tiny volcanic islands in the middle of the Banda Sea – which has a maximum depth of 7,440 metres – only 4 degrees south of the Equator. They are so small that they are only to be found on specialised maps, and they form only part of the Moluccan Spice Islands. The Molucca province is an area in modern Indonesia, which is half as big as Europe. Far to the north, roughly 1,000 kilometres from the Bandas, are the other Spice Islands of Ternate, Tidore and Makian. The closest island, Amboyna[41], lies 200 km north of the Bandas. The only place where cloves were originally grown was these last four islands, but nutmeg only grew on the Bandas. This is presumably due to the unique microclimate caused by the deep Banda Sea and the quality of the volcanic soil, which was only found here, resulting from the regular eruptions of Gunung Api[42]. The little island of Run was particularly generously endowed: it was thickly covered like a park with nutmeg trees from the coast to the mountain peaks. Today nutmeg is also grown in other places in the world, such as Madagascar, South America and the Caribbean.

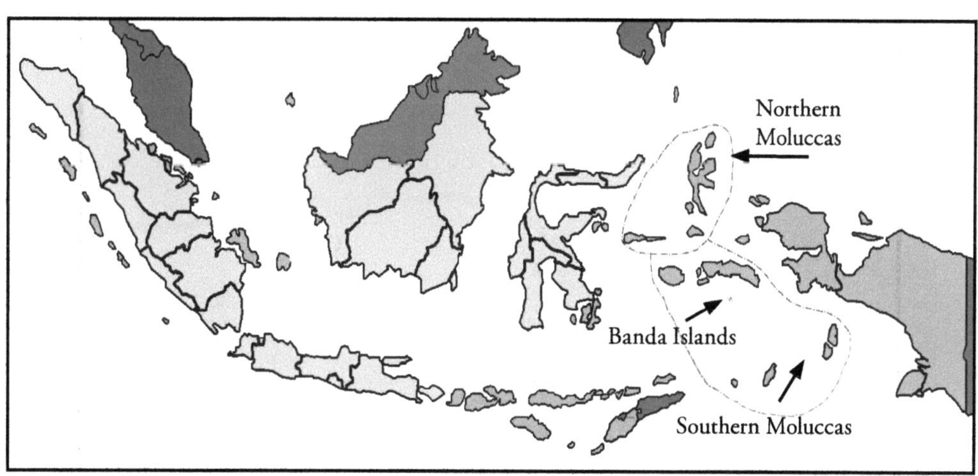

Ill. 3-1, The position of the Moluccas in Indonesia
Northern Molluccas - Banda Islands - Southern Moluccas

---

40   In his book *Suma Oriental*
41   I will follow contemp. custom and use the name Ambon for this island from now on.
42   Also known as Banda Api (Fire of the Bandas)

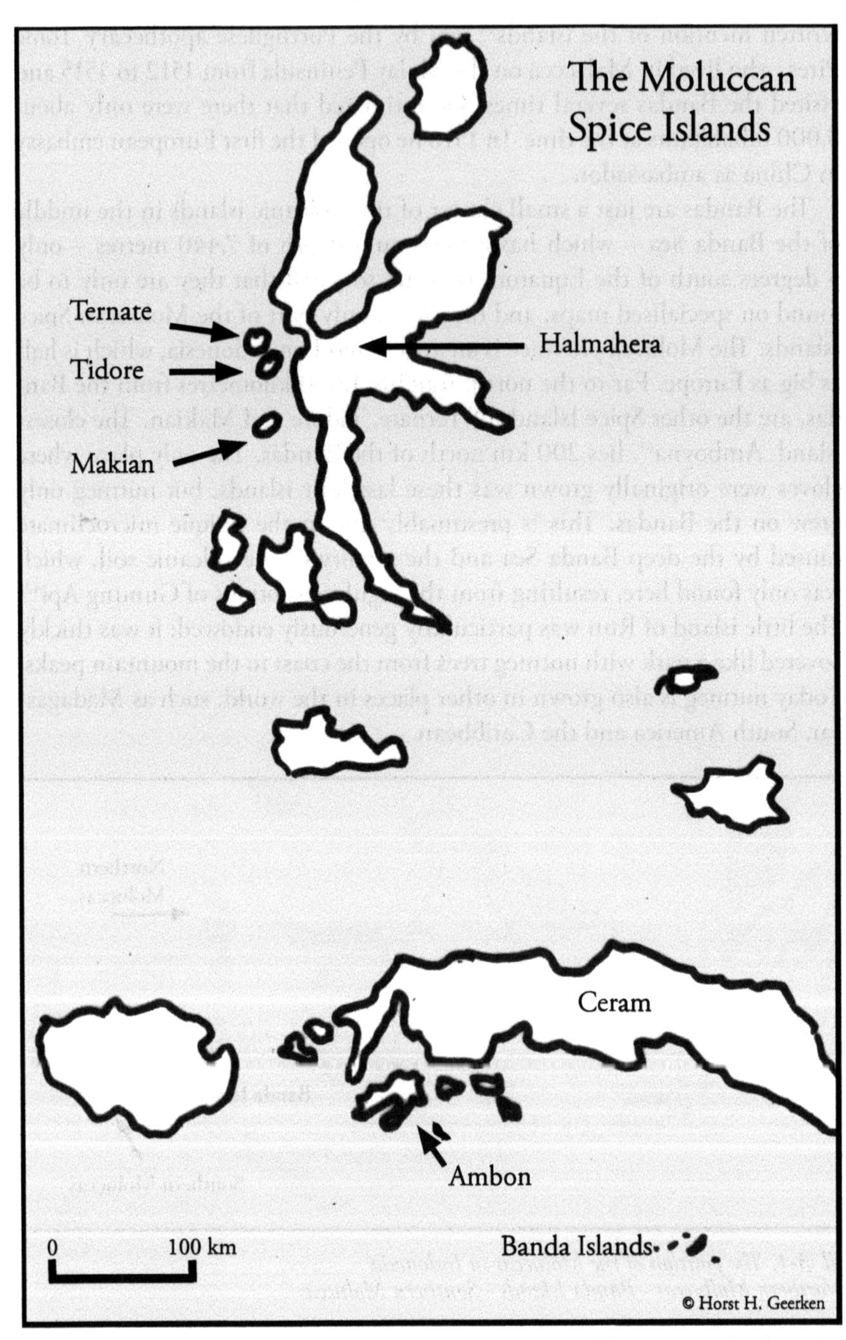

Ill. 3-2, The Moluccan Spice Islands. The islands of Ternate, Tidore, Makian and Ambon produce cloves, the Banda Islands nutmeg and mace.

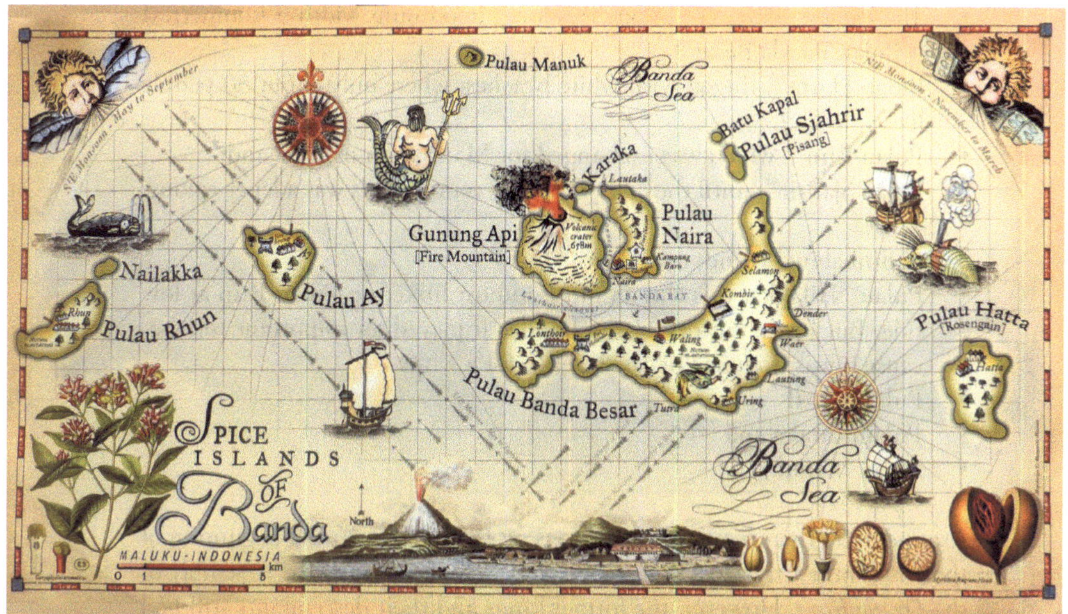

Ill. 3-3, The Banda Islands[43]

The *Kenari* nut tree also grew solely on the Bandas. It is only in the shade of these trees – which grow up to 40 metres tall – that the 20-metre nutmeg trees flourish. The *Kenari* is a very fatty nut, similar to the almond. Today *Kenari* trees have also become native to Papua[44]. The nuts have been used in Bandanese cuisine from time immemorial.

Today the Banda Islands have about 14,000 inhabitants. The inhabited islands are:
- The main island, Banda Neira. It is about 3 kilometres long and 1.3 kilometres at its widest point
- Directly next to this, separated only by a 100-metre strait[45], lies the volcanic island of Pulau[46] Gunung Api. Only a few dozen people live there on the coast opposite Banda Neira
- Pulau Ai[47]

---

43   ©Abba, Cilu Bintang Estate
44   New Guinea
45   Previously called Strait of the Sun, *Zonnegat* in Dutch
46   Pulau = Island
47   Aka Pulau Ay

- The biggest island (12 kilometres long, maximum width 3 kilometres) is Pulau Banda Besar[48]
- Pulau Hatta[49], ringed with white beaches, where only about 50 people live
- Pulau Run[50], which was exchanged for Manhattan in 1667 and
- Pulau Sjahrir[51]: until the end of the 19th century this was a leper colony.

Tiny uninhabited islands are
- Pulau Nailakka: this tiny island is almost linked to Pulau Run at low tide. But in the history of the Bandas it played an important role because it was occupied by the English for a while
- Pulau Kapal
- Pulau Karaka and
- Pulau Manuk.

Around 1500 there were still four kings on the Bandas. At the beginning of the 16th century, they lost their power and were replaced by the Assembly of the *Orang Kaya*. However, the former kings and their descendants still had a place of honour in the Assemblies. The *Orang Kaya* were the 'rich, old or influential gentlemen' in every village. As a result, each village was a small republic. There were mostly about 44 of them, a 'Council of Elders' who exercised sovereignty and dispensed justice. They also organised the nutmeg trade. They were a merchant oligarchy within Bandanese society, an upper class who liked to display themselves under silken parasols held by their servants. An important sign of their high culture was indubitably the fact that they worked together for defence against external enemies.

The nutmeg and mace trade was not the only business on the Bandas; the Bandanese were also influential middle men in the trade in cloves from Ternate und Tidore, as well as the plumage of birds of paradise from the Aru Islands and New Guinea. In return, they acquired rice from Java, or cloth. Trade with the Arabs, Malays and Chinese flourished and always ran smoothly. Until the first Dutch ships arrived, the Bandas were ruled by the *Orang Kaya*. When the Dutch entered the race for the nutmeg the lives of the Bandanese changed dramatically.

---

48   Also known during Dutch colonial times as Pulau Lonthoir (also Lontar and Lonthor)
49   Pulau Rozengain (also Rosengain) in the colonial period, changed to Pulau Hatta in 1955
50   Aka Rhun
51   Aka Pulau Sjahrir. Pulau Pisang during the Dutch colonial period. The name was changed to Pulau Sjahrir in 1955

Ill. 3-4, Orang Kayas, Detail from a picture in the Banda Neira Museum

Ill. 3-5, Orang Kaya, Painting in Banda Neira Museum

It is interesting to see what early encyclopaedias wrote about the Banda Islands. For example, the 1875 edition of the Encyclopaedia Britannica has an extensive entry about the Bandas in Volume III pages 309/310:

BANDA ISLANDS, a group in the East Indian Archipelago, lying to the S. of Ceram, in lat. 4° 30′ S. and long. 129° 50′ E. They are ten or twelve in number, and have an area of about 7150 square miles. Their volcanic origin is distinctly marked. Banda Lantoir, which derives its name from the *lontar* or Palmyra palm, is the largest of the group. From the sea this island appears lofty,—its sides being steep, and crowned by a sort of table-land which extends nearly from one end to the other. The whole is one continuous forest of nutmeg and *Canari* trees, the latter being planted to screen the former from the wind. The unhealthiness of Lantoir has prevented it from becoming the seat of government, for which in other respects it would naturally be chosen. The village of Selam contains the ruins of the chief Portuguese settlement. A considerable fort, called Hollandia, commands the harbour. Banda Neira lies S. of Lantoir. It is the seat of the Dutch resident, whose jurisdiction extends not only over the Banda Islands, but also over a part of Ceram and several other small groups. Fort Nassau, which was built in 1609, is the chief defence of the islands ; and to the right and left of it extends the village of Neira. Gunong Api is to the north of Neira, and derives its name—Fire Mountain—from its large cone-shaped volcano, which rises 2320 feet above the level of the sea, and is constantly emitting smoke. The peak was ascended by Professor Reinwardt in 1821, by M. S. Müller in 1828, and in 1865 by Mr Bickmore, who has given an interesting account of the adventure. Eruptions took place in 1586, 1598, 1609, 1615, 1632, 1690, 1696, 1712, 1765, 1775, 1778, 1820, 1824 ; and earthquakes without eruptions occurred in 1629, 1683, 1710, 1767, 1816, and 1852. On the last occasion the sea swept up in an enormous wave over Fort Nassau. Pulo Way—The Water Island—lies north of Neira. It is about 400 or 500 feet high, consists of coral rock, and is esteemed the healthiest of the group. Pulo Rond or Roon—the Chamber Island—is about four miles further N., and was at one time the seat of an English "factory." Rosyngain, about seven miles S.E. of Lantoir, is likely to become of some importance for its gold-mines. It was formerly a convict station for Amboyna. Pulo Pisang—Banana Island—two miles N.E. of Neira, produces fine fruits. The other islands Craka, Capella, Sonangy, &c., are uninhabited. In the space between Banda Lantoir and the islands of Banda Neira and Gunong Api there is a very good harbour, formed with entrances both from the E. and W., which enable vessels to enter it from either of the monsoons. These channels are well defended with several batteries, particularly the western one, which is very narrow. Between Gunong Api and Banda Neira there is a third channel into this harbour from the N., but it is navigable for small vessels only. The principal articles of commerce in the Banda group are nutmegs and mace. The native population having been cleared off by the Dutch, the plantations were worked by slaves and convicts till the emancipation of 1860. The introduction of Malay and Chinese labourers has since taken place. The plantations or *perken* can neither be sold nor divided. About 700,000 ℔ or upwards of nutmegs are obtained in a year, with a proportionate quantity of mace. The imports are provisions, cloth, and iron-ware from Batavia, and various native productions from the Aru Islands, Ceram, &c.

The Banda Islands were discovered and annexed by the Portuguese Abreus about 1511; but in the beginning of the 17th century his countrymen were expelled by the Dutch. In 1608 the English built a factory on Pulo Way, which was demolished by the Dutch as soon as the English vessel left. Shortly after, however, Banda Neira and Lantoir were resigned by the natives to the English, and in 1620 Pulo Roon and Pulo Way were added to their dominions ; but, in spite of treaties into which they had entered, the Dutch attacked and expelled their British rivals. In 1654 they were compelled by Cromwell to restore Pulo Roon, and to make satisfaction for the massacre of Amboyna; but the English settlers not being adequately supported from home, the island was retaken by the Dutch in 1664. They retained undisturbed possession of their conquests in this quarter of the globe until the year 1796, when the Banda Islands, along with all the other Dutch colonies, were conquered by the British. They were restored by the treaty of Amiens in the year 1800, again captured, and finally restored by the treaty of Paris concluded in 1814. In the Presidency of Banda there are 111,194 inhabitants of whom 6000 belong to Neira.

Ill. 3-6, The Banda Islands in the Encyclopaedia Britannica, 1875

In the German *Pierers Konversations-Lexikon* of 1889 there is also an entry about the Bandas in Volume II, page 378 though it is not as detailed as the Britannica item:

Banda 1) (Banda-Inseln), niederländ. Inselgruppe, Ostindien, südlichste Hauptgruppe der Molukken, 44 qkm, vulkanisch, mit häufigen Erdbeben, steil, hoch, üppig bewachsen, früher sehr ungesund, jetzt dagegen Sanatorium; 6 kleine u. 4 größere Inseln; die größte B. (Lontor, 16 km lang, 3,5 km breit) mit Fort Hollandia; Neira (7,4 km lang, 3,7 km breit) mit dem Hauptort u. Freihafen B., dem Gunong-Api, einem thätigen Vulkan (530 m), oft mit furchtbaren Ausbrüchen. Hauptprodukt: der Muskatnußbaum, lange Zeit v. den Niederländern auf die B. beschränkt. Etwa 6000 Ew., Malaien, Papua u. Mischlinge beider. Die B. sind eine Abteilung der niederländ. Residentschaft Amboina; 1512 vom Portugiesen Abreu entdeckt, 1600 v. den Niederländern besetzt, denen sie 1796, bez. 1810 v. den Engländern abgenommen, aber 1801, bez. 1814 zurückgegeben wurden.

Ill. 3-7, The Banda Islands in Pierers Konversations-Lexikon, 1889[52]

Although there is still detailed information about the Banda Islands in the 1965 edition of the Encyclopaedia Britannica (Vol. 3, p. 78) the 1953 German *Großer Brockhaus* devotes a meagre four lines to them.

BANDA ISLANDS, in the Banda sea, Indon., lie 130 mi. S.E. of Amboina and 66 mi. S. of Ceram. The ten islands cover only 72 sq.mi. Pop. (1956 est.) 13,686. The three largest are Bandalontar or Great Banda (6 mi. long), Bandanaira and Gunungapi, grouped around an inland sea which forms Banda harbour; Bandalontar, sickle-shaped, lies south and east, Bandanaira to the north, with Gunungapi to the west. Undoubtedly these three islands form part of the rim of a crater.

West and southwest of Gunungapi are Ai and Run, and north and northwest, Pisang and Suwangi. Channels on either side in the south of Banda harbour enable vessels to enter with safety during either monsoon, while a northern passage, between Gunungapi and Bandanaira, is navigable for small vessels. Bandalontar has coral rock to a height of 400 ft., with lava and basalt above, and is certainly volcanic, while Gunungapi (2,152 ft.) is an active volcano which caused destruction in 1820 and 1852. It is covered with bushes to within 700 ft. of the summit, which exhibits various shallow and extinct crater basins and a hot, smoking plain, sending forth sulfurous vapours and covered with split lava blocks. The volcanic soil, however, is admirably adapted to the growth of the

---

52 Translation see Appendix V

nutmeg, which is indigenous. Other products are cloves, coconuts,
tapioca and various tropical fruits and vegetables. The population of the islands is 10,000 of whom 6,000 live in Bandanaira,
the capital, on the island of that name, the port for the group.

  The people are a mixed race, mostly descendants of Javanese,
Macassarese and people from neighbouring islands brought in by
the Dutch as slaves to work the nutmeg plantations in the place
of the Bandanese, who refused to do so and were either killed
or banished. A colony of exiled Bandanese continued to exist on
one of the neighbouring islands of the Kai group. They, alone,
use the old Bandanese language. On Gunungapi there is a small
colony of Butonese. On Bandanaira there are many Arab and
Chinese traders and some Malays, with a few Europeans and Eura-
sians, officials and persons engaged in business. Agriculture and
fishing are the occupations of the inhabitants, many of whom are
Christians.

  Trade is in Chinese and Arab hands. Regular ship service con-
nects Bandanaira with Amboina. There are roads sufficient for
the needs of the population, and a radio station. The approach,
especially from the north, is beautiful, as is the scenery about the
inland sea. The marine gardens beneath this sea are probably
unrivaled.

  The Banda Islands were discovered and annexed by the Portuguese Antonio d'Abreu in 1512, but early in the 17th century the
Dutch expelled the Portuguese and established themselves, in spite
of native opposition, on Bandanaira and built a fort there. The
Dutch East India company allotted the nutmeg plantations (Dutch
perken) to deserving former servants, the so-called "perkeniers."
but kept the monopoly on the nutmeg trade. For 300 years the
perkeniers, who gradually became of mixed blood, were the aristocracy of the islands. The English tried to establish themselves
in the islands at the same time as the Dutch. After some unsuccessful attempts—among them that of Capt. David Middleton—
English influence made headway on Bandalontar, Run and Ai, and
in 1621 the Dutch, anxious to make an end of native rule, proposed
a joint Anglo-Dutch conquest of the islands. The English declined to co-operate, whereupon the Dutch crushed Bandanese
resistance and ruled the islands under a governor, soon eliminating
the English element. Alleged English participation against the
Dutch in a native revolt on the island of Run led to the Amboina
massacre (*see* AMBOINA). As a result, in 1654, under pressure from
Cromwell, Run was awarded to the descendants of those who
perished in Amboina. It was held until 1664, when the Dutch
captured it. In 1796 the islands were taken by a British naval
force, restored to the Dutch in 1800, retaken during the Napoleonic War and restored finally by the treaty of Paris of 1814.
Japan occupied the islands in World War II.   (J. O. M. B.)

Ill. 3-8, The Banda Islands in the Encyclopaedia Britannica, 1965

4. The first explorers and the quest for the Spice Islands

The urge to explore the as yet unknown world of the Orient sprang from the desire for spices and the immense wealth to be made from trading in them. The spices that had long been familiar, like pepper and vanilla, played a lesser role in this; it was nutmeg and cloves that promised the greatest profit, and all that was known about them was that they came from far away, from the unknown lands of the Orient.

In the quest for spices the four most important explorers of the 15th and 16th centuries, Christopher Columbus, Vasco da Gama, Bartolomeu Dias[53] and Ferdinand Magellan, sailed off in their ships into as yet unknown oceans, and an as yet unknown world. Since Spain was occupied with the *Reconquista* of those parts of its territory occupied by Arabian Muslims until 1492, the Portuguese were able to get a head start in their conquest of the seas. Portugal, the most south-westerly country in Europe, was interested in finding a route to the Spice Islands in an easterly direction, while Spain aimed towards the west. By 1419 Portugal had occupied Madeira and by 1431 the Azores. To prevent conflict between them, the 1479 treaty of Alcáçova laid down that the Canary Islands should fall to Spain, leaving the rest of the Atlantic and all the areas south of the Canaries to the Portuguese.

When Christopher Columbus returned from his first westward voyage in 1493, he had discovered not Asia, but a whole series of still unknown islands in the Caribbean. Nor did he bring any spices back with him, but gold and silver stolen from the Incas. Spain now wished to establish its rights over the newly discovered lands. In 1494 Pope Alexander VI drew a line from pole to pole, which was to divide the Spanish and Portuguese possessions. This line at roughly 38° west ran about 320 miles west of the Cape Verde Islands.

The Portuguese were less than happy with this division, and the Portuguese King, Fernando of Aragon, protested to the Spanish queen, Isabella of Castille. Tough negotiations followed in the small northern Spanish town of Tordesillas on the banks of the River Duero. Tordesillas looks just like any other town in the region, with a market, an old town and a few old churches, but in 1494 the decisions that were reached changed the world.

On the 7th of June 1494 the Treaty of Tordesillas was concluded: the dividing line was shifted west to 46° west, and so was now about 1185

---

53 Aka Diaz

miles west of the Cape Verde Islands. The world was now divided between the two great Catholic sea powers, Spain and Portugal. The inhabitants of the areas concerned were not involved in the negotiations, and their land was distributed without their consent. South America had not yet been discovered.

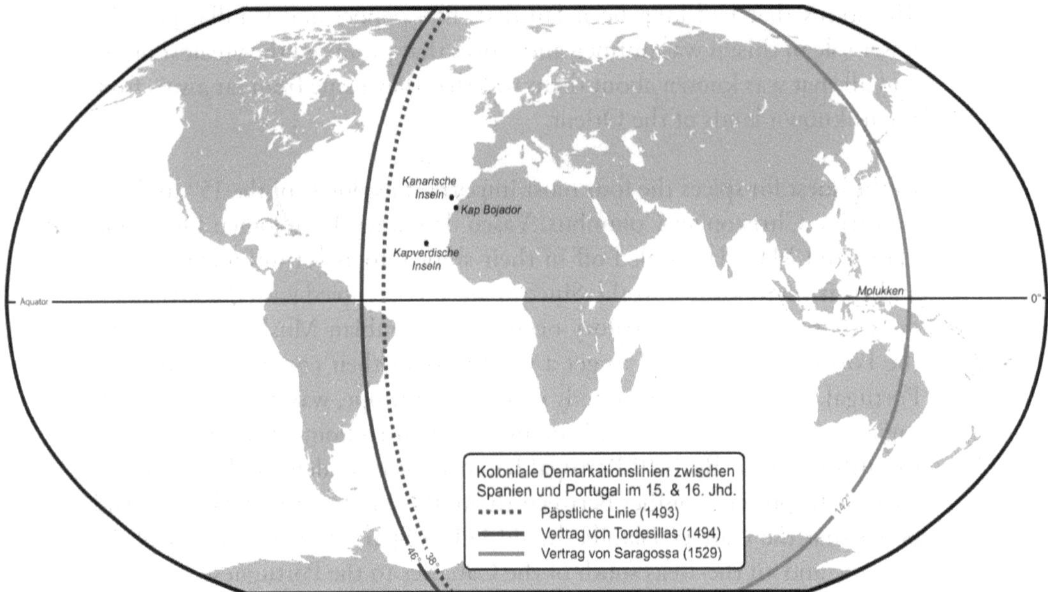

Ill. 4-1, Division of the world according to the Treaty of Tordesillas[54] and Saragossa between Spain and Portugal in the 15th and 16th Century

As we will see, the Portuguese were very fortunate that the line was moved westward. Prince Henry of Portugal, the fourth son of King John I, founded a school of navigation in Sagres in southern Portugal. He became known as Henry the Navigator, even though he himself never took part in any voyages of discovery. He was a patron of sea travel, and initiated a programme for the development of a sea route to the east, into the unexplored oceans around Africa. With the help of foreign astronomers and Arabian navigators, new navigational instruments were developed, such as the astrolabe, the sextant, the quadrant and the compass. Now the angle of altitude of the sun could be measured more accurately when calculating latitude.

---

54 From Lencer - Eigenes Werk, CC BY-SA 3.0, https://commons.wikimedia. org/w/index.php?curid=2649268

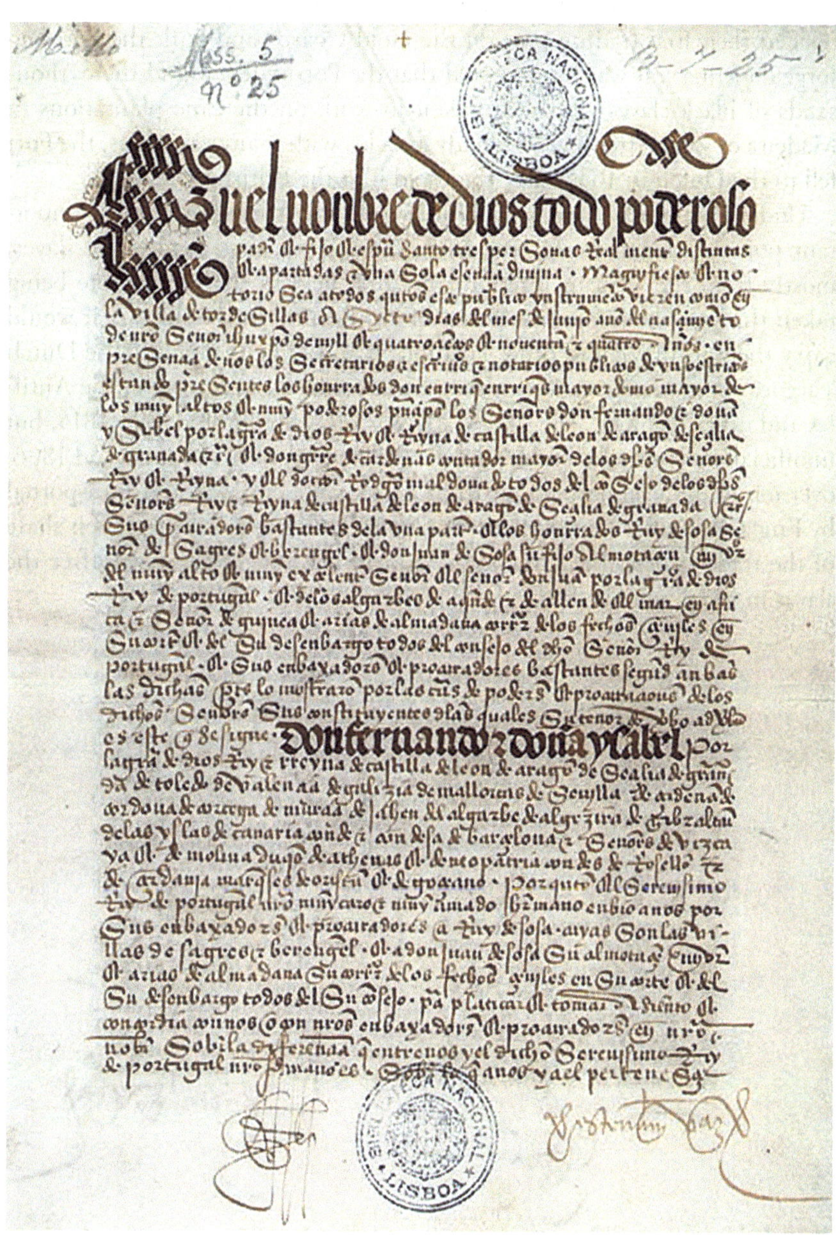

Ill. 4-2, First page of the Treaty of Tordesillas[55]

55   Wikipedia Public Domain

The Portuguese now sailed south along the African coast. In 1482 they opened their first trading post on the Gold Coast[56] and built the Fort São Jorge da Mina[57]. It was human gold that the Portuguese found there, thousands of black slaves who were taken to work on the cane plantations in Madeira or sold. After several bloody attacks, with many casualties, the Fort fell to the Dutch in 1637; they then sold it to the British in 1872.

Under Portuguese, and later Dutch, rule the fort was the most important point of departure for the later transatlantic slave trade. The slaves, mostly from the African interior, were first held in the Fort before being taken through the infamous 'Door Of No Return' to the ships that would carry them to Brazil and other Portuguese and Dutch colonies. The Dutch 'cargoes' went to the territories they had conquered in Surinam, the Antilles and other colonies. The slave trade was officially forbidden in 1814, but unofficially it continued for several decades longer. Between 1560 and 1866, over ten million human beings from Africa were enslaved and transported by England, France, Portugal and Holland. Dutch estimates put their share of the trade at 5%. The Dutch government was one of the last to free the slaves in its colonies in 1863.

Ill. 4-3, Monument to Henry the Navigator in Lisbon[58]

---

56 Now Ghana
57 Fort St George
58 From Plenumchamber - Eigenes Werk, CC BY 3.0, https://commons.wikimedia.org/w/index.php?curid=3467938

46

But in the beginning Brazil hadn't even been discovered. Starting from Fort St George, the Portuguese wanted to find a route to India following the coast. In 1487, Bartolomeu Dias became the first Portuguese to round the Cape of Good Hope. After his return, his records came into the hands of the German cartographer Henricus Martellus Germanus, who prepared a new map on the basis of this information. This is the first map to show East Africa and the Indian Ocean, and to show the Cape of Good Hope. It is, however, greatly distorted because of errors in reckoning longitude. Nevertheless, it served as an inspiration and model for subsequent world maps, such as the German world map of Martin Waldseemüller in 1507, or the first globe[59] produced by Martin von Buchheim in 1492. On the basis of information from Amerigo Vespucci, America was first shown as a new continent on Waldseemüller's map, but in very distorted form, as the west coast of America was as yet unknown.

After Bartolomeu Dias rounded the Cape of Good Hope, Vasco da Gama decided to venture further. He left Lisbon on the 8th of July 1497 with four ships.[60]

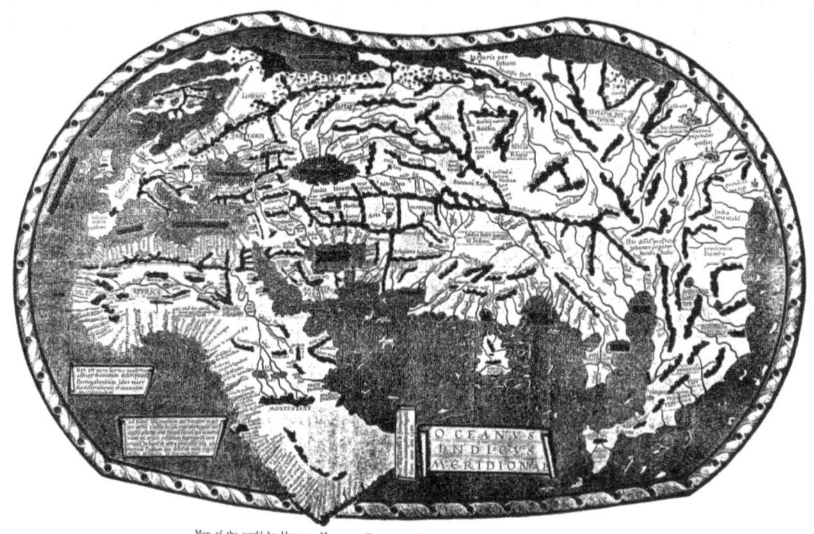

Map of the world by Henricus Martellus Germanus. After D. José de Lacerda. (Original size 0.47 × 0.495 m.)

Ill. 4-4, Henricus Martellus Germanus' world map, 1490[61]

---

59 A German: he named his globe the *Erdapfel* [Earth apple – ironically, this is a modern German term for potato].
60 His brother, Paulo da Gama, captained one of them.
61 British Library, Wikipedia commons

He first sailed down the familiar route to the Cape and then worked his way north up the east coast of Africa, taking advantage of several opportunities to stock up on provisions for his journey into the unknown. For the Portuguese, the Indian Ocean was a new, unexplored sea. In the port of Malindi[62] Vasco da Gama was fortunate enough to meet an Arabian captain who had already crossed the Indian Ocean several times. To his great surprise the captain had a detailed chart of the ocean. With the strong south-westerly winds of the summer monsoon they were blown to India in just four weeks. Ten months after leaving Lisbon, Vasco da Gama became the first European to reach the west coast of India on the 18th of May 1498.

In Calicut[63], they first sent a *degredado* ashore. This was the normal tactic employed to find out if the natives they met were friendly or hostile. A *degredado* was normally a converted Jew or a criminal whose life was worth very little in their eyes. In the meanwhile the rest of the crew remained in safety aboard ship. He returned unscathed: he had met two Tunisian merchants with whom he had been able to speak Catalan, and informed Vasco da Gama that Calicut was the most important trading centre for spices on India at the time. Merchants from the East brought their cargoes here from the Spice Islands. The Malabar Coast was also the centre for pepper[64], which was grown there. For this reason, the coast was also called the Pepper Coast.

Ill. 4-5, Calicut in 1572[65]

---

62 In modern Kenya
63 Now Kozhikode on the Malabar Coast with a population of about 500,000
64 Piper nigrum
65 Wikipedia Commons, Atlas Civatates Terrarum

I've been to Calicut several times. Nothing has changed even today where growing pepper and the spice trade are concerned. In December in particular, when the peppercorns are harvested, you can see peppercorns laid out on cloths to dry in every available free space. But little remains of the old Calicut due to the vicissitudes of time and many wars.

Archaeological excavations have revealed many Greek and Roman coins, some of them dating back to 123 B.C., so there must have been active trade with the west here for centuries.

Vasco da Gama's negotiations with the Zamorin, the King of Calicut, didn't go as planned. Da Gama expected that he could trade here with worthless glass beads and other trinkets, as he had done on the west coast of Africa. He was surprised to see that the cultured Indians and Arabs would only sell their goods for gold and silver. Merchants from Arabia, China and the Malay Archipelago ridiculed the worthless gifts da Gama presented to the King. This led to a somewhat tense atmosphere between the two of them.

Vasco da Gama was nevertheless still able to load some of his ships with valuable spices before leaving Calicut on the 5th of October 1498. The first of his ships made land in Lisbon on the 10th of July 1499. He himself didn't reach Lisbon until the 9th of September that year, as he had been caring for his mortally ill brother Paolo on the Azores. Of the 170 men who set sail in 1497, only 50 returned to Lisbon alive; most of the rest had died of scurvy, even in the early stages of the voyage. Vasco da Gama noted that they had been given oranges to eat by the natives in East Africa, after which the sick were quickly healed. But it was many decades before the problem was understood.

Of the four ships of the original fleet, only two returned to Lisbon. Still, even though Vasco da Gama returned to Portugal with a relatively small cargo of spices, the profit was several times more than the cost of the expedition.

The material loss and the cost in human lives in these early expeditions was extremely high. It was mainly scurvy, a disease caused by vitamin C deficiency, that caused the mortality. Since there was no cold storage, vegetables and fresh fruit would rot within a few days of departure. And then the only provisions for several months were salt pork and beef as a source of protein, and ship's biscuit. The preserving method was only partly successful. By the time the meat had been stored for a long period, it was full of maggots. The water, stored in barrels, was soon foul and only drinkable when mixed with wine. It only took a few weeks for the first cases of disease to appear; gums became sore, teeth fell out, the victims became short of breath and became feeble. The first deaths were not long in coming.

The German soldier Johann Jacob Saar – who served in the Dutch East Indies many decades later – describes how he improved the quality of the monotonous food on board ship as he returned, keeping himself healthy at the same time. He put layers of hot red chili peppers between fish that had been fried in butter. He then poured vinegar and olive oil over the whole mixture. By means of this method of preservation the fish – he writes – kept for at least four months. Unlike many of his comrades, he didn't suffer from scurvy, presumably because the chilis contained a lot of vitamin C. But no one knew that at the time.

James Cook[66] was told by the Scottish ship's doctor and scientist James Lind[67] that German sauerkraut and lemon juice were effective in combatting the disease. Lind had published his discovery in 1753 in his book *Treatise of the Scurvy*[68]. Cook was the first to include sauerkraut and lemon juice on the ship's menu during his circumnavigation voyages. He made them compulsory, in spite of the objections of his ship's doctor and his crew. Sailors who refused to eat the sauerkraut were flogged. Nevertheless, lemon juice was not used as a prophylactic: it was dispensed by the ship's doctor as a medicine when symptoms of the disease appeared. The success of this measure could not have been clearer: not a single man died of scurvy on Cook's circumnavigations. However, thousands of sailors died on subsequent expeditions to the Spice Islands, because it took another 200 years until this remedy for scurvy was generally accepted.

King Manuel I was without doubt the most important King of Portugal. During his reign, the Portuguese discovered the sea route to both India and Brazil, to set up bases in the Indian Ocean and to create the first colonial empire.

After Vasco da Gama's return, King Manuel I immediately set about equipping another, even bigger expedition, this time with 13 ships and 1,300 crew and soldiers under the command of Pedro Alvares Cabral. The fleet set sail from Lisbon on the 8th of March 1500. At first it followed the same route as Vasco da Gama, south along the West African coast. But then, at the latitude of the Cape Verde Islands, Cabral caught the trade winds and sailed far to the west, discovering the unknown continent of South America. A ship was laden with precious woods and sent back to Lisbon to inform the King of their discovery.

---

66 1728-1779
67 1716-1794
68 Gordon, Maurice Bear, *Naval and Maritime Medicine during the American Revolution*, p. 93

Now the shifting of the dividing line to the west in the Treaty of Tordesillas paid off. Since the rump of Brazil sticks out far to the east in the Atlantic, the area was, according to the treaty, in the Portuguese half of the world. This is also the reason why they speak Portuguese in Brazil, and Spanish in the rest of South America. When gold and diamonds were discovered in Brazil in the second half of the 17th century, Portugal became very rich. Brazil also played an important role in Portugal's history at the beginning of the 19th century. When the Napoleonic wars reached the Iberian Peninsula in 1807, the Portuguese royal family fled to Brazil. Rio de Janeiro became the capital of the Kingdom of Portugal. In 1822 King John VI returned to Lisbon and shortly afterwards Brazil declared itself independent.

To the south of South America the fleet caught the winds that constantly blow between 40° and 50° south, the Roaring Forties. In a storm off the Cape of Good Hope several ships were lost. The seven ships that succeeded in making the voyage to India anchored in Calicut on the 13th of September 1500. This time they made sure to give the Zamorin suitably valuable gifts to ensure his favour. This did not help a great deal: when the king refused to accede to the Portuguese demands that he trade with them alone and expel all Muslims, the Portuguese destroyed the city and, in an act of piracy, captured Arab ships and took their cargoes. There was unrest, in which 53 Portuguese were killed and 17 taken prisoner.

Only six of the thirteen ships that originally set out returned to Lisbon on the 20th of July 1501. King Manuel I threatened anyone who revealed the new, quicker route via the Roaring Forties or maps of the newly discovered territories in South America to their rivals in Spain or Venice with the death penalty.

Portugal tried with all its might to conquer a permanent base on the Indian subcontinent. King Manuel I ordered every expedition to gain control over the Indian Ocean and the spice trade in the name of the Christian Church. It was only after several further expeditions, involving heavy casualties and setbacks, that they managed to establish themselves in Goa on the west coast of India in 1510. Goa became the capital of Portugal's empire in the East and remained a Portuguese colony for 450 years.[69] The western part of the Indian Ocean, which until then had been free for any merchant to sail, was now controlled by Portugal. The European market for spices from the Moluccas had now shifted – much to the Italians' annoyance – from Venice to Lisbon.

---

69 Goa was annexed by the newly independent (since 1947) state of India in 1961

Ill. 4-6, The Strait of Malacca

Ill. 4-7, Malacca 1726[70]

70 Wikipedia Public Domain

After building a fort in Goa, the Portuguese' next goal lay further to the east: the legendary Spice Islands. They first advanced to Ceylon[71], where they were able to purchase cinnamon from the King of Galle in 1505. This was the most important entrepot for spices in the Far East. It took Alfonso de Albuquerque several tries and many casualties to conquer Malacca in the west of the Malay Peninsula with a fleet of 15 ships and 1,000 soldiers in August 1511. The Sultan of Malacca fled. The first Portuguese governor of Malacca permitted Hindu, Malay, Chinese and Japanese merchants to continue trading, but Arabs and Muslims were expelled or killed. Now, because the Malacca Strait is so narrow, the Portuguese were able to control the entire spice trade.

After Albuquerque's campaigns had firmly established the Portuguese in Goa and Malacca, they wished finally to press on to their ultimate goal, the Spice Islands, whose unknown location was something of a mystery. Only a few months after the seizure of Malacca, three Portuguese ships under the command of Albuquerque's friend, Captain Antonio de Abreu, set sail, guided by Malay navigators. The expedition was financed by the German banking house of the Fuggers in Augsburg. Among the party was Ferdinand Magellan, a Portuguese who only seven years later led the first circumnavigation of the globe as captain of the flagship of a fleet of five ships commissioned by the Spanish crown.

The Malay navigators on board the ships were familiar with the waters in the East and had travelled to the Spice Islands many times. We don't know whether they voluntarily piloted the Portuguese through these unknown waters, or whether they had to be forced to do so. I think it's more likely to be the latter, because all the Malay and Arabic navigators had always done their best to keep the position of the Spice Islands a strict secret. The expedition had been ordered by Albuquerque simply to trade and not to attempt to seize the islands. The laws and customs of the native population were to be observed. Looting was even to be punishable by death.

The chief navigator was the Malay, Nahkoda Ishmael[72]. The little fleet sailed south through the Strait of Malacca and then eastwards along the north coast of Java. Off the coast of the island of Madura, one of the ships ran onto a reef and was lost. They passed Bali, Lombok and Sumbawa.

---

71 Now Sri Lanka

72 In *Die Muskatnuss* [The Nutmeg] by Dr O. Warburg 'Nakhoda Ismael'. According to Warburg's account, written in 1897, Ismael sailed ahead to inform the Bandas about the impending arrival of the fleet. The fleet itself sailed first to Gresik on Java and only afterwards to the Bandas

At Flores they set course northwards over the open Banda Sea. Because of strong winds, the two ships had to shelter off the south coast of the island of Ceram[73] for a whole month. After the monsoon changed, they sailed south, and the first thing they saw was the perfect cone of the Gunung Api volcano rising sheer out of the sea. It was spring in Europe, and the season of nutmeg blossom on the Banda Islands. Even miles away from the islands, they must have caught the intoxicating scent of the much-coveted nuts.

In the first months of 1512 the Portuguese were the first Europeans to reach the legendary Spice Islands, the little Banda Archipelago, in the middle of the deep, stormy, perilous Banda Sea. The captain of the expedition may have lost a ship, but not a single member of the expedition was lost. Germany also contributed to the discovery, through the finance provided by the Augsburg Fugger Bank. Of course, we cannot really talk about a 'discovery' of the Bandas by the Europeans, because there had been lively trade between them and Java, Arabia, China and India.

Ill. 4-8, Banda Neira 1600-1700[74]

The Portuguese received a friendly welcome from the Bandanese. They were quite happy to have another trading partner alongside the Arabs, Indians, Chinese and Malays. Until then the spices from the Bandas had passed through the hands of many intermediaries as they travelled through deserts or over the sea to the Mediterranean at Constantinople or Venice. Every intermediary doubled the price of the goods. By the time they reached Europe, the spices were ferociously expensive.

---

73 Aka Seram, in the Moluccas
74 View from Gunung Api, Wikipedia Public Domain

Initially, the Portuguese did not attach much importance to setting up a fortified base on the Bandas. They simply traded with the Bandanese and filled their ships with nutmeg and mace, erroneously called nutmeg flower[75]. The cloves they purchased there came from the more northerly islands of Ternate and Tidore: the Banda Islands were an important transit market for the spice. They waited for a favourable wind, and then began their homeward voyage via Malacca, which they reached twelve months later. They had bought the spices at such a good price on the Bandas that they were later able to sell them in Lisbon at a profit of 1,000%. The expedition had been a gigantic financial success – for the Augsburg Fugger Bank too, of course.

Another Portuguese fleet under the command of Miranda de Azevedo arrived in the Bandas in 1513. From then on, trade between the Portuguese and the Spice Islands flourished. Initially they simply wished to trade, and in general accepted the rules imposed by the native aristocracy, the *Orang Kaya,* described previously.

The islands of Ternate and Tidore lie in the northern Moluccas. In 1512, the second commander of the first Portuguese expedition, Captain Fransisco Serrao, managed to become the personal advisor of the King of Ternate. As a result of this good fortune, the Portuguese made the island their base for the spice trade, building forts on the islands of Ternate and Ambon. They only occasionally visited the Bandas to buy nutmeg, or when their ships needed to seek shelter from strong winds and high waves in the Banda Sea. Trade with the Bandanese continued to run peacefully. For example, there were visits by the Portuguese Captains de Brito in 1522, de Melo in 1524 and Garcia in 1526.

When, however, the Portuguese captain and merchant Garcia returned to Banda Neira in his carrack[76] in 1529, this previously harmonious relationship turned sour. He had brought a large number of soldiers with him, and began to build a fort, without previously asking the *Orang Kaya* for permission. In the face of the fierce resistance of the Bandanese, Garcia abandoned his plans. He was driven from the island. From then on, the Portuguese once more restricted themselves to trade.

When the first cargoes of nutmeg and other spices arrived in Lisbon, the Spaniards decided that they wanted a share of this lucrative trade. In accordance with the treaty of Tordesillas they had to sail west to find the route

---

75 The aril of the nutmeg
76 A Spanish-Portuguese type of ship with three, and later also four, masts

to the Spice Islands. At the end of the 15th century Christopher Columbus embarked on the first of four voyages of discovery to the west, although in October 1492 he discovered not India but the previously undiscovered continent of America; however, until the day he died Columbus was convinced that he had reached India. But even on subsequent voyages, Columbus was unable to find the way to the Spice Islands.

At the end of the 15th and beginning of the 16th century, Amerigo Vespucci[77], an Italian in the service of the Portuguese crown made several voyages along the east coast of South America. He was the first European to realise that this was not India, but a new continent. Until then the land mass had been thought to be part of India. In his honour, the new continent was called America (based on his first name) by the German cartographer Martin Waldseemüller.

I have already mentioned the Portuguese mariner and navigator Fernando de Magellan, who took part in the first Portuguese expedition to reach the Bandas in 1512. Magellan was desperate to find a way of returning to the Bandas: he was sure that in South America there must be a way through to the Pacific. He was no longer able to take part in Portuguese expeditions, because during a campaign in Morocco he fell into disgrace with the Portuguese King as a result of an alleged act of treason.[78] He was dismissed from Portuguese service in May 1514. He then went to Spain and offered his services to the Spanish king. He was certain that, under the terms of the Treaty of Tordesillas, the Spice Islands were in the Spanish hemisphere.

The Spanish King Charles V recognised Magellan's abilities and gave him command of a fleet of five ships. His mission was to find a passage to the Pacific and the Banda Islands. The expedition was financed by the Spanish Crown, a Spanish shipping company and – as with the Portuguese expedition – the Fugger bank in Augsburg. At that time the Fugger bank had achieved global prominence.

The voyage began in August 1519. Magellan was Admiral and captain of the flagship *Trinidad*. The crews were mainly Spanish, but there were also Portuguese, Italians, Frenchmen, Germans, Greeks, and a Malay slave as interpreter in the multicultural mixture. The fleet took on supplies in the Canaries. At the latitude of the Cape Verde Islands they used the trade winds to reach the South American coast. They crossed the Equator and reached the coast of Brazil on the 6th of December 1519. They worked their way slowly and carefully south down the coast in order not to miss the passage to the Pacific. When they arrived in Patagonia, it was winter in the

---

77 1451(?)- 1512
78 Other sources say it was for illegal trading with the Moors.

Southern Hemisphere, and so from March onwards they overwintered in the sheltered bay of Puerto San Julián (so named by Magellan). Here, there was a mutiny, because the daily rations had been cut and some of the crew wanted to return to Spain. The miscreants were hanged and calm was restored. In August 1520 Magellan left his winter quarters. A good year after setting sail from Europe, in October 1520, he found the passage through to the Pacific, through the strait that is now named after him. One of the ships refused to accept Magellan's orders and sailed back to Spain.

Magellan naturally had no idea of the dimensions of the vast Pacific Ocean and he sailed westwards through the warm waters, driven by the prevailing wind. After three months on the open sea, the food supplies began to run out. The sailors ate the crumbs of the ship's biscuits, sawdust, rats and strips of water-softened leather. After three months and twenty days on the open sea, during which they only saw two tiny uninhabited atolls, they reached the Mariana Islands at the beginning of 1521. At least 19 sailors had died of hunger and disease on the voyage. Now they could collect food supplies and fresh water.

I find it incredible that the crew didn't feed on fish, which they could have caught on the open seas. I have crossed the Indian Ocean – and the Atlantic several times – in a sailing ship on the trail of the early explorers. I always succeeded in catching quite large fish using a set line. On the sailing ships of those days, it would have been perfectly possible to supplement their food supplies with freshly caught fish – and in those days the oceans had not yet been over-fished.

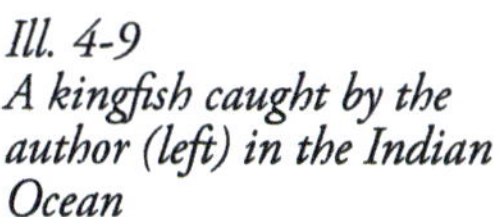

Ill. 4-9
A kingfish caught by the author (left) in the Indian Ocean

On the 16th of March 1521 Magellan reached the Philippines and discovered that he was quite close to the Spice Islands. With his three remaining ships, *Victoria, Trinidad* and *Conceptión* he visited several of the Philippine Islands. He was unable to acquire spices here, and so he changed his sphere of activity to missionising. He succeeded in converting the inhabitants of several islands to Christianity. Because of missionary activity during the subsequent Spanish colonial rule, the Philippines are still today the only Asiatic state with a majority Christian population: over 80% of the inhabitants are Catholic.

By contrast, the Dutch VOC[79] was run exclusively by merchants who were only interested in profit and therefore – unlike Spain and Portugal – had no time or money to invest in Christian missionary work. But for the Dutch there was also another reason not to missionize: in the eyes of God all humankind is equal. They certainly did not want that! For them, the natives were second class human beings, even though at the time their level of culture was higher than that of the Dutch. But the Dutch had better weapons.

However, the Philippine island of Mactan refused to be converted and rejected the Spaniard's claim to sovereignty. When Magellan tried to take over the island by force, there was a battle. On the 27th of April 1521. Magellan and 35 of his crew were killed. The rest only just managed to escape.

Ill. 4-10
Magellan Monument on the Philippine island of Mactan[80]

---

79 Vereenigde Oostindische Companie, Dutch East India Company
80 https://commons.wikimedia.org/wiki/File:Magellan_mactan.jpg

Since they no longer had enough sailors to crew the remaining three ships, they had to scupper the *Conceptión*. They sailed on to Borneo[81] with just two ships, the *Victoria* and the *Trinidad*, remaining there for 35 days. The two ships were presumably repaired during this time, since even then there were, as there are today, many ship-building wharfs where they build the *phinisi*, big sailing ketches. These are Indonesian freighters with a raised transom.

On the 6th of November 1521, the two ships reached the Spice Islands they had been so yearning for, but only Tidore, which lies south of Ternate. On Ternate, the northerly sister island, the Portuguese had already built a permanent base. Ternate and Tidore had been rivals from time immemorial. Cloves were the only one of the spices the Europeans so desired that grew on these islands. For nutmeg and cinnamon from the Bandas they simply acted as entrepots.

The *Victoria* and the *Trinidad* were filled to the brim with spices for the voyage home. It was only then that the crew realised that the *Trinidad* was so unsound that it would not survive the voyage back to Spain. It would have to be thoroughly overhauled. On the 21st of December 1521 the *Victoria* set off alone on the home journey with a crew of 47 Europeans and 13 Malays. Juan Sebastián Elcano was elected captain even though he was only a simple boatswain.

On the 6th of April 1522 the *Trinidad* finally also set sail from Tidore in a westerly direction with a 48-man crew. Since the Spanish ship now clearly found itself in the Portuguese half of the world, it was captured by the Portuguese. It was only five years later, that just three members of the crew returned to Spain from Portuguese captivity.

The *Victoria* sailed south over the Banda Sea. She was more fortunate than the sister ship *Trinidad*: the ship was not discovered by the Portuguese. They didn't sight the Banda Islands, since early Spanish charts do not show this group of small islands. On the 6th of February 1522 the *Victoria* moored off the island of Timur[82] to take on more supplies. It was not until half a year later that the ship touched land again at the Cape Verde islands. Supplies had run out and 21 crew-members had died of scurvy and exhaustion. Finally, after almost three years, the ship returned to Spain. They had made the first circumnavigation of the world and the spherical shape of the Earth had been demonstrated. Of those who originally set out on the five ships, only 18 men returned to Spain alive. The simple boatswain Juan Sebastián Elcano, who had safely steered the *Victoria* with its

---

81 Now Kalimantan
82 Also Timor

precious cargo from the Spice Island of Tidore to Spain, was officially made a captain by the King of Spain and knighted.

Since Spain had now also discovered the Spice Islands, Portugal was concerned about its recently acquired monopoly, and claimed sole ownership rights on the basis of the Treaty of Tordesillas, which divided the world between the two nations. It was no problem to keep to the treaty in the Atlantic, through which the dividing line ran quite close to home. There were already plenty of quite accurate maps and charts of this western region. But in the Indian Ocean and the Malay Archipelago much still needed to be explored, and those few maps that existed in the 16th century were extremely inaccurate. As a result, the Spaniards were able to claim that, when the dividing line was extended from the Atlantic through the Malay Archipelago, the Spice Islands in the Moluccas fell in their half. When a commission of enquiry, after five years of dispute, was unable to reach agreement about the competing claims, the Spanish King Charles V sold his claims to the Spice Islands to Portugal for 350,000 gold ducats in the Treaty of Saragossa.

The problems between Portugal and Spain had been solved, but Portugal's internal weakness and mismanagement meant that their colonial power grew ever weaker. Now England, and later Holland, also began to show an interest in the Spice Islands, and both nations rejected the regulations of the Treaty of Tordesillas. A new race for the spices began, and the conflicts renewed.

The Portuguese poet Luis Vaz de Camões[83] is one of Europe's outstanding lyric poets. His chief work, *Os Lusiadas*[84] was first translated into English in 1798 under the title *The Lusiad*[85]. This work describes the discovery of the sea route to India, using Greek and Roman mythology in imitation of the classical epic. Camões himself visited Goa, the Malabar coast and Macao. It has been suggested that he also visited the Banda Islands.

Illustration next side:
Ill. 4-11, In a Spanish naval chart of 1601[86]*, the Bandas are not shown*

---

83   c. 1524-1580
84   First Edition 1572
85   Lusitania is the Latin name for Portugal
86   Plate 14 from *Herrera's Descripción de las Indias Occidentales* (Madrid, 1601)

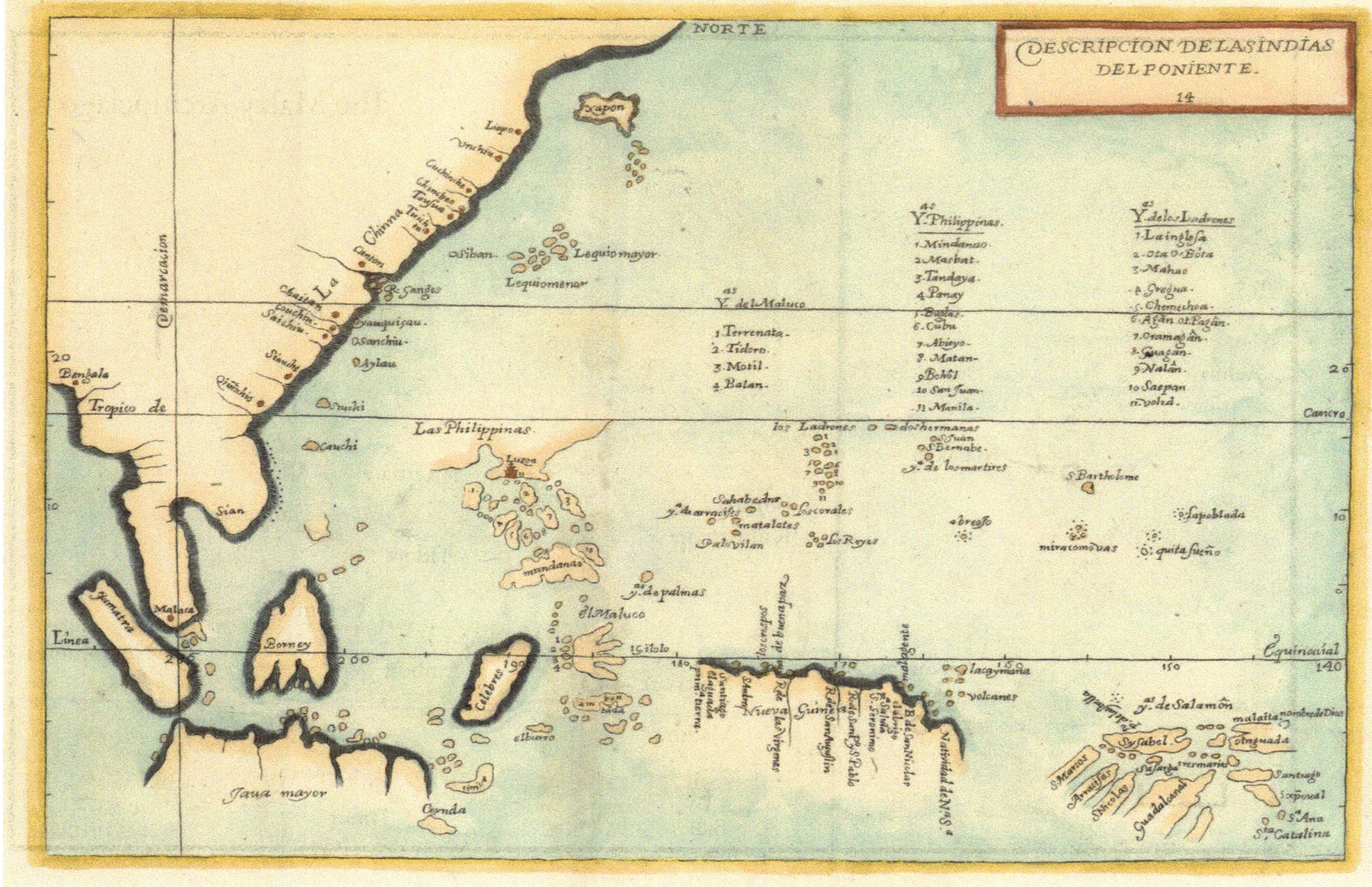

DESCRIPCION DE LAS INDIAS DEL PONIENTE.
14
NORTE
Demarcacion
Tropico de
Linea
Equinocial
Cancro
La China
Iapon
Liapo
Unchia
Cuchinha
Chimpeo
Toysua
Canton
Siban
Lequio mayor
Lequiomenor
R. Sanges
Chasian
Leuchiu
Satchiu
Pyanquiçau
O. Sanchiu
Aylau
Siaube
Qiuihiu
Suchi
Cauchi
Bengala
Sian
Las Philippinas
Luzon
mundanao
Y. de palmas
El Maluco
Sitolo
Calebes
Borney
Sumatra
Malaca
Iaua mayor
Oçnda
4.ᵃˢ Y. Philippinas.
1. Mindanao.
2. Marbat.
3. Tandaya.
4. Panay.
5. Buglas.
6. Cubu.
7. Abuyo.
8. Matan.
9. Bohol.
10. San Iuan.
11. Manila.
5.ᵃˢ Y. del Maluco
1. Terrenata.
2. Tidoro.
3. Motil.
4. Balan.
6.ᵃˢ Y. de los Ladrones
1. La inglesa
2. Ota O. Bota
3. Mahao
4. Gregua.
5. Chemechoa.
6. Agân ol Pagân.
7. Oramagân.
8. Guagan.
9. Nalân.
10. Saspan
11. volid.
los Ladrones
dos hermanas
S. Iuan
S. Bernabe
Y. de los martires
S. Bartholome
Sehabedra
y. de arracifes
los corales
matalates
Palo Vilan
los Reyes
brug
S. a poblada
mira como vas
quita sueño
los crespos de buenapaz
Nueva Guinea
R. de las Virgenes
R. de San Agustin
R. de San P. S. Pablo
S. Seuerino
B. de San Niclas
Natividad de N.ᵃ S.ᵃ
la cymana
volcanes
Y. de Salamon
malaita nombre de Dios
Y. sabel
tres marias
treguada
S. Marcos
Arrecifes
Nicolao
Guadalcanal
Santiago
S. poual
S. Ana
S.ta Catalina

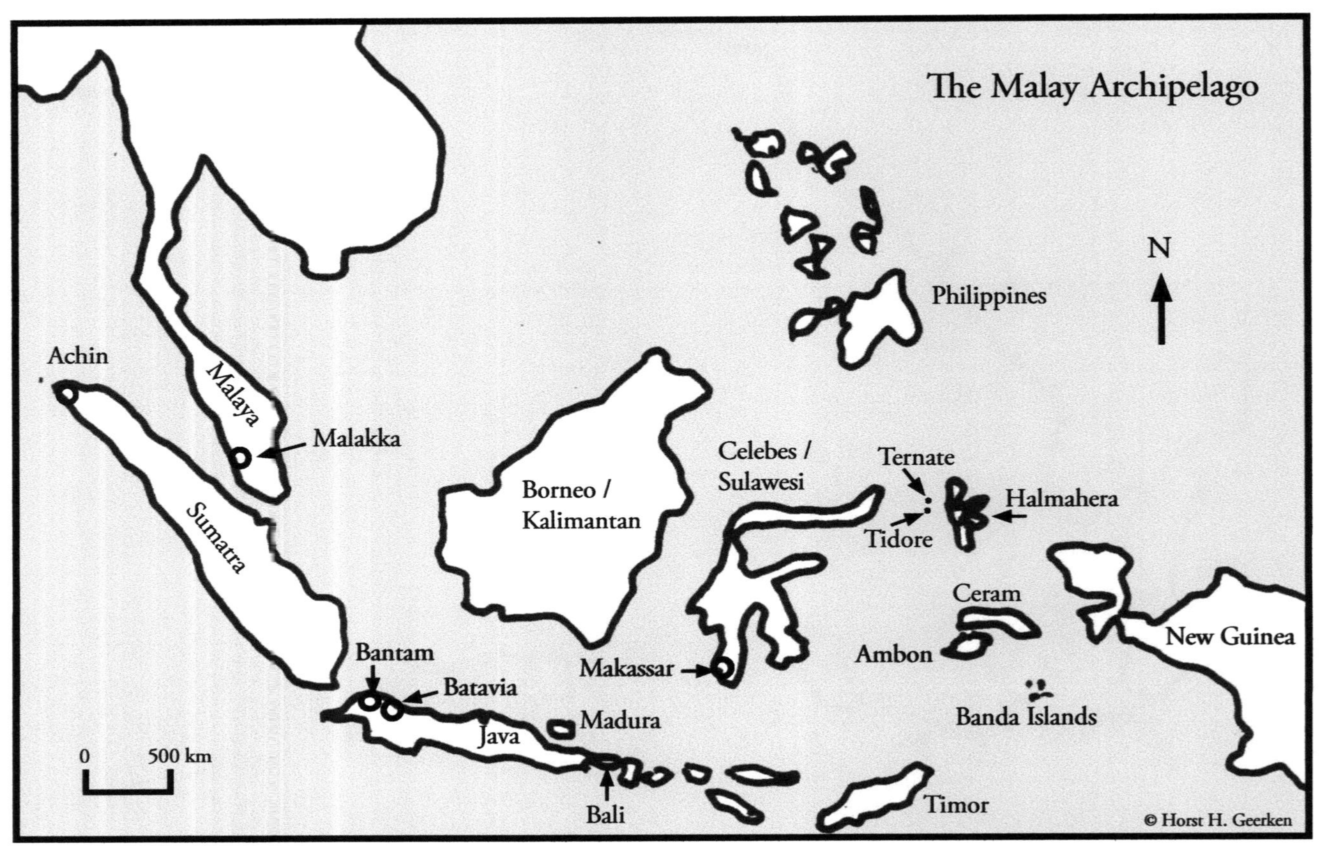

Ill. 4-12, The Malay Archipelago

5. The English wished to trade, the Dutch to conquer and possess

Forty years after the Portuguese began trading with the Spice Islands, the English decided that they too should have a share of this profitable trade. The Portuguese had already reached the Spice Islands in an easterly, the Spaniards in a westerly direction. A corporation of merchants, the Merchant Adventurers (later superceded by the British East India Company[87]), made it their goal to find their own land or sea route to the Spice Islands. They decided for the northern polar route, seeking a north-east passage. They wished to spare themselves the long voyage round Africa. If successful, the route they planned would have been some 3,500 km shorter. And they didn't want to encounter the Portuguese, who already had fortified bases along the entire eastern sea route.

It was a bad choice; the expedition was doomed to failure from the outset. The captains were not qualified for the task, and some of them were inexperienced, the equipment for the icy polar region was inadequate, they didn't have enough food supplies – some of the food was already rotten when it was taken on board, and the wine poured out of leaky barrels.

The expedition set sail on the 23rd of June 1553 with three ships, the flagship *Edward Bonaventure* commanded by Captain Richard Chancellor, the *Bona Esperanza* commanded by Captain Hugh Willoughby, who was inexperienced in northern waters, and the *Confidentia*. After they were caught in an Arctic storm north of Norway, one ship ran off course. None of the three ships was able to discover a north-east passage. Some years later, an English naval search party found the *Bona Esperanza* and *Confidentia* and their frozen crews crushed in the ice. Only Richard Chancellor and a few of his crew succeeded in making the 1,000-kilometre trek on foot to Moscow.

It was not until 24 years later that the English renewed their attempts to reach the Spice Islands. For the Portuguese, on the other hand, the trip across the Indian Ocean to trade with the Spice Islands had been routine for decades.

On the 13th of December 1577 Francis Drake sailed west with five ships under his command. He followed the same route as Magellan. In Patagonia he lost two of his ships, and another passing through the Magellan Strait. The other companion ship set out to return to England in a storm. Drake then sailed up the west coast of South and North America in the Pacific.

87   British East India Company, until 1707 English East India Company

Drake was neither an explorer nor a merchant, but rather a pirate, a freebooter. He was involved in the slave trade from Africa to the Caribbean. Queen Elizabeth I granted him letters of marque permitting him to board Spanish ships and confiscate their cargoes. On his voyage north he attacked numerous Spanish ships and plundered Spanish settlements on the west coast of South America. Fully laden with his booty of gold and silver, he began the Pacific crossing. After Magellan's poor experiences, he was well aware that it was necessary to have adequate provender for the long voyage. After several intermediate stops he reached the Spice Island of Ternate on the 4th of November 1579. Here, Drake made a trade agreement with the Sultan.

Drake's return voyage took him through the western Banda Sea, so that he did not approach the Banda Isles. South of Java his ship ran aground on a reef and was severely damaged. With great difficulty, Drake reached the port of Cilacap[88] on the south coast of Java. After the repair he sailed directly back to England with only one stop in Sierra Leone in West Africa, arriving on the 26th of September 1580, after 1018 days. It was England's first successful circumnavigation of the world. The voyage was a great success for the investors, who made a profit of 4,700%. Queen Elizabeth knighted Drake – a scoundrel whose wealth derived from plunder and multiple murder.

The British Corporation of Merchant Adventurers began a new attempt to reach the Spice Islands on the eastern route around the Cape of Good Hope. In 1582 Edward Fenton was commissioned to lead the expedition. Fenton could not have been a worse choice. He was devoted only to his own interests and had little understanding of sailing. He just sailed around in the Atlantic – in the meantime trying to get himself elected King of the Isle of Elba, a venture that failed in the face of his officers' and crew's opposition. Like the previous northern expedition, this was a costly failure for the English corporation.

Forewarned by the bitter failures of the English, the Dutch prepared their own expedition particularly carefully. In this, they were aided by information from Jan Huyghen van Linschoten, who had spent nine years in South-East Asia. He knew what languages were spoken on the various islands, what goods were most popular on the Spice Islands, where one could put into port to refresh supplies and so on. He reported that nutmeg sharpened the brain and the memory, warmed the stomach, purified the breath and prevented flatulence. It would even cure diarrhoea and alleviate bodily pain. The nutmeg was then, at the end of the 16th century, a universal panacea!

---

88   Previously Tjilatjap

Dutch merchants sent Cornelis de Houtman to Lisbon as a spy, to gain top secret information from Portuguese navigators and their charts. He was to discover details of the Portuguese' profitable trade, as at that time Portugal had a monopoly of the spice trade. He brought back important information and a world map drawn using the German cartographer Gerhard Mercator's[89] projection. Mercator worked at the newly founded University of Duisburg. Admittedly, the projection he developed does distort the shapes of countries the further north or south they are located, but it is the conformality of the projection that was a breakthrough for marine navigation. Mercator's first map was also stated to be solely for 'marine navigational use'. The projection is still in cartographic use.

Mercator's map gave the Dutch a decisive advantage for many years. Dutch cartographers now made their maps using this projection. Using the information provided by Mercator's map and information from Dutch mariners the Dutch cartographer, astronomer, geographer and pastor Petrus Plancius published a map of South-East Asia in 1594 which far surpassed all previous maps for accuracy.

With the aid of this map, which was state-of-the-art for the time, the organisers in Amsterdam were able to raise the funds for the first Dutch expedition to the East Indies. Now it was no longer a voyage into unknown waters

Though the expedition was extremely carefully prepared – there were, for example, spare masts, sails and anchors – the choice of leading personnel was equally extremely negligent. Houtman was given the position of chief merchant on the *Mauritius* and also had a seat on the fleet council. As we will see, he was not suited for either position.

In the spring of 1595, a fleet of four ships – the *Amsterdam*, the *Mauritius*, the *Hollandia* and the *Duyfken* – set sail. Houtman was ordered to avoid all Portuguese-controlled ports and also the Strait of Malacca.

By the time they rounded the Cape of Good Hope, 71 men had already died of scurvy. When the captain of the *Amsterdam* then also died, the crews' discipline collapsed completely: there was continual unrest on the ships, which degenerated into violence. While they were stopping over in Madagascar, a large number of the sailors were killed in brawls between the crews of the different ships. The bay in which they were anchored is still called The Dutch Cemetery. They were unable to sail on until some months later. The armada finally sailed through the Sunda Strait into the port of Bantam[90] on the northern coast of western Java. Up to this point they had lost more than a hundred men on the voyage.

---

89   1512-1594
90   Now Banten

ORBIS TERRARVM TYPVS DE INTEGRO MULTIS IN LOCIS EMENDATVS auctore Petro Plancio 1594
Europa
Asia
Mexicana
Peruana
Magallanica
Africa
AMERICA SIVE INDIA NOVA
AFRICA
MAGALLANICA SIVE TERRA AVSTRALIS
TERRA AVSTRALIS MAGALLANICA
MAR PACIFICO
OCEANVS PERVVIANVS
EL MAR

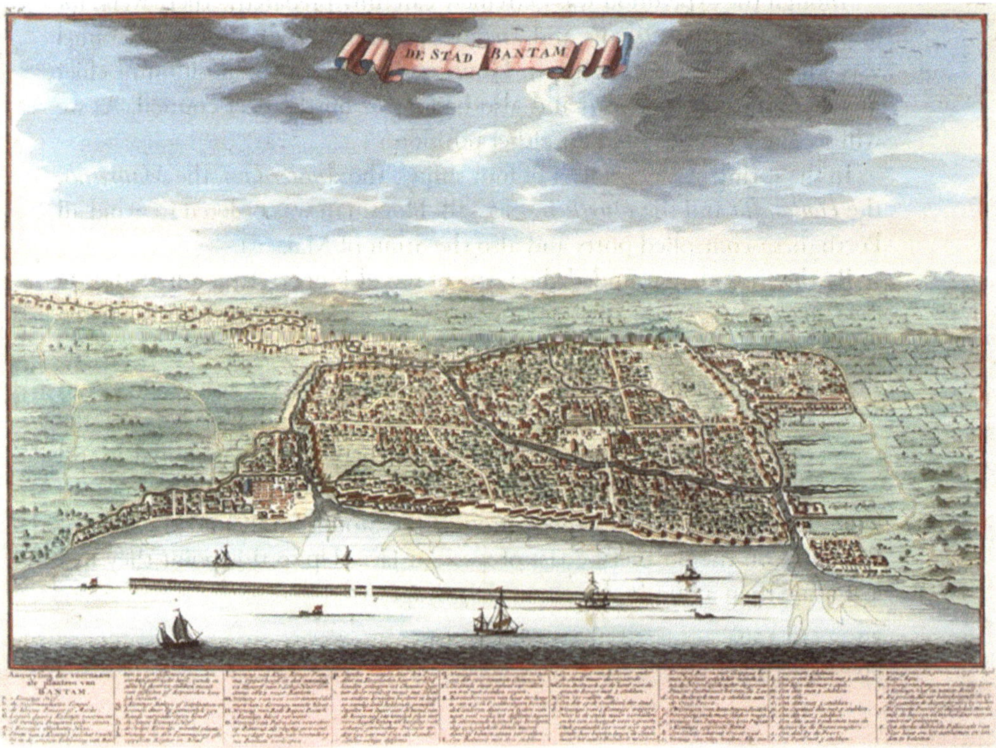

DE STAD BANTAM

When the Dutch landed on Java, they were expecting to find 'savages' like the ones Columbus had found in the New World. But on Java everything was very different. They encountered an advanced culture and sophisticated people, and nevertheless they still treated them as savages. Java already had cities, governments, water supply and sewage system, art, literature and temples. The native people planted trees, harvested spices and had traded with China, India, Arabia and the coast of Africa for centuries. Members of the upper ranks of Javanese society were intelligent and highly educated. The market-place in Bantam was – to the surprise of the Dutch – thronged with merchants from Malacca, the Malabar Coast, China and the Spice Islands who were all trading peacefully with one another.

The Dutch behaved with unparalleled brutality – something that was to continue throughout their centuries of colonial rule. Houtman was arrogant and hot-headed. As the Javanese merchants refused to exchange spices for cheap glass beads and Houtman did not want to pay the regular price they demanded, on the spur of the moment he captured two junks in the harbour of Bantam in an act of piracy. They were loaded with nutmeg and cloves. In response, the Sultan von Bantam had all the crew members of the four ships who were on land at the time arrested, only freeing them when Houtman had paid compensation for the damage he had caused. When all his men were back on board, he bombarded the city with his ships' cannon in a fit of rage at his discomfiture. The Sultan's palace was destroyed. Captured Javanese were tortured and killed in the most gruesome manner. The brutality with which the Dutch introduced themselves to the Malay Archipelago was indescribable. When they had wreaked enough destruction, they sailed off to the east and sought out another port on the north coast of Java.

News of the aggressive behaviour of the Dutch had naturally quickly spread throughout Java. When the ships dropped anchor near Tuban[91], vengeful Javanese succeeded in storming one of the ships and killing twelve Dutchmen. Houtman weighed anchor once more.

Illustrations left page:
Ill. 5-1, Orbis Terrarum: map by Petrus Plancius (1594)[92]
Ill. 5-2, Bantam in a 1724 illustration[93]

---

91   West of Surabaya
92   Petrus Plancius' Map (1594), Maritime Museum, Rotterdam. Wikipedia Commons
93   Wikipedia Public Domain

Off the island of Madura, a large flotilla of small boats approached the Dutch fleet. In the middle was the elegantly decorated barge of the Sultan of Madura. They were approaching with peaceful intentions, because the murderous character of the Dutch had not been reported in Madura, an island off the east Javan coast. But Houtman suspected an ambush and ordered a massacre. All the cannon on the four ships fired on the little boats, and then when they were sunk the Dutchmen lowered their boats and shot the survivors individually. Some of them seem to have suffered a bad conscience as a result of this brutality. One member of the crew wrote in his diary that he was surprised *that merchants had suddenly been transformed into bloodthirsty cutthroats*. After the massacre no Dutch ships were allowed to land on Java.

The Dutch ships were already in a poor state: the *Amsterdam* was so rotten that it had to be set on fire and destroyed. When the fleet moored off Bali to take on water and provisions, two of the men decided to remain in Paradise and went to ground. After a mutiny, the fleet council decided to discontinue the voyage to the Spice Islands and to begin the home voyage with the three remaining ships. The first Dutch expedition to the East Indies from April 1595 to August 1598 went very badly and ended as an utter catastrophe. The ships brought only a small quantity of spices back to Amsterdam and of the 249 men who had set out only 87 ever saw their homes again. Because of their aggressive and arrogant behaviour and their gratuitous acts of murder, the Dutch lost the trust of the native population from the very outset.

Ill. 5-3, The German translation of the Dutch account of the voyage, 1598[94]

---

94 Wikipedia Commons

Ill. 5-4, Bombardment of the city of Bantam by the Dutch, 1596[95]

Levinus Hulsius in Nuremberg published a series of 26 travel reports. In
1598 he published a booklet containing the German translation of the
Dutch report on Cornelis de Houtman's voyage. The book is in the archives
of the Saxon State Library in Dresden; there is another copy in the Library
of the Catholic University of Eichstätt-Ingolstadt.

Apparently, the gentlemen in Amsterdam had learned nothing from Cornelis Houtman's failure, since only six months after his return in 1598 they
gave him the command of a new expedition to the East Indies. He was
accompanied by the Englishman John Davis as helmsman and navigator.

95 Wikipedia Commons

After his return, John Davis went back to the East Indies, but this time for the newly founded English East India Company.

In the five years following the return of Cornelis Houtman[96] more than 60 other Dutch ships sailed to East Asia. The Portuguese monopoly was broken. The Dutch had now taken over the majority of the spice trade and extended their position in the Malay Archipelago.

In 1600 Portuguese influence in the Moluccas was still very minor. They traded, but they only had fortifications on the islands of Ternate and Ambon. They had neglected the Banda Islands, the richest islands in the Moluccas, even though the first European to visit them had been the Portuguese Miranda de Azevedo as early as 1513. The English now planned to sail to these remote and isolated islands and raise the English flag there. Neither the Portuguese nor the Spanish had yet built a fort on the Bandas. It had become an accepted tenet of international law among the European nations that they could only claim possession of a territory by building fortifications there. There was therefore still an opportunity to claim the Bandas, the richest of the Spice Islands, for the English Crown.

After James Lancaster's successful voyage, subsequent English expeditions ended in disaster: one expedition under Captain Benjamin Wood even disappeared without trace. Now all the hopes of the London merchants were placed in a new expedition led by Lancaster. He was invited to command a fleet of four vessels, the *Susan,* the *Hector,* the *Ascension* and the *Red Dragon.* John Davis, the experienced navigator and re-discoverer of Greenland, who had just returned from a Dutch expedition was appointed chief helmsman: the East India Company's expedition was thus in good and experienced hands.

It was in February 1601 that the fleet, with a force of around 470 men, left England. On board they had a number of factors[97], who were to found branches in East Asia. The Queen granted them almost unlimited powers. For example, they were to have a monopoly of all trade east of the Cape of Good Hope. However, they had to guarantee that they would undertake a new expedition every year. Queen Elizabeth even had special coins minted for the English East India Company, portcullis money. They were silver coins which were only minted between 1600 and 1601, with a portcullis on the reverse. Unfortunately, the coins were not internationally accepted.

It took until September 1601 – seven months – for the fleet to reach South Africa to take on provisions. Lancaster's flagship, the *Red Dragon,*

---

96   Houtman returned to Holland in 1598
97   Merchants/Agents

70

had an ocean-go-
ing pinnace in dis-
mantled form on
board, which they
assembled during
a stopover in Madagascar. They next touched land at the Nicobar Islands,
where they once more took on provisions and then sailed on to arrive at the
flourishing port city of Achin[98] in north Sumatra on the 5th of June 1602.
Unlike the Dutch, the English were very welcome here. Lancaster brought a
letter from Queen Elizabeth which he handed over to the Sultan of Achin,
Alauddin Shah, in which she asked him to grant regular trading relations
and a trading post. All the English Queen's requests were granted, and mutual gifts exchanged. The agreement was sealed by multiple banquets, where
they were toasted with a great deal of alcohol, in spite of the fact that northern Sumatra was Islamic even then.

Today no occasion including alcohol would be possible. I visited Aceh
several times in the 1960s and 1970s (it is now called Banda Aceh[99]). It
was almost impossible to get hold of alcohol. In the Chinese restaurant
you could still secretly drink beer in teacups poured from a teapot in those
days.[100] Today even that is impossible: strict Sharia reigns.

Lancaster left Achin in November 1602 and set his course for Bantam in
western Java since the price of spices was lower there than in Achin. The *Ascension* was already fully laden with its precious cargo for the voyage home.
Lancaster also received a friendly reception from the King of Bantam, and
the ships were loaded for a pre-arranged price. Shortly before the fleet set sail
on the homeward voyage in February 1603, Lancaster selected eight crew
and three merchants to stay at the newly opened trading post in Bantam.
They were to purchase spices for a future expedition and store them in a
small warehouse. They were also to attempt to reach the Bandas in the pinnace, which was left with them for that purpose.

---

98 Called Kuta Raja under Dutch rule; now Banda Aceh
99 Formerly Kuta Raja, also Kuta Radja and Koetaradja
100 See Horst H. Geerken, *A Gecko for Luck,* p. 190 ff

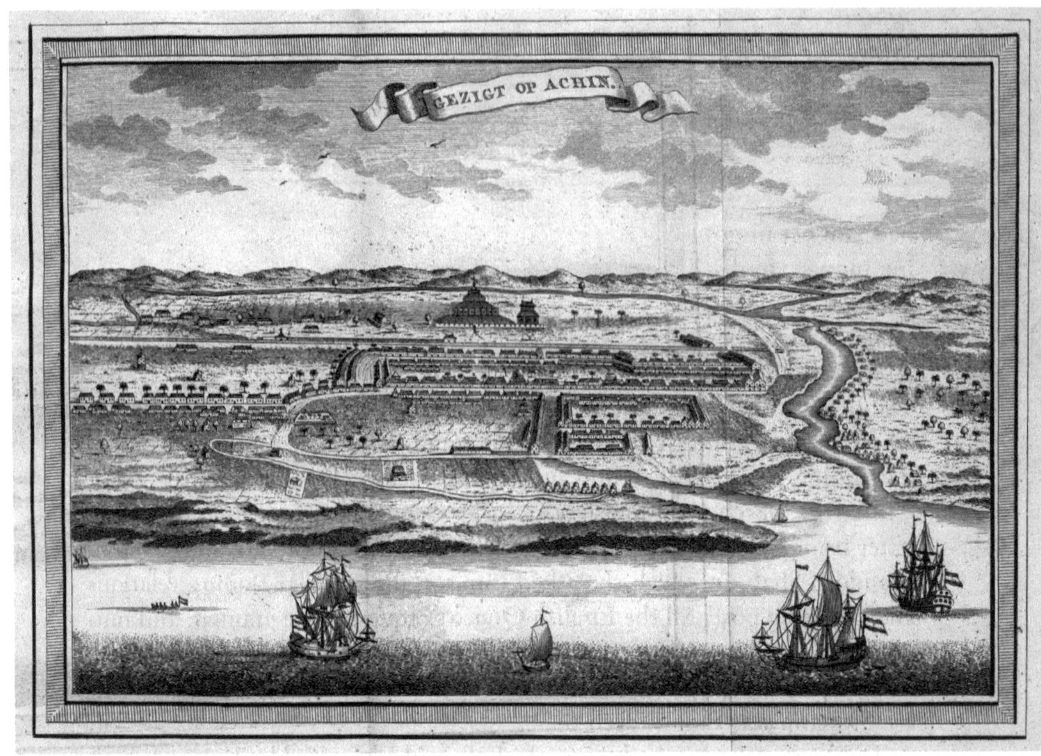

Ill. 5-6, An old view of Achin[101]

In September 1603 the fleet arrived back in London. Lancaster brought all his ships back fully laden. His voyage had been a great economic and diplomatic success. Nevertheless, he had lost nearly half his men to scurvy and other diseases on the two-and-a-half-year voyage.

Detailed historical writing about the Banda Islands only actually begins with the arrival of the first Dutchman in 1599. This was Vice Admiral Jakob van Heemskerk, who arrived on the *Gelderland* off the island of Banda Besar[102] – the largest and most fertile of the islands – with a company of 200 merchants and soldiers on the 15th of March 1599. The next day the *Zeeland* arrived at the island. This date, the 15th of March 1599, is still deeply engraved in the memory of the Bandanese, because it was the beginning of the misery and injustice. The *Gelderland* and the *Zeeland* were only part of a Dutch expedition of eight ships commanded by Admiral Jacob van Neck.

---

101 Wikipedia, Public Domain
102 Then Lonthoir, also Lonthor

72

The Bandanese received the blonde Dutchmen with reserve. Their contacts with Europeans over more than 100 years made them distrustful of the newcomers. And there was also the fact that the Gunung Api volcano, which had been inactive for a long time, erupted with unusual force, vomiting fire, ashes and lava. Another reason for their anxiety was the prophecy made by a Muslim holy man five years previously, that strangers from a far distant land would try and conquer and exploit their islands.

The Dutch paid their respects to the *Orang Kaya,* 'rich, old or influential gentlemen', and handed over gifts. From the very beginning they made it clear that the Portuguese and the English were their enemies. Van Heemskerk was much more diplomatic and restrained than all his successors. He won a certain degree of trust from the Bandanese and was able to begin trading with the merchants from Java, China and Arabia. They had long been settled on the Bandas. It was a tedious process, as each merchant had only a small stock of spice available, and they had to deal with each of them individually. It took three and a half months for the two ships to be fully laden with mace and nutmeg from the Bandas. During this time, the price of the spices rose by 50% because of the increase in demand. Even so, they were sold later in Amsterdam – after deducting all the costs involved – at a profit of 430%.

It is interesting to note how the ships were loaded with the spices. Down at the bottom of the hull of the ship there were jars full of ginger; then came a layer of pepper on top of them. And only then was the nutmeg stored on the very top. According to the the German naturalist Rumphius the nuts were simply poured into the hold. As a result of oxidation, the spices produced heat and poisonous gases, so that the hold could not be entered during the voyage. This storage method was something of a fire risk, and so the hatches had to be kept permanently open for ventilation. I am unable to understand why they used this particular technique. It was only towards the end of the 19th century that they began to use sacks, crates and barrels as containers.

On the 16th of July 1599 the *Gelderland* and the *Zeeland* began their return voyage to Holland. Vice Admiral Jakob van Heemskerk left 22 of his men behind on the islands of Banda Besar and Banda Neira. They were to purchase as large a quantity of spice as possible for the next expedition. In the spring of 1600, van Heemskerk returned to Holland with his two ships.

The success of the Dutch alarmed the Javanese and the Portuguese in Malacca. With the help of 1,500 Javanese allies, the Portuguese decided to destroy the Dutch trading posts. Shortly before the planned attack, two

Dutch ships, the *Morgensterre* and the *Maan*[103], arrived off Banda Neira on the 9th of May 1600. They were on their way to Ambon and were seeking shelter from a storm. When the Javanese saw the two gigantic ships, they lost heart and sailed back to Java.

The English followed in the footsteps of the Dutch. Soon after Lancaster left Bantam, five of the men who had been left behind set sail in the pinnace to seek the Banda Islands. Master Mariner Keche captained the ship. Very little is known about this expedition, as all the reports the mariners wrote have been lost. All we know is that they had to battle with high West-Monsoon winds and high seas for two months to reach the island of Run, the most remote of the Bandas and the most difficult to reach. Because of the monsoon winds, the Bandas were normally only accessible from Bantam in the second half of the year.

Run is surrounded by dangerous shallows, strong currents, coral reefs and cliffs. It was a masterly achievement – unless it was pure luck – to reach the island unscathed through all these obstacles (which are still there today). The five men were given a friendly welcome on Run. They were allowed to trade and to build a small storehouse in the north of the island.

They were the first Englishmen to reach the Banda Islands, and the first to be allowed to build bases on the islands of Run and Ai. The inhabitants of Run saw in them allies against the Dutch. A treaty was agreed with the *Orang Kaya*, which transferred all rights over the islands of Run and Ai to the English. They were the first English possessions in Asia. The English flag flew over both islands for decades, much to the annoyance of the Dutch. The Dutch hadn't taken possession of the islands, because it was barely possible to reach the islands from Banda Neira under sail during the West Monsoon, and this is still so today. And Run was at a safe distance from the belligerent Dutchmen on Banda Neira. There are a good eighteen kilometres of open sea between the two islands.

How long the Englishmen stayed on the island – and whether they sailed back to Bantam in the pinnace – is unknown. In the meanwhile, Queen Elizabeth I had died, and James Lancaster was knighted on his return by her cousin, the newly crowned King James I. The King now proudly listed his titles as 'King of England, Scotland, Ireland, France, Puloway[104] and Puloroon'[105].

---

103 Aka *de Maen*
104 Pulau Ai, Island (of) Ai
105 Pulau Run, Island (of) Run

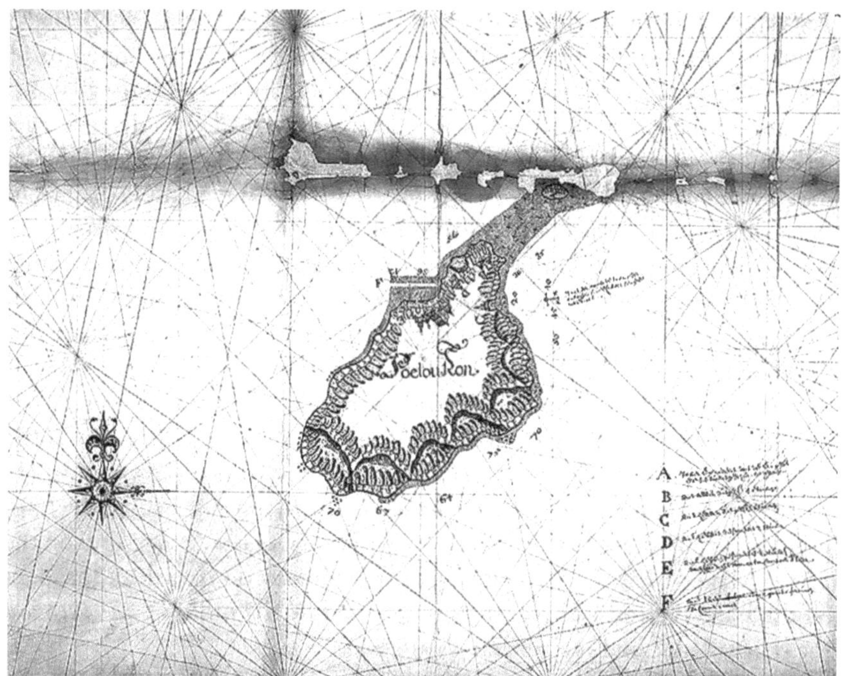

Ill. 5-7, The first known map of the Island of Run, 1623[106]

The English immediately planned another expedition to the Malay Archipelago with the same four ships. Lancaster had no desire to undertake the dangerous voyage again, and so command of the expedition was given to the experienced Captain Henry Middleton, who had already sailed with Lancaster. The fleet sailed directly to Bantam on Java, arriving on the 22nd of December 1604. The *Hector* and the *Susan* were laden with spices and immediately despatched on the voyage home. The *Red Dragon* and the *Ascension* headed for the Spice Islands. By the time they reached the port of Ambon, many of the crew had died of amoebic dysentery.

While Henry Middleton was at anchor in the port of Ambon with his two ships, nine Dutch ships with an accompanying auxiliary fleet arrived with hostile intent. They were commanded by Admiral van der Hagen. After bombarding the Portuguese fort, they occupied the bastion. Both English ships fled the scene without loading any spices. Middleton wrote in his log: *If this frothy nation may have the trade of the Indies to themselves, their pride and insolencie will be intollerable.[107]* The ships separated, the

---

106 Wikipedia, Public Domain
107 Giles Milton, *Nathaniel's Nutmeg,* 1999, p.109

Red Dragon sailing to the northern Spice Islands, and the *Ascension* under Captain Colthurst to the Banda Islands, where the English hoped to be able to buy nutmeg without any vexatious competition. Colthurst planned to put into the Island of Run, but was deterred by the dangerous reefs that lay just beneath the surface. He therefore abandoned his attempt to land on the island, but was able to buy spices on the islands of Ai, Banda Neira and Banda Besar. Then the *Ascension* rejoined the *Red Dragon*. They made the voyage home together. Unfortunately, the surviving documents concerning this and subsequent English voyages to the Banda Islands and to Run in particular are extremely sparse. At the end of 1608 the English pinnace *The Hope* came to Run and left two Englishmen[108] there.

The commander of the Dutch base on Banda Neira was Admiral Hermanszoon, who arrived with the *Utrecht* and the *Zeeland* in February 1602. He did his best to make the lives of the English as difficult as possible. He stirred the Bandanese and the merchants on the islands up against the English. He even managed to make a treaty with some of the *Orang Kaya* on the 23rd of May 1602 which gave the Dutch a monopoly on the sale of spices on all the Banda Islands. This treaty was rejected by the other *Orang Kaya* on the other islands and the general population.

Trading with the native population by exchange was difficult for the Dutch at first. They only had knives, fabrics that were far too heavy, and other goods that were totally unsuitable for the tropical climate. And the Bandanese were interested in rice, sago and vegetables, for which they exchanged their nutmeg. They got these goods from merchants from Java and Ambon. And goods from China, like porcelain, metal goods and medicines, were of far better quality than what the Dutch had to offer. English competition was therefore more than welcomed by the Bandanese. They refused to accept the treaty that the Dutch had extorted from the people of Banda Neira.

However, it was precisely this extorted treaty that the Dutch referred to when they announced their claim to the islands of Run and Ai. Admiral Hermanszoon's interlude on Banda Neira and Banda Besar was only short lived. He left the islands again in June 1602, leaving ten men behind to look after the two Dutch bases on the island.

When the next Dutch ship put into the Banda Islands with Admiral van der Hagen in 1605, both bases were abandoned and neglected. What had happened? They were told that two of the ten Dutchmen who had been left behind liked the life on Banda Neira so much that they had abandoned their Christian beliefs and gone over to Islam. They wanted to stay on

---

108 Brown and Sydell

Banda Neira for ever with their charming Bandanese companions. Their fellow Dutchmen found this scandalous, and murdered them. The Bandanese stormed the bases and murdered five of the Dutch. Three succeeded in escaping.

Admiral van der Hagen's fleet, consisting of thirteen ships and a force of at least 1,500 men, was at first in action in the northern Moluccas. Van der Hagen went to the Bandas with only one ship and a pinnace. The mission the VOC, the Dutch East Indies Company founded on the 20th of March 1602, gave to Admiral van der Hagen was to drive the Portuguese and English from all the Spice Islands and create a trade monopoly by any means possible, either by treaty or by violence. Trading and military stations should be established on all strategically important islands. We have already seen how van der Hagen carried these instructions out in Ambon using cannon fire. Van der Hagen was irate when he heard that the English Captain Colthurst had reached the Banda Islands before him, and returned to the fleet in Ambon to discuss the matter.

Ill. 5-8, The Headquarters of the VOC in Amsterdam [109]

109   Wikipedia Public Domain

In the meanwhile the English Captain William Keeling had established himself firmly on the islands of Run and Ai with only 30 musketeers. He cruised between the islands to buy spices in his ship the *Hector*. He was surprised to be greeted in a friendly manner even by Dutch merchants. On those lonely and remote islands, the merchants were glad of any diversion.

This changed dramatically on the 8th of April 1609 when the Dutch Admiral Pieterzoon Verhoeven arrived in the Bandas with an initial force of six ships. Within a few days seven more ships arrived. On board were 1,000 armed soldiers, mostly Dutch, though there were some Japanese mercenaries who were executioners. Captain Keeling withdrew to the safety of the Island of Run.

On the 19th of April 1609 Pieterzoon Verhoeven landed on Banda Besar with 250 heavily armed men to negotiate a monopoly with the *Orang Kaya*. The Bandanese played hard to get, finding ever more excuses – at least partly because of the Muslim holy man's prophecies and the activity Gunung Api. Pieterzoon Verhoeven lost patience and landed another 750 soldiers on the neighbouring island of Banda Neira. Without consulting the *Orang Kaya,* He began on the construction of a fort, which later became Fort Nassau, on the site where the Portuguese had begun to build nearly a hundred years before, though they had been driven away by the Bandanese. One big advantage was that the massive stone foundations were still there.

The inhabitants of Banda Neira were forced to leave their homes and put them at the disposal of the soldiers. The *Orang Kaya* of Banda Neira, who had not been present at the talks on Banda Besar, were simply brutishly ignored. The Bandanese watched the activities of the Dutch from a hill behind the fort and plotted revenge. Fort Belgica was later built on that hill. In military terms, the Bandanese had no chance at all, because the Dutch were far better armed.

On the 22nd of March 1609 the *Orang Kaya* requested a meeting with Admiral Verhoeven, who immediately agreed, as he thought that the Bandanese were now ready to give in to his demands. Towards mid-day he and his captains and merchants went to the agreed place near the coast in the east of Banda Besar, bringing armed guards with them. The *Orang Kaya* had retreated to a nearby wood, and let it be known that they were afraid of so many soldiers, and that Verhoeven should come alone. He left his guards behind and went into the wood with just his unarmed captains and merchants. They were walking into a trap. There were 200 armed Bandanese hiding in the wood. Verhoeven and about 30 of his companions were immediately beheaded; others were cut down as they fled. This all happened very quickly. When the guards went into the wood, all they found were decapitated corpses. The Bandanese population had vanished into thin air. One witness of the event – in Holland it is called *Het verraad der Bandan-ezen van 1609* [The Bandanese treachery of 1609] – was the young Jan Pieterszoon Coen, a junior merchant under Verhoeven's command. He later became Dutch Governor-General, and was to wreak terrible vengeance on the Bandanese for what they had done.

The *Orang Kaya* of Banda Besar offered to trade with the Dutch, but only under two conditions: all Dutch soldiers must return to their ships, and the partly completed fort must be dismantled. Both conditions were rejected by the Dutch. Upheaval and skirmishes followed. Dutch merchants were murdered on Banda Besar. Admiral Simon Janszoon Hoen was chosen as Verhoeven's successor as new commander of the mission. He ordered his soldiers to loot villages and to burn the natives' houses and fishing boats. The Bandanese resisted, and killed and injured many more of the Dutch. The Dutch laid down more regulations for the Bandanese, who circumvented them as much as was possible.

Fort Nassau was now so far completed that Admiral Hoen was able to leave the Bandas for the Northern Moluccas. The merchants, together with a strong garrison, were now able to entrench themselves in the Fort and store and collect supplies of spices. Hendrik van Bergel was appointed Governor of the Banda Islands. The Dutch continued to regard themselves as rulers over all the Bandas. They planned several attacks on Run and Ai, which were still in the hands of the English, but their ships were always blown back by the strong monsoon winds, so that they never actually came to blows.

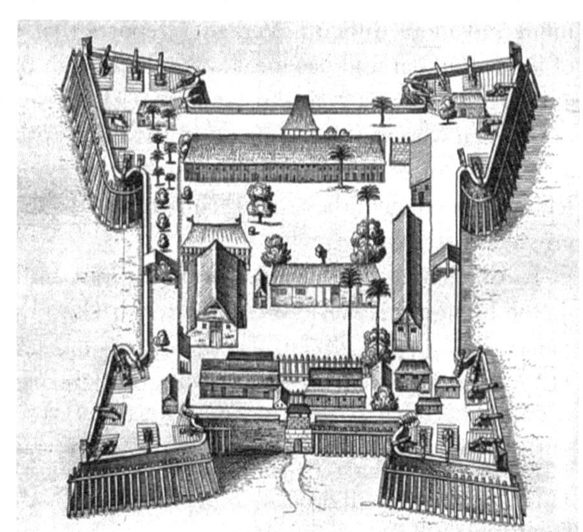

Ill. 5-9
Fort Nassau, etching
from 1646[110]

---

110 Wikipedia
Public Domain

79

The English merchants on Run and Ai were now able – with a certain degree of schadenfreude – to acquire spices from Banda Neira and Banda Besar, even though according to the enforced monopoly they were supposed to be destined for the Dutch. In the course of time the Bandanese actually supplied the English with more nutmeg than the Dutch. Relations between the two countries became increasingly tense. The Dutch blamed the English for the fact that there were such high Dutch casualties in the attacks on the villages. The English on Run did in fact train the Bandanese in modern military tactics and the use of muskets, so that they could collaborate in standing up to the Dutch.

In February 1610 the English Captain David Middleton[111] arrived in the Bandas in the *Expedition.* In the course of the year, he travelled to and fro between the Bandas, Ambon and Ceram in the pinnace[112] *Hopewell* buying spices. He had set up a base on Ai to which the Bandanese could bring their harvest. He frequently chartered ships from local merchants to carry the spices first to Ceram and then to Bantam, where they were transferred to English ships. The Dutch were now not getting enough spices to fill their own ships and so, in order to enforce their monopoly, they increased their pressure on the Bandanese. Secret meetings took place between Middleton and the *Orang Kayas* on the *Expedition.* They discussed how they could continue to get round the Dutch monopoly, and the *Orang Kaya* asked for more support against the Dutch. The Bandanese fought back against the Dutch reprisals and killed every Dutchman they could catch outside Fort Nassau. Any venture outside the Fort was now dangerous: it took a whole company of 60 armed men to harvest fruit near the Fort. Life in the fort became more and more difficult. Verken[113] reports that they were running short of food. Rat, cat and bat meat was sold at high prices. When a VOC ship anchored off Banda Neira in January 1611 it brought, much to the dismay of the men who were hanging on in the Fort, nothing but some arak[114] and a few sacks of beans. The ship's crew had no sympathy with their starving fellow-countrymen: they sold their own rations to the soldiers in the Fort at grossly inflated prices.

To the delight of the directors of the East India Company David Middleton brought his precious cargo safely back to England.

111 David was Henry Middleton's younger brother
112 A small light vessel, usually having two schooner-rigged (originally square-rigged) masts, often in attendance on a larger vessel and used as a tender or scout, to carry messages, etc. (OED)
113 A German in the service of the VOC, see Chapter 8
114 A high proof spirit distilled from palm wine. On the Bandas 20 *perkeniers* were licensed to distil and sell this spirit

In 1615, much to the disappointment of the Bandanese, it was only merchants and not soldiers who came to Run. In Bantam the Bandanese now requested muskets, gunpowder and rice. Their desire for some English soldiers was finally granted by the gentlemen of the Directory.

In April 1610 the sixth East India Company fleet set sail for the Banda Islands, under the command of Sir Henry Middleton, who had experience in sailing to East Asia. The fleet consisted of the *Trade Increase,* the biggest ship so far to sail to East Asia, the *Peppercorn* and the *Darling.* On board was Nathaniel Courthope, who was to be left on the island of Run with other factors to promote friendship with the Bandanese and to acquire and store nutmeg and mace for future expeditions.

Middleton had been ordered to make a trade treaty with the Sultan of Oman. Instead, there were disputes which led to the imprisonment of Middleton and some of his crew. It was not until the following August that they were able to continue their voyage – without the treaty. When they finally arrived at Bantam the supplies on the ships had all run out and the *Trade Increase* was so worm-eaten that they had to scuttle her. The *Darling* was also not in a fit state to make the return voyage, and was only used for trips between the islands. Only the *Peppercorn* made it back to England. The whole unsuccessful enterprise had taken three and a half years.

The crews of the *Trade Increase* and the *Darling* had to hang on in Bantam. When the next English ship – from the seventh fleet – arrived in Bantam they were faced with a ghastly sight. Most of the crew and the Captain, Sir Henry Middleton, had died of an inexplicable disease. Only a handful of men, among them Nathaniel Courthope, had survived.

Bantam was always the first port of call for English ships, and the centre point of their activities. The English warehouses and factory[115] were there. The climate was unhealthy: it was hot and humid and surrounded by foul swamps in which malarial mosquitoes bred. There were constant arguments and fights, and not just between English and Dutch sailors, but also between the sailors of the various English ships. One had to be constantly on one's guard against thieves and bandits. Bantam society was always looking for a fight. It was also a den of iniquity; Javanese, Chinese and Indian women were all too ready to offer their services to the sexually frustrated sailors. In October 1616, After Courthope had recovered, and also carried out a mission in Borneo[116], he was given command of two ships, the *Defence* and the *Swan.* Their orders were to sail to Run via Macassar. Run is one of the smallest inhabited Banda Islands, but also one of the richest, with nutmeg

---

115 Trading post
116 Now Kalimantan

trees covering the slopes from the coast to the mountain tops. Yet, as we know, it was also, because of the dangerous reefs and currents, one of the most difficult to reach.

On the 25th of December 1616 Nathaniel Courthope and a few dozen soldiers arrived at Run in the *Swan*, to defend it and Ai against the territorial claims of the Dutch. The mission was ordered directly by King James I and was top secret. The courageous Courthope was to play a particularly important role for England and the Banda Islands.

The English had been instructed to develop a firm friendship with the Bandanese. The inhabitants of Run were delighted to see two English ships in their harbour. They were unable to feed themselves on what the island produced. No rice grew there, hardly any sago and very few vegetables. The only thing that flourished was the nutmeg. Food had to be brought in from other islands, but since the Dutch were blockading Run, the majority of the inhabitants were on the verge of starvation. The situation was made worse by the large number of refugees from Ai. Nathaniel Courthope could only help them temporarily, as his ships had only been partly provisioned in Macassar.

The provision of drinking water was a major problem. The islands of Run and Nailakka have no freshwater springs. They had to use rainwater, which was collected in large pots and cisterns. And the increase in population exacerbated the problem. The Dutch blockade meant that they could not import water either. They had to limit their daily consumption to a minimum.

Courthope renewed the treaties with the Run *Orang Kaya*, confirming England's sovereignty over the island. The Bandanese trusted Courthope completely. Both sides regarded themselves as allies against Dutch aggression. The Bandanese collaborated with the English on building fortifications on Run and Nailakka. It was absolutely necessary for the English to retain possession of the latter, a small uninhabited islet, because it had particularly rich fishing grounds and had ships sailing in from Banda Neira in its line of fire. They took the heavy cannons from the two ships and mounted three each in Fort Defence on Nailakka and Fort Swan, west of the port of Run. The dangerous reefs and currents round the island meant that there was only one practical entrance to the harbour, which was easy to defend. It was a bit exaggerated to call the two artillery positions forts, since they only consisted of dry-stone walls. Observation posts were established on higher ground and musket positions along the west coast. The Dutch could no longer come within range of the cannons and it would be extremely difficult for them to take the island. However, none of these preparations affected the blockade, and there were still limited supplies of food and gunpowder.

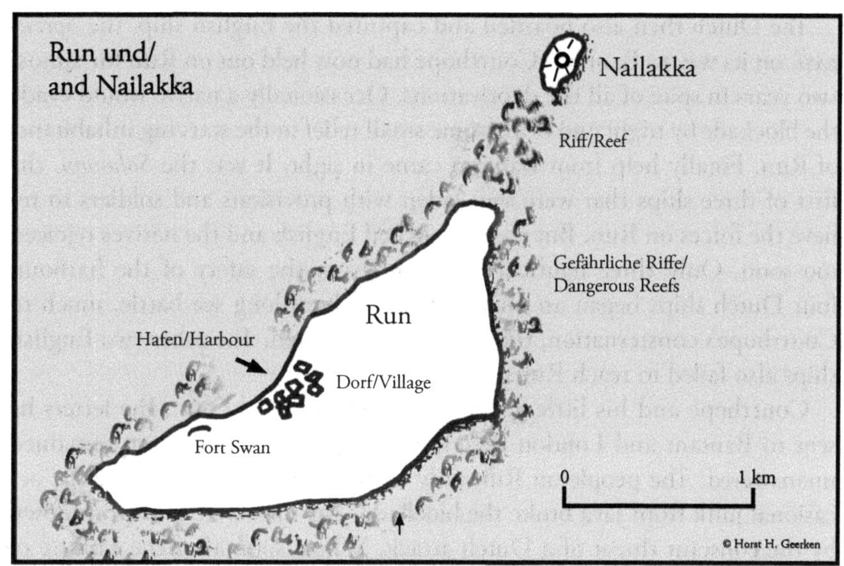

Ill. 5-10, Map of the islands of Run and Nailakka

When supplies of drinking water threatened to run out, the *Swan,* captained by John Davis sailed to Ceram to fill up the casks. Before doing so he headed for the island of Bandalontar[117] whose *Orang Kaya* had requested, along with the island of Rozengain[118] to be taken under English protection. Captain Davis received the documents attesting to this commitment.

On the return voyage from Ceram to Run the *Swan* was attacked by the Dutch ship the *Morgensterre.* The *Swan* was very vulnerable, because its cannons were in position on Run and Nailakka. After a bloody struggle on board the *Swan,* the ship was captured and plundered by the Dutch. She was towed to Banda Neira and Captain Davis and the surviving members of his crew were imprisoned in Fort Nassau.

For Courthope this was a severe loss, especially as the *Defence* was also stolen by deserters from his own crew. He could now only hope for outside help: his situation was hopeless. In the spring of 1617, he sent several men to Bantam in a pinnace to ask for help and support. But the new head of the factory, George Ball, was too concerned with himself and his private affairs and refused. And now there was an increase in encounters between Dutch and British sailors in Bantam; they went for each other with knives. English reports frequently complain about the uncontrollable violence of the Dutch.

117 Now Banda Besar, earlier also Pulau Lomthoir
118 Now Pulau Hatta

The Dutch then also boarded and captured the English ship, the *Speed-well*, on its way to Bantam. Courthope had now held out on Run for almost two years in spite of all the deprivations. Occasionally a native would evade the blockade by night and bring some small relief to the starving inhabitants of Run. Finally help from Bantam came in sight. It was the *Solomon,* the first of three ships that were sent laden with provisions and soldiers to relieve the forces on Run. But the entrenched English and the natives rejoiced too soon. Only three nautical miles out from the safety of the harbour, four Dutch ships began an attack. After an hour-long sea battle, much to Courthope's consternation, the *Solomon* capitulated. The other two English ships also failed to reach Run.

Courthope and his little garrison continued to hold out. The letters he sent to Bantam and London describing his precarious situation remained unanswered. The people on Run only managed to survive because the occasional junk from Java broke the blockade. The men were also worn down by the constant threat of a Dutch attack. When, soon after the capture of the *Salomon,* the Dutch attempted a landing on Run they suffered a crushing defeat at the hands of the Bandanese, who in the meanwhile had been trained in the use of muskets and artillery.

Native spies kept Nathaniel Courthope up to date about the Englishmen from the captured ships, who were imprisoned on the islands of Banda Neira and Ai. The dungeons in Fort Revenge on Ai were particularly disgusting and degrading. The Dutch found it funny to urinate and defecate on the Englishmen who were imprisoned in irons beneath them. Anyone who complained was left out in the cold winds and rain at night and under the merciless tropical sun by day. Their only food was mouldy rice, and the water was foul.

Everywhere in the Malay Archipelago the reputation of the English was untarnished, and generally better than that of the Dutch. As a proof of their superiority the Dutch would take English captives with them in cages as they travelled the archipelago, and show them to the natives who thronged to see them. Any means of establishing their claim to power was acceptable to the Dutch.

In January 1619, Courthope received the good news that Sir Thomas Dale had arrived in Bantam with a fleet of five ships. The plan was to conquer Java and then continue to the Banda Islands to free them from the Dutch. But that never happened – to the great disappointment of the English garrison on Run – because the flagship, the *Sun,* was shipwrecked off the coast of Java.

There was a naval battle with the fleet of the new Dutch governor, Jan Pieterszoon, who fled the field when his defeat was obvious and sailed to the Bandas with his fleet. Sir Thomas let him escape unhindered and, to the further dismay of Courthope who was still holding out on Run, set sail for India, where he died.

A good friend of Courthope's, John Jourdain, then took over command of two of the fleet's ships. He set sail immediately to support his friend on Run. He was about to load his ship with provisions for Run in a port on the Malay Peninsula when he was attacked by three Dutch ships. After only a short battle it became clear that the English were going to lose, and so Jourdain raised the white flag and offered to surrender. On his way to negotiate this, John Jourdain was shot dead by a Dutchman.

For the Dutch there was now only one fly in the ointment, and that was Nathaniel Courthope, who was still holding out on Run with his men under the most difficult of conditions. His garrison was diminishing as one after another died of hunger or disease. But Courthope always knew how to inspire his men not to capitulate. He and his crew had been left to their fate on this little island for almost four years now.

On the 18th of October 1620, when Courthope heard that the inhabitants of Banda Besar were rebelling against the detested Dutchmen, he planned a joint attack. That very night – against the advice of his men – he set out for Banda Besar in a sailing boat with his manservant and a few musketeers. He wanted to meet the leaders of the rebellion and discuss plans to make a joint attack. But the Dutch had been informed of his intent by a spy on Run, and waited in ambush with two ships. Courthope and his men had no chance, between two and three in the morning off the island of Ai they were cut down by a hail of bullets.

There are several versions of how Courthope died. One says that he fell off his boat into the sea, another that the Dutch had salvaged him and his boat and buried him on Ai. Yet until this day no trace has been found of his grave. Courthope was a hero who, in impossible circumstances, resisted the superior forces of the bloodthirsty Dutch for over 1,540 days. I have not been able to find a picture of him in any archive or on the Internet, even though he worked for the East India Company in the Malay Archipelago for ten years. The hero of Run seems to have been forgotten.

The English garrison on Run didn't hear of Courthope's death until nine days later. They elected his deputy, senior merchant Robert Hayes, as their new leader. But the English will to resist was now, without Courthope, broken. They were half starved and had suffered far too long as they held out on their lonely island. Their ammunition supplies were depleted. Now that their chief opponent Courthope had been killed, the Dutch saw their chance to integrate Run into their sphere of influence.

When the Dutch arrived off Run with 25 ships and an army of several hundred soldiers, the Bandanese inhabitants of the island wanted to fight and defend their home to the last man, but when the English, whose garrison was already severely diminished, no longer showed any will to fight, the Bandanese also gave up. They would have no chance against such superior forces.

The Dutch landed without a shot being fired. In their fury they subjected both the Bandanese and the English to deep humiliation. They had to hand over their weapons and raze all their fortifications to the ground. They had to destroy the English trading post and storehouses. The landing stage that protruded into the sea had to be dismantled. The cannons the English had brought were sunk in the sea. The goods stored by the English were stolen by the Dutch.

All the Bandanese chiefs were taken into captivity and had to submit to the Dutch. They had to swear that they would never again resist the Dutch and that they would only trade with the VOC Now the Dutch ruled all the islands of the Bandas where the nutmeg grew. But it was a rule enforced by violence, suppression, humiliation and exploitation.

The English on Run were allowed to withdraw to the tiny island of Nailakka, which remained an English possession. There they were free. Nailakka was of no interest to the Dutch: there wasn't a single nutmeg tree there. The English on the other islands were worse off: they were imprisoned either in Fort Revenge on Ai, Fort Nassau on Banda Neira or on Dutch ships.

Nailakka, which is an atoll less than 200 metres long, is only a stone's throw from Run. At low tide it can even be reached on foot over the coral banks. The tiny English Fort defence with its three cannons had been there until it was torn down. Though the island has a beach of fabulous white sand there are no fresh water, no vegetables, no fruit, no nutmegs. The only thing that grows there is the coconut palm. But in the shallow waters around the island there were abundant fishing grounds. I believe that the destitute English were now supplied with food by the Bandanese on Run.

There is no record of how many Englishmen survived the tribulations of the long blockade, not how long they were there. It was until at least May 1621, since a letter from the Dutch Governor General Coen has survived, in which he asked the English on Nailakka to take part in a punitive expedition against the Bandanese – which degenerated into a massacre.[119] The English firmly refused.

The men held out on Nailakka until a ship finally passed which was prepared to take them to Ambon or Bantam. One source says that they were only able to leave the island in 1628, but I can hardly believe that they survived for so many years on the tiny atoll. Nevertheless, one Englishman remained on Run till the end of his days. The first officer had fallen in love with a pretty young Bandanese woman, and married her.

Ill. 5-11, The Island of Run and on the right the tiny, flat island of Nailakka with its white beach of white sand[120]

119 Massacre on the 8th of May 1621 see next chapter
120 Free Wikimedia, Photograph: Hans Peter Grumpe

6. The Dutch Governor General Jan Pieterszoon van Coen and the Banda Massacre

Before their conquest by the Dutch, prosperity and orderly life reigned in the Banda Islands for centuries. This only changed when the Dutch arrived at the Bandas about a hundred years after the Portuguese. The Dutch didn't want to buy and trade, they wanted to take over, and proceeded on the Bandas – as they had already done on Java and Ambon – with cannon fire and a brutality it is almost impossible to imagine today.

The Dutch demanded that the Bandanese give them a monopoly over the spice trade, even though they had been trading freely with Arabia, India, China and other countries for centuries. It wasn't just the Bandanese for whom this was unusual: monopolies were unknown in Asian trading culture. For example, the Dutch couldn't supply vegetables or rice as the merchants from Java had done for centuries in exchange for nutmeg. These things were absolutely necessary for the Bandanese to survive, as they are today. In the beginning the Dutch could only offer warm fabrics and other goods from Europe, for which the Bandanese had no use. As a result, the Bandanese, a proud and free people, refused to cooperate with the Dutch.

Since the arrival of the Dutch, tension and strife had reigned between the Native population and the newcomers. The Bandanese felt that they were being oppressed and exploited. When the new Governor, Jan Pieterszoon van Coen[121], came to the Dutch East Indies the situation became dramatically worse. Coen was known to be a particularly ruthless and brutal man. His vision was a Greater Dutch East Indies that would stretch from India to Japan. He also had a masterplan in his pocket for the Banda Islands, one that exceeds all imagination for cruelty and ruthlessness. His recipe was violence, and yet more violence against the Bandanese. They would ultimately have to *eat out of his hand*. Van Coen had no intention of negotiating any longer. He wanted to mete out personal vengeance on the Bandanese people for the betrayal and the murder of Admiral Verhoeven and his fellow campaigners.[122]

Jan Pieterszoon van Coen was born in Hoorn on the Zuiderzee. He made several voyages to the Dutch East Indies in the service of the VOC. In 1607 he accompanied Admiral Verhoeven to the Banda Islands as a junior mer-

---

121 1587-1629
122 See Chapter 5

chant, and was present when Verhoeven and his officers were killed. In 1612 he returned to the East Indies, this time as a senior merchant. In 1613 he became Director General of the VOC in South-East Asia and in 1618 the VOC's Governor General of the Dutch East Indies.

Ill. 6-1, Jan Pieterszoon van Coen[123]

123 Wikipedia, Public Domain

Although a peace treaty had been signed between Holland and England in Europe in 1619, its contents reaching the Banda Islands on the English ship the *Bull,* hostilities between Holland and England continued there. The English based their claim to Run on the fact that they were the first to land on the Bandas. They had also made a treaty with the *Orang Kaya* of Run.

The Dutch based their claim on a treaty concluded between them and only a few of the *Orang Kaya* of Banda Besar, which nevertheless was supposed to include all the Bandas. These *Orang Kaya* had been under extreme pressure from the Dutch to sign the treaty, even though they had no mandate to make decisions for other islands. With this treaty, which the Bandanese could neither read nor understand, they gave up their sovereignty. The Dutch were particularly concerned that the English on Run and Ai were training the Bandanese in the use of muskets and artillery. The Bandanese on Run wanted to be able to defend themselves against Dutch attacks.

There was one fundamental difference between the claims of the two nations: the Dutch based their claim on a treaty which they had extorted from the Bandanese by force. By contrast, the English had been asked by the inhabitants of Run and Ai to place them under the protection of the English king, to protect themselves against the Dutch. They had voluntarily given up their sovereignty.

In early 1621 there was a naval battle – already mentioned above – between the English and the Dutch off Jakarta. The battle was sparked by Coen commanding that the English fort and the Javanese prince's palace should be burnt down. The English wanted revenge for this. When it became obvious that the battle was heading for an English victory, Coen fled with the remainder of his fleet, first to Ambon and then to the Spice Islands. Since he could not achieve a monopoly by treaty, he now decided to solve the problem by force.

He still had an impressive fleet of 19 big ships, three smaller ships and 36 junks. On board were 1,655 European soldiers and 80-100 Japanese mercenaries, including a good dozen executioners. They also had almost 300 Javanese slaves as oarsmen and porters. With the other 250 soldiers in Fort Nassau on Banda Neira and their superior armament, the Dutch had a considerable strategic advantage. With this superior force at his disposal, Coen intended to make an example of the recalcitrant Bandanese. Coen's entire life was characterised by boundless hate for the Bandanese and the English. His ultimate goal was to drive every last Bandanese and Englishman permanently from the Banda Islands.

The Japanese mercenaries were hired in the town of Hirado[124] in Nagasaki province. Hirado was then an important centre of foreign trade in Japan. In 1609 the VOC had been permitted to open a factory there, the first Dutch commercial presence in Japan. It continued to function until 1639, when the Dutch had to move to the Bay of Nagasaki.

An English trading post was opened in Hirado in 1613 with Richard Cocks as the merchant in charge. The post was presumably closed by the year of 1623.

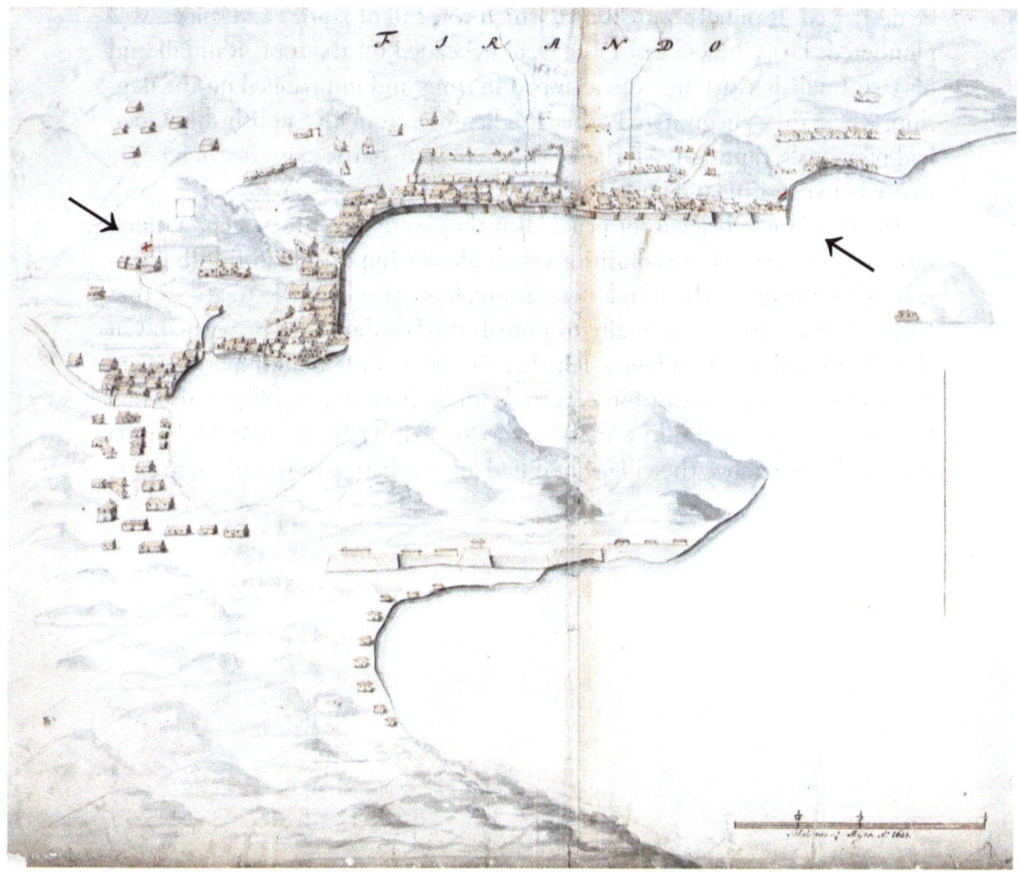

Ill. 6-2, Old drawing of the Bay of Hirado, 1621.[125] *On the coast on the far right the Dutch factory with the red, white and blue flag. On the left, a little bit inland, the English East India Company's post, recognisable by the white flag with the red cross of St George.*

124 Aka Firando
125 Nationaal Archief, The Hague, Atlas van Isaac de Graaff

On the 7th of March 1621 the entire fleet sailed around Banda Besar to find a suitable landing place for an invasion and on the 11th of March the Dutch troops landed at several widely distributed places on Banda Besar. Coen had invited the English, who were still entrenched on Nailakka, to participate either actively or passively in this punitive expedition, but they categorically refused. By the following day the Dutch troops had taken the last Bandanese positions in bloody fighting, and the power of the *Orang Kaya* was broken. The battle for Banda Besar had been won.

First of all, Coen ordered Randall's English factory on Banda Besar to be destroyed. Randall's warehouse, which was full of fabrics and spices, was plundered. His Chinese assistants were beheaded on the spot. Randall and his two English assistants were clapped in irons and imprisoned on the flagship, where they encountered other Englishmen from an English ship Coen had previously captured. All these crimes, in spite of the existence of a peace treaty between England and Holland!

The Bandanese begged for peace. But they were forced to accept a much more rigid treaty, whose conditions were almost impossible to fulfill. Coen was just waiting for the Bandanese to break an article of the treaty so that he would have an excuse finally to punish the Bandanese as he wished. On the other hand, the Bandanese felt that they were only bound by the treaty when there was a superior force in their immediate vicinity. Coen also had his soldiers begin to build a massive fort on Banda Besar: Fort Hollandia was on the hill above the village and had an excellent panoramic view.

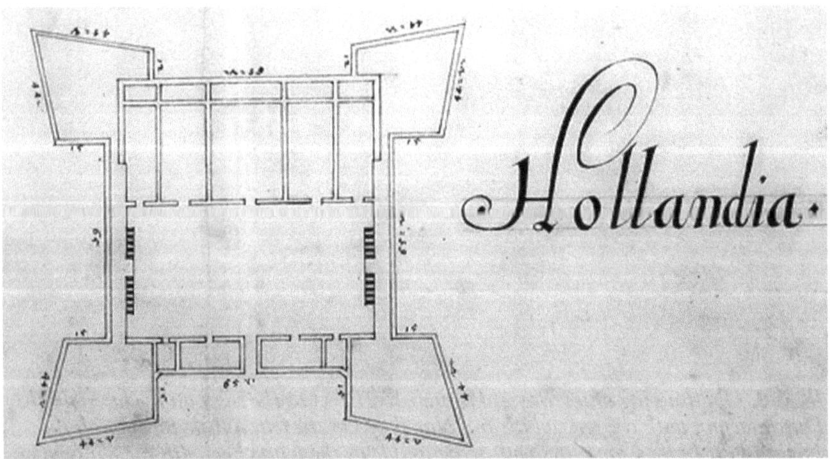

Ill. 6-3, An old plan of Fort Hollandia on Banda Besar [126]

126 Wikipedia Public Domain

The inhabitants of Banda Besar had fled into the mountains and woods on the island in the face of the Dutch invasion. And now the nutmeg was rotting on the trees. Through intermediaries, the Dutch appealed to the Bandanese to return to work on the plantations, but all in vain, in spite of the promise of a general amnesty. The Bandanese continually ambushed the troops, killing and injuring Dutchmen. Up to this point, Jan Pieterszoon van Coen's expedition had simply brought costs, and he was not one step closer to the monopoly he so desired. Whole villages were burned as punishment, boats were destroyed, and natives slaughtered, not just on Banda Besar, but also on other islands. Captives, mostly women and children were transported to Java and sold there as slaves. The total number is unknown. However, there is evidence that just one of the Dutch ships involved transported 890 people from the Banda Islands to Java, of whom about 230 did not survive the voyage. Those who did survive were enslaved and sold. In order to destroy Bandanese culture, the Dutch – as well as using other cleverly calculated 'devices' – even went as far as to encourage the natives to smoke opium.[127]

The inhabitants of the islands were driven into the mountains and starved out by a blockade. When the Dutch finally stormed the interior of the islands, they found many fresh graves. Dead women and children were lying at the roadside. Those who were still alive were killed or enslaved. Many Bandanese escaped the massacre by committing suicide. After Banda Besar had been 'cleansed' of the native population, the islands of Run and Rozengain[128] suffered the same merciless fate.

It is estimated that the population of the Bandas until that time had been around 15,000. A few hundred succeeded in escaping in their fishing boats to the Kei Islands, about 250 kilometres away. Their descendants still live there in the villages of Banda-Eli[129] and Banda-Elat[130] on the island of Kei Besar. It was the end of the West Monsoon. Many Bandanese must surely have perished on their flight over the stormy open sea in their little fishing boats. In those two villages on Kei Besar – and only there – the original language of the Bandas, Bandanese, still survives today.

It is still possible in the villages today to see how cultured the Bandanese are. Their sleek black hair and bronze complexion makes it possible to classify them – unlike the widespread curly-headed type from New Guinea – as pure-blooded Malays. To whitewash the brutal extermination of the

---

127 Dr O. Warburg, *Die Muskatnuss,* 1897, p. 124, note 1
128 Now Pulau Hatta
129 Aka Wadan El
130 Aka Wadan Elat

Bandanese, the Dutch called them – and treated them like – second-class human beings.

On the 8th of May 1621, the Dutch began a barbaric massacre on Banda Neira. First, the 44 most important *Orang Kaya* were tortured on board Coen's flagship, the *Dragon* and then taken to Fort Nassau on Banda Neira, where they were herded together like sheep outside the fort. One after another they were beheaded and quartered. Many were quartered alive before being beheaded. In the past this was the cruellest method of execution. Japanese mercenaries and executioners were used to do this dirty work. The relatives, wives, children and parents, were forced to watch the cruel massacre before being executed themselves. The body parts were hung on bamboo frames and the victims' heads stuck on bamboo stakes and displayed at various places on the island as a deterrent.

When the atrocities became too much for three Dutchmen and one of the Japanese executioners and they stopped killing, the Governor General ordered all four to be hanged for indiscipline. Coen was merciless.

In the *Rumah Budaya Banda Neira* Museum there is an old, rather faded painting of the massacre. No one could tell me when the painting was made, or by whom.

Afterwards all the male inhabitants of the islands older than 15 were massacred or enslaved. Young women were sold as slaves or kept as slave mistresses; older 'useless' women were executed. Almost the entire population of the Banda Islands – estimates suggest over 90% – were slaughtered or enslaved. The Banda Massacre was the first genocide in modern history. A whole population group was obliterated. A few months after the massacre nine more *Orang Kaya* were executed: they were quartered alive.[131]

There are no exact population figures for the islands before the massacre – some old documents suggest 15,000. And there are no figures for how many were killed or enslaved or succeeded in escaping. It is assumed that fewer than 1,000 survived the massacre, and they were mostly the Bandanese who lived on Run and were protected by the English.

The Banda Islands were now depopulated. The directors of the VOC in Amsterdam had given Coen the job of overwhelming the Bandanese by force and repopulating the islands with young Dutch families. Coen, a practising Christian, had achieved his goal and was rewarded for his success by the VOC with a bonus of 3,000 Guilders.

---

131 Dr O. Warburg, *Die Muskatnuss*, 1897, p. 107

Ill. 6-4, Picture of the massacre in Banda Neira Museum

Ill. 6-5, Detail from Ill. 6-4

Ill. 6-6, Detail from Ill. 6-4

Ill. 6-7, The victims' heads were displayed on bamboo stakes as a deterrent

Later similar massacres were also perpetrated by the Dutch on the more northerly Molucca Islands, like Ceram, Kelang and Goram. For example, during a *hongitocht*[132] on Goram in 1653 all the villages were burned and all inhabitants who resisted were murdered.[133]

The native inhabitants of the Moluccas suffered much injustice during the *hongitochten* and the punitive campaigns. All they wanted was to live in freedom on their own land, to defend their rights and to trade with whomsoever they wanted. It was not until 1824 that the *hongitochten* were finally and permanently abolished by the VOC.[134]

The Banda Islands were now 'pacified', but the surviving Englishmen on Nailakka were still a thorn in Coen's flesh in spite of the treaty that had been signed in Europe. To make Run unattractive to any English who might think of conquering it, the Dutch cut down all the nutmeg trees, or destroyed them by stripping the bark. They also wanted to avoid overproduction and a consequent fall in the price of the nuts. Nevertheless, in the years that followed the English constantly renewed their claims to Run even they no longer had a presence there. The few native inhabitants who remained on Run could now no longer harvest the nuts. They had been robbed of their traditional source of income and became impoverished.

The situation became particularly precarious for the surviving English in the Bandas in 1623. The Dutch had perpetrated another terrible massacre, this time of the English on Ambon, and the Banda English feared that the same thing would happen to them. This massacre entered history as the *Complot van Ambon* (Conspiracy of Ambon) in Holland and the Massacre of Ambon in England. I will give more details of this in Chapter 20, which deals with Ambon. In any case, the English on the islands feared for their lives. It is probable that the last of them only managed to leave Nailakka in 1628.

Jan Pieterszoon van Coen returned to Holland in 1623. He had a second term as Governor General of the Dutch East Indies from 1627 to 1629, though he never went back to the Banda Islands. In 1629 he died in the fort in Batavia – of dysentery, according to the Dutch. There were, however, claims by the Javanese that they had killed him during an attack on the fort.

If Coen had been able to visit the Banda Islands again a hundred years after the massacre he instigated, he would have seen that his dream of an efficient colony of Dutch settlers had been fulfilled – for a time. The islands had become a Dutch plantation and produced even higher levels of profit.

---

132 A *hongitocht* was an expedition undertaken to deal with rebellious natives, something like a press gang: many natives were captured and enslaved by this process.
133 Dr O. Warburg, *Die Muskatnuss*, 1897, p. 125
134 Ibid., S. 129

Ill. 6-8, A portrait of the monstrous Jan Pieterszoon van Coen in the Banda Neira Museum

But the excessive dividends that the VOC paid out to its shareholders and increasingly widespread corruption finally drove the VOC to bankruptcy in 1790. This rang the knell for the economic decline of the Bandas, and this once so important group of little islands in the Banda Sea fell into oblivion.

Jan Pieterszoon van Coen definitely remains an extremely contentious character. He was a brutal, unscrupulous man. As a strict Calvinist, he committed his crimes in the name of Christianity! Even so, in his birthplace of Hoorn in Holland this mass murderer is still honoured with a statue.

You can still occasionally see VOC emblems in Banda Neira, carved in the stone floor of the old church, for example. When I visited the old church with an educated Bandanese, a boat and restaurant owner, he pointed to the VOC emblem carved in the floor and said, *This is a symbol of hate! The Dutch were terrorists!* Please note that it was the Bandanese who said that, and not I: that would not be fitting for me as a German citizen, given our past in the Third Reich. The same thing was said by Bandanese to an Australian film-maker who was working on a documentary about the Bandas. I mention this because I see all the events of the Dutch colonial period from an Indonesian perspective. What the Bandanese said shows that the wounds inflicted on them in the past by the Dutch have still not healed.

On the Banda Islands every schoolchild knows about Jan Pieterszoon van Coen's massacre, but I am always surprised when I talk to young people from the Netherlands when they are in Indonesia. They tour Indonesia, a country they exploited and ruled for centuries, and yet they have no idea of the crimes committed there by their ancestors. In Dutch schools the 'dark side' of their history is excluded or at least minimised. But the Dutch were not always the victims – though that is how they like to portray themselves – they were also perpetrators, even as late as the period after the Second World War when Indonesia was already independent in 1945. They wanted to reconquer their former colony of the Dutch East Indies and to continue to oppress and exploit the Indonesians. In the colonial war, which lasted more than four years, there were hundreds of thousands of victims on the Indonesian side before the Dutch were finally expelled.[135]

The genocide instigated by the Dutch Governor General Jan Pieterszoon van Coen on the Banda Islands and the subsequent enslavement of thousands of innocent people are among the darkest chapters of Dutch colonial history. He was called King Coen by the Dutch; for the Bandanese he was, and remains today, The Butcher of Banda.

---

135 See Horst H. Geerken, *A Gecko for Luck*

7. Perkeniers[136]

After the Dutch massacre of the Bandanese, the Banda Islands were suddenly empty and uninhabited. Governor Jan Pieterzoon van Coen planned that the Banda Islands should now become a colony inhabited solely by settlers, independent Dutch burghers, with slaves to do the work. The plantations had been totally neglected since the massacre, and were no longer producing any profit. Coen's plan was to resettle the islands as quickly as possible. He divided them into 68 sections, which were called *perken*.[137] In the literature of the time these *perken* were often called nutmeg plantations, garden concessions or nutmeg parks. As I walked through nutmeg plantations during my visit to the Bandas, I did actually get the feeling that I was in a park. The borders of the individual *perken* were drawn on the map more or less at random. There was no need to consider the ownership rights of the previous native inhabitants since they had all fled or been killed or enslaved.

The Dutch created 34 *perken* on Banda Besar[138], 31 on Ai and three on Banda Neira. They now set about finding people to farm these plantations successfully. These people, known as *perkeniers,* came mostly from the merchant, administrative or military classes. They had to guarantee that they would settle permanently on the Bandas and be loyal servants of the company. The nutmeg plantations were to be maintained in good condition. They would receive an agreed price for the nutmeg. They were also allowed to grow coconut palms, bananas and other plants for their own use. The Bandas were to become exclusively Dutch plantations.

But Coen was not at all satisfied with the first settlers sent by the VOC. He complained that all he got from Holland was 'drunks and whoremongers'. It was well known that the VOC would give an advance to any Tom, Dick or Harry who turned up and send him to the East Indies. The Dutch regarded the conditions and climate on the Bandas as very unhealthy. They got fat and bloated with oedema. Of the 243 European soldiers stationed there in 1817, more than half died the same year. It was probably, however, because of an unhealthy diet and excessive consumption of the local spirit, arak. In the same year only 11 of 60 Ambonese and 66 of 326 Javanese in the service of the VOC on Banda Neira died.[139] Today the Bandas are thought to be extremely healthy, presumably because of improvements in hygiene.

136 In Dutch also *Leenheeren*
137 In Dutch the system was known as *perkeniersstelsel*
138 Then Pulau Lonthor
139 According to Reinwardt in Dr O. Warburg, *Die Muskatnuss,* p. 158

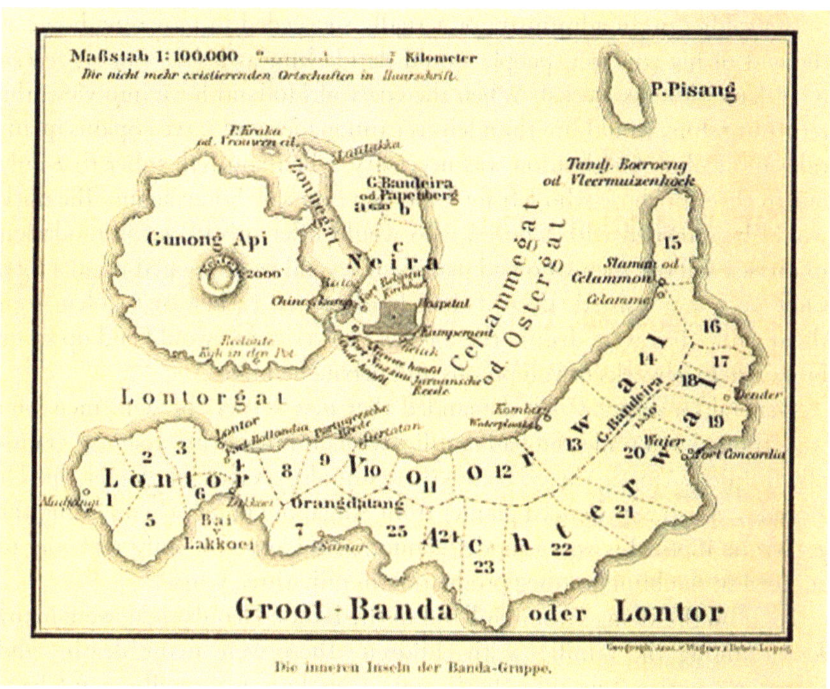

Ill. 7-1, Coen's plan of the individual perken[140]

Ill. 7-2, Nutmeg plantation on Banda Besar

140 *Die Muskatnuss*, Dr O. Warburg, 1897, p. 64

If a soldier or an administrator actually succeeded in returning home at the end of his contract, people would deride him as a *heer van zes weken* (Gentlemen for six weeks). When the coast of Holland hove into view, the returning ships would fire thunderous cannonades and serve copious quantities of alcohol. Celebration was necessary, when you remember that only one in three of those who left for East Asia ever saw home again. The dock would be crowded with whores, who would offer private accommodation to the sex-starved men who had just spent several years cooped up in a fort. Only very few resisted. Even if their hard-earned cash wasn't stolen from them while they were drunk, these *heren van zes weken* would end up stony broke after six weeks of voluptuous and debauched living.

General Governor Coen demanded that new settlers be sent: men who were trained in a trade and had families with children. This wish was gradually fulfilled. Among the *perkeniers* there was also a German planter, one Dr Brandes. As an experienced planter from Singapore noted when visiting the *perken* in 1856, this was a model plantation. He was the only *perkenier* to succeed in doubling nutmeg production in only three years.[141]

Even on the voyage from Holland to the Banda Islands there were many losses among the families with children. There were many deaths, and sometimes entire ships, like the *Batavia,* were lost, as we will see in Chapter 12.[142]

The soldiers were very badly fed. They had to eat not just rotting salted meat, but also cats, dogs and other vermin. A soldier wrote that *victuals did come from Bali and Java, but only the well-off could afford them.* For many years a posting to the Bandas was therefore regarded as a punishment, and yet the Bandas were not really unhealthy: many of the native inhabitants lived to be over 100.

The Dutch also had the terrible habit of burying the dead in their houses, beneath the bedroom. This contaminated the air, especially at night. In 1816, when the house of the Resident of Banda Neira collapsed during an earthquake, they found seven corpses in the ruins, all quite well preserved.[143]

In 1859 there were still 850 convicts and 900 contract workers on Banda Besar.[144] There were far too few coconuts for them to eat, as most of the crop was used to make palm wine for the *perkenier* families. About the only fruit

141 Dr O. Warburg, *Die Muskatnuss,* p. 208
142 See Chapter 12, Abrolhos
143 Oliver, *Reisen,* p. 156
144 van der Crab, *De Moluksche Eilanden,* (1861)

on the market were bananas, and they were too dear for the convicts and contract workers. The small amount of rice provided for them by the VOC was sold on the black market by the *perkeniers*. Instead of rice they fed the slaves on sago, which was cheaper. They feathered their own nests with no thought of the workers' health.

On this rich volcanic soil other fruits flourished brilliantly. According to Oxley[145], they experimented with European grapes on the Bandas in the 19th century. They succeeded very well and bore copious fruit. Unfortunately, they did not go on to grow them, since I found no grapes on the Bandas when I was there. Oxley was an experienced English planter who visited the Bandas in 1848 and 1856 and published several reports, particularly statistical information about the nutmeg.

There was often hunger on the islands when supplies failed to arrive from Java or Ambon in the monsoon season. The islands couldn't be reached because of stormy seas and adverse winds. Although the fishing grounds around the Bandas are extremely rich, they didn't exploit them enough.

The land, the *perken*, could be inherited or sold, the VOC claiming 25% of the proceeds. In return the VOC guaranteed to provide the *perkeniers* with rice at cost price plus a small surcharge. The most important thing, however, was that the VOC provided 25 slaves for each *perk,* male and female, between the age of 15 and 30. If a slave died, the VOC would provide a replacement.

In Governor General Coen's massacre only about 50 male Bandanese were spared; they now had to pass on their knowledge of nutmeg farming to the inexperienced *perkeniers*.[146] Some of the female slaves were Bandanese who had previously been captured by Coen's troops and sold in Batavia. Now they had to work as slaves in their own homeland. The VOC was also responsible for the defence of the islands against English attacks or slave uprisings.

All these agreements were drafted in haste. The islands had to start producing a profit again as quickly as possible. This frequently led to friction between the *perkeniers*. For example, the boundaries of the *perken* were very ill-defined. And then there was conflict between the *perkeniers* and the VOC. The former received a fixed amount for the nutmeg they harvested. When they heard that their product was being sold in Amsterdam at a profit of more than 1200%, they wanted a bigger share of this profitable business. They complained that they were being exploited even worse than the Ban-

145 Oxley, *Banda Nutmeg Plantations,* 1856
146 Dr O. Warburg, *Die Muskatnuss,* 1897, p. 107

danese had been previously. There was continuous strife, about money or about the non-delivery of goods, such as the rice and fabrics the VOC was committed to provide. Everything was made worse by the fact that in their haste they had failed to make written contracts with the *perkeniers.*

By 1627 all 68 *perken* were occupied, but the provision of the agreed number of 1700 slaves, 25 for each *perk* created difficulties. The slaves came mainly from New Guinea, Ceram, Java and Borneo, though some were from East Africa and the Malabar Coast. The traders were from Arabia, mainly from the Hadramaut in modern Yemen, and from China.

The *perkeniers* would buy extra slaves to supplement the ones provided by the VOC, so that on a small *perk* there would be about 50 and on a large one 160. Slave mortality was extremely high. For example, Rumphius[147] writes that *the owners lose many slaves because of cold, discomfort and other mishaps.* Many had only skimpy clothing and had to go around almost naked. Others died as a result of brutal mistreatment by their Dutch owners.

The annals of the VOC note that of the 2,199 slaves who were toiling on the Bandas in 1638 13 % were Bandanese men, women and children.

Wurffbain[148], a German working for the VOC on the Banda Islands, estimated that a quarter of the Bandanese slaves were male, and three-quarters female. For slaves with other origins the proportions were roughly 50-50. Presumably the female Bandanese slaves were younger than the others, or more attractive. We know that during the 1621 massacre the Dutch spared a large number of young women. They then selected the most attractive. Those who were not so chosen were killed.

After a mass attempt to escape from the Island of Run 160 slaves were executed. Wurffbain[149] wrote that after a suicide attempt a female slave was flogged and branded, and, moreover, that *tot meeder afschrik voor anderen* – as a greater deterrent to the others – her cheeks were slit to the ears.[150] Other 'traitors' were tortured to extract information. The soles of their feet were *cut open with a sailor's knife, and hot pitch and sulphur poured into the open wound.*[151] Most of them confessed. The Dutch, as colonial rulers, used inhumane methods to maintain their power.

The VOC had to constantly supply new slaves, to make up for the losses due to the high level of mortality. The slave population of the Bandas was

---

147 See Chapter 21
148 See Chapter 8
149 See Chapter 8
150 Dr O. Warburg, *Die Muskatnuss,* 1897, p. 113
151 Peter Kirsch, *Die Reise nach Batavia,* p. 208a

remarkable for its low level of reproduction. Major slave-hunts, the *hongitochten,* took place in 1658, 1665 1673, 1694, 1713 and 1792. The Dutch made lesser *hongitochten* every year on the more remote islands and on New Guinea. They were carried out with the help of the military. For example, Captain Junker, who served under a Scot named Jacob Couper, wrote: *We pursued the fugitives for three days and brought back great spoils, including many women.* He wrote that the 'spoils' were meagre compared with the previous year. They had collected 103 *head of Macassar girls* who were sent to Batavia to be sold. But in the forest they *captured 400 women and shared them out as spoils.* In the camp the soldiers passed their time playing dice and cards and ... *anyone who lost all his money would go and lie with a lovely woman of 22 or 23.*[152] Many villages went up in flames. Thousands of men, *useless old women* and children were beheaded during these raids.

A soldier called David Tappe wrote in his diary: *Now we had more or less cleansed the country of thieves and natives...*[153] *No prisoners were taken; they were all shot or put to the sword!*

Elsewhere Captain Junker describes how the Dutch dealt with 2,500 prisoners in their usual way: *Their hands were tied behind their backs, they were taken into a large flat field and there cut down within a quarter of an hour.*[154] The old documents contain many appalling descriptions like this.

Smaller numbers of slaves were also frequently purchased, for example in 1622, about 325 slaves were brought from the west coast of India to Banda Neira.[155]

According to Saalfeld[156], there were 2,190 slaves on the Bandas in 1638: 835 men, 881 women and 474 children over 12, who mostly came from other islands. In the same year there were only 50 people living on the devastated island of Run.[157]

As well as Wurffbain, many thousand men left their homes in Germany to serve as sailors, craftsmen, merchants or administrators for the VOC in the Dutch East Indies. At the end of the 18th century Duke Carl Eugen of Württemberg even sent a mercenary army of 2,000 officers and men to support the VOC in the Dutch colony for the sum of 300,000 guilders. Most of these soldiers married native women and settled there. Though there are

---

152 Deventer, M.L. van, *Geschiedenis der Nederlandsers op Java,* 1886
153 Kirsch Peter, *Die Reise nach Batavia,* S. 201
154 Peter Kirsch, *Die Reise nach Batavia,* p. 200
155 Ibid., pp. 110ff
156 Saalfeld, *Geschichte des holländischen Kolonialwesens in Ostindien,* 1812
157 Dr O. Warburg, *Die Muskatnuss,* 1897, pp. 110ff

diaries written by some of them in Dutch archives, relatively little is known about their lives. However, the books are still an interesting source of information about the age of the spice trade.

In the international literature, the Dutch *perkeniersstelsel* is uniformly described as the most brutal and ruthless slave-ownership system. Java, Timor, Macassar, Malacca, the Malabar coast, even far-off Muscat in modern Oman shared in this profitable slave trade. In 1794 there were still 4112 slaves on the Bandas. They made up over three-quarters of the population, over 50% of them being the private property of the colonists. It is surprising that, on the Bandas where the slaves far outnumbered the colonists, there was never a slave revolt against the white population. But on the Bandas the majority of slaves were female and had little to gain from a revolt. It was generally customary for them to have an intimate relationship with their masters, which put them in a better position than their male fellow-slaves.

During the colonial period almost every Dutchman had a relationship with a native woman, known as a *nyai*.[158] Until 1860 the *nyais* were slaves. They were almost exclusively Muslims. Afterwards, when slavery was banned, they became free wives or concubines. The mixed race – mostly very attractive – children born of these liaisons were much in demand among the next generation of Dutch colonists in the Indies.

Temporary mixed marriages between white colonial officials and native women were legalised by the Dutch government in 1898, which improved the status of the *nyais*. They entered quite gladly into relationships of this kind, because it increased their prestige in their native environment, and because they were well provided for. Nevertheless, they were almost always temporary marriages: when the Dutchman returned to his family at home, the marriage was dissolved as simply as it had been made. The wife remained behind with her children and had to find a way to get on with her life. The quickest way to survive was usually to take a new partner: the *nyai* was simply handed on to a successor, with whom she made a new temporary marriage.

The children of these relationships created what was called the 'Indian branch' of the family tree. After two or three generations, these descendants usually disappeared namelessly – that is, without carrying on the Dutch name – into Indonesian society.

There was a great deal to do. Because of the years of war and unrest the nutmeg plantations had been neglected. It took years to clear and re-estab-

---

158 A Balinese term for the lowest class of woman; used by the Dutch as a term for mistress, though other sources suggest that it is a Javanese word for sister.

lish them. From planting, the nutmeg takes seven or eight years to bear its first fruit. The early years were very hard for the new settlers. Newly built houses and storehouses were frequently destroyed by earthquakes, hundreds of slaves sickened and died, and, last but by no means least, Gunung Api kept on spewing out fire and ashes. This often meant that the islands had to be evacuated in panic. But a good ten years after the genocide of the original Bandanese inhabitants the islands began to flourish again, bringing enormous profits to the VOC. The *perkeniers* were now the aristocrats of the Banda Islands.

In the mid and late 18th century many *perkeniers* became immensely wealthy – particularly from illegally lining their own pockets. For example, one over-proud *perkenier* on Ai had 1200 slaves. When he was put in chains for killing a fellow-planter, he offered the government 100,000 guilders to allow those chains to be made of gold![159]

The *perkeniers* were mostly young men in the prime of life, but who didn't have a wife. What Dutchwoman would want to live on a remote island like that, which could only be reached after months on board a sailing ship? There was no entertainment, no diversion. One day was very much like another: planting, harvesting, supervising the slaves. And the evenings were devoted to drinking staggering amounts of the local arak. It was a coarse, masculine society. Initially, Coen didn't succeed in settling the Bandas with whole families with wives and children, and as we will see in Chapter 12, whole shiploads of families headed from Amsterdam on the perilous voyage out to the Bandas were lost at sea.

In the colonial period, the men were initially forbidden to marry native women without the express permission of the Governor. If a secret amorous liaison between a Dutchman and a slave was discovered, they would both be publicly flogged. Only when a young slave girl had converted to Christianity and been baptised and adopted did the young couple have a chance of gaining the Governor's permission to marry.

To deal with the shortage of European women on the Bandas – which was the case in the whole colony – the VOC used to send *compagniesdochters* [daughters of the Company] out to the East Indies. They were orphans, prostitutes, and women from Dutch poorhouses. Since the ships always arrived in Batavia first, the most attractive of them would find a relationship there, and remain in the lively capital. Very few of these daughters of the Company – and only the 'second best' – made it to the isolated islands in the Banda Sea, and so the Dutchmen on the Bandas linked up mainly with the younger – and prettier – slave girls.

159 Dr O. Warburg, *Die Muskatnuss*, 1897, S. 187

If a higher-ranking colonist married an attractive slave woman, even if, as in most cases, it was a temporary marriage, then she was no longer a slave, but the lady of the house. She didn't breast-feed her children herself, but handed them over to slaves as wet-nurses, who then brought them up. These children were brought up in the lap of luxury. They were totally dependent on others and had no idea how to deal with real life. One major fact was that the girls were extremely attractive – and well aware of it. As Vogel, a mine manager and ensign in the Company's service wrote, *they were extremely coquettish, and when they walked by, under a parasol carried by a slave girl, they could take your breath away. Their hair was worn down and gleamed seductively with coconut oil and scented essences. Yellow and red hibiscus blossoms adorned their glorious coiffure.*[160]

Christian Burckhard, a German soldier, wrote: *they are extremely cleanly and wash themselves from head to toe twice a day, especially after marital activity and after relieving themselves.* This was something completely new to the Europeans, who in those days washed very seldom and often did not change their clothes for several weeks – and on the ships for several months. Soldiers wore their uniforms day and night. No wonder they stank of sweat in that heavy clothing. The native inhabitants, with their sense of hygiene, were obviously put off by this, and accordingly kept their distance from the Europeans, whom they thought of as dirty pigs. One still senses this attitude in Asia, given that washing the body after using the lavatory still isn't customary in western civilisation.

In Java at that time it was common for the Javanese, if a Dutchman passed by, to hold their noses and often to spit in disgust. Because of this, the soldiers were given the order to give everyone who disrespected his 'master' a hefty box round the ears. Frik[161], a surgeon from Ulm wrote about his: *Then you might have seen a wonder, the way the blows rained down, until finally this shameful Javanese custom fell into disuse ...*[162] The colonial rulers never even considered the idea of becoming clean themselves and adopting hygienic habits. They could have learned quite a bit from the native population!

The Dutch *perkeniers* and officials were of course envied for these attractive *mestizas* by the *common European soldiers* who only had *one free night a week* to go to a brothel, called *kasies*. A European *perkenier* or craftsman,

---

160 Johann Wilhelm Vogel from Altenburg in Ludwig Richter, *Beschreibung von Java und Sumatra 1678-1687,* published 1704
161 Aka Frick
162 Christoff Frik, *Beschreibung von Java, Ceylon und Bali,* 1692

on the other hand, could keep slaves and could *sleep with his women every night.*[163]

Another contemporary writer says that over time these mixed-race females became *excessively lazy and haughty and were consumed by an implacable desire for revenge.*

A mixed-race generation resulted, a culture combining European and various Asiatic elements, a mixture of peoples not to be found anywhere else in the world. The freedwomen and their offspring were initially very industrious. The nutmeg harvest grew from year to year. If a *mestiza* had a child with a white man, the child was called a *castice.* The child of a white man and a *castice* was a *postice.* The skin of a *postice* would be very pale. Her social status would rise, and such a woman would be treated almost as a European. But after three or four generations the industriousness began to decrease. Over the generations they fell back into tropical lethargy, only wanting to enjoy *la dolce vita.* They no longer took an interest in the plantations, which degenerated more and more over time. In the middle of the 19th century, van der Crab wrote: *They detest work. They do not even wish to trade. This was then done by the Chinese and the Arabs. There were about 150 of them on the Bandas. They knew how to make profitable deals.*

In 1633 the VOC's programme of sending *compagniesdochter*s to the Archipelago was wound down. At the same time, they were increasingly frequently prepared to accept alliances between their employees and native women. In 1898 mixed marriages between white colonial officials and native women were legalised by the Dutch government, which improved the status of the *nyais.*

When Governor Jan Pieterszoon van Coen divided the islands into *perken,* the Island of Run was left out because, even though it was occupied by Dutch soldiers, the English still laid claim to the island. In 1638 a new English expedition came to Run. Slaves and material were landed on the island. They intended to re-plant the island with nutmeg trees. Either it was too lonely on the island for the English, or the work was too hard, because they left soon afterwards, leaving all the slaves behind. The slaves used up the supplies that had been left with them, and then vanished in their turn. In 1648 and 1662 there were further failed English attempts to settle and re-cultivate Run.

It was only in 1667, after the Peace of Breda[164] that calm returned to the island. But it was of no practical use to its new Dutch colonial rulers, be-

---

163 Ibid.
164 See Chapter 9

cause they had themselves cut down all the nutmeg trees. The situation did not improve until 1862, when the Dutch also divided Run into *perken* and offered the land to new settlers from Holland.

The hundred years following the Peace of Breda were a tranquil period for the Dutch, and for the VOC it was the most successful period of their rule over the Bandas. Calm and obedience reigned, and the nutmeg and mace trade flourished. But it was the calm of a prison which could only be upheld by capturing and selling slaves. More and more slaves died of ill-treatment or fled. Slowly but surely corruption caused the decline and fall of the VOC. *Perkeniers* became wealthy through smuggling and other shady activities. Honest officials became impoverished and regarded the Bandas as a prison. The Company's position was hopeless. The colony became a loss-making business requiring subsidies, and the level of debt rose. The Company was not officially dissolved until 1808.

By the 18th century the population of pure Dutch citizens Governor General Coen had envisaged[165] for the Banda Islands no longer existed. As we have already shown, the result of the relationships between Dutchmen and native women and female slaves was that Dutch society in the Indies was already quite mixed. Chinese, Japanese, Javanese, Arabs and freed slaves now called themselves citizens of the Banda Islands. They regarded themselves as belonging to the exclusive class of the Dutch, even though the latter still treated them as second-class citizens. Freed slaves later made up the greater part of the Bandanese middle class.

In the course of several generations the *perkeniers* began to feel that they were the owners of the *perken* that the VOC had let to them. They sold, mortgaged, and left the land in their wills, mostly without any sanction on the part of the VOC. When it came to conflict, the cards were stacked against the VOC, because there had been no binding written contracts when the *perken* were allotted. Thus all the *perken* ultimately ended up in private hands.

Soon afterwards the perkeniers began to ignore the restrictions placed on their ability to trade. They bought fast ships and sold most of their produce on the markets in Macassar or Timor. The proceeds ended up in their own pockets. Corruption and fraud mushroomed: the VOC lost control.

After the brutal and genocidal depopulation of the Banda Islands in 1621, the *perkenier* system produced a new breed of people. The mixture between the Dutch colonists and the original Bandanese inhabitants as well as slaves from all over the world produced a new race which is probably unique in the

---

165 By importing Dutch *burghers*

world. Governor Coen wanted to create a white colony of Dutch citizens, and this just about worked for a few generations. The Bandas flourished and produced extremely profitable returns for the VOC. But with today's hindsight we can see that this success was short-lived, since the slaves then established themselves in *perkenier* society and achieved legal status on the islands.

Today the descendants of the *perkeniers* and their slaves live on the Banda Islands. But the time when you could get rich quick with a nutmeg plantation is long past. Today the plantation owners have to do the hard work themselves to make ends meet. Instead of the big plantations with their monocultures, we now have a small-scale culture that provides work and an income for many people.

I saw many beautiful and attractive faces. It is well known that racial mixing produces particularly beautiful women. Many have an unmistakable trace of the Arabian. You see light skin and dark skin, smooth and curly black hair, narrow and broad noses, and many similar differences. The people here are a pot-pourri of the most different races, and of course the mixing goes on, so that in a few centuries we would expect a greater degree of convergence. The people who now live on the Bandas describe themselves as *orang campur,* mixed people.

Ill. 7-3, Two friendly owners of a kiosk in Banda Neira

The slaves, who came from all over the world, had to agree on a common language for daily communication. They had no common ancestors and no mutual traditions. Malay had for generations been the region's *lingua franca*. After only two generations most of the Dutch descendants of the *perkeniers* could no longer speak their ancestral mother language.

The dialect of Bahasa Indonesia spoken by the Bandanese today is also unique within the Archipelago. As early as 1876 a Dutch linguist classified the dialect spoken on the islands as Banda Malay. I will say more about this in a later chapter.

Ill. 7-4, A young woman and her child from Run

*Ill. 7-5
Cheerful child-
ren on Banda
Besar*

*Ill. 7-6
Nyello, a jolly
man from Banda
Neira, a diving
instructor who
knows a few
words of
German*

After slavery was officially abolished in Holland in 1863, the slaves were re-classified as *orang kontrakt,* contract coolies or contract workers. This was in essence no different from slavery. The coolies could expect severe penalties if they didn't conform to every detail of the contracts they were given. They called themselves *jual jiwa* [we had to sell our souls].

Although in the past the Banda Islands had been capable of producing fantastic profits, the decline of the little archipelago had been on the cards for decades. It wasn't just the corrupt and voracious descendants of the *perkeniers* that contributed to this, it was also the forces of nature. In the fragile volcanic strata on which the Bandas tower out of a depth of 4,000 metres there were continuous cataclysmic eruptions of Gunung Api, earthquakes and tsunamis that caused massive damage.

But in the last decade of the 19th century the Bandas experienced one last boom. The little village of Banda Neira became chic, a popular place for planters and rich Dutchmen to live.

After several generations the *perkeniers'* descendants had become too comfortable and lazy. They left the administration of the plantations to poorly-paid overseers and went to live in Banda Neira, where they lived in luxury and squandered their ancestral wealth. The simple little village of Banda Neira became a tiny sophisticated 'capital'. Property prices rose until they were almost comparable with those in major world cities.

The *perkeniers* no longer cared about the VOC. They forged reports on the nutmeg harvest and sold their crops directly in Java or Macassar, keeping the profits for themselves. At the same time, the slaves had to grind away, getting cheap sago from Ambon instead of the rice they were entitled to. Most of the *perkeniers* were brutal, beating and torturing the slaves for the most trivial reasons. Human life was cheap, there would always be more forthcoming from the VOC. Fearing the vengeance of the slaves, they employed overseers to supervise them. They took no interest in the plantations and lived in luxurious houses in Banda Neira near the two forts. This was the VOC's military headquarters, and they could go out even by night without fear of being attacked and killed. But the overseers were also working for their own interests, and the plantations fell into increasing decline.

Arabs and Chinese also enjoyed this life of luxury. They all vied to outdo one another. Exclusive villas with polished marble floors and crystal chandeliers were built in Banda Neira. Antique furniture made with the most expensive woods and mirrors with golden frames were imported. When money ran short the land of the *perken*, in spite of the VOC's opposition, was so heavily mortgaged that it would barely be possible to redeem it.

On Banda Neira they lived in an extravagant cloud-cuckoo land of stunning parties. Every evening they dressed up and promenaded up and down the pier and the only main street to the music of a military band. Their only aim was to see and be seen. It must have been, as Somerset Maugham writes, 'a Dutch *Arabian Nights*'.[166] The descendants of the once hard-working *perkeniers* had lost their energy. They surrendered themselves to a voluptuous and dissipated life and got up to their ears in debt.

When the Dutch Governor General visited the Banda Islands in 1860, he thought that the islands were as rich as they had ever been. The whole of Banda Neira was decorated with flowers and garlands and bands played on the streets. But for the Dutch in Amsterdam the Bandas had already become a loss-maker. The Dutch Governor was recalled, and the young descendants of the *perkeniers* decided they preferred the more exciting life in Amsterdam and emigrated to Holland *en masse*. The older descendants of the *perkeniers* continued to enjoy life in Banda Neira and livened up their declining years with frequent parties.

During my stay on the Bandas I kept asking people if they were descended from a *perkenier,* or if they knew someone who was. I got no answer. They simply didn't know. It was not only the islands that had fallen into oblivion, but also the *perkeniers.*

---

166 W. Somerset Maugham, *The Narrow Corner,* pp. 121ff

8. Germans in the service of the VOC on the Bandas

In the 17th century many young men in Germany were unable to find work. They dreamed of making their fortune in far-off lands and volunteered to serve as soldiers in the Dutch East Indies with the VOC in Amsterdam. They were often forced to do so because of abject destitution. Poverty was the best qualification for a military career. Many of these soldiers became wealthy by looting, because one of the privileges attached to service in the VOC was that plunder became their private property. They could also acquire wealth through private trade; though this was strictly forbidden by the Company it was common practice. They were not necessarily the best of men; many were drunkards and ruffians. There was a Dutch saying: *Useless in Holland, good enough for the colonies!*

There were also Germans who wished to emigrate because they were in danger of being prosecuted for debt, theft or murder. They chose the VOC and South East Asia to avoid punishment. In the Indies they were subject only to the jurisdiction of the Company, which didn't care about crimes committed in the past.

A third group of emigrants included educated men like doctors, scientists and engineers, as well as craftsmen like carpenters and bakers, all seeking their fortunes in the Netherlands Indies.

Although the VOC didn't pay very well, many of them succeeded in making a career for themselves. The normal term of a contract – which only began when the newcomer was on the spot after the long voyage out – was five years. Anyone who was still alive after five years and extended his contract would be promoted and receive a pay rise.

There were thousands of Germans who entered service of the Vereenigde Oostindische Companie, but only a few of them kept diaries and even fewer of these accounts – a mere handful – have survived. Only one in three of the emigrants made it back to Germany. Many documents went down with the ships and many who had lived long enough to return preferred to fill their luggage with spices rather than paper. There is very little information about trade, profits or the business processes of the Dutch in the surviving documents, because the Dutch regarded that as their business, and would not let outsiders get a look in.

At the end of the 18th century[167] Duke Carl Eugen of Württemberg sent a mercenary army of 2,000 officers and men to the Dutch colony to sup-

---

167 1787-1808

port the VOC.[168] Hardly any of them returned to Germany. The majority of the soldiers married Javanese women and remained out there. There are Indonesian historians who claim that, as a result of the activities of these soldiers, at least five percent of Indonesians today have Württembergish blood in their veins. That would come to some 13 million! But the story of the Württemberg Regiment, also known as the Cape Regiment, seems to have vanished from Württemberg's history. All that is known is that some units were stationed on Java and in Fort Rotterdam in Macassar on the Island of Celebes.

Visiting the National Archives in Jakarta in the 1960s, I discovered the names of descendants of members of the Württemberg Regiment, for example, officers called Wolzogen and Winckelman. The name Franquemont, the surname of Duke Carl Eugen of Württemberg's six illegitimate sons, was still extant. Four of them served in the regiment. All were married on Java.

In the mid-1960s I discovered an Upper Swabian Baroque cupboard – over 200 years old – in an antique shop in a Jakarta suburb. I bought it. Three of the Duke's illegitimate sons had cupboards in their luggage. I managed to find two more, similar Baroque cupboards in Indonesia. One was in the Indonesian President's palace in Jakarta, the second was in the private home of Ibnu Sutowo previously the very influential chairman of Pertamina, the Indonesian oil company. These are presumably the three cupboards that the Duke's sons took to Indonesia at the end of the 18th century. The cupboard is still in my living room.

Ill. 8-1
18th-century Upper Swabian Baroque cupboard

---

168 See also Horst H. Geerken, *A Gecko for Luck, pp.* 25 f

Although several of these German mercenaries must presumably have been sent to the Banda Islands from the nearby Fort Rotterdam in Macassar, I found very little evidence of this.

One of the Germans who did serve on the Banda Islands was Corporal Johann Verken from Meissen[169]. He sailed for South East Asia from Texel in Holland in December 1607 on board the *Geuineerde Provincien,* one of a fleet of thirteen ships. The fleet was commanded by Admiral Pieter Willemsz Verhoeff; its mission was to find the Spice Islands and to sink ships of the Portuguese East Indian fleet. All of this under the watchword *ryche retouren* [rich returns], that is, profit – which was always the most important thing for the Dutch.

After a short stay in Bantam on Java the *Geuineerde Provincien* sailed on to the Banda Islands. For days – writes Johann Verken – he was able to see the volcanic cone of Gunung Api, but the ship was unable to reach the island because of contrary winds. The voyage lasted seventeen months, and it was not until the 8th of April 1609 that the *Geuineerde Provincien* dropped anchor off Banda Neira. Eleven days later, on the 19th of April, Verken, together with 250 soldiers and sailors, set foot on the island. He writes in his diary that the islands are the best and most delightful in the whole of the Orient. He marvels at the dense, blue-green forests which stretch from the mountain peaks to the seashore.

Verken describes in detail the meeting between Admiral Verhoeff and the *Orang Kayas* on Banda Besar (as mentioned above in Chapter 6). The *Orang Kayas* were in full armour with massive sabres, hardwood spears 2.5 metres long and big shields, and were accompanied by other warriors. There were around 200 Bandanese gathered under a big Waringin tree.

As we already know, the Dutch demanded a monopoly of the nutmeg trade and the consent of the Bandanese to the building of a fort on Banda Neira, both of which were rejected. Verken writes that the Dutchmen were supposed to have been killed at this point, but that the Bandanese didn't dare to attack because the Dutch warships were just off the coast with loaded cannons and the master gunner standing by with his slow match already lit. We know the story of the ambush and killing of Admiral Verhoeff with his officers and senior merchants on the 22nd of May 1609; but we didn't know until now that Corporal Verken, after cries were heard from the woods, was the first to force his way into the grove with six other men and engage in a

---

169 S.P. L'Honoré, *Reisebeschreibungen von deutschen Beamten und Kriegsleuten im Dienst der Niederländischen West- und Ost-Indischen Kompanien 1602-1797* [Travel writing by German officials and military personnel in the service of the Netherlands West and East India Companies 1602-1797]

skirmish with the Bandanese. 47 Dutchmen died on that and the following day. Verken received a head wound from a wooden spear. It was the second wound he had received in VOC service. He was lucky: *within six days I was healed and fit again.*

Building work on Fort Nassau had progressed enough for Verken and 200 other men to be quartered there. He was promoted to sergeant and a little later – since the tropical climate had caused other deaths and they were short of men – to ensign. The first of many punitive raids made on the island's population by the Dutch was on the village of 'Labetacke'[170] in the north of Banda Neira. Verken describes it as follows: *…it then came to great carnage, because we spared no one, but shot or stabbed everyone, woman and child, old and young, on the spot. Afterwards the soldiers plundered the town, burning it to the ground, leaving nothing but ashes.*

Verken reports that in 1611 a new fleet brought the first Governor General of the VOC, Pieter Both, to Banda Neira. He took drastic measures to maintain discipline among the soldiers, and new campaigns against the Bandanese population began. Both had brought fresh troops. After two years, three month and nine days on the Bandas, Verken was discharged. He set sail on the return voyage to Europe on board the *Middelburg*. He writes that many people who had been looking forward so much to getting home died on the voyage. On the 18th of July 1612 the *Middelburg* anchors off Holland, and then we lose track of Ensign Johann Verken from Meissen.

Another diary and documents written by Johann Sigmund Wurffbain[171] of Nuremberg have survived. He has already been mentioned in Chapter 7. He too was in action for the VOC on the Banda Islands. More is known about Wurffbain and his life, since books and articles have by and about him been published.

Wurffbain[172] came from a wealthy family. His father, Leonhard Wurffbain, was a member of Nuremberg City Council. He had made a name for himself with books about Charlemagne and the expansion of the Habsburgs. He could afford to give his son a first-class education.

Wurffbain was born in Nuremberg on the 20th of August 1613. After leaving school, he trained as a merchant in his home city. When he had completed his training, he went to Amsterdam on the advice of his father to apply for a job with the VOC. He had high hopes of being employed by

---

170 Now Lantaka, or Lewetaka
171 Also Wurfbain
172 1613-1661

them as a merchant, because as well as German he spoke fluent Dutch and French. But he was disappointed, because in January 1632 he was only employed as a soldier of the lowest rank, an *adelborst[173]*. Later, on his return to Germany he told his fellow-countrymen about his experiences and advised them never to become a soldier in the service of the Dutch, the Portuguese or the English.

He first travelled to Batavia, where he was assigned to a command that was tasked with carrying out a punitive campaign[174] in the Spice Islands against rebellious natives who would not bow to the Dutch monopoly. In May 1633 he arrived at the island of Ambon; he was now twenty years old. Fort Victoria on the Spice Island of Ambon was at that time the centre and most important base of the VOC's operations in the East Indies. He took part in several punitive expeditions along the coast of the neighbouring island of Ceram – against *disobedient and rebellious* villages and their inhabitants. They set sail with seven European ships, four sloops and about 750 soldiers and sailors. Wurffbain was in a company of 47 men commanded by Lieutenant Bertram Duyvel. Whenever they found them, they set fire to the smugglers' ships and villages. All the clove trees they could find were destroyed, as were the coconut and sago palms which were necessary for the native inhabitants' subsistence. In spite of the bad weather – it was the West Monsoon period – the Governor of Ambon, Artus Gisels, spurred the soldiers on to ever greater atrocities. As Wurffbain wrote, whole islands were depopulated and laid wastes, there were murders, rapes, arson and destruction. Finally, on the 6th of May 1633, they set fire to the last of the smugglers' ships. It was not only the murdered natives who died – many VOC soldiers also lost their lives in the conflict. But as Wurffbain says, the unhealthy air on Ambon wiped out more Europeans than the weapons of the natives. Next, Wurffbain is transferred to the Banda Islands. But the punitive campaigns continue for 14 more years in the northern Moluccas under Governor Giesels' successor, Arnold de Vlamingh. Thousands of clove trees and sago palms are destroyed. Vlamingh wrote to the Directors of the VOC in Amsterdam: *Once we make the rebels destitute beggars and vagabonds, it will be greatly to the advantage of the Company.*

In April 1633 Wurffbain arrives on Banda Neira. He writes that nutmeg farming is now centralised on the three islands of Banda Neira, Lontor[175] and Ai. *The Good Lord has so generously blessed these islands above all others with so many trees that they [...] could amply supply the whole world.* The is-

---

173 Midshipman or cadet
174 Called *hongitocht* by the Dutch (see also Footnote 129)
175 Now Banda Besar

lands of Run and Rozengain[176], which were difficult to keep under control had ... *already been robbed of their glorious fecundity.* He also writes that the Bandas were known among the soldiers as the *Hungry Isles,* because apart from the nutmeg there were hardly any vegetables, and no cattle or poultry. Salt meat, cheese, olive oil and wine came from Batavia, *but a poor devil of a soldier can hardly afford such luxuries.*

Five years after his arrival on the Bandas, in 1638, he was already a senior assistant merchant. He took part in a census, whose results were as follows: Before the arrival of the Dutch the Bandas had had an estimated population of 15,000. Now there were only 3,842 inhabitants, 2,190 of them slaves. There were only 560 of the original inhabitants, the Bandanese, mainly young women. Wurffbain states that the church and administrative systems on the islands are good, and that schools are free. Christian religious education and Dutch language form an important part of the curriculum. But when the native pupils grow older, they turn away from the 'true religion' and revert to being *blind heathens.* Wurffbain himself was a Lutheran.

The VOC appoints him assistant merchant in Fort Nassau, so that he can now practice the profession he was trained for. He has to keep the books, logging the goods that come in and go out; he also registers the severe sentences passed by colonial justice. In the five years of his service in the Bandas, 25 people were condemned to death: *two burned alive, one broken on the wheel, nine hanged, nine beheaded, three strangled or choked and one 'arqvebussed'*[177]. *52 people were flogged, and of them 44 were branded once and three branded twice. One had his tongue pierced with an awl and another had both cheeks slit from the mouth to the ears.* The crimes were mainly treason, smuggling nutmegs, and love. For example, one man who had made his wife's sister pregnant was burned alive, while the poor woman was strangled *for committing such a sin.* The executioner on the Banda Islands was – Wurffbein tells us – Thomas Mosch, a *baptised Japanese.* With his Japanese sword – only about 60 centimetres long and two fingers wide – he could behead his victims with one one-handed stroke. When Mosch one day killed an innocent Dutchman while drunk, he suffered the same fate.

In the eyes of the VOC, homosexuality on land or sea was an inexcusable and capital crime. If two sinners were caught on board ship they were tied together back-to-back and thrown into the sea alive.

There were also cruel punishments on land. Wurffbain reports on such a case on Banda Neira. A slave was caught committing an *abhorrent sodomitic abomination* with a dog. Slave and dog were burned alive together.

---

176 Now Pulau Hatta
177 Shot. An arquebus is a muzzle-loading gun.

Even if the perpetrator was a long-term servant of the company, they still applied the punishment for homosexuality. For this 'crime' a captain who had just arrived in Batavia after the long voyage from Europe was strangled and burned, and his 13-year-old partner was drowned. Even the Commissioner and Counsellor of the Dutch East Indies, Justus Schouten, whose position was second only to the Governor General, was strangled and burned in Batavia for homosexuality.

In March 1638 Wurffbain's five-year term of service in the East Indies came to an end. By then he had spent four years and eleven months in Fort Nassau on Banda Neira. The Governor offered him a promotion and a better salary, but Wurffbain had had enough of the 'Hungry Isles'. In Batavia he was promoted to VOC junior merchant and transferred to Surat on the west coast of India, where he traded in coffee beans from the Yemen and precious stones. He played a major role in the spread of coffee consumption in Europe. In 1644 he was promoted to senior merchant and at the same time made responsible for diplomatic relations with Indian princes and rulers, a substantial position which also allowed him the opportunity to trade for himself. After six years and three months in Surat he returned to Batavia in April 1645.

After 14 years in the service of the VOC, Wurffbain asked to be discharged. He travelled home on the *Henriette Louise*. As a senior merchant, he was responsible for keeping the ship's books concerning the cargo, as well as all the ship's papers. In June 1646 he returned to Holland a wealthy man, arriving in his home town of Nuremberg in September of the same year. Wurffbain married in Nuremberg, had two sons and died there on the 2nd of August 1661.

Wurffbain's account of his travels was only published in part during his lifetime. The full account was published posthumously by his son.[178] It is an excellent description of Dutch colonial rule at the times, and of the VOC's trading activities. It is one of the first works to describe the situation in the Dutch East Indies, and was not superceded in that century.

His father Leonhard[179] had already published a book made up of Wurffbain's letters and other material from East India in 1646. He wanted to give

---

178 A digital edition of this rare work can be found under Ioannis Sigismundi Wurffbain in the Herzogin Anna Amalia Library in Weimar

179 Called Leonhartum Wurffbain in the book *Joh. Sigmund Wurffbains vierzehnjährige Ostindische Kriegs- und Oberkaufmanns-Dienste, in einem richtig geführten Journal- und Tage-Buch.* [Joh. Sigmund Wurffbain's fourteen-year service as soldier and senior merchant in the East Indies, in a properly kept journal and diary], Nuremberg 1686, Tübingen 1688.

his son a pleasant surprise on his arrival in Nuremberg, but unfortunately did not succeed. The book had so many errors that Johann Sigmund bought up and destroyed all the copies he could get hold of. The work can be found under *Monographier Digital*[180]. It was advertised as follows in 1646:

Ill. 8-2, Allegorical frontispiece of Johann Sigmund Wurffbain's travel memoirs.[181]

180 https://0ra-web.swkk.de/digimo_online/digimo.Sammelband?, Herzogin Anna Amalia Bibliothek, Weimar
181 The angel on the left is holding a portrait of Wurffbain

Description of the Travels [of] Joannis Sigismundi Wurffbain, a Citizen of Nuremberg, which he undertook in the Name and the Service of the Honourable East India Company, with its Seat in the Netherlands, setting forth in the Month of April in Anno Christi 1632 in the Name of God and Honour and completing his journey in the month of June 1646. Produced by his Father Leonhart Wurffbain at his own Press and Cost.

Ill. 8-3, Johann Sigmund Wurffbain: Reise Nach den Molukken und Vorder-Indien 1632-1646 [Journey to the Moluccas and the Indian Sub-Continent 1632-1646][182]

---

[182] *Reisebeschreibungen von deutschen Beamten und Kriegsleuten im Dienst der Ostindischen Kompanie* [Travel Writing by German Officials and Military Men in the Service of the East India Company], Nuremberg 1646, Reprint 1931

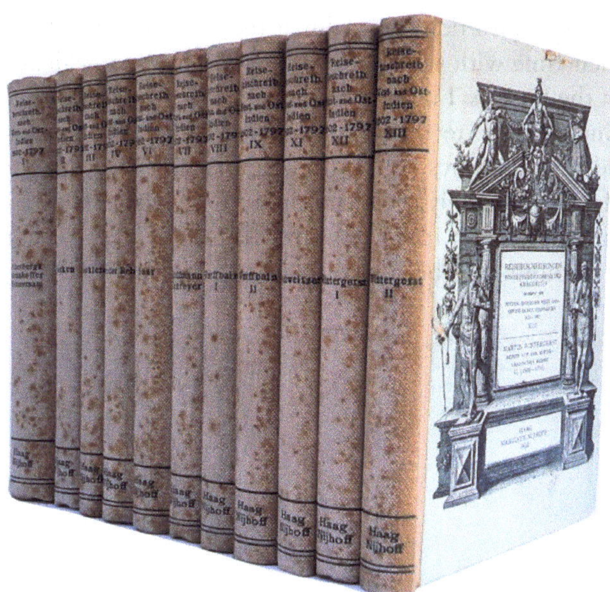

Ill. 8-4
It was a 13-volume work

The Nuremberg grammar-school teacher and poet Christoph Arnold[183] was interested in the history of East Asia. He collected material and also interviewed Johann Sigmund Wurffbain. In the miscellany published by Arnold in 1663 – two years after Wurffbain's death – entitled *Wahrhaftige Beschreibung zweyer mächtigen Königreiche, Jappan und Siam* [*True Description of Two Mighty Kingdoms, Japan and Siam*] – there is an interesting contribution by Wurffbain with instructions on how to go about organising a voyage to the East Indies.

It is interesting that in this work Wurffbain mentions an expedition by three Germans – Michael, Piemp and Schiller – which they embarked on in 1634 with some Dutchmen, to the as yet unexplored New Guinea. I have not found any other reference to this expedition.

There were many other German soldiers, administrators and merchants who served in the Dutch East India Company, like mining engineer Johann Wilhelm Vogel, who published his book on *Bergmännisches Rechnen* [*Mining Calculations*] and his *Reiseberichte* [Account of his Travels] in 1694,[184] and ship's doctor Johann Jacob Merklein, soldiers David Tappe, Christian Burckhardt from Halle, Christoph Schweitzer, Volquard Iversen, Martin Wintergerst, Christoph Langhanß and Johann Jacob Saar, or ship's surgeons

---

183 1627-1685
184 1690 and 1696 also in German in Frankfurt and Leipzig

Johann Schreyer, and Christoff Frick from Ulm at the Danube. They have all left accounts of their time with the VOC, but I could find no evidence that they were ever in the Bandas. I do suspect, however, that one gardener, George Meister did intend to go to the Bandas because his profession was very much in demand there for forestry and maintenance work in the nutmeg plantations. Unfortunately, only the first part of his travel writings has survived. The many other Germans in the service of the VOC either did not keep diaries, or their accounts have been lost.

1132 Oſt=Indianiſche

Johann Sigmund Wurfbains
INSTRUCTION,
oder
Kurtzer Bericht/
Wie eine Reiſe / ſowol zu Waſſer / als zu Land / nach Indien anzuſtellen ſey :

Die Reiſe zu Land / von Conſtantinopel aus.

Alls Europa nach Orientaliſch Indien zu reiſen / muß ſolches per terram oder per mare geſchehen; über Land muß man ſich erſtlich nach Conſtantinopel oder Alexandretta verfügen. Die von Conſtantinopel aus / nehmen ihren Weg über Land nach Alcair, und weiter bis nach Sues, den äuſſerſten Ort an dem mari rubro gelegen; allda begeben ſie ſich insgeſamt zu ſchiffen / (*) bis nacher Mocha, welche Stadt nicht mehr als ungefähr 16. Mei-

(†) *Bis nacher Mocha.*] Dieſe Stadt ligt in dem glückſeeligen Arabien / gerad im Munde des rothen Meers / auf der Höhe von 13. Grad. 28. Min. Norderbreite : Sie iſt ſehr groß / und ohne Mauren / an der Waſſerſeite gelegen; auf einem dürren und unfruchtbaren Boden. Vor 90. oder 100. Jahren war daſelbſt ein Fiſcherdorf / aber ſeit der Großtürk darüber herrſchet / iſt ſolche Stadt zu einem Haubtplatz worden. Sie beſtehet

Reis=beſchreibung. 1133

beſtehet aus Türken / Arabern / Benjanen / und Juden. Von Alters her iſt allhie / von dem erſten Mertz an / bis auf den halben September / groſſer Zulauf des Volks / geweſt; indem das groſſe Schiff Manſouri (welches / im September vom euſſerſten Theil des rothen Meers abreiſt) allhie anlandet. Solches Schiff aber komt / wegen des groſſen Sultans von Conſtantinopel; der es / auf der Kaufleut Fracht / hin und her fahren läſſt. Man muß alsdann 10. pro cento, vom hundert / von der Kauffmannſchaft bezahlen ; und / auſſer dieſem Schiff / dürfen keine andere Schiffe dieſelbige Reiſe thun. Diß zuvorbeſagte Schiff komt von oben herab / ſehr köſtlich beladen / bisweilen 25. oder 30. hunderttauſend Realen von achten werth ; welches theils in paaren Realen / Venetianiſchen und Mohriſchen Ducaten ; theils aber in Welſchen / guldenen Stücken / Camelotten / Safran / Queckſilber / allerhand Krämereyen / und groſſer Menge Chriſten Weiber / Männer und Kinder / ſo gegen Oſten eröbert und bekommen worden ; die meinſtentheils Griechen / Ungern / Italiener / auch aus Cypren / und andern Inſeln gebürtig ſind. Diß Schiff verreiſt gemeiniglich den erſten Jenner / mit Specereyen / und allerhand Indianiſchen Wahren wol und reichlich beladen. So hat man auch gemeiniglich alle Jahre / im Anfang / oder um die Helfte des Mertzen / allhie eine Caffila oder Caravvane ; ſo über die 1600. Camelen ſtark: Die beſtehet in lauter Kauffleuten / ſo meinſtentheils Türken / Araber / und Armenier ; neben noch andern fremden Nationen. Dieſe kommen über Aleppo, und Alexandria ; ſind gemeiniglich zwey Monath unter wegs / und reiſen nicht mehr / dann drey oder vier Holländiſche Meilen / des Tags. Die Kauffmannſchaften / ſo ſie mitbringen / ſind Neh = und Stickſeiden / guldner Drath / rothe Corallen / Vermelion / Saffran / allerhand (zuvor theils in Oſt = Indien / theils auch in Afrika berühmte) Nürnberger = wahren / Nablen / Brillen / Scheere / Meſſer / Spiegel / ꝛc. Solche Caffila verreiſt gemeiniglich im December / mit allerhand Indianiſchen Wahren / alſo daß ſie / mit Hin = und wiederreiſen ein gantzes Jahr zubringen. Ferner dienet zu wiſſen / daß

Cccc iij   Mocha

Ill. 8-5, Johann Sigmund Wurffbain's instructions concerning the various routes and modes of travel to the East Indies with commentary by Christoph Arnold.[185]

---

185 From Christoph Arnold: *Wahrhaftige Beschreibungen dreyer maechtigen Koenigreiche Japan, Siam und Corea* [True Descriptions of Three Mighty Kingdoms, Japan. Siam and Korea], Nuremberg, 1672.)

9. The island of Run exchanged for Manhattan

Henry Hudson the English explorer had already made two voyages under the auspices of the English merchants' association, the Muscovy Company, attempting to find a route to China and the Spice Islands via the North-East Passage. He didn't find the passage, though he did discover a number of unknown islands in the North Sea. He approached the London merchants for the funds to make a new expedition. He firmly maintained that he now knew where the route through the northern polar seas was, but the merchants, disheartened by all the previous failures, flatly refused any further financial involvement.

The Dutch directors of the VOC heard about this. They scented an opportunity to take advantage of this route to the Spice Islands, which was roughly 3,500 kilometres shorter than their current route, and invited Hudson to a meeting in Amsterdam. They quickly reached an agreement, and only a few months later, in March 1609, Hudson sailed north in the *Halve Maen* in the employ of VOC. Because of constant disputes among his mixed crew of Englishmen and Dutchmen, Hudson broke off his quest in the polar sea and sailed westwards. When the pack ice became too thick, he sailed south along the east coast of America. On the 11th of September 1609, Hudson reached the mouth of the river that now bears his name and the island that is now known as Manhattan, a part of the modern city of New York.

When Hudson, on his return, told of the great fertility of the land, of the profusion of wild fruit that grew there, of the immeasurable quantity of skins and furs and of the wide expanses of forest, a group of Dutchmen set out and settled there, living in simple log cabins. Since the south of Manhattan provided the best moorings, this was the first part of the island to be settled in 1611. Then in 1623 whole families followed them out in the *Nieuw Holland*. They named the town Nieuw Amsterdam, New Amsterdam. The south of the settlement was dominated by Fort Amsterdam. It was an exact copy of Fort Nassau on Banda Neira.

On the 2nd of February 1653 New Amsterdam was made the capital of the Province of New Holland, which encompassed what is now the city of New York, New Jersey, Long Island, Connecticut and parts of Delaware. The Dutch had purchased the land for the sum of 24 dollars, which would now be over 1,000 dollars. By now, New Amsterdam had grown into a town of barely 1,000 inhabitants. The first Dutch governor of the province was Peter Stuyvesant, whose strict rule made him quite unpopular.

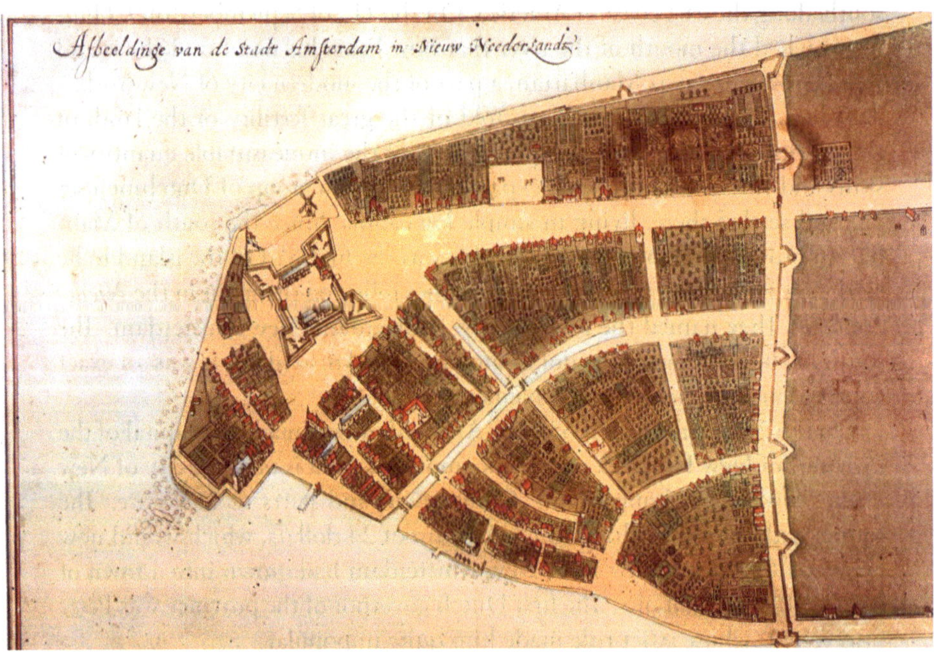
t' Fort nieuw Amsterdam op de Manhatans
Afbeeldinge van de Stadt Amsterdam in Nieuw Neederlandt

Since New Amsterdam was in a state of constant expansion due to the arrival of new settlers, a defensive wall was built as extra protection. Wall Street, one of the most famous streets in the world, runs along the course of that wall.

When hostilities broke out between England and Holland over the Ambon Massacre[188], in which many Englishmen were tortured to death by the Dutch – and which I will describe in detail in Chapter 20 – the Dutch confiscated the Island of Run and deported the English who lived there to Bantam on Java. There was an interminable tug of war between the two colonial powers for the possession of the tiny island. It changed ownership several times during the hostilities, being sometimes Dutch and sometimes English again.

James I of England swore vengeance for the Ambon massacre. In the English Channel, the English confiscated Dutch ships on their way to or from the East Indies. After King James' death, his successor, Charles I, renewed the English claim for compensation from the Dutch. When a Dutch delegation came to London, the confiscated ships were soon returned to them. Rumours circulated that the king had been bribed.

But the merchants of the English East India Company gave him no rest. They had invested too much money in their expeditions, and insisted on Run being returned. In 1632 and 1636 ships were sent from Bantam to Run, but because of the contrary winds they had to return to Java having achieved nothing. It wasn't until later in 1636 that an English merchant succeeded in reaching Run. He was horrified to discover that the island was almost uninhabited. The buildings had been destroyed, the bigger nutmeg trees had been cut down, the smaller ones uprooted. He found a bare island with almost no one living on it. The Dutch had made it worthless.

Demands for compensation were renewed, supported by heaps of documents which were sent to Amsterdam. In only two decades, 150 Englishmen had been killed by the Dutch, and at least 800 people who worked for the English had been sold as slaves. They demanded that Run should be newly planted with nutmeg trees and returned to the English.

---

186 Wikipedia Public Domain
187 Wikipedia Public Domain
188 In historical literature: The Amboyna Massacre

But England was in a poor state at the time. Civil war was raging, and the English East India Company was deeply in debt and nearing the end. If any of their ships managed to load a cargo of spices, it would usually be captured by the Dutch. On the 14th of January 1657 the company declared itself bankrupt. Had all the effort of the earlier expeditions been in vain? Had thousands of human lives been lost for nothing? The government intervened and on the 19th of October 1657 the English East India Company was transformed into a modern joint stock company.

But the trade in spices was now in decline, and the main focus of English trade was now India, where there were fine fabrics and chemicals. The English legal claim on Run was never abandoned, but they lacked the finance necessary to equip a fleet to win back the island for the kingdom.

A war between England and Holland fundamentally altered the situation. In was the first of four wars between the two rivals, which lasted from 1652 to 1654. In the peace negotiations, England held the better cards. The resulting treaty stated that the Island of Run was to be returned to the English, and there was an agreed sum of compensation for the Ambon massacre. On the 8th of May 1654, the Treaty of Westminster was signed by both parties, giving it legal force. But the Dutch had no intention of observing the treaty. On the Banda Islands hostilities between the English and Dutch companies carried on unchanged. The Dutch governors in the outposts were a long way from Amsterdam. They had their own ideas – and their own military forces.

An employee of the English company from Bantam visited Run and reported that the native inhabitants who had remained would look favourably on the return of the English, and that they would like to re-afforest and re-settle the island in co-operation with the English. When this news reached London, the Company planned the establishment of a model colony on Run. A ship carrying carpenters, gardeners, farmers, smiths and other craftsmen set out for Run, but it didn't get to Run because a renewal of hostilities between England and Holland seemed likely. Captain John Dutton therefore preferred to stop over first on the island of St Helena in the South Atlantic. In May 1659, the British East India Company took possession of St Helena. They built Fort Jamestown, a garrison and a first settlement.

It was not until a year later that the situation between the two opposing nations relaxed enough for a fleet of colonists under the command of Captain John Hunter[189] was able to set sail, this time with four ships. The fleet sailed first to St Helena, where they took Captain John Dutton – who

---

189 John Hunter later achieved fame as an explorer in Australia and Tasmania

was to be the Governor of Run – and some of the settlers he had with him on board. However, some of the colonists intended for Run wanted to settle permanently on St Helena. They formed the foundation of today's British Overseas Territory of St Helena, Ascension und Tristan da Cunha.

The Dutch Governor General in Batavia found threadbare excuses to refuse permission for the English fleet to sail on to Run. Since the Company had given the expedition's captains the order to take the island by force if necessary, they sailed on to the Banda Islands in spite of the Governor's embargo. But the Governor of the Bandas also refused to hand Run over to the English as had been agreed in the Treaty of Westminster, saying that if the English were to try and land on the island, the Dutch would use their firepower to prevent them. The Dutch had lied to the English. They had never seriously intended to return Run to the English. Captain Dutton wanted to take action, but Hunter, his deputy, refused to become involved in a military conflict.

The merchants back in London were outraged and desperate. The Island of Run had brought them nothing but losses. Finally, the English did succeed in occupying the island. On the 23rd of March 1665 two ships – unnoticed by the Dutch – moored in the harbour of Run. The English took the island without a shot being fired. The Dutch who were living there at the time left the islands with their possessions and sailed to their Dutch headquarters on Banda Neira.

The English joy at the liberation of Run was only short lived. Shortly afterwards the Dutch took the island back. To make it permanently unattractive to the English, they cut down the trees and burned everything. All that was left, was a bare island.

As a reaction to the decades of violent actions by the Dutch in South-East Asia, from the Ambon massacre to the several times they had illegally captured Run, the English began to plan their retaliation.

On the 8th of September 1664, at the instigation of the Duke of York[190], English troops attacked New Amsterdam in North America and captured the town. Fort Amsterdam had fallen into disrepair, the weapons available were out of date and most of them were unserviceable. New Amsterdam was therefore an easy target, and was quickly overrun. The English now renamed it New York. War was raging once more between the two states in Europe, the Second Anglo-Dutch War, which lasted from 1665 to 1667. It was once more a war for economic dominance in world trade. A battle for mastery of the seas, in which dozens of ships were sunk and thousands of seamen and soldiers lost their lives.

190 James, later James II, brother of Charles II

The Dutch protested at the capture of New Amsterdam, but the English rejected their protests, pointing out that they had done the same with the Island of Run. The plague and the Great Fire of London had weakened the power of the English financial world, and Holland too was becoming tired of war. Both countries were now ready to negotiate. Holland claimed possession of the Province of New Holland in North America with its capital New Amsterdam, though this was now occupied by English troops and was now called New York. On the other side of the globe, England had claims on the Bandanese island of Run, which was occupied by Dutch forces.

A historic exchange was made. The Dutch were determined to keep the island of Run in their sphere of influence, in order to finally establish a monopoly over all the Banda Islands and the nutmeg trade. The English voyages to the Bandas had long been a thorn in the flesh of the Dutch, since the Bandanese gave the English preferential treatment in the nutmeg trade.

Ill. 9-3, Fort Amsterdam around 1730. Under the English it was renamed Fort George[191]

191 Wikipedia Public Domain

132

That even went so far that the English were sometimes able to export more nutmeg from the Bandas than the Dutch. To definitively possess Run, the Dutch were prepared to make major concessions. The island they themselves had devastated had now become incredibly valuable.

The Treaty of Breda, signed on the 31ˢᵗ of July 1667, was in part an attempt to tidy up international borders in the aftermath of the Second Anglo-Dutch war. The English exchanged the tiny island of Run in the East Indian Archipelago not only for the considerably larger island of Manhattan on the east coast of North America, but also for the whole province of New Holland. Tiny as Run is, it was invaluable asset, and was the most important item pledged by the English in the exchange. The English delegation at the negotiations was led by Lord Sandwich.

In addition to the island of Run, the English recognised Dutch sovereignty over Dutch Guyana[192] in South America. The English had founded a settlement there in 1651, but it had been conquered by a Dutch expeditionary force in 1667, before the conclusion of the Treaty of Breda. It is interesting to note that the descendants of the thousands of slaves transported from Java to Dutch Guyana to work on the sugar cane plantations still mostly speak Javanese or Malay even today in this part of South America.

New Amsterdam now became New York and the old Native American path in Manhattan that bisected the island from north to south, built up by the Dutch and named Breede Weg, is now Broadway. The nutmeg had been exchanged for the Big Apple!

Still, Run had no economic value for its new Dutch colonial rulers, since they had themselves cut down the nutmeg trees to hinder a return of the English. They also wished to avoid over-production in order to keep the price as high as possible.

When I visited Run at the end of 2018, I saw that there were once more nutmeg trees growing there and that recently new plantations are being created. Even though the nutmeg trade is not as lucrative as it once was, it looks as if an old tradition is being revived there.

I believe that there is nothing in the world to compare with the different development of those two islands, which were once regarded as of equal value. The Treaty of Breda had more portentous consequences than almost any other ever concluded. The tiny island of Run with its one small village slumbers like Sleeping Beauty. The scarcely one thousand people who live in their little huts on the island live mainly from fishing. There is not a single car on the island, just a few motorcycles that putter about the narrow roads.

192 Now independent Surinam

Ill. 9-4, The Congress of Breda, contemporary print[193]

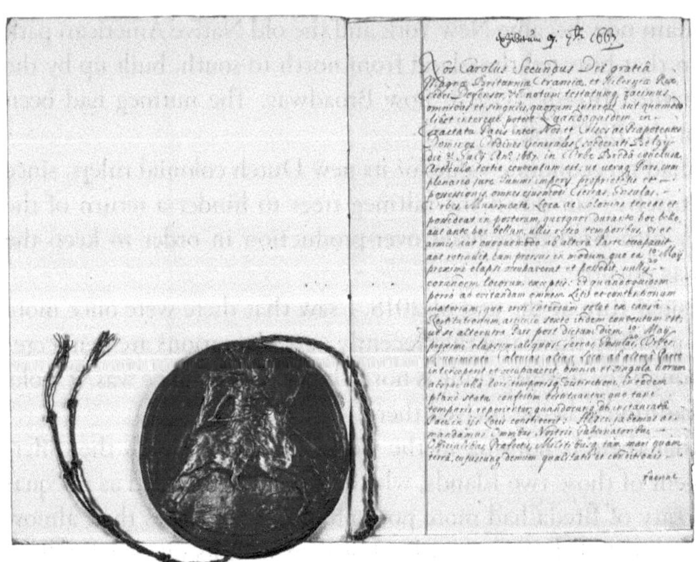

Ill. 9-5, The last page of the Treaty of Breda with the seal[194]

---

193 Wikipedia Commons
194 Nationaal Archief, Staten-Generaal Archiefinventaris 1.01.02 Inventarisnummer
12589.127

Ill. 9-6, The Peace of Breda was such an important event that a coin was minted to celebrate the signing of the treaty.[195]

Hardly any of the inhabitants know about their island's importance in history. If the people of Run want to experience something out of the ordinary, they have to take a two-hour trip by speedboat to reach Banda Neira, the capital of the island group, which is hardly less sleepy. The nearest larger city is Ambon, at least ten hours away by ship.

Manhattan, on the other hand, developed into a pulsating financial and economic metropolis, perhaps the biggest in the world, with a population of millions and countless skyscrapers. You can hardly imagine a greater contrast.

In November 2017, in the context of a Banda Festival that ran from the 11th of October to the 11th of November, an anniversary was celebrated: it was 350 years since the exchange of Run for Manhattan. Although the Treaty of Breda was signed on the 21st of July 1667, it took some time for the exchange to be organised. The commemoration of the event therefore took place a bit later with VIPs from the USA and Indonesia, like Said Assagaff, the Governor of the Moluccas, and the US Ambassador to Indonesia, Joseph R. Donovan were there.

---

195 A restrike mint, Wikipedia Public Domain

Since the VIP delegation – as I was told – only visited Banda Neira on a day excursion by special flight, it had not been possible for them to visit Run, the island which was the reason for the whole event. One of the inhabitants of Run, who had been at the celebrations, said to me jokingly: *Now we're just waiting for President Trump to build a tower on Run too, just like in Manhattan!*

On the island of Banda Neira, almost exactly on the other side of the world from New York, the day of the 350th anniversary of the handover was solemnly celebrated with dancing, debates about the history of the islands, an exhibition of old photographs and maps, and local culinary specialities. By contrast, in New York it was a day like any other, no one seems to have been interested in this historic anniversary.

And so we seem to have come to a full circle. In those days the Banda islands, including Run, were of great political importance, the centre of the world. The Spice Islands were on everyone's lips, while New York was an unassuming village with a population of a few hundred.

Times and positions have changed. In Wall Street, Manhattan today has the most important stock exchange in the world. Everyone knows New York, but who has even heard of the island of Run? When the price of nutmeg fell, the Banda islands also fell into oblivion. Even in Indonesia I have never found anyone who knows offhand where the little island group is. And Pulau Run? Never heard of it, not in Indonesia and even less in the rest of the world. But who can be aware of such tiny details, in an Indonesian Archipelago that has over 17,000 islands?

But I practically imbibed the Banda Islands with my mother's milk, which is why this little faraway archipelago has fascinated me and been with me my whole life long.

10. The nutmeg and Pierre Poivre

For millennia, because of the unique microclimate and the special qualities of the volcanic soil, the nutmeg grew only on the Banda Islands, and nowhere else in the world. After the brutal conquest of the islands by the Dutch, and when production of the spices returned to normal after the genocide and brutal eradication of the Bandanese population, the Dutch maintained a strict monopoly for the next 150 years. The sale of nutmeg and mace created untold wealth for the VOC and the Dutch. They achieved profit margins of up to 60,000 %.

The nutmeg always had an aura of fascination, and so it is little wonder that it entered the realms of poetry. In the early 13th century, when the nutmeg was a rare and precious spice whose origins were most mysterious, the German mine-singer Wolfram von Eschenbach wrote in his *Parzival*[196]:

... swâ man ufen teppech trat
cardemom, jeroffel, **muscat**,
lac gebrochen undr ir fuezen
durch den luft suezen ...

Translation (the extract chosen is printed in bold type):
When [the King's] bitter suffering
Caused him sharp pangs of pain,
The air was sweetened
To disguise the stench of the wound
Before him on the carpet were strewn
Allspice and terebinth resin,
Musk and aromatic herbs.
To sweeten the air there was also
Theriac and precious amber
Whose aroma was pleasant.
Whenever they stepped on the carpet,
cardamom, cloves and nutmeg
Were crushed under foot
To sweeten the atmosphere,
So that by treading on the spices

---

196 From *Parzival*, Book XVI, 789,21-790,8 [Translator's note: This describes the scene in the hall of the Fisher King, whose suppurating and incurable wound can only be healed by the actions of the Grail knight (Parzival)]

They disguised the dreadful stench.
The logs in his fire were lignum aloe (agar wood)
As I told you before.

His contemporary Albrecht von Halberstadt[197] wrote in his version of Ovid's
Metamorphoses:
Cynaras gewan ein kint
die wart ein maget sinnes blint,
die durch ir unkûsche wart
zeinem boume verkart
der die mirren nu treit.
Der boum mûze uns verseit
Nû und iemer mêre sîn
Muschât *unde zinemin*
und der edle wîrouch
mûzen uns verbern ouch
daz icht in disme lande
won sus getâne schande,
daz wir des icht begân
der dô Mirrâ het getan.

Translation:
Kynyras begot a daughter;
She grew up to be a foolish young woman,
Who because of her unchastity
Was turned into a tree
Which now produces myrrh.
Let us abhor this tree
Now and for evermore.
Nutmeg and cinnamon
And noble incense:
We must abstain from them
So that in this land
We do not have such shame,
And do not commit the crime
That Myrrha committed there.[198]

---

197 Albrecht von Halberstadt, *Metamorphosen* X, 300ff
198 The point Albrecht is making here is that it is better to live in a country where we do not have crimes of the kind Myrrha committed with her father, even if it
means doing without luxurious spices.

In the 13th century there were many other German writers who mentioned the nutmeg: in Konrad Fleck's *Flore und Blanscheflur* of 1230, in Freidank's *Bescheidenheit*, in Konrad von Würzburg's *Goldener Schmiede*, in Hugo von Langenstein's *Martina*, in Heinrich von Neustadt's *Apollonius von Tyrland* (and possibly his *Von Gotes Zuokunft*) and many others.

Ludwig Uhland immortalised the nutmeg in his *Volksliedern* [Folk Songs], 1844:
Bei meines liebsten Bette, da stond drei beumelein
*Das ein treit **muscatblüt**, das ander negelein[199];*
*Die **muscat** die ist süsse, die negelein die seind gut*

[By my beloved's bed there stand three trees
One of them bears nutmeg and the other cloves
The nutmeg is sweet and the cloves are good]

and Martin Luther wrote:[200]
Exactly as if those learned, serene, wise beasts, the sows, decided in their parliament: We sows ordain that no one shall maintain that nutmeg is a noble spice.

B. Waldi in his 1548 poem *Epos* [Epic] writes:
*Der **muskat** wird die kuh nicht froh*
ir schmeckt viel basz grob haberstro

[Nutmeg doesn't please the cow
She much prefers coarse oaten straw]

And in another place:
wie man auch sonst giebt zu errathen
*wozu sollen der kuh **muscaten**?*
Sie frisst wohl Haberstroh.
[No matter how you try to explain
What use is nutmeg to the cow?
She actually feeds on oat straw.]

'Feeding nutmeg to the cow' was proverbial at the time, meaning much the same as the Biblical 'Casting pearls before swine', which is still current (and is also what Luther is referring to).

---

199 Negelein=Nägelein [Translator's note: [literally a little nail], another term for clove. Compare the French 'clou [nail] (de girofle), which gives us the English clove.]
200 Luther 5, 297a

The important role that the Banda Islands played in the German popular imagination of the time, and the fact that the islands were known all over Europe – unlike today – is shown by an extract from the writings of Daniel Parthey, published in 1698[201], which mention the mountain Gumanapi[202] [sic] *which burns perpetually,* and say that the famous quack doctor, magician and soothsayer Johann Georg Faust[203], who provided the basis for the protagonist in Goethe's *Faust,* claimed that *he could travel there in the twinkling of an eye and bring fresh nutmeg back to Europe.*

There are many such examples, and the list could be extended right down to modern times. But the decreasing popularity of the nutmeg as a spice in Europe is also noticeable in the sphere of literature.

The 18th century is regarded as the peak in the medicinal use of nutmeg. In 1704, Dietzius published a 900-page dissertation in Latin dedicated solely to the nutmeg. According to him 138 diseases can be cured with the nutmeg, often in combination with herbs. 18th-century women in England and America used nutmeg to produce a miscarriage.

The works of Rumphius[204], a German naturalist, botanist and zoologist, and Valentijn[205], a Dutchman, are the classic works on the Moluccas. Both lived there for a long time around 1700, and described the nutmeg tree in great detail. Rumphius says: *the leaves are like those of the pear, but more pointed, longer and without indentations, deep green on the surface and rather greyish underneath; the tree itself is also like the pear tree in terms of shape and size....*

Rumphius often makes comparisons with European fruit trees, but I could not find any similarity with the pear tree. Rumphius' description of the nutmeg tree, the blossoms, the stamens, the fruit, the trunk, the roots and so on, go on for pages. It is only of interest to experts, but it is the first, most detailed and most accurate description of the nutmeg tree.

Illustrations right page:
Ill. 10-1, Almost ripe nutmeg fruit on the tree
Ill. 10-2, Open fruit casing, showing a nut which is still in its aril, the red mace

---

201 Daniel Parthey, *Daniel Parthey Burgers in Franckenberg/Ost-Indianische und Persianische Neun-jährige Kriegs-Dienste* [The Nine-Year East Indian and Persian Military Service of Daniel Parthey, citizen of Frankenberg], Nuremberg, 1698, p. 137
202 Gunung Api, a still active volcano in the Banda Islands
203 1480–1541?
204 See Chapter 21
205 Valentijn, *Oud- en Nieuw-Oost Indie,* 1726, p. 197

Ill. 10-3
Nutmeg juice and nutmeg jam from Banda Neira

Ill. 10-4
Candied nutmeg peel

The nutmeg tree[206] is an evergreen tree with thick, dark-green foliage which can grow to a height of 20 metres. The nutmeg itself is found in an ochre-yellow almost spherical fruit with a diameter of about 5 centimetres, which reminds me of a large apricot or a peach. From blossoming to the ripening of the fruit normally takes 9 months. A fully grown tree produces about 2,000 fruit every year. There is no particular fruiting season, and so the ripe fruit can be harvested all year round. However, the main harvest times are the months of April, August and December, though – as Rumphius says – August the best harvest month. The nutmeg tree needs protection against strong winds. A good worker can harvest 1,000 – 1,500 nuts a day.

The shell which contains the kernel – the nutmeg – is enclosed in a shiny, blackish-red aril, the mace, which is still sometimes erroneously described as *Muskatblüte* [nutmeg blossom]. Mace has a finer taste and is also considerably dearer than nutmeg. They have both been – and still are – used in cookery as well as medically in naturopathy and cosmetics. As soon as the fruit is ripe, it bursts open, showing the nut enclosed in its bright red aril. When the nutshell is broken open, the kernel, the nutmeg, is revealed.

206 Myristica fragrans

If the fleshy outer peel of the nutmeg is put in a shallow trench and covered with some earth and twigs, it produces a growth medium in which the delicious edible fungus *Jamur Pala*, the nutmeg fungus, flourishes. According to Rumphius, it is a gill fungus with a thick stem and a round, greyish black, bell-shaped cap. Rumphius gave it the Latin name *boletus moschocaryanus*. He only found this fungus on the Bandas. He says it is the *most delicious and best of mushrooms*. He calls it a gill fungus, although today the term *boletus* is confined to the fungi with hymeneal pores. But, even mycologists sometimes get mixed up.

The nutmeg used to be propagated exclusively by pigeons who – says Wurffbain – are particularly fond of nutmeg. The number of nutmeg trees used to be increased simply by collecting wild saplings from the forest and transplanting them in the plantations. The species of pigeon that spreads the nutmeg is particularly large: it is known as the nuteater[207] or nutmeg bird. These blue pigeons are also a delicacy on the Bandas when roasted. Rumphius thinks that the roasted pigeon tastes best when cooked while you can feel the whole nut still in its stomach.[208] He names the bird *pala-ala* or *pala-ala-manay*. They didn't succeed in growing nutmeg from seed in the *perken* until 1662. According to Rumphius this only succeeded with half-ripe nuts whose mace aril was not yet red.

There is no doubt that the nutmeg has possible toxic effects. Rumphius writes that excessive consumption of the popular puree that is made on the Bandas from the green outer peel of the nut can cause drowsiness and numbness. When a whole grated nutmeg is eaten, it can result in impaired consciousness, including hallucinations and speech impairment. Medically, it is used in small quantities to reduce stomach pain. Ayurvedic medicine suggests that an extract of nutmeg has effects that include increasing libido and potency. In India and Sri Lanka even today nutmeg is used in Ayurvedic medicine as a heat-generating medium. Ingesting five nutmegs is said to be fatal for adults. Nutmeg oil[209] is used on the Bandas – in addition to its use in cooking – as an external medication for rheumatism and muscle pain – usually warmed.

The peel that covers the mace and the nutmeg is fleshy, and makes a wonderful jam, as well as juice and a candied sweet. In past centuries, the candied peel of the young fruit was a quite important commodity in Europe. Today this delicacy is totally forgotten in Germany. In his books Rumphius describes the preserving of the fruit while still green in some detail. He also

---

207 Dutch *Noteneeter*, Indonesian *Burung Pala*
208 Dr O. Warburg, *Die Muskatnuss,* 1897, S. 319
209 In Malay *Minyak Pala*

says that if you eat this confection every day, *head and heart fill with a dense mist. This results in a drowsy state in which people dream and become forgetful.* Candied nutmeg peel tastes delicious. Such a pity that it is not to be found outside the Bandas.

Nutmeg can be pressed to produce what is called nutmeg butter.[210] It is a reddish-brown vegetable fat with an intense smell and taste of nutmeg. The butter is made of 'bad nuts' – the Dutch called them *rompen* [rumps]. The *rompen* are unripe nuts that have fallen from the trees in bad weather. As the nuts are an oily fruit, they could also be burned in the stove, because as Rumphius[211] wrote, *one could cook a meal with them, since they produce a clear flame and great heat.*

In England in particular – even at Elizabeth I's court – they ascribed important medical qualities to nutmeg butter. It was called nutmeg balm, and used to treat abdominal pain, queasiness and nausea. It also played a role in pharmacies on the continent in the 17th century. It was very expensive, and arrived in Europe – as Valentini, a doctor, reports in 1704 – in porcelain jars. Small pieces wrapped in banana leaves found buyers in Europe as medicinal nutmeg soap.[212] In my experience, nutmeg butter is an acquired taste: rather bitter, hot and too spicy.

Nutmeg is also used in the manufacture of perfumes in the form of ground nutmeg, powdered mace or the nuts' essential oil. Nutmeg is also found today in many toothpastes, bath additives and skin lotions. Even the world-famous *Original Eau de Cologne*, produced in Cologne since 1743, cannot be produced without mace, along with lemon, orange, bergamot, cedar and other herbs. It is still made to the original recipe.

All these products – nutmeg jam, nutmeg juice, candied nutmeg and nutmeg butter – are on sale in every kiosk in Banda Neira. They all sell the same things. But I have not been able to find any of these products outside the Banda Islands, not even in the best supermarkets on Java and Bali. I tried them all, of course, the jam, the juice and the candied peel, and they all tasted excellent.

Illustrations right page:

Ill. 10-5, The author beside the buttress roots of a kenari tree in a plantation. In the front on the left, you can see a nutmeg tree growing directly out of the root of a kenari tree.

Ill. 10-6, In this plantation there were the nutmeg, still in its red mace aril, black kenari nuts and the bark of kayu manis tree, cinnamon.

---

210 The Dutch called nutmeg butter *Bandazeep* or *Muskaatzeep*
211 See Chapter 21
212 Dr O. Warburg, *Die Muskatnuss*, 1897, p. 522

Nutmeg trees can reach an age of up to 100 years. I was shown trees on Banda Besar which had been planted in Dutch colonial days. A young tree starts to bear fruit after 8 years, and is at its most productive at about 15. As you already know, they prefer to grow in the shade of the Kenari tree, which can be up to 40 metre high. It produces the kenari nut, a kind of almond, that is used in almost all dishes in the Bandanese cuisine. It also produces a sweet-smelling oil which reminded me of olive oil.

After the Dutch drove the Portuguese out, they could consider themselves Lords of the Spices until the end of the 18th century. Their monopoly was ultimately broken not by war, but by the French governor of the island of Mauritius[213] Pierre Poivre[214], who was, among other things, a horticulturalist. The French were determined to grow the nutmeg in their own sphere of influence, and Monsieur Poivre enabled them to do so. He had originally been a missionary in East Asia. On his second voyage there in 1745, he was captured by the English near Sumatra. He was released in Batavia and got to know the spice trade. In 1749 he went to Cochinchina[215] for the French Compagnie des Indes, after which he was sent on a secret mission to Manila.

In 1754 he sailed on a small frigate, *La Colombe,* to Timor, where the Portuguese governor acquired some nutmeg plants from the Bandas and some fresh nutmegs for him. It later turned out on Mauritius that the nutmegs were already too old to germinate, and all the nutmeg trees died. Today we know that fresh nutmegs are only capable of germinating for a week. Poivre returned to France, where he was made a member of the Académie des Sciences.

In 1768 Poivre was appointed Governor of Mauritius. In the corvette *Le Vigilant,* accompanied by a smaller vessel, *L'Etoile du Matin* he sailed to the southern Philippines, where the Prince of Jolo[216] promised to help him in his quest for spices. On the 24th of June 1770 the two ships returned to Mauritius with 450 nutmeg saplings, 70 clove plants and 10,000 germinating nutmegs. The plants were cultivated in the governor's garden. Poivre had even brought plantation workers from the Moluccas to care for the plants, but the results were not up to expectation.

Poivre made a second expedition to the Moluccas, where he was able to get hold of more young saplings and germinating nuts. On the 8th of April 1772, his ship had to leave the Moluccas in a hurry. The Dutch had got wind

---

213 Then Île de France
214 1719-1786
215 Later French Indochina
216 In the Sulu Sea (southern Philippines)

of what he was doing and wanted to proceed against him. In June 1772 both ships returned to Mauritius with their precious cargo. Poivre planted the majority of the saplings in the garden near the harbour called Monplaisir[217]. When he returned to France in the October of that year, 956 of the nutmeg plants were still alive, but only 58 of them grew into trees. In 1776 the first 11 nutmeg trees blossomed, and they harvested their first 6 ripe nutmegs in December/January 1778/79. In spite of all the reverses the project was finally a success.[218]

There is no evidence that Poivre was ever on the Banda Islands. He presumably got natives to smuggle the saplings out for a suitably large payment. Now they could create nutmeg plantations in Mauritius and in other French colonies. After a good many setbacks, they found similar soil and climatic conditions to those in the Banda Islands in Madagascar, the Seychelles and South America, and planted nutmegs there. The only real success was the small Caribbean island of Grenada. The spice was globalised, and a new market emerged. The golden years of the Dutch monopoly were coming to an end. Profits in the nutmeg trade decreased year by year.

In 1769 Poivre described his coup in his book *Voyages d'un philosophe*.[219] Perhaps the title *How Monsieur Pepper got away with the nutmeg* would have made more of a sensation than *Voyages of a Philosopher*.

Ill. 10-7
Title page of Pierre Poivre's book, 1769

---

217 Later this park was renamed, first *Jardin du Roi* and then *Republic Jardin Français*
218 Dr O. Warburg, *Die Muskatnuss*, 1897, p. 215
219 English translation, *Travels of a Philosopher* published in 1769

In the century before last, in 1897, Dr Otto Warburg published his extremely detailed book on the nutmeg under the lengthy title: *Die Muskatnuss, ihre Geschichte, Botanik, Kultur, Handel und Verwertung, sowie ihre Verfälschungen und Surrogate. Zugleich ein Beitrag zur Kulturgeschichte der Banda Inseln.*[220] Over 664 pages he leaves no questions about the nutmeg unanswered. It is still the international standard work about the nutmeg, its range, propagation, care and so on. To carry out his research he made several long stays on the Bandas. In 1913 he published his two-volume work *Die Pflanzenwelt* [The world of plants].

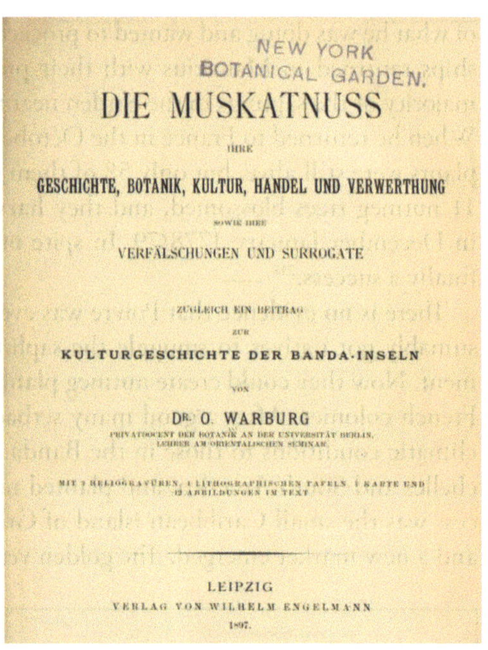

NEW YORK BOTANICAL GARDEN.

DIE MUSKATNUSS

IHRE

GESCHICHTE, BOTANIK, KULTUR, HANDEL UND VERWERTHUNG

SOWIE IHRE

VERFÄLSCHUNGEN UND SURROGATE

ZUGLEICH EIN BEITRAG

ZUR

KULTURGESCHICHTE DER BANDA-INSELN

VON

DR. O. WARBURG

PRIVATDOCENT DER BOTANIK AN DER UNIVERSITÄT BERLIN,
LEHRER AM ORIENTALISCHEN SEMINAR.

MIT 3 HELIOGRAVÜREN, 1 LITHOGRAPHISCHEN TAFELN, 1 KARTE UND
12 ABBILDUNGEN IM TEXT

LEIPZIG
VERLAG VON WILHELM ENGELMANN
1897.

Ill. 10-8
Title page of Dr O. Warburg's book Die Muskatnuss, 1897

Ill. 10-9
Illustration of a nutmeg tree from Warburg's book

220 In the Archive of the New York Botanical Garden

Ill. 10-10, Illustration with details of the nutmeg from Warburg's book

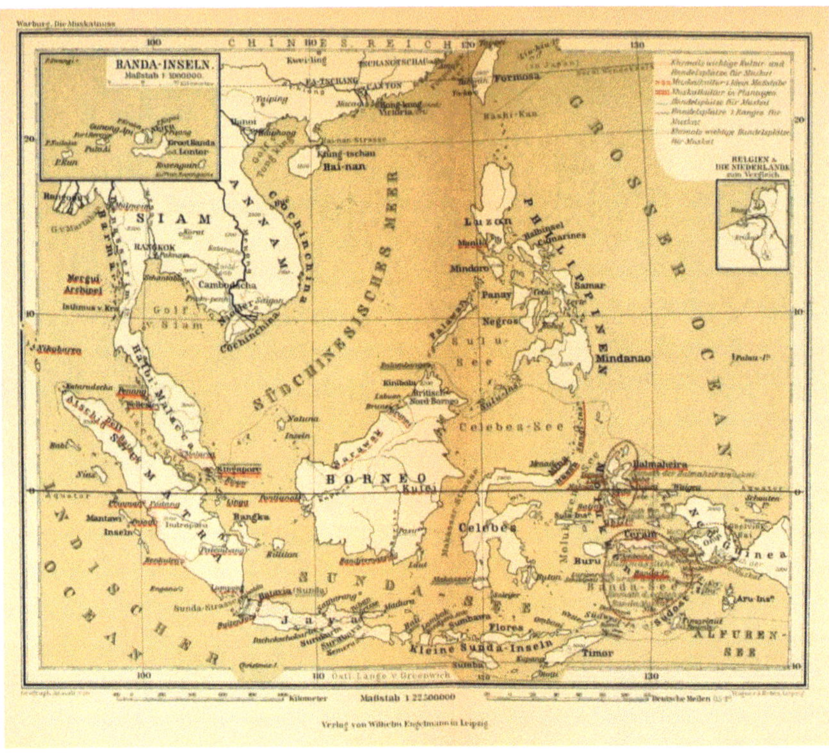

Ill. 10-11, 1897 map of the Spice Islands from Warburg's book

Holland's star now set, once more as a result of war. In 1799, the VOC, which had once been so fabulously rich, went bankrupt because of debt and corruption. Its successor organisation was the semi-governmental NHM[221]. But now vanilla cost more than nutmeg. For almost 300 years the Spanish were able to maintain a monopoly with their plantations in Mexico. But then Edmond Albius, the child of slaves on the French island colony of La Réunion, succeeded in pollinating vanilla flowers manually. And so that monopoly too was broken.

The end of the spice monopoly in the 19th century meant that ordinary citizens could finally afford the spices, which had once been so excessively dear. The Indonesian nutmeg now also grows in great profusion on the Antilles Island of Grenada. Indonesia and Grenada now supply about three quarters of the world market in nutmeg, which are traded on the stock exchanges of New York, London, Hamburg and Kuala Lumpur. Smaller quantities are

221 Nederlandsche Handel-Maatschappij

150

produced by Malaysia, Sri Lanka, New Guinea and India. The main nutmeg importers are the European Union and the United States of America. Although the nutmeg is an Indonesian crop, it is hardly ever used in Indonesian cuisine, except in the Moluccas, and most of all in the Bandas, where nutmeg and the native kenari nut are found in every dish.

Ill. 10-12, Aubergines in a kenari-nut sauce

Although nutmeg and other spices no longer have the status they once had, they still possess a certain magic. When the scent of cinnamon or vanilla wafts from the kitchen in the run-up to Christmas, our thoughts wander back to childhood – or to far-off lands.

It is interesting that the Banda Islands provide ideal conditions for growing the nutmeg, while almost all other vegetables, from tomatoes to cabbage, do not really prosper here. That must surely be because of the volcanic soil. Most vegetables for daily use have to be brought in by sea from Java or Ambon.

11. Fort Belgica and the English

For this chapter we need to return to the time before the Treaty of Breda, which sealed the exchange of Run for Manhattan. As I have already said, the Dutch Governor Pieterzoon Verhoeven began by building Fort[222] Nassau on the island of Banda Neira on the foundations of a fort that the Portuguese had started building 100 years before, abandoning the project when the Bandanese protested. Directly beside Fort Nassau there is a hill, from the top of which it was possible to look down into the fort and observe what was going on inside. The Bandanese continually took advantage of this to watch the Dutch and then kill them outside the fort when the opportunity arose.

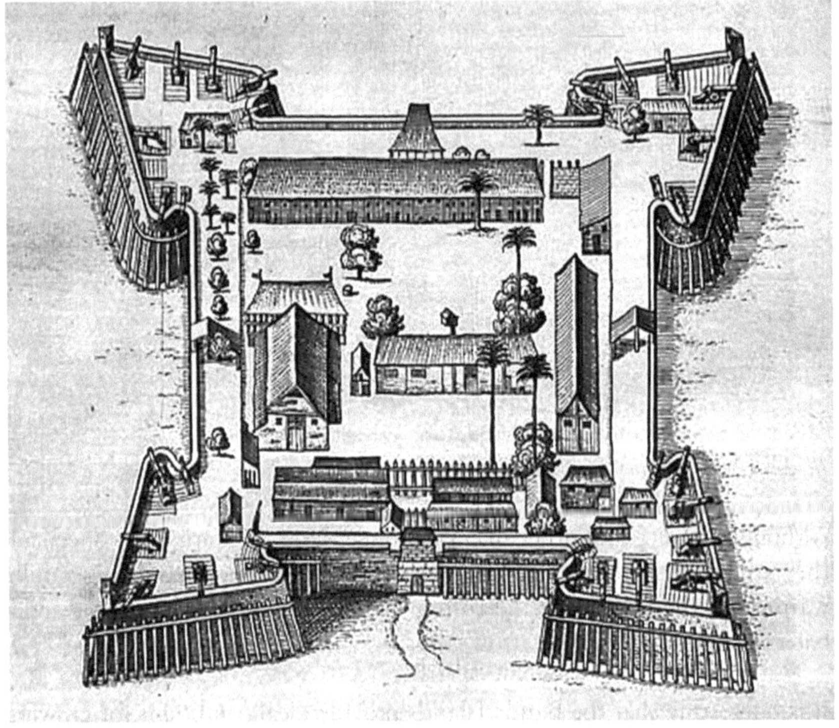

Ill. 11-1, Fort Nassau in 1646[223]

---

222 Fort in Indonesian: Benteng, thus Benteng Nassau and Benteng Belgica
223 Wikipedia, Public Domain

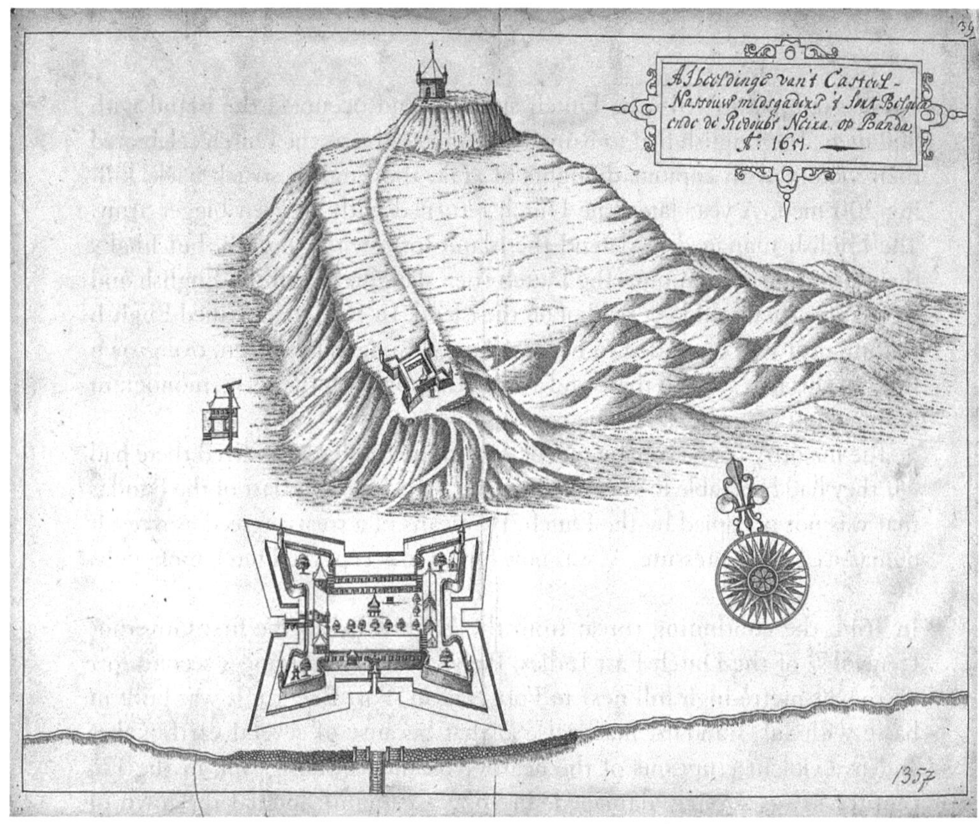

Ill. 11-2, Fort Belgica in 1651[224]

Both forts on Banda Neira were meant primarily as a bulwark against the English, who had already established themselves on Run and Ai by means of treaties with the *Orang Kaya* on both islands, though the Dutch refused to recognise the treaties. The Dutch felt permanently exasperated at the trading activities of the English, since the English outbid the prices they offered. It went so far that the Dutch had to pretend to be English to acquire enough spices to fill their ships.

There was constant friction and conflict between the two nations, with hundreds of casualties on the islands. At the request of the Bandanese, England built fortified trading posts on Run and Ai, and the Dutch had occupied the other islands by forcing them to accept treaties. There was fierce fighting, especially on Ai, where the Bandanese brought the nuts to the British they should have delivered to the Dutch. The island changed hands several times. There was no end to the rivalry – here, too, the ground was soaked in blood.

---

224 Ibid.

153

For example, in 1615 the Dutch attacked and occupied the island with 900 men. The English fled to Run. That same night, as the Dutch celebrated their victory with copious draughts of arak, the English struck back, killing 200 men. A year later, the Dutch returned with an even bigger army. The English managed to defend the island for a whole month, but finally their ammunition ran out. The Dutch then slaughtered all the English and Bandanese they could get hold of on the island. In 1616 the fortified English trading post was expanded to become Fort Revenge. The green, overgrown walls of this fort are still there and a rusty cannon with the VOC monogram is aimed out over the deep blue sea.

The majority of the inhabitants of Ai and the English who lived there had – if they had been able to – escaped to Run, which was the last of the Bandas that was not occupied by the Dutch. By means of a treaty agreed as a result of massive Dutch pressure, Ai was now forced to accept the Dutch monopoly.

In 1614, the continuing threat from the English led to the first Governor General[225] of the Dutch East Indies, Pieter Both[226], building a second fort on the 30-metre-high hill next to Fort Nassau, Fort Belgica. It was built in haste with sub-standard materials, so that because of several earthquakes and five violent eruptions of the nearby volcano, Gunung Api, in the 17th century it was severely damaged. In 1629 a tsunami flooded the town of Banda Neira and Fort Nassau, destroying the town.

In 1667 Governor Cornelis Speelman therefore ordered that Fort Belgica on its hill should be renovated and strengthened. The stone needed was brought from Ambon. Six years later, in 1673, Fort Belgica was finished in its present state, a pentagon with five circular bastions. It was now on two levels. It was armed with 50 cannons and had room for a garrison of over 400 men. It has only one entrance which is reached by a flight of steps. An underground passage originally linked Fort Belgica with Fort Nassau. This passage has now collapsed and cannot be used any more.

The hill where Fort Belgica was built was of great strategic importance to the Dutch. With their powerful cannons, they could now reach all the Banda Islands from here, with the exception of Run. Fort Belgica is regarded today as the most imposing and best preserved of all the forts that were built all round the world by the Dutch VOC.

Illustrations right page:
Ill. 11-3, The gateway to Fort Revenge
Ill. 11-4, The ruins of Fort Revenge

---

225 1610-1614
226 1568-1615

In 1904 Fort Belgica was partly dismantled, but in 1919 the damage was repaired. The Indonesian Defence Ministry has had Fort Belgica completely restored to the state we see today. In 2015 it was included in the UNESCO[227] World Heritage list, thus showing the unique nature of the building.

In spite of the strongly fortified Fort Belgica and the far greater military superiority of the Dutch, the provocation and the military actions continued. Sometimes the Dutch would blockade Run; then the English would recapture Banda Neira. Here are just two particularly interesting examples.

In 1796 an armada of several English warships sailed through the narrow strait between Banda Neira and Gunung Api, and took up position opposite Banda Neira. The Dutch surrendered without a shot being fired. Was Fort Belgica thinly garrisoned and so unable to defend itself, or did the Dutch just wish to avoid a military encounter? We don't know. The occupation of Fort Belgica lasted only seven years: in 1803 it was handed back to the Dutch.

The Dutch colonial troops were no heroes anyway. It was mostly drunkards, or men with a murky past who allowed themselves to be lured into serving in the colonies. As Claire Hake, a Swiss woman, wrote: *they drank a lot of beer and arak, and on manoeuvres the soldiers had their native 'servants' behind them, carrying camp chairs. They treated the natives inhumanly and without respect.*[228] And when the Dutch didn't want to get their own hands dirty, they employed mercenaries from Japan, as in Pieterszoon van Coen's massacre in Fort Nassau in 1621. Centuries later, under Japanese occupation in the Second World War, the Dutch in the East Indies experienced for themselves what it is like to be treated without respect.

But the peace didn't last long. On the 9th of August 1810 there was another attack on Fort Belgica by the English. It was during the Napoleonic Wars, and this time the English had ambitious plans. They wanted to occupy all the Banda Islands and steal nutmeg trees.

Four ships under the command of Captain Christopher Cole[229] arrived in the Banda Islands. They were the frigate *HMS Caroline,* armed with 38 cannons, *HMS Piedmontaise,* also with 38 cannons, *HMS Barracouta* with 18 cannons, and the supply ship *HMS Mandarin.* Under cover of darkness, an English force led by Captain Cole succeeded in scaling Fort Belgica using ladders. Cole was an experienced Royal Navy officer, who had already been involved in successful military actions in Surinam and the Caribbean.

227 United Nations Educational, Scientific and Cultural Organization
228 Claire Hake, *Mein geteiltes Herz* [My Divided Heart], 2011, p. 266
229 1770-1836

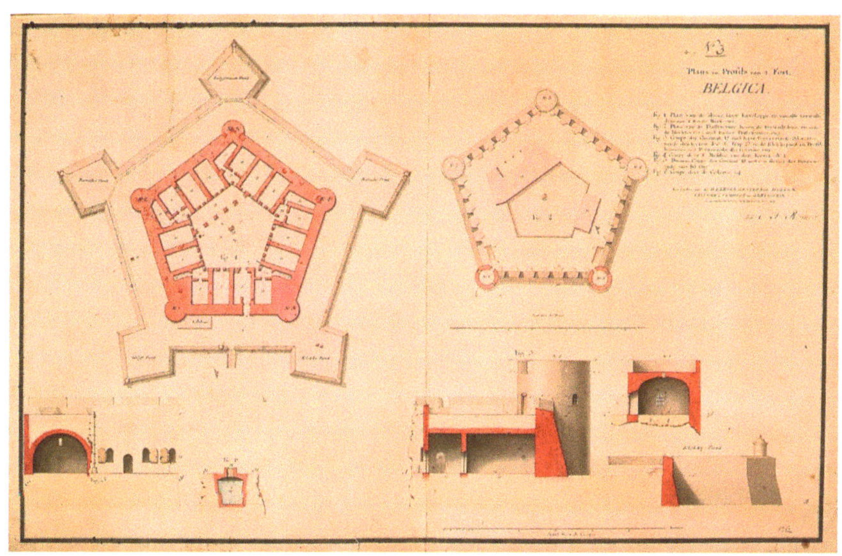

Ill. 11-5, Fort Belgica, new plan, 1667

Ill. 11-6, Fort Belgica, Print from 1824[230]

230 Wikipedia Public Domain

Ill. 11-7, Fort Belgica today. There is only one entrance

Ill. 11-8, Fort Belgica with Gunung Api volcano

It was a stormy night with heavy rain. No one in the garrison was expecting an attack. The small English force of only 180 men surprised the Dutch garrison – normally at that time over 500 men – in their sleep. Even the men on guard duty, who would normally have been patrolling the walls, were nowhere to be seen in the rain. Cole's surprise attack caught the Dutch napping. After a brief exchange of fire, the garrison capitulated. Fort Belgica was in English hands. Cole himself described the attack as follows:[231]

'The gallantry and activity with which the scaling ladders were hauled up after the out-work was carried and placed for an attack on the inner-work, under sharp fire from the garrison exceed all praise. The enemy, after firing their guns and keeping up an ineffectual discharge of musquetry for ten or fifteen minutes, fled in all directions through the gateway, leaving the Colonel-Commandant and ten others dead, and two officers and 30 prisoners in our hands.'

However, the mission that had been entrusted to Captain Cole by London was not yet complete. He still had to take Fort Nassau, which is below Fort Belgica. The Dutch had entrenched themselves there. Now the strategic advantages of Fort Belgica's position became apparent. He aimed his cannons at Fort Nassau and bombarded them from above until they surrendered. A surprise attack had put the Bandas in English hands once more. The English suffered no casualties.

Bloody battles have taken place on the Bandas. Fort Belgica's cannons still point out to sea, where the Dutch and English sailing ships used to anchor. Now there are only little fishing boats scurrying to and fro. From Fort Belgica I look down into the courtyard of Fort Nassau, which Captain Cole bombarded from up here. Now cows are grazing there peacefully, and a couple of children are playing football.

Compared with the Dutch, the English were very humane rulers on the Bandas. The English governor, Sir Thomas Stamford Raffles[232], who also visited the islands wrote that *the Bandanese are unhappy but submissive subjects.*[233] In 1812 Raffles introduced a ban on the slave trade.

Captain Cole's troops occupied the islands for seven years. During that time, they dug up vast numbers of nutmeg saplings and shipped them, together with tons of the unique volcanic soil, to the English territories in Ceylon, Malaya and Singapore. In their familiar Bandanese soil the trees flourished and after only six or seven years English nutmeg production outperformed that of the Bandas, since production there had diminished

---

231 Quoted from Ian Burnet, *East Indies,* 2013
232 See Horst H. Geerken, *A Gecko for Luck,* pp. 39, 65, 126 and 188
233 Dr O. Warburg, *Die Muskatnuss* 1897, p. 168

Ill. 11-9, Courtyard of the Fort. In the centre is the entrance to the collapsed tunnel link to Fort Nassau

dramatically, in part because of the loss of the young trees that had been removed.

But it wasn't just Captain Cole, who rang the knell of the wealth created by the nutmeg trade, it was also the descendants of the Dutch *perkeniers* who had become idle and unimaginative. Their only interest was in spending their lives in the luxury provided by their inherited wealth. The Dutch young people, on the other hand, were drawn to the pulsating life in Holland, a country which they so far only knew from their family tales, and whose language they no longer spoke.

Captain Cole only stayed on Banda Neira for a year, after which he was involved in the successful invasion of the island of Java, which began on the 6th of August 1810. In just 45 days the English occupied Java. This swift success was ascribed to Sir Stamford Raffles, the founder of Singapore. In 1812 Cole was knighted. After 34 years' service at sea for the Royal Navy, he became a Member of Parliament in London.

Ill. 11-10, View of the Island of Banda Besar from Fort Belgica

The house Captain Cole lived in on the main street of Banda Neira, built in Dutch colonial style with massive pillars, is still there and can be visited. In the 1930s, Mohammad Hatta and Sutan Sjahrir, nationalists and freedom fighters exiled here by the Dutch, gave school lessons to Bandanese children in this house.

After seven years the trees planted in the English territories bore their first fruit. The mission was accomplished, and Captain Cole's forces were able to leave the Bandas in 1817. The Dutch monopoly was finally broken.

During the English occupation of the Bandas from 1810 to 1817, many Chinese and Arab merchants settled permanently on the islands. It didn't take long for them to establish a retail monopoly for themselves.

Now the Dutch were once more masters of the Banda Islands. The English ban on the slave trade was more or less rescinded by the Dutch in 1819. Instead of being called slaves, they were now known as *perkhoorige,* more or less serfs tied to the *perken,* but this didn't improve their situation in the slightest.

Ill. 11-11, Captain Cole's residence in Banda Neira

Ill. 11-12, Plaque on the house

Only when the new Dutch Governor General van der Capellen visited the Bandas in 1824 and saw for himself the lamentable circumstances under which the slaves had to work did anything improve. Until then the Resident's word had been law, and everyone feared him. They had to work from dawn to dusk: cutting grass, preparing plots, transplanting, transporting the nuts and so on. Women and children took over the harvest. In the late afternoon they went to the storehouses, where they removed the rind and the mace from the nuts. At six o'clock they were sent home and when the watchmen called out at 8 o'clock they had to go to bed. It was a hard life.

Reforms were now introduced. The Governor General announced the abolition *of all restrictions on individual liberty and tortures, as long as they were not immediately necessary for maintaining the monopoly.* The *hongitochten* – slaving and revenge expeditions – were discontinued, and importing slaves was forbidden. The law of the 8th of September 1853 even made Banda Neira a freeport. The inhabitants were allowed to trade freely, though not with the monopoly items nutmeg and mace. Even so, the decline of the monopoly system as a result of foreign competition could no longer be halted. The golden days of the *perkeniers* were slowly coming to an end.

12. The Abrolhos Islands and the *Batavia*

There was active maritime traffic between the ports of the European naval powers and the Spice Islands. Individual voyages were only sketchily reported, but there were horrible dramas on these months-long voyages. There were ships that grounded on sandbanks or were shattered on rocks; some crews got involved in fights, others mutinied or were locked up. There were always many diseases and deaths on board ship. Whole ships and their crews vanished without trace. Every voyage was an adventure with an uncertain outcome. At this point I am simply going to tell you about the voyage of the Dutch ship *Batavia*. The passengers and crew of this ship went through particularly horrific experiences.

Initially, the Dutch sailed from the Cape of Good Hope along the coasts of Africa, Arabia and India through the Indian Ocean. Eventually a Dutch navigator, Hendrik Brouwere, found a new route which would take the ships to the East Indies more quickly: from the Cape Verde Islands they took the Trade Winds to Brazil. South of Tierra del Fuego they took the powerful winds that blow constantly west to east. These winds reached gale force blowing the sailing ships along at hitherto unknown speeds. Most of the ships took on fresh provisions at the Cape of Good Hope, but there were also ships that sailed far to the south of the Cape to the southernmost point of Western Australia, Cape Leeuwin, the most south-westerly point of the Australian continent. This cape was named after the Dutch ship *Leeuwin* which first sighted and described it in 1622.

Australia was of no interest to the early explorers: it was too dry, and they could find nothing edible to refresh their supplies, though the main reason for this lack of interest was that there were no spices there! The Dutch only landed sporadically on the west coast. They just used the southerly prevailing wind to get to Java and then on to the Spice Islands as quickly as possible. In October 1616[234] Dutchman Dirk Hartog made landfall in the VOC ship *Eendracht* of Amsterdam near what is now Shark Bay in Western Australia. It is the first documented landing by a European in the west of Australia.

In the 1980s I travelled all over Australia in my VW campervan. I visited Geraldton several times on these trips. It is a town whose population was then about 30,000, making it the fifth largest town in Western Australia. It is an important port, the centre of the fishing industry in the region.

234 Other sources say that Dirk Hartog landed around 1622-3.

The waters around Geraldton, and especially around the Abrolhos Islands, a group that is off the coast of Geraldton, are home to large numbers of rock lobsters (langoustes), so that Geraldton is popularly known as the Rock Lobster Capital of the World. They were the main reason that I returned to Geraldton, because I love eating them – and nowhere else in Australia are they as big and as fresh as they are there. On one of these occasions, I met John, a young lobster fisherman, who told me about his work on the Abrolhos. They are a group of 22 uninhabited islands and islets about 60 kilometres off the coast of Geraldton. They were discovered as early as the end of the 16th century by Portuguese seafarers. Even in those days the area around the Abrolhos was regarded as dangerous for navigation because of its many shallows and coral reefs. One explanation of the name Abrolhos is that it derives from the Portuguese phrase *'abri vossos olhos'* – keep your eyes open!

Like some other lobster fishermen, John had a little hut on the islands, which he used to go to and stay in several days at a time during the lobster season, which is from March to June. The fishermen were the only people allowed to land on the islands, because it was a nature reserve. We became friends, and I was able to visit the islands with him several times. The trip, in his Crayfish Carrier Boat, was no pleasure cruise. Not only did the speedboat with its two powerful outboard motors crash into every single wave, there was also an appalling stench. John always had a couple of sacks of half-rotten sheep's heads with him to use as bait in his lobster pots. In the waters around the flat Abrolhos there were large numbers of brightly coloured buoys floating on the surface. They were attached by long lines to the lobster-pots lying on the sea-bed. Each fisherman had his own colour scheme. We were welcomed by John's fishermen friends on Beacon Island[235] with a friendly can of beer. John's hut was, of course, very sparsely furnished with a table, chairs, an absorption refrigerator, a paraffin stove and two camp-beds to sleep on. After the smell of rotting flesh on the boat, there was now a penetrating odour of fish to cope with. From John and his fishermen friends I learned the gruesome story of the Dutch merchant ship, the *Batavia*, that was wrecked on the perilous coral reefs in 1629.

In 1619 the Dutch astronomer and navigator Frederick de Houtman[236], younger brother of the Cornelis de Houtman mentioned in Chapter 5, first mapped the Abrolhos. He was on a voyage of exploration along the west coast of Australia when he visited them. To ensure his own immortality, he named this group of islands the *Houtman Abrolhos*, prefixing his own name.

---

235 The Dutch called the island *Batavia's Kerkhof* [Batavia's graveyard]
236 1571–1627

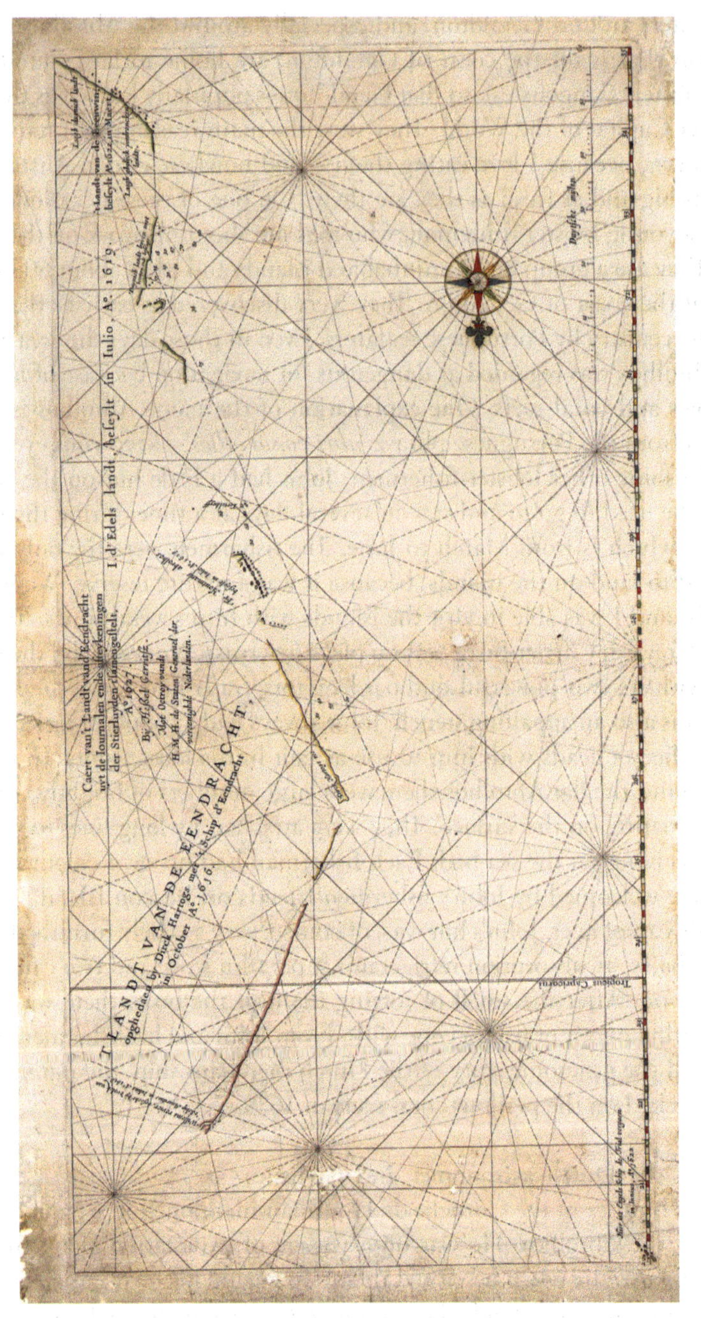

Ill. 12-1, The Houtman Abrolhos are first mentioned on a marine chart of 1627. It is based on records in Dirk Hartog's 1616 log.

Ill. 12-2
Detail with the
Houtman Abrolhos

The *Batavia* was the flagship of the VOC, built on the Peperwerft [literally: Pepper Wharf] in Amsterdam. On the 29th of October 1628 the three-master set sail from Texel for her maiden voyage to the East Indies, accompanied by two other ships. There was a full crew, and the winds were favourable. She was 56.6 metres long and could reach a speed of five knots[237] if the wind was good. There were 341[238] people on board: as well as the officers and men, the carpenters, sailmakers, coopers, cooks, a chief surgeon and several barbers there were many Dutch families, men, women and children as passengers who, after a stopover in Batavia, were to be taken to the Banda Islands. This was in line with Governor General Pieterszoon van Coen's plan to settle the Bandas with families with children and young women from orphanages after his massacre of the native Bandanese.

237 5.76 mph
238 Some sources give 322, others 316

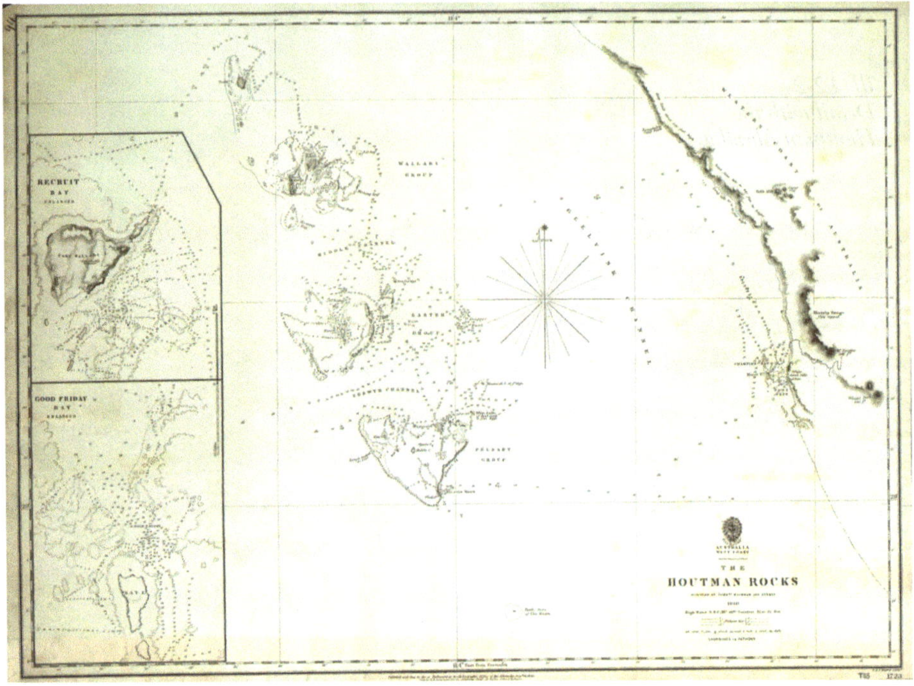

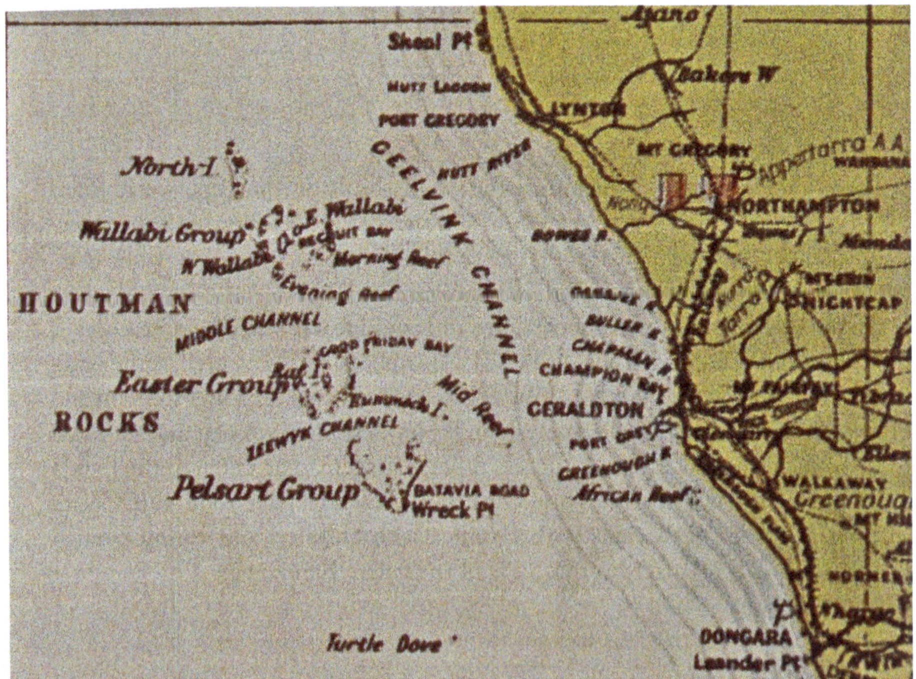

Ill. 12-3, British Admiralty map of the Houtman Rocks, 1840
Ill. 12-4, 1897 map

The voyage out was free for these families, and they were also given start-up financial aid by the VOC. I have been unable to discover how many families, how many women and children intended for the Bandas, were on board. But there are the names of some of those who were there: Provost[239] Pieter Jansz from Amsterdam with his wife and child, Gysbert Bastiansz with his wife, their grown-up daughter Judith and five other children, Claudine Patoys with her child, a man called Harmansz with his wife and several children, an unnamed woman with her three-month-old child[240], Mayken Soers, who was pregnant, sisters Trynt and Zussie Frederics, and other women: Lucretia van der Mylen[241], Anneken Gunner, Margaret Louys, Janneken Gist and Anneken Hardens. There were at least 38 women and children on the ship.

There were almost certainly also some *handschoentjes* on board, as there were on almost every VOC ship. These were women who had been married in Holland by proxy to a man who was living in the East Indies. This kind of ceremony was known in Dutch as *met de handschoen trouwen*, marrying with gloves on.

There were frequently also women who slipped on board dressed as men to try and get to the colony. All these women said that their reason for doing so was to try and find their husbands – from whom they had not heard for years. The families with children and the women lived in the upper parts of the ship in a hut where the trumpeters were also lodged, so that during the voyage they would not come into contact with the men, particularly the common sailors. They lived crammed together in the most cramped space. There was no privacy on board.

The trumpeters were there to give signals and to encourage their own side with their trumpet calls. There was often also a singer to lead the sea shanties the sailors sang while working.

The *Batavia* was what was called a *retourschip* [return ship], which was intended to return to Holland with a valuable cargo. Smaller or older ships were generally left in the Malay Archipelago to be used for local transport between the islands. The return ships had large holds, which meant that they were relatively lightly armed with only 28 cannons, 7 of which were bronze. The officers, non-commissioned officers and passengers were accommodated in the stern of the ship, while the soldiers and sailors were squashed

---

239 Senior administrator at a university, something like a vice-chancellor, or possibly a minister of religion
240 She must have given birth to the child on the *Batavia*
241 Later Lucretia Jans

into two forward decks. The lower deck was only one metre high. Anyone living there had to crawl to reach his mattress or hammock. Each sleeping space was divided between two people, so that one could only sleep while the other was on watch. The conditions were awful, and behaviour was coarse; one wonders how the sailors and soldiers managed to put up with this life for months on a swaying ship on rough seas. The sailors did have their daily routine tasks on deck and up in the rigging, while the soldiers trained with their muskets every day. New recruits had to learn the ropes until the processes became an automatic routine. The morning religious service, at which attendance was compulsory, provided some diversion, but even so tension between the soldiers and sailors was always high, and in the course of the voyage discipline left increasingly much to be desired. The officers had to hand out severe punishment to keep any kind of order.

Shortly before a fleet sailed one of the directors of the VOC would read out the *artikelbrief* on every ship. This was the list of rights and duties to which everyone on board would be subject. Anyone who missed divine service would be fined and have his wine ration stopped for a long period. If someone was found with cards on his person, he would have to spend a week on bread and water in a small punishment cell. If anyone drew a knife on another person, his hand would be nailed to the mast by the same knife.

Keel hauling was the severest corporal punishment. The sailor was tied to a line looped beneath the vessel, thrown overboard on one side of the ship, and dragged under the ship's keel, either from one side of the ship to the other, or the length of the ship (from bow to stern). The underside of the ship would be rough and covered in sharp barnacles – and at a depth of six or seven metres. If the victim became stuck, his head would be pulled off. The victims were usually keel-hauled three times, and those who survived this triple torture would then be given 100 lashes. Only one out of ten survived the ordeal.

A man who murdered another would be tied to his victim and thrown into the sea alive. The most minor of offences were dealt with extremely severely. When a sentence was carried out, the rest of the crew were made to watch the grim spectacle as a deterrent.

The death penalty, for mutiny, for example, was quickly carried out. The instigator and his followers were hanged from the main mast and later thrown overboard. Miscreants were often left on an uninhabited island with some water and biscuits, which was more or less equivalent to a death sentence. Flogging was the punishment used most frequently on board VOC ships. The sentence could be up to 500 lashes. After 20 lashes most of the victims became unconscious. Many of them died as a result of internal injuries.

They would load nine months' provisions: salt meat, salt fish, ship's biscuit, salt cod, bacon and cheese. Many of the voyages, however, lasted for a year or more, meaning that food had to be rationed. On VOC ships, Thursday and Sunday were meat days – meaning that they were given salt meat that could be several years old, with peas or beans. For the officers and passengers there were a few more pleasant things, like spices, honey and raisins. The sailors and soldiers could only imagine the delicacies that were eaten by the captain and a few select people. Shortly before departure, live piglets and chickens were taken aboard to provide fresh meat. As well as drinking water, there were also vast quantities of beer in barrels and the Rhenish wine that was so popular with the crews.

At the tables below deck where the crew and the soldiers ate, a curious ritual was carried out after every meal. After finishing the last morsel and putting down his spoon, everyone had to *let one rip*. Anyone who failed to do so had to clear the table and wash the dishes and spoons. Given the ship's high-fibre diet, there cannot have been many who ended up as *calefaktors*[243], as they were called then.

On the 27th of October 1628 the great sails thunder into action as they fill out with the wind. The *Batavia* begins her long voyage from Texel to South East Asian. The soldiers' pay only starts from this moment. The – frequently long – periods spent at anchor waiting for a favourable wind didn't count. For many soldiers – depending on their contracts – higher pay only began when they arrived in the East Indies.

242 Old print, Wikipedia Public Domain
243 Dogsbody

Ill. 12-6, The author on an Atlantic crossing on the four-masted clipper Star Flyer, on the yardarm known as the widow-maker

Shortly before the ship set sail, some chests of gold and silver for trading in the Indies were also loaded. The commander of the fleet was Senior Merchant[244] Francisco Pelsaert, the captain was Ariaen Jacobsz. As commandant of the fleet, the senior merchant was allowed to give orders to the captain on VOC ships. The junior merchant[245] was Jeronimus Cornelisz, a bankrupt apothecary who was leaving for East Asia to avoid imprisonment in Holland. From the very beginning, there was hostility between Pelseart and Jacobsz, arising from a previous incident. Their personalities could not have been more different, and any collaboration between them was doomed from the start. In the course of the voyage the situation got increasingly worse because there were constant disputes between them over two of the women on board, Lucretia van der Mylen and her maid Zwaantie Hendrix.

In the strong wind and high waves the ship rolled into the North Sea. The first soldiers – all of them landlubbers – were already feeling seasick and

244 *Opperman*
245 *Onderkoopman*

172

the experienced sailors maliciously made fun of them. The captain and the navigator sought out the prevailing winds and currents in the Atlantic to get the ship across the ocean as quickly as possible. Life in the cramped conditions on board ship carried on as usual. The youngest scrubbed the decks. The soldiers trained until they could operate their muskets in their sleep, and the passengers accustomed themselves to boredom.

The ship passed the Canaries and the Cape Verde Islands. Warm winter clothing was now finally put away in the cabin trunks. When a storm neared, the unwieldy sails had to be reefed in. This was a difficult and dangerous task on the rolling ship, as the sailors crawled out along the yardarms on their stomachs to haul in the sails. A man could so easily be caught by a raging wind or a fluttering sail and knocked into the sea.

When the big-bellied ship rolled in the turbulent sea, all its joints creaking, and the raging storm meant that you couldn't hear yourself speak, there were no meals and sleep was unthinkable anyway. The chests on the deck and in the cabins slid from port to starboard and then back again. It became increasingly difficult to relieve yourself as the beakhead, a platform that protruded out over the bow of the ship, was continuously washed by the wild seas. Nowhere on the ship was dry anymore. Below deck there was a sour stench of vomit. Everyone, both the crew and the passengers, just had to wait for the unchained elements to calm down. In weather like this, they just let the ship go where the wind took it, riding out the storm. Their only thought was survival. Water got in everywhere in the wooden ship. Sailors and soldiers toiled day and night at the bilge pumps, collapsing exhausted on their mattresses when the watch was changed.

In a storm you often didn't see the sun for days. The navigator had no idea where the winds might have driven the ship. When the first rays of the sun broke through the navigator would use his cross-staff and the less accurate astrolabe to measure the height of the noonday sun to get a rough idea of their latitude.

To establish a ship's latitude there was only the log. This was a triangular wooden board on a line, with knots at regular intervals along the line. When the log was in the water, they would pay out the line, counting the number of knots that were paid out in 15 seconds. To measure the 15 seconds each ship had a special sand glass. This was the only way of establishing – roughly – the speed of the ship and therefore its rough geographical position. It was not until 1759 that an Englishman, John Harrison, developed a chronometer that was accurate enough, to allow them to measure longitude more accurately.

It is amazing to think how the navigators of the time managed to find such remote and tiny islands as the Bandas, thousands of kilometres from home, without radar, radio or GPS. They were expert oceanographers who used clouds and currents, seabirds and flotsam to orientate themselves.

The *Batavia* was now south of the Equator and when the wind dropped the heat was crippling. The water began to go off and to smell. To purify it they dropped red-hot iron bullets into the barrels – but it could still only be drunk mixed with wine. The result was a series of diarrhoeal diseases.

Because of the heat, the poor and unvarying diet and the already failing health of many of the women and men, the number of deaths began to increase on the ship. The Dutch – and the English – were very concerned with cleanliness on their ships. The decks were scrubbed and disinfected with vinegar every day. To relieve themselves they had to use the beakhead – the 'garden'. Anyone who used a pot or a bucket to 'do his business' was severely punished.

There were often infectious diseases brought on board by the crew, because there were no medical examinations before getting a post in the VOC or working in the colony. Nevertheless, the catastrophic death rate on the voyage out was mainly due to scurvy. They knew even then that the disease departed quite quickly when people landed and ate fresh fruit and vegetables, but they thought it was the fresh meat, that was responsible for the recovery. This idea was even taken as far as killing the rats on the ships, and first boiling them in water, sugar and wine. They were then roasted and served to the sick. As I previously said in Chapter 4, it would be a long time before they discovered that the disease – which caused you, as a contemporary said, to rot alive – is due to vitamin C deficiency.

Another disease that was widespread on 17th- and 18th-century ships was epidemic typhus, called jail fever[246] at the time, which was transmitted by lice. Since they hardly ever changed their clothes during the voyage and were often unable to wash properly for months, lice were a real problem for everyone. The disease often ended in delirium.

After so many monotonous weeks at sea, apathy began to spread among all the travellers, but joy returned when the Cape of Good Hope hove into view. The Dutch had built a fort and a trading post next to Table Mountain. Nearly all VOC ships called in here on the way to Asia, just as the return ships did in the other direction. At last there was fresh water again, as much as you could drink, as well as vegetables and fruit in profusion. The Dutch farmed vast agricultural estates here, worked by slaves. Fat cattle and sheep

---

246 The Dutch called it *rotkoortsen* [red fever]

174

grazed on green meadows. After a good week the *Batavia* had loaded fresh provisions: cabbage, radishes, onions, fruit and live cattle. The crew and the sick had recovered to such an extent that it was possible to embark on the second half of the voyage towards Australia and Batavia. The *Batavia* now headed east.

So far it had been a normal outward voyage like those the VOC ships had made many times before. But now the Captain, Ariaen Jacobsz, and the Junior Merchant, Jeronimus Cornelisz, began to conspire against the Senior Merchant, Francisco Pelsaert. Jakobsz and Cornelisz planned to mutiny, plunder the ship and begin a new life of luxury somewhere in the world with the gold and silver treasure on board. The *Batavia* offered rich pickings: 12 chests of gold and silver coins and one full of valuable jewels intended as gifts for Malay rulers. The *Batavia* was the VOC's newest and most modern ship. She was twice as big as the *Bounty* or Captain Cook's *Endeavour*. It was intended to create a big impression in the Colony.

The two leaders of the conspiracy had already been able to gather a group of sailors and soldiers who were prepared to join the mutiny. Mutiny and piracy were quite common at the time, and were a profitable business. When the fleet reached the south of West Australia, Captain Jacobsz deliberately took a different course and left the fleet so that he could take control of the ship off the coast without being seen by the other ships. There was a storm at the time, and the different ships of a fleet often lost sight of each other for a while in those conditions.

Jacobsz had erred wildly in his last calculation of their position. The course the *Batavia* took was too far to the east. In the early morning hours of the 4th of June 1629 the ship hit the deceptive reef that encircled a group of small islands. What the people on board saw in the light of dawn were nothing but insignificant, forlorn, windy sandbanks, each of them smaller than a football field. Miserable treeless sandbanks littered with washed-up lumps of coral.

Jacobsz tried to float the ship free by making it lighter. All the cannons, unnecessary chests and barrels were thrown overboard. They even unstepped the heavy topmast. But in vain, because the ship had grounded on the reef at the very peak of a spring tide, and there was no chance of freeing it. The *Batavia* might break up at any moment.

They then began to transfer people and materials to the nearest two islands, later named Traitor's Island[247] and Batavia's Graveyard[248] by the crew.

---

247 *Verrader's Eylandt*
248 *Batavia's Kerkhof* later renamed Beacon Island

By evening they had managed to ferry about 180 of the 341[249] people on board, including all the women and children, and some water and bread to the little islands. There was no water and no edible vegetation on either island.

Water was suddenly more precious than all the gold and silver on board. Since survival would be impossible on these arid islands without fresh water, Senior Merchant Pelsaert and Captain Jacobsz decided to sail to Batavia to get help. They went in the longboat[250] carried on the ship, taking 30 men, two women and a baby with them. They set off the morning after the accident. Further attempts to save those left on the wreck failed because of contrary winds and high seas. About 40 men drowned trying to swim to Traitor's Island, which was closest to the wreck.

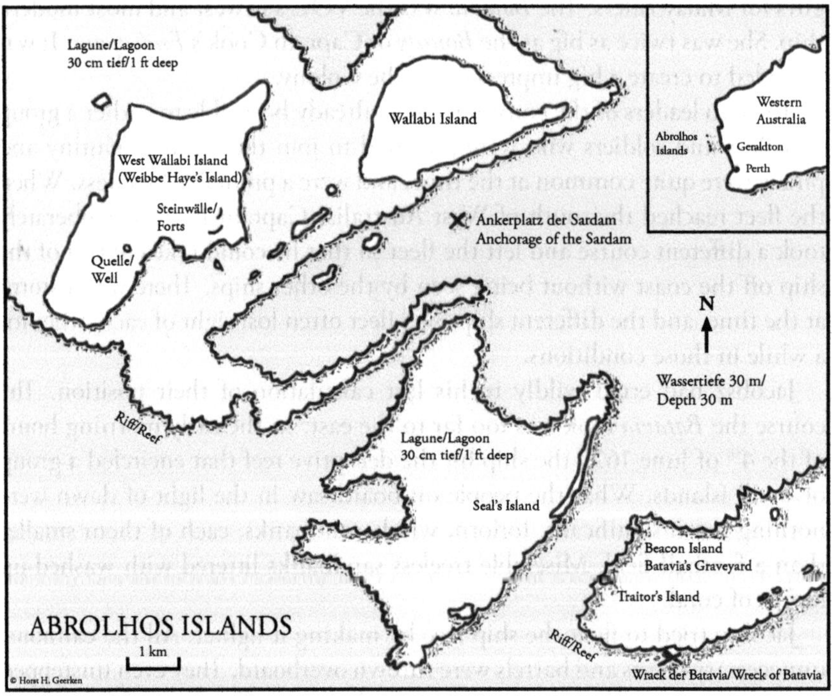

Ill. 12-7, Map of the Abrolhos Islands

---

249 In Batavia the few survivors later gave differing statements about the numbers of passengers, victims of murder and those drowned, and so the numbers given here may vary
250 A 9-metre sloop

Ill. 12-8, Old print from 1647[251]

Ill. 12-9, Beacon Island

251 Wikipedia, Public Domain

Junior Merchant Jeronimus Cornelisz remained alone on the wreck for almost a week. He couldn't swim. But as the ship began to break up he was washed ashore on one of the ship's timbers. As the highest-ranking VOC officer, he took over command. But the boat carrying Pelsaert and Jacobsz had hardly disappeared over the horizon when Jeronimus Cornelisz's reign of terror began.

Cornelisz hadn't given up his mutinous plan. With his accomplices, who numbered about 20, he planned to kill everyone except for a few women. Then, when the rescue ship arrived, they would capture it. He thought that the drinking water should be enough to last until then for the much reduced number of survivors. However, they first needed to take control of the island. Cornelisz would need to act swiftly to save himself and his confederates. In his eyes, it was stupid to *waste bread and water on useless mouths*. His problem was the armed soldiers, who were still loyal to the Company. He needed to get rid of them first. Weibbe Hayes caused him particular concern. He was a private soldier, a brave, honest and experienced servant of the VOC, and had been elected as the surviving soldiers' leader. Cornelisz sent Hayes and his soldiers to what is now West Wallabi Island[252] – without their weapons – ostensibly to look for water and collect birds' eggs. They were to send up a smoke signal when they were ready to return. Cornelisz, however, had no intention of going to get them. He was sure that there was no water there and that they would die of thirst. When, a few days later, they saw the smoke signal from the other island – it was somewhat larger – no boat was sent. But his plan failed. Hayes and his men found enough water and food on West Wallabi to survive for months. There were wallabies living on the arid island, and there were plenty of birds' eggs, oysters and seals.

Cornelisz divided the remaining survivors into three groups and distributed them on Traitor's Island, Beacon Island, and the long thin strip of Seal's Island. Now things were easy for him. Their temporary society quickly collapsed. The survivors stranded on the islands were terrorised by a group of mutineers led by Cornelisz, the bankrupt apothecary, and the majority of them were murdered.

The open sloop carrying Pelsaert and Jacobsz arrived in Batavia 33 days after leaving the site of the wreck, on the 7th of July 1629. Immediately on arriving, Pelsaert was summoned to report to the Governor General, Jan Pieterszoon van Coen. Captain Jacobsz was arrested for negligence in navigating his ship and Pelsaert was ordered to return to the site of the disaster as quickly as possible in the fast sailing yacht *Sardam* to save lives and recover the valuable gold and silver treasure.

252 The survivors called it Weibbe Hayes' Island

Ill. 12-10, An old print from 1647, showing the massacre[253]

The *Sardam* left Batavia on the 15th of July 1629. In the meanwhile, Cornelisz had killed almost all the survivors on Traitor's Island and Beacon Island. When he then went to Seal island to kill the roughly forty other survivors there, some of the women managed to escape to West Wallabi Island floating on driftwood. By now, Cornelisz and his men had killed over 125 people in the most gruesome manner. At first the mutineers had killed people in order to survive, but after a while they did it for fun, because they were bored.

The women – as is unfortunately so often the case in such situations – suffered the worst. They either had to be prepared to satisfy the sexual demands of the mutineers any time day or night, or they were killed. Cornelisz took Lucretia van der Mylen as his personal concubine. She was on the way to her husband in Batavia, having been married *met de hantschoen*. Cornelisz's second in command, Coenraat van Huyssen, took Judith Bastiansz as his concubine. The two sisters, Trynt und Zussie Fredrix, and Anneken Gunner, Anneke Hardens and Margaret Louys were designated by *general use*. The two last-named were later also murdered. Wybrecht Claes was stabbed on the spot when she refused a man. The mutineers had got a taste for blood.

253 Wikipedia, Public Domain

When Wiebbe Hayes was told by those who had escaped that Cornelisz had perpetrated a massacre, he was outraged, and made preparations to defend the island against the mutineers. 47 men remained at Hayes' side. They made themselves simple weapons like spears and missiles out of driftwood and nails. They had had to leave their muskets on Beacon Island on Cornelisz' orders. The muskets would have been of no use anyway, as most of what little gunpowder that had been saved from the *Batavia* was damp. They built defensive walls out of lumps of coral and sandstone. They also now outnumbered the mutineers. To make sure that there was timely warning of an attack, Hayes set watches on guard round the clock. They covered the springs they had found with large, flat stones so that the mutineers would not be able to find them.

As expected, an attack came, because the mutineers' supplies of water were running out and they wanted to capture the springs on West Wallabi Island, but the experienced soldiers under Hayes' command were able to ward it off. A week later there was a second attack, which was also dealt with by Hayes' soldiers. Four of the attackers were killed and Cornelisz was captured and put in irons.

On the 17th of September 1629, the remaining mutineers began a final attack, this time with their muskets. Fortunately, the *Sardam* came into view. Hayes was able to warn Pelsaert and the *Sardam*'s crew in time, so that when the mutineers tried to take the ship, they were ready for them. When the mutineers reached the ship, they were looking down the barrels of loaded muskets and cannons, and the gunners were standing ready with lighted matches. They had no chance and surrendered without a shot being fired. By then the *Batavia* had been broken up by the surf on the reef; some parts sank, others were stranded on the reef.

Since the risk of taking so many criminals on a week-long voyage to Batavia in a small yacht loaded with treasure would have been too great, the worst of the mutineers were sentenced there and then. The hearings, held by Pelsaert, lasted ten days. Some of the mutineers confessed immediately, others only when they had been subjected to the 'water cure'[254] that was customary at the time. Meanwhile the casket of jewels had been found, along with ten of the chests of gold and silver. The jewels alone were valued at 58,000 guilders: the monthly income of a common soldier or sailor was 10 guilders.

---

254 This method of torture (today declared illegal), called waterboarding in the USA, was authorised once more by US President George W. Bush in 2002 and used far too frequently in the camp Guantanamo Bay. This authorisation was not rescinded until 2009 under the presidency of Barak Obama.

The sentences were carried out on Seal's Island, where *Sardam's* carpenter had built a gallows out of the wreckage of the *Batavia*, on the 2nd of October 1629. All the survivors of the *Batavia* and the crew of the *Sardam* were present. Jeronimus Cornelisz had both hands cut off, and then he was hanged. Two others only had their right hands cut off before being led to the gallows. Others were just hanged. The sands were red with the criminals' blood. When Jeronimus Cornelisz was dragged to the gallows, his stumps bleeding profusely, he shouted *Revenge! Revenge!* until the noose cut him short. One after another they were led to their deserved punishment. At the last moment an eighteen-year-old youth, Jan Pelgrom, was provisionally pardoned. The less dangerous mutineers were clapped in irons to be taken to Java for trial.

Six weeks later, on the 15th of November 1629, the *Sardam* began her return journey to Batavia. Slightly to the north of the Abrolhos Islands, near where the coastal town of Kalbarri is situated today, Jan Pelgrom, the youth who had been pardoned, and Wouter Looes were marooned one day later near a river on the desolate western Australian coast. Documents written by Pelsaert show that they were given toys from Nuremberg, which they could use to befriend any natives they met. In those days Australia, called the Southland, was thought to be an arid, uninhabited island. No-one had seen any aborigines, and being marooned – 200 years before Western Australia was settled by the English – was as good as a death sentence. The two Europeans were never seen or heard of again. But perhaps they had been luckier than their fellows.

George Gray was the first to explore the region around the Murchison River in April 1839. He discovered that some of the aborigines in the area had a strikingly pale skin. Had the two marooned men been accepted in aboriginal society? Today a DNA test could establish this immediately. This would surely be very important for the history of Western Australia, since that would mean that Pelgrom and Looes were the first Europeans to settle in the west of Australia, 200 years before the English. But it would be difficult to find a real aboriginal inhabitant of the Murchison Region, since the English massacred most of them in 1838.

On the 5th of December 1629 the *Sardam* arrived back in Batavia. The mutineers, who had been transported there in chains received far more severe sentences than those who had been hanged on Seal Island. On the 31st of January 1630, after all the evidence had been heard and assessed, there was a great, bloody, public spectacle outside the fort in Batavia. The mutineers had all been convicted of mutiny and raping women, and sentenced to death by hanging. The death sentences had all been passed by the new VOC Governor General, Specx, as Jan Pieterszoon van Coen had died in the interim. Many of the convicted men were tortured and had their bones broken before they were hanged on the gallows as a warning and deterrent to the spectators.

The captain of the *Batavia,* Ariaen Jacobsz, who had deliberately taken the ship off course, was tortured for two more years before his execution. Then all his bones were broken on the wheel and he was quartered.

Weibbe Hayes was celebrated as a hero and saviour, and was promoted to the rank of sergeant. The commander of the fleet, Senior Merchant Francisco Pelsaert died a few months after his return. Bastiansz, who had wanted to settle permanently on the Banda Islands as a *perkenier* with his wife and six children, had lost his entire family. He and Lucretia van der Mylen were the only surviving eyewitnesses of the massacre. He married again and died in Banda Neira in 1633. Lucretia van der Mylen married and died as an aged grandmother in Holland.

None of the women or families on the *Batavia,* whom Governor General van Coen had wanted to establish on the Banda Islands ever got there. There were many other ships, which suffered a similar fate; but this was the only one I found in the course of my research where there had been a massacre. Most loss of life occurred when ships went down in storms.

Perhaps one day more documents will emerge to cast more light on this terrible incident. For example, different figures are given for the number of passengers, those murdered and the survivors. The number of those murdered by the mutineers is mostly given as more than 125. If the number of passengers was, as has been stated, 341, then if we take into account of the number of those who died in the wreck, the soldiers on Hayes Island, the passengers who were taken to Batavia in the longboat, the murdered women and those who died of thirst on the islands, the total of those who were killed by the mutineers must be at least 150. Whatever the numbers, it was a dreadful event which still has echoes today.

For over 300 years the *Batavia* lay on the seabed, until she was once more remembered and the search for the wreck began. After five years the remains of the ship were found on the reef off Beacon Island, as the island is now called by the fishermen. Its previous name was *Batavia's Kerkhof, Batavia's* Graveyard. The *Batavia* ran aground on the reef about 1.5 kilometres from the island.

In 1963 the work of raising parts of the *Batavia* and the treasure that was still lying on the seabed in two chests began. The divers and their boats now found it easier to move between the reefs and sandbanks. In 1840 the Royal Navy had surveyed the island and produced accurate charts.[255] There were also excavations, which discovered bottles, coins and mass graves. The view on the long, narrow Seal's Island was particularly gruesome: there were dozens of sun-bleached skulls, bones and skeletons protruding from the sand.

Ill. 12-11, 'Fortification' of piled up stones on West Wallabi Island[256]

In the 1980s, when I was on Beacon Island and took a little walk around the island before going to bed, my flesh crawled and the few hairs I had even then stood on end when I suddenly thought of all the blood that had been shed on this piece of earth. The island was strewn with the sun-bleached skulls of the sheep's heads the fishermen had used as bait. In the moonlight

255 See Ill. 12-3
256 Wikipedia Public Domain

they looked like human skulls staring at me from their empty eye sockets. It was eery on the island at night, and it is no secret that the locals talk about ghosts that still walk the blood-soaked ground of the Abrolhos. On West Wallabi Island, which Weibbe Hayes was able to defend with his soldiers and some of those who had escaped, you can still see the stone walls they put up.

On one of the smaller islands there is a blow-hole among the corals, which can be heard from a distance groaning and whistling in the night. It has been called Pelsaert's Ghost. The lobster fisherman told me that they would never land on that island after sunset – the island was too creepy.

After three or four days, having collected the lobsters from the pots, we set off for Geraldton again, where they were immediately deep-frozen in a refrigerated warehouse. The main customer for the lobsters was the USA. In John's house – furnished in very modern style – I was served a lobster dinner and a cool beer. John preferred steak. Understandable, if you think that he was surrounded by the creatures all day. I imagine the earnings from the lobster trade are not bad.

I had lost contact with John – I hadn't seen him for a good eight years – when we ran into each other by chance in Munich, at the Oktoberfest, which is very popular among Australians. We had to drink to that, of course. In return for his hospitality, I took him to see all the sights of Munich the next day. I got the feeling that culture wasn't his thing, and that he was much more interested in the Oktoberfest beer tents. He wanted to get back to his mates as quickly as possible.

When I was back in Perth, I told my English friend Michael about my adventure, and also about how long Weibbe Hayes and his men had survived on West Wallabi[257] without any supplies from the ship. They lived only on what the island and the sea provided. Michael suggested that we should try that too. No sooner said than done. We got ourselves a lobster pot and some stinking bait, a fishing rod, sleeping bags and some water. We rationed the water so that it would last for two weeks. We also had a box of matches and a knife – and that was all! We didn't even take salt with us. We intended to cook our catch in seawater, or to scrape salt from the rocks of a nearby saltpan. They were meant to be the same conditions that Weibbe Hayes and his men had overcome.

The ferry took us to Rottnest Island, which we reached in an hour. Unlike the Abrolhos Islands, there were traces of Aborigines on Rottnest, dating back thousands of years. Perhaps the Abrolhos were too far out at sea from

---

257 Then called Weibbe Hayes' Island

the coast for the Aborigines. They weren't visible from the mainland. That was not the case with Rottnest.

Then we set off on a long footpath to the lonely south of the island – it is 11 kilometres long. We'd brought along a handcart to carry the heavy water containers. After looking around for quite a while we found a little cave right on the water's edge – more of a rocky overhang, really. This would shelter us from the rain. We took the lobster pot and put it in a spot that seemed likely to us and I spent the rest of the afternoon trying my luck with the fishing rod. I'd brought bait along for the first day, but nothing bit and the lobster pot was also still empty by the evening. We made a little fire in our cave and got into our sleeping bags with rumbling stomachs.

But sleep was not on the agenda. First of all, there were thousands of mosquitos whining around our heads – and then the quokkas arrived. They are small marsupials of the kangaroo family which are only found in the south of Western Australia and the off-coast islands. A Dutchman called Vlamingh visited the island in 1696 and named it Rottnest – the Dutch for rats' nest – because he thought the quokkas were just big rats. At first there was just one quokka, who came up to us quite trustingly and looked at us quizzically as if to say, 'What are you doing here, then?' Initially, we found that quite cute. But then there were five, then ten, then at least twenty. The rumour must have got around among them that there were strange creatures on view in the cave. We were hardly able to fend them off. Were the little beasts stupid, or just inexperienced? Had they never come across a fire before? They jumped boldly into the fire – and then out of it onto us. Again and again. There was a strong smell of singed fur. In the early hours of the morning – dawn was just breaking – I fell into a brief doze, then I was suddenly wide awake again. A quokka had landed right on my face – and they weigh two to three kilograms. They are nocturnal, and sleep among the bushes during the day. Had we landed in their regular night-time playground?

In the morning we found a big langouste in our pot. We boiled it in sea-water and breakfasted on langouste *au naturel*. Even on that very first day I'd have preferred a fresh roll. I fished all day without success. On the third day there were two langoustes in the pot. Even after eating both of them our stomachs were still rumbling. In five days we didn't catch a single fish. And when we were unable to catch any more langoustes in the pot our hunger became almost unbearable. We didn't want to kill a quokka, because they are an endangered species. On the evening of the fifth day we abandoned our experiment and allowed ourselves a cold beer in the pub on the island. We admitted that the life of Robinson Crusoe or a hermit is not for us. We had nothing but admiration for the way Weibbe Hayes and his men survived so long on West Wallabi island.

Beacon Island, where the *Batavia* was wrecked on the reef in 1629 is being restored to its natural condition by the West Australian Museum and the Department of Fisheries in Perth. All the lobster fishermen's huts were removed in 2014. The natural flora and fauna are now being restored on the Abrolhos. Parts of the *Batavia* wreckage, as well as cannons, coins and pottery, are on display in the Museum of Geraldton, the Western Australian Museum in Perth and the Shipwrecks Museum in Fremantle near Perth. The last time I was in Geraldton, one of the bronze cannons from *Batavia* was mounted outside the municipal buildings. The oldest coin found in the wreck by the divers dated back to 1575. It came from one of the two treasure chests that Francisco Pelsaert failed to salvage when he returned to the Abrolhos in the *Sardam*. It is interesting that most of the coins recovered were German Reichstalers[258]. In those days, German talers were the most important currency in Europe and parts of Asia. The silver coins were minted in Brunswick and Lüneburg (Luneburgum).

Ill. 12-12, A treasure trove of silver Reichstalers was found in the wreck[259]

---

258 The word Dollar is derived from Taler. Until 1901 the German spelling was Thaler
259 Wikipedia Public Domain

Ill. 12-12-1, One of the coins found in the wreck. It has the imperial eagle at the centre, and the inscription reads FERDINANDUS II · D.G ·ROM· IMP · SE · AU (Ferdinandus II Dei Gratia Romanus Imperator Semper Augustus) [Ferdinand II by the Grace of God (Holy) Roman Emperor Eternally Magnificent][260]

Ill. 12-13, Part of the Batavia's hull[261]

---

260 Western Australian Museum, Perth
261 Wikipedia Public Domain

Archaeologists from the University of Western Australia in Perth excavated bones and skeletons. New, so far undiscovered graves continue to be found – graves of those slaughtered by the bloodlust of Jeronimus Cornelisz and his henchmen. Perhaps one day it will be possible to discover the victims' identity.

Ill. 12-14, Skeleton of a man of about 35 years old, with a shattered shoulder-blade.

Ill. 12-15, A replica of the Batavia

Between 1985 and 1995 a replica of the *Batavia* was built by the Bataviawerft in Lelystad in the Netherlands. In 1999 she was transported to Australia and displayed in the National Maritime Museum in Sydney. Today the ship is back in Holland.

In 1973 the Australian film director Bruce Beresford produced the film *The Wreck of the Batavia*. Surprisingly, the film attracted little attention.

Things were very different at the time of the wreck and the murders. When the news reached Holland, all the news media were filled with reports of the catastrophe. I found material from 1628, 1629 and 1642. It was in the headlines for years.

Ongeluckige Voyagie,
VANT
SCHIP BATAVIA,
NAE
OOST-INDIEN.
Uyt-gevaren onder de E. François Pelsaert.
Gebleven op de Abrolhos van Frederick Houtman, op de hoogte van 28. en een half graden / by Zupden de Linie Æquinoctiael.
Vervattende 't verongelucken des Schips, en de grouwelijcke Moorderyen onder 't Scheeps-volck, op 't Eylandt Batavia's Kerck-hoff; nevens de straffe der handtdadigers in de Jaren 1628. en 1629.
Hier achter is noch by-gevoegt eenige discoursen der Oost-Indische Zee-vaert / als mede de gantsche gelegentheyt der Koopmanschappen die men in Indien doet.

'tAMSTERDAM,
Voor Joost Hartgers, Boeck-verkooper in de Gasthuys-Steegh / bezyden het Stadt-huys / in de Boeck-winckel. 1648.

Ill. 12-16
Journal: Ongeluckige Voyagie van't [disastrous voyage of the] Ship Batavia

Ill. 12.17
The first page of the journal

JOURNAEL,   Pag. 1
Ende   1628.
Historisch verhael van de On-   ――――
geluckige Reyse gedaen naer   Octob.
OOST-INDIEN,
Door
FRANCOIS PELSAERT van Antwerpen,
Koopman op het Schip BATAVIA. Den 28.
October 1628. uyt Texel gezeylt.

Naer dat den Heer Generael Pieter Carpentier in Junio des jaers 1628. met by-rijcke retour-Schepen uyt de Oost-Indien behouden in 't vaderlant gekomen was: en dat de Bewinthebberen haer by ghearresteerde Schepen / verleden Jaer met den Commandeur Ian Karstensz van Embden (uyt Suratta gekomen) van 't beslagh uyt Engelant ontslagen hadden / heeft sulcks geen kleyne couragie / ende gelegentheyt tot nieuwe equipagie ghegeven: weert weder een vloot van elf Schepen derwaerts gesonden / met welcke de Heer Generael Jacob Specks mede varen souderop dese Schepen heeft hem begeven de wel-besochte Mathematicus Iohan Walbeeck, zijnde een persoon curieus ende neerstig om de natuer ende gelegentheden der Oostersche landen naeuw te onder soecken. De Heeren Bewinthebberen ter Kamer van Amsterdam / twee Schepen ende een Jacht by tijdts ghereet hebbende / hebben (om gheen tijdt te verliesen) de selvige voor naer Texel afghevaerdight / ghenaemt zijnde als volgt: Batavia, op 't welck als Commandeur was François Pelsaert van Antwerpen Dordrecht, tot Opper-Koopman op hebbende den Fiscael Isaac van swaenswijck van Leyden: ende het Jacht Assendelft, daer als Onder-Koopman mede voer Cornelis Vlack van Amsterdam: zijn den 28. October / uyt Texel in Zee gheraeckt.

Haer reyse vervorderende / ende door storm ofte andere ongelegentheden van den anderen geraeckt zijnde / noch niet sonderlinghs als ghemeyne coursen / ende dagelijcksche Scheeps-dingen voorvallende / niet waerdigh om in 't licht ghebracht en door den druck gemeen gemaeckt te werden / bevintis den Leser sulcx door de veelhoudige gedruckte reysen te verdrietigh valt; soo sullen wy niet van dat gedenck waerdigh is door den dagh brengen.

Het Schip Batavia sich alleen bevindende / ende haer tijdt op de reyse voorgebracht hebbende tot den 4. Junij 1629. zijnde den tweeden Pincxterdagh / mede gekomen op de hoogte van 28. en een derde graet Zuyder breete / ontrent 9 mijlen [1629. / Junius.]

AA 2

13. The Banda Islands in the turmoil of the 20th Century and a Bandanese called Des Alwi

After the German Empire acquired its colony of German New Guinea[262] in the 19th century, the Banda Islands were connected to the outside world by regular shipping services. The age of the steamer had begun. This brought some relief into the monotonous everyday life of the Bandanese. The Dutch now offered several connections between the Bandas and neighbouring regions: for example, the KPM[263] had routes between Banda Neira and Ambon, Ceram and the Aru Island of Wokan. The Dutch mail steamer now also regularly put in to Banda Neira.

On the 3rd of November 1884 the Bismarck Archipelago in New Guinea became a German protectorate. One and a half years later the first liner[264] subsidised by the German Empire sailed for German New Guinea. The North German Lloyd shipping line set up a regular service between Friedrich-Wilhelmshafen[265] in German New Guinea and Singapore. Every four weeks – once on the outward journey and once on the return journey the steamer would put in to Banda Neira, which was roughly in the middle of the long voyage.

Ill. 13-1
The Imperial Mail Steamer Prinz Waldemar[266]

---

262 The Protectorate of German New Guinea included Kaiser-Wilhelms-Land, the Bismarck Archipelago, the Carolina and Palau Islands and the Marianas
263 Koninklijke Paketvaart Maatschappij
264 Probably the *Otilie*
265 Now Madang
266 The ship on which the artist Emil Nolde and the tropical doctor Professor Leber sailed on their South Sea expedition to German New Guinea in 1910/11. See Horst H. Geerken, *A Gecko for Luck*, pp. 26 and 132, and *Hitler's Asian Adventure*, p. 86

Ill. 13-2, North German Lloyd advertising poster, 1898

Another NDL service ran fortnightly from Friedrich-Wilhelmshafen via Banda Neira and Ambon to Macassar[267]. Other shipping lines, the Hamburg Sunda Line and the Kingsin Line, also had shipping routes in the region, but they only visited the Banda Islands at irregular intervals. At the beginning of the First World War, there were 31 Imperial Mail Steamers in service between Germany and East Asia and in East Asia. It appears that the Banda Islands had better connections with the outside world then than they do now.

I find it hard to imagine that many passengers embarked or disembarked in Banda Neira. Probably a few rich Europeans or nature researchers, for whom this isolated island world was an interesting area for study. New species were continually being found in the Banda Sea, All the steamers that moored here were combination carriers which could carry freight – nutmeg, for example – as well as passengers.

Hans Minssen was captain of the Imperial Post Steamer *Manila,* which regularly sailed the route between Singapore and New Guinea. On the voyage described in the pamphlet, the ship first sailed from Singapore to Batavia. The voyage then continued via 'Pulo Laut'[268] on Borneo and Macassar to Ambon. The next port was Banda Neira. Captain Minssen describes Banda Neira in his 1944 book *Maschine Achtung – Leinen los*[269] [Stand by engines – Cast off] as follows:

Banda is a dream island, a sleeping beauty, a fairy-tale world and – too fine for Europeans, who would only want to turn it into part of the tourist industry. So it's lucky for everyone who goes there that this little island is out-of-the-way and as good as unknown in the wider world.

But what Banda calls its 'harbour', Banda Neira, is a narrow bay, about as big as the Potsdamer Platz in Berlin, surrounded by land on three sides. The fourth side is a dangerous bank of coral; a gap that is narrower than the Manila is long is the only way in, and just before that there is, to crown it all, a sandbank with palm trees growing on it, which seems to threaten to deny entrance to any outsiders.

Captain Minssen also describes how difficult the manoeuvres necessary for the *Manila* to turn and put out to sea in the narrow strait between the volcano and Banda Neira were. From there the journey continued to New Guinea. Funnily enough, he doesn't mention nutmegs or the extraordinary history of the islands in his remarks about the Bandas.

---

267 On Celebes, now Sulawesi
268 To take on coal
269 Hans Minssen, *Maschine Achtung – Leinen los,,* Berlin 1944

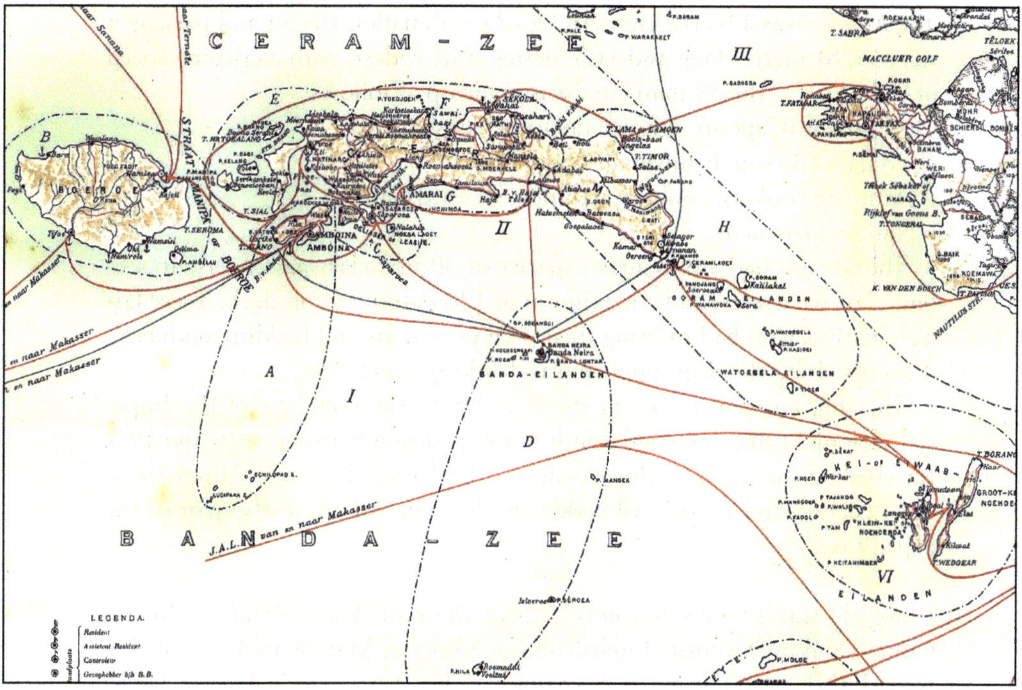

Ill. 13-3
Dutch map of the shipping routes in the region in 1915. The First World War seems not yet to have reached South East Asia.
Red: Dutch KPM routes
Blue: North German Lloyd Routes

Ill. 13-4
Pamphlet about the Imperial Mail Steamer Manila: Zwischen Singapur und Neu-Guinea [Between Singapore and New Guinea] by Captain Hans Minssen[270]

270 Extract from his book Maschine Achtung – Leinen los, Berlin 1944

The *Manila* was a North German Lloyd combination freight and passenger steamer, 81 metres long and 11.3 metres at its widest, with a cruising speed of eight knots. The 55-man crew was made up as follows:
11 Germans (Captain, officers, doctor, chief steward)
15 Malays (Bo'sun, helmsman, carpenter, sailors)
25 Chinese (stokers, cooks, watchmen, stewards) and
6 Natives (oarsmen)

The *Manila* had a passenger capacity of 30 first-class passengers, 16 second-class passengers and a maximum of 120 passengers on deck. These last were natives who had to bring their own provisions and bedding on board. The only thing the ship supplied was drinking water.

The ship entered service in the year 1904. The members of the Imperial Colonial Office's second South Sea Expedition between 1910 and 1911 travelled on the *Manila*. The expedition's leader was Professor Alfred Theodor Leber[271]. The artist Emil Nolde and his wife Ada were also part of the expedition.

I love old travel books and novels about the East Asian islands by Joseph Conrad and my favourite English author Somerset Maugham. I've probably read all their works, some of them twice. When I travel to Indonesia, I usually take novels or short stories by Somerset Maugham along. In the early tropical evenings, I enjoy immersing myself in his stories of the colonial past, with his apt descriptions of adventurers, romantic islands and failed colonial officials. In the 1920s, Somerset Maugham visited the Banda Islands in the course of his visit to the European colonies in South East Asia. Many years ago, on a visit to Indonesia, I took his novel *The Narrow Corner* with me. At the time I hadn't taken such a close interest in the book, so that I didn't realise as I read it that the story is set on Banda Neira.

I had the novel with me in my luggage this time, too. What better place to read this novel on these islands? The dreamy little town of Banda Neira is given the literary disguise of Kanda Meria, the islands are the Kanda Islands and the Banda Sea is the Kanda Sea. He writes about the narrow strait between Banda Neira and Gunung Api, the marble palaces of the Dutch, the fort and nutmegs, but doesn't mention the massacre of the Bandanese at all. Have even crimes like these fallen into oblivion with the passing of time? Or have they just become unimportant?

In the novel the main character is on a sailing ship in the Banda Sea in a raging storm. The ship has to seek shelter on the remote island of Banda Neira. Maugham describes the island as follows:

---

271 See Horst H. Geerken, *Hitler's Asian Adventure,* pp. 84 ff.

It's a fine place. It's the most romantic spot in the East. [. . .] We live on our memories. That is what gives the island its character. [. . .] The old Dutch merchants were so rich here in the great days of the spice trade, they didn't know what to do with their money. There was no cargo for the ships to bring out and so they used to bring marble and use it for their houses. If you're not in a hurry, I'll show you mine. It used to belong to one of the perkeniers. And sometimes, in winter, they'd bring a cargo of nothing but ice. Funny, isn't it? That was the greatest luxury they could have. Just think of bringing ice all the way from Holland.

Somerset Maugham realised even then that the remaining descendants of the Dutch *perkeniers* on the island were living in a dream of an idealised colonial past. It seemed to him that time had stood still here. People in the Bandas were living in a different era. After the First World War, the colonial rulers – and not just the Dutch – had become weak. In Europe, too, resistance to colonial rule was growing in Holland, the United Kingdom and France.

After the First World War Germany lost her colonies and the Bandas sank back into their dreamy existence. They were cut off from the outside world again, and were forgotten. It was only when leading figures in the Indonesian nationalist movement were exiled to the Bandas by the Dutch that they once more became a focus of international interest.

In 1927 the foundations of the PNI, the Partai Nasional Indonesia were laid by Sukarno, later the first President of Indonesia. The party's goal was to throw off the fetters of Dutch colonialism and to create an independent Indonesia. Because of the charismatic Sukarno's talent for rousing people's enthusiasm – from the simplest peasants to intellectuals from all ethnic and national groups – it became a mass movement. He was respected and venerated as the teacher and father of his people. The Indonesians all suddenly regarded themselves as one big family, regardless of any cultural, religious or linguistic differences. Holland recognised the danger posed by the PNI. In 1930 they threw Sukarno and other PNI leaders in prison, and the party was banned.

In 1932 Mohammad Hatta[272] and Sutan Sjahrir[273] founded a new national association with a different name, but the same objectives. Sukarno was briefly released in 1933, but sent back to prison when he made contact with Hatta and Sjahrir. The Dutch then began to regard Hatta and Sjahrir as dangerous as well. They were arrested in 1934 and also imprisoned. A lit-

272 1902-1980, aka Muhammed Hatta. Popular nickname Bung Hatta (Brother Hatta)
273 1909-1980, aka Sutan Sjahrir

tle later they were sent to the infamous Dutch Boven Digul[274] concentration camp in the swamps of Papua New Guinea. It was Hell! Because of diseases like malaria, insufficient food and a lack of medical facilities, countless thousands of Indonesian freedom fighters never left the concentration camp alive.

Ill. 13-5, The house where Tjipto Mangoenkoesoemo was interned

Ill. 13-6, The living room

Ill. 13-7, Tjipto Mangoenkoesoemo was interned here from 1928 to 1940

---

274 See also Horst H. Geerken, *A Gecko for Luck*

In 1935 Hatta and Sjahrir were interned on the remote and forsaken Banda Islands, where they met Tjipto Mangoenkoesoemo[275], Sukarno's mentor and co-founder of the PNI. In 1927, after fomenting a revolt in the KNIL[276], the Royal Netherlands Indian Army, he had been exiled to the Bandas by the Dutch. The KNIL was an army under Dutch leadership, which since the First World War had consisted mainly of natives of the Ambon Islands. While on the Bandas, Mangoenkoesoemo ceased to be politically active. Many years later, in 1942, he was released by the Japanese and died shortly afterwards.

The two newcomers also encountered Iwa Koesoemasoemantri[277], another of Sukarno's fellow campaigners and a member of the PNI, on the Bandas. Because he too supported independence from the Dutch, he was imprisoned by the Dutch in 1929 and afterwards exiled to Banda Neira. After Indonesia declared independence on the 17th of August 1945[278], he was appointed Minister for Social Affairs in President Sukarno's first cabinet. When the Dutch attempted to regain Indonesia as a colony in an almost five-year war, he was temporarily made Minister of Defence with responsibility for the Indonesian armed forces.

Hatta and Sjahrir had experienced several forms of imprisonment by the Dutch. After months in the Boven Digul concentration camp, Banda Neira must have seemed like paradise to them, especially as they shared their exile with people they already knew: Tjipto Mangoenkoesoemo and Iwa Koesoemasoemantri, patriots of the older generation, who shared their views. Judging by the houses they were lodged in, the exiles seem to have lived quite comfortably.

Much to the annoyance of the roughly one hundred Dutch people living on Banda Neira, Hatta and Sjahrir were allowed to move freely around the island. The Dutch found it scandalous that they were able to impart their idea of a free and independent Indonesia to the youth of Banda Neira. In the house of Captain Christopher Cole[279], who had captured the Banda Islands in 1810, they set up a school. One of the pupils was Des Alwi, a bright boy just nine years old, who had met Hatta and Sjahrir on the 11th of February 1936 in the port of Banda Neira when they arrived on the island.

275 1886-1943, in the reformed spelling Cipto Mangunkusumo
276 Koninklijk Nederlandsch-Indisch Leger
277 Reformed spelling: Iwa Kusumasumantri, aka Iwa Kusuma Sumantri
278 The 17th of August is now celebrated every year as Hari Raya Kemerdekaan, Independence Day, with banners, flowers and other celebrations. Independence Day is still not recognised by the Dutch government.
279 See Chapter 11

Ill. 13-8, The house where Mohammad Hatta, later Vice-President of Indonesia, lived in exile in Banda Neira

Ill. 13-9, Mohammad Hatta's living room

Ill. 13-10, Mohammad Hatta's study with his old typewriter

Ill. 13-11, The house where Sutan Sjahrir, later Prime Minister of Indonesia, lived in exile in Banda Neira

Des Alwi was born on Banda Neira on the 7th of November 1927. His father came from the Sultanate of Ternate, the clove-producing Spice Island in the northern Moluccas. His mother was a Bandanese, a member of the Baadilla family, a family of Arab origin. The head of the family was Said Baadilla, then the richest man in the region. He ran a fleet of 80 pearl-fishing boats. The Queen of England's crown is adorned with more than 100 pearls that came from Said Baadilla and the Banda Sea. Des Alwi's father worked for Said Baadilla as captain of one of the pearl-fishing boats.

Des Alwi[280] spent a happy childhood on the islands. Every day he hung around the harbour with his friends. There was nothing to do but swim, sail or fish. However, the arrival of two pale, emaciated men who had been in the Boven Digul concentration camp on New Guinea radically changed his life. They were Mohammad Hatta and Sutan Sjahrir. At first they both moved into a large, empty house in the middle of Banda Neira town, owned by a former *perkenier*. It was built in the Dutch Colonial style with massive pillars and spacious covered verandas at the front and rear. A few months later, they moved into separate quarters. Now they could read undisturbed, commit their thoughts to paper and hold discussions with Bandanese visitors. They were both well-educated, speaking English, German and French as well as Bahasa Indonesia and Dutch. They were extremely popular with the Bandanese children who were very eager to learn. They now met regularly in their homes.

They hardly ever came into contact with the Dutch in the town, who just went on heedlessly partying every evening. Both of them thought that Dutch society was completely decadent, and there was mutual aversion between them from the very start. According to Sjahrir, the Dutch and their mixed-race descendants were degenerate. He said that the remoteness of the islands and the resultant in-breeding were to blame for this.

Sjahrir had very close contacts with the locals. He particularly enjoyed meeting a group of fishermen. He was surprised to hear that the local natives still believed in ghosts and vampires, despite being Muslims.

According to their letters, the only friendly personal contact they had on the island was with a German clergyman. They also had more official contact with the Dutch Inspector, who was supposed to keep them both under more or less close surveillance. I have tried to find out more about the German clergyman, but unfortunately without success so far.

A Chinese merchant in Banda Neira clandestinely supplied Sjahrir with a small short-wave radio, which – even though it was, of course, forbidden – allowed him to keep both himself and the local population up to date about

---

280 His full name is Des Alwi Abubakar

the advance of the Japanese Army in South-East Asia during the Second World War.

The school was right next door to Sjahrir's house. Since he felt quite lonely, Sjahrir constantly sought out conversations with the school's pupils. While doing this, he was struck by a particularly intelligent and outgoing boy who regularly came to these meetings in his home. It was Des Alwi. Very soon, Des Alwi brought his sister Lili along, as well as their cousin Mimi, who was not yet school age. The three children, who all belonged to the influential Bandanese extended family, the Baadillas, became such close friends with Sjahrir that in the course of time he adopted all three.

It was the 31st of January 1942, just 30 minutes before the Japanese air force bombed the Dutch ships in the port of Banda Neira for the first time, when Mohammad Hatta und Sutan Sjahrir were flown out to Java in a Catalina seaplane by the Dutch, who didn't want them to be freed by the Japanese. Three children were allowed to fly with them, Sjahrir's adoptive children Lili and Mimi and a third Baadilla child, little Ali, who was only three. The flight took them to Surabaya. The next day they were taken on by train to Sukabumi in the mountainous west of Java, where they were all imprisoned.

Ill. 13-12, The school in which Hatta and Sjahrir taught Bandanese children.

When the Japanese took control of Java, the prison governor freed them. Sjahrir, Hatta and the three children struggled through to Batavia, which was now called Jakarta, where they formed part of Sukarno's circle. Des Alwi followed them by sea. Among his baggage were two large, heavy cases containing Sutar Sjahrir's collection of books, which he hadn't been allowed to take on the plane. In Jakarta he rejoined Sjahrir and Hatta. Since Des Alwi played an extraordinary role in the Indonesian independence struggle and for the future of the Banda islands, I will return to him in more detail later.

A little later the Banda Islands were taken by the Japanese without any resistance. The Dutch had already fled the islands for Java. Shortly before the Japanese surrender, there was an extremely unfortunate event. At the beginning of 1945, an American bomber attempted to attack the Japanese ships anchored in the port of Banda Neira. Instead of the ships the bomb hit a wedding party in the town. More than a hundred Bandanese wedding guests lost their lives in the attack. It was – as the Americans now equivocally say – collateral damage. Shortly before its end, the horrors of the Second World War had reached the isolated Banda Islands and claimed innocent victims even there.

During the Japanese occupation of the Dutch East Indies there were food shortages on the Bandas. There were no deliveries from Java and Ambon because the Japanese forces had already requisitioned them from the producers. There may have been an abundance of nutmeg and mace on the Bandas, but you could not live on that. The Japanese were not interested in nutmeg and mace, because they are not used in Japanese cooking. As we know, the soil on the Bandas is not good for growing vegetables, but many nutmeg trees had to be felled to make way for planting tapioca roots and potatoes. These clearances meant that nutmeg production fell to about 20% of its pre-war level. There was no more rice, and there were very few sago trees. Hunger reigned, especially on Run, which was even less self-sustaining than the other Banda Islands.

During the Japanese occupation of the Dutch East Indies there were often Japanese warships – and also freighters – moored in the strait between Banda Neira and Gunung Api. Older residents of Banda Neira told me of a very unusual event, when a submarine moored at the pier in Banda Neira. No one could tell me if it had been a Japanese or a German submarine. Most of the people telling me about it had heard the story from their fathers or grandfathers. It could quite possibly have been a German submarine, since they also operated in the Banda Sea on their way to Japan. At the beginning of World War Two German freighters also put into ports on North Sulawesi to buy raw materials.[281]

When Hatta and Sjahrir – like Sukarno, who had been imprisoned or exiled for 16 years by the Dutch – were once more free because of the Japanese occupation, the young Des Alwi also joined those who were fighting for independence from the Dutch. From then on, Sjahrir lived with the children and educated them until regular schooling started up again. The children got to know the Indonesian freedom fighters – not just familiar faces from Banda Neira, but also the future President Sukarno.

Two days after the Japanese capitulated, on the 17th of August 1945, Sukarno proclaimed the Indonesian Republic, encompassing the territories within the borders of the Dutch colony, with himself as first President, and Hatta as Vice-President. Sutan Sjahrir, the third great man of the revolution became Prime Minister. Indonesia was now free and independent – but only on paper. Things were somewhat different in reality, since for Indonesia the Second World War was far from over. The Dutch were not going to let the Indonesians become independent with impunity, and began a brutal colonial war that lasted nearly five years.

When the Second World War ended, the Dutch returned to Indonesia – now independent – with their entire armed forces to reconquer and exploit their former colony. In the war that followed, hundreds of thousands of Indonesian lives were lost. In Europe – thank God – the concentration camps had closed. At the same time, in Indonesia thousands of freedom-loving Indonesians were imprisoned by the Dutch in newly-opened concentration camps. In the Second World War, the Dutch were not just victims – they were also perpetrators. Nevertheless, they seem to have managed to sweep the darker aspects of their history under the carpet. Up to now!

Even as a teenager – he was now already 18 or 19 – Des Alwi involved himself in the struggle for independence from the Dutch. He was a member of the youth militia, *Pemuda Republik Indonesia*. During the famous – and infamous – battle for Surabaya[282] at the end of 1945, in which the British played an ignominious part, he acted as a courier between the Indonesian units and the national leadership. Even though British troops took the city, this battle became a symbol of national resistance, and Surabaya became the City of Heroes.[283]

---

281 See Horst H. Geerken, *Hitler's Asian Adventure*
282 For details see Horst H. Geerken, *A Gecko for Luck* and Horst H. Geerken, *Hitler's Asian Adventure*
283 See Horst H. Geerken, *A Gecko for Luck,* pp. 144 ff.

On *Radio Pemberontakan*, Rebellion Radio, a Scotswoman, Surabaya Sue, who is better known in Indonesia as K'tut Tantri[284], broadcast anti-colonial propaganda against the Dutch and British. In those post-war years, international journalists listened with great interest to her live reports directly from the thick of the independence struggle. She brought Indonesia's battle for independence to international attention. Des Alwi also worked in the headquarters of the underground radio transmitter. He was responsible for the technical side of the transmissions. He remembered that Surabaya Sue had a high, thin voice which wasn't really suitable for radio. *But she spoke English*, said Des Alwi, *and that was good enough!* She kept on repeating her appeal to the Indian troops who were fighting for the British, and encouraging them to give up: *You'd better go back to where you came from. Don't bring us the Dutch back!* [sic][285] Surabaya Sue became a legend of the Indonesian independence struggle far beyond the borders of Indonesia.[286]

When the Dutch were finally driven out of Indonesia in December 1949, Des Alwi worked in the Yogyakarta studio of the Voice of Indonesia, the Indonesian State radio station. Then his foster father Sutan Sjahrir sent him to England for training. As well as studying, he worked in the office of the Indonesian Information Office in London. He returned in 1950 and a year later he was appointed – at the age of only 24 – Indonesian representative at the International Telecommunications Union in Geneva. From 1952 he worked for the Indonesian Foreign Ministry[287] as Press Attaché in London, Bern and Manila.

Des Alwi then fell into disfavour with Sukarno because he took part in the PERMESTA[288] rebellion. North Sulawesi, North Sumatra and the Moluccas were the centres of this rebellion, which was mainly about a fairer distribution of state finances. These regions felt that they were being put at a disadvantage by the government, which was dominated by the Javanese. When the USA, using the CIA, began to support the PERMESTA rebels with vast supplies of military material, and even sent American bombers and fighters to the region, President Sukarno intervened with his forces – by now well-trained – and successfully put down the rebellion.[289] Des Alwi

---

284 She gave herself more than 15 different names. It is most likely that she was born Muriel Stuart Walker in Glasgow on the 18th of February 1899. She died in Sydney on the 27th of July 1997. In accordance with her wishes, her ashes were scattered in Bali. See also K'tut Tantri: *Revolt in Paradise,* 1960
285 https://www.journal21.ch/surabaya-sue
286 See also Horst H. Geerken, *A Gecko for Luck,* p. 147
287 Departemen Luar Negeri Indonesia
288 *Piagam Perjuangan Semesta*
289 For detail, see Horst H. Geerken, *A Gecko for Luck,* pp. 159ff

could no longer remain in Indonesia. He was welcomed in Malaysia by the Prime Minister Tengku Abdul Rahman and the Deputy Prime Minister Tun Razak, becoming their advisor on Indonesian matters. The three of them had been friends since their student years in London. It was the era of *konfrontasi,* confrontation with Malaysia. *Ganyang Malaysia,* smash Malaysia, was now on everyone's lips in Indonesia.

The cause of the tension was that Great Britain was trying to increase its influence in the region by the creation of Malaysia. Borneo was split into four parts, the Indonesian Province of Kalimantan, the Sultanate of Brunei and two British colonies, Sarawak and North Borneo. North Borneo was later renamed Sabah. As it pulled out of its South East Asian Colonies, Great Britain wished to unite all its colonies in Borneo and the Malay Peninsula in a single state, Malaysia. This met with massive resistance from the Philippine authorities and President Sukarno in Indonesia.

After negotiations between the British and the Philippines and Indonesia, all three states declared that they were prepared to accept Malaysia after a UNO referendum, provided that a majority of the population voted for the confederation. In September 1963, when Great Britain and Malaysia unilaterally announced that the confederation of the states would take place **before (!)** the publication of the results of the vote, President Sukarno regarded it as a breach of the agreement and a further example of British imperialism.

The oil-rich Sultanate of Brunei in Borneo had decided from the outset against joining the confederation and remained a British protectorate. Singapore, which in the British colonial period was a part of Malaya, later left the confederated state of Malaysia because the rights of their Chinese majority were not given sufficient consideration. Tension grew. The Philippines and Indonesia broke off diplomatic relations with Malaysia and Great Britain. There was unrest in Jakarta and the British Embassy was burned down.[290]

Initially, there was a guerrilla war with Malaysia and slogans like *Gerakan Ganyang Malaysia*[291] and *Konfrontasi*[292] boomed out continuously on Indonesian Radio. The Singapore Embassy building in Jakarta was also demolished and set on fire. The war along the border in Borneo escalated. The Royal Navy sent warships and aircraft carriers, the Royal Air Force over 100 fighters. 14,000 British soldiers were already on the ground. Australia then also sent troops. The situation was deteriorating.

---

290 See Horst H. Geerken, *A Gecko for Luck,* pp. 160 ff
291 Smash Malaysia
292 Confrontation

Ill. 13-13, Inauguration of the radio transmitter by President Suharto.[293]

Since every war is also a war of words, Indonesia needed to acquire a powerful short-wave transmitter with a directional antenna for propaganda broadcasts attacking the enemy, Malaysia, as quickly as possible. As I was the representative of a major German industrial concern which produced large transmitters, I was summoned to negotiations in President Sukarno's palace. Without being aware of it, I was now an opponent of Des Alwi. While Des Alwi was trying to mediate between the opposing parties from Kuala Lumpur, I was trying to sell Sukarno a powerful transmitter to broadcast propaganda to Malaysia. In Kuala Lumpur, Des Alwi, using a pseudonym, was trying to calm the situation down by means of radio broadcasts. Sukarno, on the other hand, wanted to inflame the situation with broadcasts from Jakarta on his powerful new 100-kilowatt transmitter. At that time, however, I was unaware of the name and existence of Des Alwi.

The negotiations for the contract for the purchase of the transmitter project took place in President Sukarno's palace on Medan Merdeka [Freedom Square] in Jakarta, with the President's closest advisors. My most impor-

293 On the left the German Ambassador Lüdde-Neurath with his wife

Ill. 13-14, President Suharto beside the transmitter with the Minister of Information

tant opposite number was a general, head of KOTI[294], the most important decision-making committee, answerable directly to the President, which therefore had the right to make the decision and provide the funds for the project.

We quickly reached a deal. Fortunately, my company had a complete 100-kilowatt transmitter waiting ready-packed in the port of Hamburg, which was supposed to be going to Togo in West Africa. This was now diverted to Jakarta. Everything had to be done as quickly as possible.

Shortly afterwards the installation of the transmitter began in Cimanggis, on the route of the old road from Jakarta to Bogor. But Sukarno never got to use the propaganda transmitter. In 1965 he was deposed by Suharto with massive support from the CIA. The situation with Malaysia calmed down, and the 100-kilowatt radio transmitter was inaugurated in 1967 by Sukarno's successor, President Suharto. From now on, the transmitter broadcast its peaceful message to the whole world for the Indonesian State Radio RRI[295] as the Voice of Indonesia.

---

294 *Komando Operasi Tertingi*
295 *Radio Republik Indonesia*

Ill. 13-15, Des Alwi

After his return to Indonesia, Des Alwi worked for the RRI and became a successful businessperson. I was also closely involved with the leading figures in the RRI. When I was given the commission to build a complete new studio building in Jakarta in the 1970s, I met Des Alwi shortly after the building was completed. He was interested in radio technology and the new studio. With a smile, we talked about the era of *Konfrontasi,* when we had been unwitting opponents. How times had changed! In Chapter 17, The Banda Islands Today, I will write about Des Alwi's subsequent life and career.

14. Gunung Api[296]

The Banda Sea, which in places reaches a depth of up to 7,440 metres, is one of the deepest seas in the world. It is of vital importance for the currents that circulate in the Indonesian Archipelago of more than 17,000 islands. At the same time, it is recognised as one of the most seismically dangerous zones in the world. The Ring of Fire, a volcano belt that runs through the whole of Indonesia from Sumatra and Java to the Moluccas and beyond, passes through the Banda Sea. There are a great many volcanoes lined up along this plate boundary, which is many thousand kilometres in length. Of the roughly 450 active volcanoes on the planet at this moment, 330 are in Indonesia alone – and they are among the most dangerous. 90 per cent of all earthquakes occur in the vicinity of the Ring of Fire. In the Banda Sea there are earth tremors almost every day.

From west to east the Banda Sea measures about 1,200 kilometres, from north to south about 600. In the middle of this sea lie the eleven tiny, remote and forgotten Banda Islands, six of which are inhabited.

Ill. 14-1, The Gunung Api volcano looks dangerous[297]

296 Aka Api Banda and Gunung Api Banda
297 The side that was burnt in the eruption of 1988

No matter what direction you approach the Banda Islands from, the first thing that comes into view is always the majestic volcanic cone of Gunung Api, the fiery mountain. Gunung Api is the peak of a powerful active volcano that rises from the seabed, which is here 4,000 metres deep. The perfect volcanic cone towers another 600 metres above sea level. The island, almost perfectly circular, has a diameter of three kilometres.

Gunung Api lies at the central point of a caldera with a diameter of seven kilometres. The islands of Banda Besar, Sjahrir and Kapal form part of the southern and eastern walls of this caldera. To the north east this joins up with another, even bigger, sunken caldera. These calderas are evidence of gigantic eruptions in the past.

Gunung Api is one of the most active volcanoes in the region. Even though it is so remote and isolated it was the earliest volcano in Indonesia to have been documented and described in so much detail, beginning in 1586. This is because even at that early period the Banda Islands were regularly visited by the Portuguese, Spanish, English and Dutch for the reson of the spices. And they kept a detailed account of the eruptions. Sometimes it just emits ash, sometimes there are only fountains of lava, and on other occasions streams of lava flow into the sea. Sometimes there have been explosive eruptions which flung lava bombs as far as the islands of Banda Neira and Banda Besar. Gunung Api is unpredictable.

In the 17th century alone, there were several devastating eruptions with earthquakes and flood waves. In 1629 Banda Neira was flooded by a tsunami and destroyed. Such catastrophes were often followed by years of suffering and deprivation. In 1778 a large proportion of the nutmeg trees were destroyed by a powerful eruption accompanied by an earthquake and a tsunami.

Whenever the Dutch ships arrived in the Banda islands there was a powerful eruption. Major eruptions were recorded in the following years: 1586, 1598, 1609, 1614, 1615, 1632, 1635, 1683, 1690, 1694, 1696, 1712, 1722, 1749, 1762, 1765, 1773, 1775, 1778, 1816, 1820, 1824, 1825, 1835, 1855, 1890, 1901 and in 1988.

The showers of ash spewed out during eruptions caused severe damage to the nutmeg trees on Banda Neira and Banda Besar. The crowns of the trees would be burnt. By replanting with young trees, they always managed to avoid major losses.

Illustrations left page:

Ill.. 14-2, The author sailing around the volcano
Ill. 14-3, The coastline of Gunung Api is strewn with black lava rock

Ill. 14-4, Lithograph from 1846[298]

Ill. 14-5, Eruption of Gunung Api in 1988[299]

---

298 Lithograph by Louis le Breton. Produced during a French South Pole expedition. Wikipedia Public Domain
299 The photograph was supplied by Mr Ahmet Iskandar of Banda Neira.

Gunung Api's last major eruption lasted from the 17th to the 19th of May 1988. It began with an explosive eruption. The volcano only settled down again in August 1988. Satellite measurements showed that the plume of the eruption reached a height of 16 kilometres. Streams of lava flowed down to the sea from five craters. Red-hot lumps of stone flew as far as the neighbouring islands. The inhabitants of Banda Neira and Banda Besar were evacuated to Ambon, 200 kilometres away. When the volcanic ash even reached Ai, which is further off, the inhabitants fled to Run, which is the furthest island from the volcano.

It is interesting that the stream of lava that flowed into the sea in 1988 is now overgrown with all kinds of beautiful new corals. The sea around the Banda Islands is still healthy. By contrast, the scars left by the lava stream on the volcano are still visible.

The devastation caused by earthquakes and tidal waves was worse than that caused by volcanic eruptions. There were particularly strong earthquakes in 1586, 1598, 1625, 1629, 1683, 1684, 1686, 1690, 1710, 1743, 1763, 1767, 1798, 1811, 1816, 1820, 1852 … and so it continues until today.

Ill. 14-6, Gunung Api with the stream of lava flowing down to the sea

The last major earthquakes were in 2009 and 2012, the latter reaching a magnitude of 6.3 on the Richter scale. Minor earthquakes are felt almost every week. For the inhabitants of the Bandas, these are just part of everyday normality. The latest smaller earthquakes, which I recently measured with an earthquake-app, were on the 27th of April 2019, magnitude 4.2, the 3rd of May, magnitude 3.2 and the 21st of May 2019, magnitude 3.7 on the Richter scale.

The earthquake on Banda Neira in 1629 caused a tsunami with a 16-metre-high tidal wave. A boat from the harbour was washed into the courtyard of Fort Nassau by the wave. Many human lives were lost, but according to Joahnn Sigmund Wurffbain[300] there was very little damage to the nutmeg plantations.

In 1683 a very severe earthquake destroyed many houses in Banda Neira and even parts of Fort Nassau. This earthquake was the reason why the Governor of Banda, who until then had lived in the Fort, moved into a residence outside it. Simultaneously with the earthquake, there was a violent eruption of Gunung Api. All the vegetation on the island of Gunung Api was destroyed.

In the following year, 1684, there was a severe earth- and seaquake. The following tsunami washed the Governor's[301] wife out of the new residence to her death.

A violent eruption of Gunung Api in 1690 was followed by an earthquake so severe that many houses of the islands were destroyed. After that, many Bandanese emigrated to Ambon and Macassar. They felt there was no future for them on the Bandas.

In 1816 the massive residence built by the Dutch Governor in 1683 and all the administrative buildings on Banda Neira were utterly destroyed. In many villages not a single house was left standing.

In 1820, most of the stone-built houses and walls in Banda Neira collapsed. However, the earth- and seaquake on the 26th of November 1852 is said to have been particularly bad. It began with an earth tremor which caused most of the stone buildings on Banda Neira and Banda Besar to collapse. The church lost its roof. Convicts who were in chains in the prison in Fort Nassau were buried under the rubble. Only the sturdily built Fort Belgica was spared. A powerful submarine earthquake followed a quarter of an hour later. The difference between the lowest and highest water level was nine metres! 60 people were swept away in the vicinity of the port. Parts of Banda Neira were flooded and some nutmeg plantations destroyed. Hourly

---

300 See Chapter 8
301 Van Zijl

214

earth tremors continued over the next three days, accompanied by subterranean rumbling. None of the buildings were habitable.

Until now the islands of Ai and Run have been spared such elemental natural catastrophes. They were, of course, further from the unpredictable volcano Gunung Api. Instead, the main problem for these two islands was the violent storms in the monsoon season. In 1778 another powerful hurricane swept the islands, destroying a whole year's harvest and many of the plantations. They live dangerously on the Banda Islands.

When I was living opposite the volcano in December 2018, it remained very tame. There was just the occasional plume of smoke from the peak or an underground rumble. But I did feel a few weak earthquakes. No-one on the Bandas worries about them – they're simply a part of everyday life.

There are hotspots beneath the surface of the water in several places on Gunung Api. At particular times thousands of sea snakes of all sizes gather here to mate. Although some of the sea snakes are poisonous, they are not aggressive. This spectacular event attracts divers and scientists from all over the world. In the spring, when the West Monsoon is over, the water is crystal clear: underwater visibility is up to 50 metres.

Here in the Banda Sea in June, August and sometimes also in September, you can, if you are lucky, observe a very special phenomenon. It is a marine luminescence, which is called the 'milky sea'. It is caused by micro-organisms which float on the surface. Unlike normal marine phosphorescence, which is caused by motor stimulus in the marine micro-organisms and produces both long and short light signals, the 'milky sea' glows constantly.

In 1904 Captain Hans Minssen was in the Banda Sea on the Imperial Mail Steamer *Manila*, under way towards Banda Neira. His final destination was Rabaul in German New Guinea (Germany still had colonies in the region in those days). Around midnight, Captain Minssen was standing on the bridge with the helmsman, gazing out into the pitch-black darkness, when he saw a 'milky sea' for the first time. This is how he describes it:[302]
Suddenly, in the water forward of us, a white patch appears, which gets bigger and brighter the closer the ship gets to it. When the distance from it is only one nautical mile, it gives the impression of a circular, foaming reef. I immediately warn the deckhand to keep his eyes peeled and keep sounding the depth. You always have to be prepared for newly formed submarine islands and reefs in this

302 Hans Minssen, *Reichspostdampfer ‚Manila‘, Zwischen Singapur und Neu Guinea* [The Imperial Mail Steamer *Manila* between Singapore and New Guinea] 1944, ed. Kapitän Fred Schmidt, Hamburg. See also Chapter 13. The artist Emil Nolde also travelled on this steamer on his South Sea Expedition in 1910/11

volcanic region. This surging circle forward of us is probably a new undersea volcano, whose vent is just below the surface of the water.

We circle this unexpected obstacle very carefully in a big arc, with the engines only at half speed, and then return to our old course.

But to the captain's dismay, a new white patch is immediately seen forward, another astern and a third to starboard. The Manila has suddenly entered a newly formed undersea crater landscape. 'Stop engines!'

Losing way, the steamer takes a zig-zag course between the shining craters. Then those on the bridge are amazed to discover that the white edge is not surf, but only stands out from the deep black of the water as a silvery glow. But not only that. Now the crew, who are gazing at the spectacle with ever-increasing amazement, see that towards the middle this circular patch shades into shimmering gold, and at the very centre into swirling, glowing red, as if a gigantic fire were raging in an unfathomable crater. The glow is so strong that the side of the ship is brightly lit up. Even the bridge and the masts can be seen in the reflection of this inexplicable, mysterious, terrifying light source. Everyone stares down spellbound, unable to explain the origin of this eerie fire on the seabed.

The further the ship sails, the closer to each other the circles become. The pitch-dark gaps between them become narrower and narrower, so that the Manila is eventually unable to proceed. But she has to, because she has a timetable to keep to, and cannot be deterred by such phantoms.

The captain orders soundings to be taken. He must take action to get away from this macabre, inexplicable colour play, because he is responsible for his ship and his passengers.

A skilful cast right into the middle of the fiery red glow shows that the sea here appears to be bottomless. The whole length of the plumbline disappears without finding the seabed. By contrast, the 'crater edges' have a normal depth of water. 'Thank God!'. With a sigh of relief, Captain Minssen gives the engine room the order 'Ahead Slow!'

The Manila sails on over the mysterious, glowing underwater circles. The hull of the ship glides unscathed through one of the circles, whose diameter is no greater than the length of the ship. The water-temperature measurements taken as she does so — which were generally expected to be near boiling point — strangely show that the temperature is normal, and not a degree warmer.

Thus far, the patches of colour have been immobile, but now, the closer the steamer gets to the volcanic island, the livelier they become. Whole combinations of rays now shoot at strikingly uniform intervals and always in the same direction from east to west from the seabed into the darkness, and disappear like the beams of a beacon, only to reappear in another position with new fiery arrows. It has all been an indescribable, incomprehensible orgy of soundless, wraithlike bolts of glowing light emerging from the depths of Hell itself, in the face of which human understanding simply fails.

That night no-one on board gets a wink of sleep. The Manila has left the ghostly lights far behind and is sailing towards the entrance to the harbour, but everyone is still heatedly discussing what we saw, but are incapable of comprehending.

'What on earth can it have been?' No one has an answer to as the question, which is repeated a hundred times. Only the Malays believe that they know: the Manila has sailed over the open gates of Hell. They now know what it looks like, and what awaits them should they ever end up there.

Captain Minssen was not the first to describe the 'milky sea' phenomenon over 110 years ago. Also Rumphius observed this phenomenon in the Banda Sea in 1670, naming it *mare album* [white sea]. Since he didn't have a microscope, he was unable to investigate the phenomenon himself. Ernst Christoph Barewitz of Erfurt also mentioned the 'white sea' in his book *Ost-Indianische Reise-Beschreibung* [Account of [my] Travels in the East Indies] published in 1751.[303] There are probably earlier references to 'white water', but without exact descriptions. The phenomenon cannot be seen every year – and it is only seen in the Banda Sea and no other ocean.

Until the end of the 19th century, the planters on the Banda Islands were convinced that the 'white sea' caused the nutmegs to burst open prematurely on the trees. It was only later that it became clear that it is a sudden change of temperature that is to blame. Both phenomena always occur simultaneously.[304]

There is a path which allows you to climb Gunung Api. The volcanic cone is quite densely wooded and from a distance, from Banda Neira, it looks as if a climb would be possible and not too difficult. I, at 85, decided that I wanted to climb to the peak. Early in the morning I got a motorboat to take me over to the volcano. I wanted to take my time and avoid the heat of the midday sun. At first it went quite well – 640 metres are not that much, I thought to myself. But the higher I got, the steeper and more difficult the climb became. The mountain was now nothing but scree and ash. With every step upwards I slid back almost to where I'd started. And the shoes I was wearing weren't really suitable for climbing in. When I'd climbed a good half of the volcano, I turned round, and went back to enjoy the view of Gunung Api in a lounger on the terrace of the Cilu Bintang Estate – with a cold Bintang beer.

---

303 p. 428
304 Dr O. Warburg, *Die Muskatnuss,* 1897, Footnote 1, p. 418

I later heard that even younger people have difficulty reaching the peak. Because of the slippery scree and the ash, the ascent is very strenuous. You have to more or less pull yourself up using the undergrowth. But if you do get to the top, the view over the Banda Islands is said to be overwhelming.

In Mai 1696 two Dutch seamen wanted to climb the mountain. They wanted – as they told their comrades – to look down into the crater. While they were climbing, they were caught in a powerful eruption and killed by a stream of red-hot lava.

The first documented ascent of Gunung Api was made by the German naturalist and botanist, Professor Kaspar Georg Karl Reinwardt[305] in 1821. There was a second ascent by M. S. Müller.[306]

Ill. 14-7, View from Gunung Api (half way up) of Banda Neira and its landing strip. In the background Banda Besar[307]

---

305 1773-1854
306 For both these naturalists see: *The Encyclopaedia Britannica*, Ninth Edition, Volume III, 1875, p. 310
307 Commons, Wikimedia

Reinwardt was born on the 5th of June 1773 in Lüttringhausen, a suburb of Remscheid. He became Professor of Natural History at the Dutch university in Harderwijk, and also Rector – Vice-Chancellor. In 1810 he was appointed Director of Science and the Arts in the Royal Commission for the Colonies. In April 1816 he arrived in Batavia. From then until the end of 1821 he toured the East Indian Archipelago, paying particular attention to the Moluccas. In his last year in the Dutch East Indies he climbed Gunung Api. In 1818, when the Gunung Guntur volcano near Garut in western Java, which is a good 2,200 metres high was in its most active eruptive phase, Reinwardt climbed it as well.

In 2006 a memorial to Reinwardt was unveiled in the Botanical Gardens in Bogor[308] on Java. Work on these world-famous gardens began in 1817, to plans prepared by Reinwardt. Perhaps there will one day be a memorial on Gunung Api to commemorate his first ascent.

The American Albert S. Bickmore[309] reached the edge of the crater on the 13th of September 1865. Bickmore was a naturalist and founder of the American Museum of Natural History in New York. As a naturalist, however, his main focus was on nature rather than science. His ascent of Gunung Api was presumably the fourth by a visitor from the West, because he found an inscription scratched on a lava block that showed that someone from the *Etna* had made the ascent before him. They could only find one man among the local population in Banda Neira who had already climbed Gunung Api, and he was taken on as guide.

He recorded his experiences on his travels in his book *Travels in the East Indian Archipelago*, which was published on the 1st of January 1867.[310] A German edition followed in 1869.[311] In volume 12 of his 1867 *A Description of the Banda Islands* he describes his ascent of Gunung Api in detail, and so I here reproduce what is probably the first documentation of the adventure.

As we read, climbing Gunung Api was no walkover. And nothing has changed, so I have no need to reproach myself for turning back – I had completed a good half of the climb.

The following extract from his description of the Banda Islands also includes information about the earthquakes and tsunamis that continually devastate the Bandas. Appendix II of this book contains the whole of his

308 Kebon Raya Bogor

309 1839-1914

310 A 2nd edition followed in 1868. This date is often erroneously given as that of the first edition

311 Albert S. Bickmore, *Reisen im Ostindischen Archipelago in den Jahren 1865 und 1866 bis 1869. Beschreibungen von Java, Sulawesi, Sumatra, Ambon, Banda, Seram und Buru*

description of the Bandas. The extract preserves the grammar, punctuation and spelling of names as they were in 1865:

A Description of the Banda Islands from 1865

[Author's Note: Extract about the ascent of the volcano, earthquakes and tsunamis]

By ALBERT S. BICKMORE, M.A.

The Governor having finished his inspecting duties, now proposed that we try to reach the top of Gunong Api. There was only one man – a native – who had ever been to the top, and 'knew the way', though, to judge from a distance, one part of the mountain was as dangerous as every other. He was engaged as our guide, and some ten others, whose duty it was to carry our lunch and a good supply of water in long bamboos. Early the next morning the coolies were ready. From the west end of the village we crossed the narrow 'Strait of the Sun' to the foot of the mountain. Some coolies who had preceded us had cleared a path up the steep declivity, but soon our only road was one of the many narrow tracks, where large masses of rocks and sand, which had loosened from some place high up the mountain, had shot down in a series of small land-slides, ploughing up the low shrubbery during its thundering descent. As long as we climbed among the shrubbery, although it was very difficult and tiring, it was not particularly dangerous until we came out on to the naked sides of the mountain; for this great elevation is not covered with vegetation more than two-thirds of the distance from its base to its summit. This lack of vegetation is caused by the frequent and wide land-slides, and by the great quantity of sulphur brought up to its top by sublimation, and washed down its sides by the heavy rains. Here we were obliged to crawl up on all fours among small, rough, black rocks of porous lava, and here all spread out until our party formed a horizontal line on the mountain side; so that when one man loosened the rocks, as every one was constantly doing, these might not come down and carry away some other man beneath him.

Our ascent now became slow and difficult, but we kept on, though sometimes the top of the mountain seemed as far off as the stars until we were within about 300 feet of the summit. Here we came to a horizontal band of loose, angular fragments of lava from two to six inches in diameter. The mountain here rose at least at an angle of 35°, and to us, in either looking up or down, it seemed almost perpendicular. This band of stones was about 200 feet wide, and so loose that, when one was touched, frequently half-a-dozen would go rattling down the mountain. I had got about half-way across this dangerous place, when the stones on which my feet were placed gave way! This of course threw all my weight on my hands, when at once the rocks which I was holding with the clenched grasp of death also gave way, and I began to slide downward. The natives on either side of me now gave a loud shout, but not one dared to seize me, for fear that I should carry him down the mountain with me. Among these loose rocks a few ferns grew up and spread out their leaves to the sunlight. As I felt myself going down I chanced to roll toward my right side and notice one particularly, and quick as a flash of light the thought crossed my mind that my only hope was to seize that fern. This I did with my right hand, burying my elbow among the loose stones with the same motion; and that, thanks to a kind Providence, was sufficient to stop me, otherwise in less than a minute, probably in thirty or forty seconds, I should have been dashed to pieces on the rough rocks beneath me. The whole certainly occurred in a less space of time than it takes to read two lines on this page. I found myself safe, drew a long breath of relief thanked God it was well with me, and, kicking away the loose stones with my heels, turned round, and kept on climbing. Above this band of loose stones the surface of the mountain was covered with a kind of crust formed chiefly of sulphur washed down by the rains. These rains had also formed many small grooves, and we made better progress here by crawling in these small gullies. At this moment the natives above us suddenly gave a loud cry, and I supposed of course that some one had lost his footing, and was going down to instant death. 'Look out! Look out! Great rocks are coming!' and the next instant several small blocks and one great flake of lava two feet in diameter bounded by us with the speed of lightning. 'Here is another!' It is coming straight for us, and it will take out one of our number to a certainty, I thought. I had stood up in the front of battle when shot and shell were flying and men were falling, but now to see the danger coming, and to feel that I was perfectly helpless, did, I must confess, make me quiver, and I crouched in the groove where I was climbing with the hope that it might bound over me and that instant a fragment of lava about a foot square leaped up from the side of the mountain and flew directly over the head of a coolie a few feet on my right, clearing him by not more than five or six inches. I then supposed that the mountain was suffering another eruption, and that in a moment we should all be shaken down its almost vertical sides; but soon the rocks ceased coming down and we continued our ascent, and in a few moments stood on the rim of the crater.

The mystery in regard to the source of the falling rocks was now solved. One of our number had reached the summit before the rest of us, and with the aid of a native had been tumbling off rocks, for the sport of seeing them bound down the mountain, having stupidly forgotten that we all had to wind partway round the mountain before we could get up on the edge of the summit, and not being able to lean over far enough to see that we were just beneath him.

*The whole mountain is merely one great cone of small **angular** blocks of trachytic lava and black volcanic sand. The crater at its top is **merely** a conical cavity in this mass. The form of the summit is nearly elliptical, **and** is approximately given in the accompanying plan and section.[312]*

*The depth of the crater is about 80 feet. Its diameter **we roughly** estimated at from 100 to 150 yards. The area at the top is about 300 **yards** long, by 200 wide. This is composed of heaps of small lava-blocks, which **are** whitened on the exterior, and in many places quite encrusted with sulphur. **Through** these heaps of stones steam and sulphurous acid gas are continually rising, **and** we soon hurried round to the windward side to escape their suffocating fumes. In a number of these places we were glad to run, to prevent the shoes from **being** scorched on our feet by the hot rocks.*

*On the western side of the crater the rim is largely composed of sand, and in one place rises 120 feet higher than on the opposite eastern side. The top, therefore, partly opens out toward the east, and from some of the higher parts of Lontar one can see most of the area on the summit of this **truncated** cone. In this western part were many fissures, out of which rose sheets and jets of gas. When we had come to the highest point, we looked over the north-west side down into the great crater, now active, one-fourth of the distance from the summit down to the sea. Dense volumes of steam and other gases were rolling **up and** only now and then could we distinguish the edge of the deep, yawning abyss beneath us. Here we rested and lunched, enjoying meanwhile a magnificent view over the whole of the Banda group, when the suffocating gases were not **blown** into our faces. Again we continued round the northern side, and came **down** to an old crater, where we found a large rock with the word 'Etna', the name of a Dutch warship, cut on one of its sides, and our Captain spent some time carving 'Telegraph,' the name of our yacht, beneath it. Great quantities of sulphur were seen here, more, the Governor said, than he had seen on any mountain in Java; for the great abundance of sulphur they yield is one of the chief characteristics of the volcanoes in this archipelago.*

*It was now time to descend. We called our guide, but he did not know where we ought to go, everything appeared so different when we looked down, from what it did when we looked upward. I chose a place where the vegetation was nearest the top, and asked him if I could go down there, to which of course he answered Yes, as most people do when they do not know what to say, and must give some reply. I had brought up with me a long stick or **kind** of Alpenstock, curved at one end, and with this I reached down and broke places for my heels in the crust that covered the sand and small stones. For **hundreds** of feet beneath me the descent seemed perpendicular, but I slowly worked **my** way downward*

312 Illustration: see complete text in Appendix 2

for more than a hundred feet, and had begun to congratulate myself on the good progress I was making – soon, I thought, I shall be down there, where I can lay hold of that bush and feel that the worst is past – when suddenly I was startled by a shout from my companions who were a short distance on my left. 'Stop! Don't go a step further, but climb up just as you went down.' I now looked round for the first time, and found to my surprise and alarm that I was on a tongue of land between two deep long holes or fissures, where great land-slides had recently occurred. I had kept my attention so fixed on the bush before me that I had never thought of looking to the right or left, generally a good rule in such perilous places.

To go on was simply impossible, so I turned round, climbed up again and passed round the head of one of these frightful holes. If at any time the crust had been weak and had broken beneath my heels, no earthly power could have saved me from instant death. As I broke place after place for my feet with the staff, I thought of Professor Tyndall's dangerous ascent and descent of Monte Rosa.

At last I joined my companions, who had found the way we had come up; and, after some slips and sprains and considerable bruising, we all reached the bottom and were glad to be off the volcano, and reaching Banda Neira, feel ourselves on terra firma once more.

For a few days I could scarcely walk or use my arms; but that lameness soon passed away – not so with the impressions made on my mind by the perils I had so narrowly escaped, and even now, when suddenly aroused from sleep, for a moment the past becomes the present, and I am once more on the tongue of land with a deep gulf on either hand, or I am saving myself again by grasping that fern.

The first European who reached the summit, so far as I am aware, was Professor Reinwardt in 1821; the second was M.S. Muller in 1828, and from that time till the 13th of September, 1865, when we ascended it, only one party had attempted this difficult undertaking, and that party was from the steamer Etna, whose name we had found on a large rock in the old crater.

The height of this volcano we found to be 707,5 metres,[313] 2321 feet. Its spreading base occupies less space, 2 miles square. In size, therefore, it is insignificant compared to the gigantic mountains on Lombok, Java, and Sumatra; but when we consider the great amount of suffering, and the immense destruction of property that have been caused by its repeated eruptions, it becomes one of the most important volcanos in the archipelago.

From Valentyn and later writers we learn that eruptions have occurred in the following years: 1586, 1598, 1609, 1615, 1632, 1690, 1696, 1712, 1765, 1775, 1778, 1820, and 1824.

---

313 Today Gunung Api is approximately 640 metres high. Presumably it has lost some of its height as a result of the eruptions that have taken place since then

That of 1615 occurred in March, just as the Governor-General, Gerard Reynst arrived from Java with a large fleet to complete the war of extermination that the Dutch had been waging with the aborigines for nearly twenty years. For some time previous to 1820, many people lived on the lower flanks of Gunong Api, and had succeeded in forming large groves, or, as the Dutch prefer to name them, 'parks' of nutmeg-trees. On the 11th of June of that year, just before 12 o'clock, in an instant without the slightest warning an eruption began which was so violent that all the people at once fled to the shore and crossed in boats to Banda Neira. Out of the summit rose perpendicularly up a great mass of ashes, sand, and stones, heated until they gave out light like living coals. The latter hailed down on every side, and as the accounts say, 'set fire to the woods and soon changed the whole mountain into one great cone of flame.' This happened unfortunately during the western monsoon and so great a quantity of sand and ashes were brought over to Banda Neira, that the branches of the nutmeg-trees were loaded down until they broke beneath its weight, and all the parks on the island were totally destroyed. Even the water became undrinkable from the light ashes that filled the air and settled in every crevice. This eruption continued incessantly for thirteen days, and did not wholly cease at the end of six weeks.

During this convulsion the mountain was apparently split through in a N.N.W. and S.S.E. direction. The large, active crater, which we saw beneath us on the north-west side of the mountain, from the spot where we lunched, was formed at that time, and another was reported higher up between the new crater and the older one on the top of the mountain. A stream of lava poured down the western side into a small bay and built up a tongue of land 180 feet long. This fluid rock heated the sea within a radius of more than half a mile, and nearer the shore eggs were cooked in it. This lava stream is the more remarkable, because it is a great characteristic of the volcanos throughout the archipelago, that, instead of pouring out fluid rock, they only eject hot stones, sand, and ashes, or mud – that is, water mingled with sand and ashes – such materials are thrown up in those volcanos where the eruptive force is known to have attained its maximum and to be becoming weaker and weaker.

On the 22nd of April 1824, while Governor-General Van der Capellen was entering the islands an eruption commenced just as had happened 209 years before, on the arrival of Governor-General Reynst. A great quantity of ashes again rose upward from its summit, accompanied by clouds of 'black smoke,' in which lightnings darted, while such a heavy thundering rolled forth that it completely drowned the salute from the forts on Neira, in celebration of the Governor's arrival. This was followed by a second eruption, succeeded by a rest of fourteen days, when the volcano again seemed to have regained its strength, *and once more ashes and glowing stones were hurled into the air, and fell in showers on all sides.*

But the people of Banda have suffered quite as much from earthquakes as from eruptions, though the latter are usually attended by slight shocks. Heavy earthquakes, without eruptions, have occurred in 1629, 1683, 1710, 1767, 1816, and 1852.

Almost the first objects that attract one's attention on landing at the village are the ruins of those houses that were destroyed by the last of these fearful phenomena. Many houses had their walls levelled to the ground, but others, that were built with especial care, suffered little injury. These walls are made of coral-rock or bricks. They are two or three feet thick, and covered with layers of plaster. At short distance along their outer side, sloping buttresses are placed against them, so that most of the houses in Banda look more like fortifications than private residences. The first warning that any one had of the coming destruction was that the water suddenly began to stream out of the enclosed bay, and this continued until the war brig Haai, which was at anchor in 8 or 9 fathoms touched the bottom. Then came in a great wave from the ocean that rose at least to a height of 25 or 30 feet over the low western part of the village, which is separated from Gunong Api by the narrow Sun Strait. Praus lying near this shore were swept up against Fort Nassau, which was so completely engulfed, that it was stated to me that one of these native boats was carried over the walls of the fort, and remained inside when the sea had receded to its usual level. The part of the village over which the floods swept contained many small houses, and nearly every one of them was carried away.

15. My journey to the Banda Islands

Twenty years ago was the first time I tried to get to the Banda Islands, which had been my dream since childhood. I waited more than two weeks in Ambon for a ship to take me to the islands, but in vain. Now I wanted to have another try. I was back in Bali at the beginning of December 2018. I gave myself just two days to recover from the long flight from Germany and to repack my luggage, since I wanted to travel light on the journey to the Bandas. I had no idea if and how I would get further than Ambon this time. Unlike earlier travellers, we now know exactly where the Bandas are, but a journey there is still an adventurous leap in the dark. Admittedly, there are now flights there in a little Cessna, but they are said to be as unreliable as the shipping services. But I was determined to try, and luck was on my side!

The journey to the 'forgotten isles' – the tiny, remote Banda Islands in the middle of the Banda Sea – was extremely interesting. How many people today are aware of these islands, which are so tiny that they can only be found on large-scale specialised maps? Yet over three hundred years ago they made history.

Anyone who travels to the Bandas needs to have plenty of time, patience, strong nerves, and even more luck. This time I had more time and more luck, but even so, the journey there was still quite an adventure. I was going to travel on one of the ships of the Indonesian state shipping line, PELNI, which can only be recommended to seasoned, hard-boiled travellers.

At 04:30 in the morning my driver Murah took me to Ngurah Rai airport on Bali. The Lion Air flight to Macassar[314] on Sulawesi[315] took off on time. After a wait of three hours, I left on the connecting flight – in a Boeing 737 – to Ambon. Situated on the island of the same name, it is the capital of the Province of the Moluccas with a population of about 300,000. Even as we took off there was a raging storm. We were violently shaken, and every time we hit an air pocket the women on board screamed loudly, while others prayed to Allah to take care of them. There was no way of calming the children, and they began to vomit. It was a dreadful flight, especially as there was a severe storm over Ambon and we had to circle the airport for 45 minutes before being allowed to land. Was I happy to be on *terra firma* once more!

---

314 Previously Ujung Pandang
315 Previously Celebes

For a few years, there has been a small airport on the main island of Banda Neira. At Ambon airport I discovered that there was a Susi Air flight in a small 12-seater Cessna the next day. Susi was the only airline that flew to Banda Neira, though there was no fixed timetable. There was information on the Internet, but it wasn't possible to book online. I soon discovered that the information on the Internet – that there were flights once or twice a week – was wildly optimistic, since the little plane sometimes didn't fly for weeks on end.

The Susi Air office was closed, but the information desk at the airport told me that there was a flight to Banda Neira the next morning at 06:15 – but it was hopelessly overbooked and there was a long waiting list. So I had no chance of a seat. I decided I was going to try anyway and took a room for the night in a simple *penginapan* [guesthouse] right next to the airport. I intended to be at the airport very early the next morning to see if I could get hold of a seat on the plane.

The owner of the *Dahalia* guesthouse was Ibu Hadji Nur, a white-robed Muslima who had visited Mecca several times. I had a pleasant and lively discussion with her about life, the universe and everything. Ibu Hadji Nur herself was just the first stroke of luck. When I told her what my destination was, she contacted her good friend Pak Umar, who she said was the local Mr Fixit where transport was concerned. That was my second stroke of luck in Ambon. But even he told me that there was no chance of getting on the next morning's flight.

I couldn't find a halfway decent looking restaurant anywhere close to the airport, and since there was still a storm and heavy rain I didn't want to have to walk too far to find one. After my strenuous day, I calmly decided just to go to bed without any dinner and try to find out more the next morning.

It took a long time to get to sleep with so many thoughts whirling around in my head. At about 4.30 AM there was a loud knock on my door: it was Ibu Haji Nur. Pak Umar had managed to get me a place on the plane. I would have to be at the airport with my baggage in 15 minutes. Take off was 6 o'clock sharp. Without washing, I hurriedly threw on my shirt and trousers and rushed to the nearby airport with my light baggage. Pak Umar was waiting for me at the entrance, and took me straight to the Susi Air desk. I paid 400,000 rupiahs[316] for the ticket, checked in my baggage, and headed off to Gate Number One. I sat down with the other 11 passengers. 'How lucky I've been this time.' I thought, 'Finding transport to Banda Neira so quickly.'

---

316 Barely 30 Euros

But I rejoiced too soon! Seven o'clock passed, then eight o'clock and nothing happened. No sign of the Susi Air plane. In the meanwhile, there was a flight to the Kei Islands. I'd always wanted to go there, but this time I was aiming for the Bandas. Shortly after eight o'clock we were informed that the flight had been cancelled because of bad weather. And when would the next flight be? Sorry, that was the last flight for 2018, and the new 2019 timetable wasn't coming out until May. Since they were losing their government subsidy the conditions would change. A ticket to Banda Neira would cost 1.45 million rupiahs, almost 100 Euros. Wow, that's a staggering price increase. And I didn't want to wait for the next flight in May: I intended to be back home in Bonn by then.

Back to the Susi desk to get my baggage; then, of course, I wanted my 400,000 rupiahs back – but they only gave me 350,000. The rest was an administration fee. Fortunately, Pak Umar was still around, and so even this problem was solved.

Now we need to get to the port straight away to get a ticket, said Pak Umar. This was because the *KM Leuser*, a ship of the PELNI line – the Indonesian state shipping line – was sailing from Ambon for the Banda Islands that evening. He drove me in his car to the port, where we bought a ticket for the ship, and then helped me to find a room for the day in a nearby hotel so that I could catch up on the sleep I'd lost that night. The *KM Leuser* was sailing at 8:00 PM. He said he'd get me to the ship on time that evening and make sure I got a bunk on the ship. Pak Umar certainly had a finger in every pie!

I knew the *KM Leuser* from a previous trip with my partner Annette. We had sailed to the islands east of Timor on her 22 years before. At that time, they had cabins for 14 first-class passengers, 40 for the second class, had dormitory space for about 920 third-class passengers. The classes were kept strictly separated. In the first class we felt as if we were on a cruise. Our cabin had two beds and a bathroom. There was even a deck reserved for just the first- and second- class passengers. In the dining room we were served by liveried waiters. At lunch and dinner there was live music played by a five-piece band. You were only allowed in the dining room properly dressed and with proper shoes. Propriety and order prevailed! In the evenings we could shake a leg to the dance band. It was pure luxury.

The *KM Leuser* was built by the Meyer shipbuilding company in Papenburg in Germany and was delivered to Indonesia in 1994. In those days the ship was still in very good shape: it was clean and, above all, there was discipline. My ticket to the Banda Islands cost now only about seven euros.

I wondered what was awaiting me, as there was now only one class: economy.[317] Pak Umar picked me up from the hotel punctually. He brought a torch with him, as all the power in Ambon was down because of the storm. The *KM Leuser* was only a few hundred metres from the hotel. Since I am half-blind at night, I was grateful for every step that Pak Umar took with me through the darkness. There were potholes, steps and all kinds of other pitfalls in the pavements. Masses of people were streaming towards the ship.

Even a hundred metres away from the ship there was already an incredible, chaotic hustle and bustle. The ship officially had room for 920 passengers in the dormitories, and everyone wanted to be first up the narrow gangway. When we finally managed to board the ship, I could hardly believe my eyes. Everywhere, in the passageways, on the decks, in the restaurant there were boxes, sacks of rice and vegetables, parcels, cases, and between them the bodies of men, women and children on sarongs or sheets of cardboard. The ship was completely overloaded, and the atmosphere was thick with the stink of human perspiration. It was perfect chaos. Everyone was fighting for a space to sleep for the night and defending their territory vociferously. Even in the former first-class dining room, where Annette and I had been served by liveried waiters to live music, men, women and children had spread themselves out on the floor. Every square metre was occupied. Where were all these people headed? I later learned that they were headed to New Guinea and not, thank goodness, to the Bandas.

They were all shrieking at once. Mothers tried to stop their babies whining by fanning the fug towards them with pieces of cardboard. To get to the purser's office, we had to climb over dozens of bodies and boxes. The Purser promised me a bunk, but said I'd have to wait until the ship had cast off. I said goodbye to my new friend and thanked him for his help with a respectable tip.

I waited patiently outside the purser's office; there were three blasts of the ship's siren, the whole ship shuddered, and we cast off. The Purser assigned a man to show me to my cabin and my bunk. It was a three-bunk cabin, and in a state that was beyond all description. All the covers for the overhead lighting and the – no longer functioning – air-conditioning were missing. Next to my bunk there were bare wires sticking out from the wall where there had once been a reading lamp. The toilet didn't flush – all the interior workings of the system had been torn out. It is unimaginable that the ship

---

317 A voyage on a PELNI ship 20 years ago – the *KM Dobonsolo* – is described in: Annette Bräker and Horst H. Geerken, *Indonesia Then and Now,* pp. 1387 ff, ISBN 978-3-7460-7532-87

could have been allowed to run down so much in 20 years. Herr Meyer, the owner of the Meyer shipbuilding company in Papenburg, would have wept to see the state it was in.

Shortly after I got to the cabin, the Purser appeared and took a sum equivalent to about 20 Euros for the bunk. Without a receipt, of course – the money vanished into his own pocket. He also told me that I should be careful of the man he had personally assigned to me – he stole things. Now he told me! They were probably in cahoots, since – even though I was very careful – money and medications were missing at the end of the voyage. How they got into my holdall is a mystery to me, since the only time the man had access to it was when he carried it through the throng of humanity in the passageways from the purser's office to the cabin. I only noticed the loss after I arrived in Banda Neira. Nothing could have been stolen during the night, as I kept tight hold on my holdall even when I slept.

Two Indonesians joined me in the cabin – the purser took the same sum of money from them as he had from me. I spread my sarong on the bed, as the bedclothes didn't look very inviting. To judge by the colour, several dozen people had slept in them before me. Even though I had a bunk, I slept very little that night: I discovered that the Indonesians have a talent for snoring in duet!

The *KM Leuser* docked in Banda Neira punctually at 8.30 AM. The journey to get there had been a long one – two flights and a ship. Very few passengers disembarked, and the ship sailed on to the eastern Indonesian islands and then to Papua[318]. As I descended the gangway, I found, to my amazement, that I was being met at the pier.

It was Abba from the Cilu Bintang Estate. He took me to his hotel on the pillion of his motorbike. What service! Pak Umar had arranged it all! He was a real gem. The second surprise was that Abba spoke perfect German. I was the only guest. If more than one guest arrives at a time, Abba is prepared: he can collect them with his motortrike workhorse.

---

318 New Guinea

Ill. 15-1, The KM Leuser in which I sailed to Banda Neira

Ill. 15-2, The Cilu Bintang Estates' motortrike workhorse

16. The Cilu Bintang Estate

My friendly contact with Pak Umar in Ambon had been really worthwhile. Without my knowledge, he had informed Abba about my impending arrival in Banda Neira and – to my surprise – he met me at the ship and took me to the Cilu Bintang Estate on his motorbike. I hadn't expected luxury on the Banda Islands, but now I was gazing wide-eyed and open-mouthed at the hotel. Abba had recreated a magnificent colonial building which gleamed with romantic flair. Everything glittered, from the marble to the crystal chandeliers. As Somerset Maugham said, Banda Neira was an island *where the sea was scented with spices and there were great marble palaces.*[319] Both were true of the Cilu Bintang Estate!

On my travels in Asia, I've always loved staying in former colonial hotels, like Falletti's in Pakistan, the Lake Palace in India, the Strand Hotel in Myanmar[320] and Raffles in Singapore. But that here, at the end of the world, I should find luxury in a magnificent colonial villa, exceeded all my expectations. A further source of amazement was that Abba spoke to me in perfect German. Since many Germans had visited the Bandas before the religious disturbances in 1999/2000, he had studied German in Ambon and afterwards stayed in Austria for some time. He had learned his English in Bali, where he had spent some time working as a pearl merchant and tourist guide.

Abba Rizal Bahalwan – his full name – is the owner of the Cilu Bintang Estate, a middle-aged man, full of energy, always active and helpful – and a treasure trove of information about the Banda Islands, which is hardly surprising, since he is the Chair of the Banda Neira Foundation. Even when he was much younger, he used to guide tourists around the Banda Islands.

Ill. 16-1, Photo of Abba and me

319 W. Somerset Maugham, *The Narrow Corner,* p. 130
320 Formerly Burma

Abba's family's roots are in the Hadhramaut, in the town of Yaman in southern Yemen. His ancestors came to Java as spice merchants and settled in Surabaya. When the Dutch took control of the Banda Islands in the 17th century, the family, who now worked for the Dutch colonial power, shifted the focus of their trade to the Banda Islands. Abba is a descendant of that family, which is still very influential in the Bandas. His long pedigree is more than impressive; and I should know, as I have just produced a history of my own ancestors.[321]

In the Hadhramaut, the Malay and Javanese languages are still occasionally in use as a result of economic links with Indonesia and close family connections. At the beginning of the 1960s almost all the hotels in Jakarta were still owned by Yemenites from Hadhramaut. Because of them there are close links to Java, since many sons of well-off families still go there for training and education.

Abba made his living mainly by selling pearls from the Banda Sea to tourists on Bali and wholesalers in Europe. In 2009 he built his guesthouse, *Mutiara*, in what was once the Christian quarter in Banda Neira. He was 35 at the time. Only two years later, in 2011, Ali bought a large plot of land behind Fort Nassau. On it there was a dilapidated colonial villa which probably belonged to Pieter van den Broecke[322] in the colonial era. After the Indonesian declaration of independence in August 1945, all Dutch property was confiscated and became state property.

Abba created the Cilu Bintang Estate on this land. He had the building demolished and built an elegant, modern colonial villa, using old plans to ensure that it was as close as possible to the original – but with modern amenities and facilities. Nevertheless, I was warned straight away that the tap water – as is the case all over Indonesia – was not drinkable. It was partly rainwater that was stored in cisterns. I was obviously aware of this, but there have always been unwitting tourists who end up in bed with stomach or bowel complaints as a result of drinking it. When you travel you are constantly reminded that clean drinking water from the mains is not – as in Germany – a matter of course.

Pieter van den Broecke was posted to the Dutch East Indies for the Dutch navy. He took part in the battle for Batavia in 1619. The VOC then appointed him Administrator of the Banda Islands. During his time on the islands, the Dutch monopoly of the nutmeg trade was imposed by incredibly extreme methods. His son was a *perkenier* who held vast nutmeg plantations

---

321 Horst H. Geerken, *My Ancestors,* 2020. ISBN 978-3-7519-4824-1
322 (1585-1640) In Chapter 17 we will encounter his descendants once more.

on Ai and Banda Besar. His descendants farmed the plantations until the post-independence confiscations.

Ill. 16-2, Portrait of Pieter van den Broecke[323] with the gold chain he received on his retirement

---

323 By Frans Hals, 1633. Original in Kenwood House in London (English Heritage), Commons

Ill. 16-3, The author with cooks Tini and Vita outside the kitchen

My room is near the kitchen. Three young ladies, Tini, Ulfa and Vita, clatter away there from breakfast time till dinner time. I can hear them laughing all day. They are Muslims; Tina and Ulfa wear the hijab, but Vita doesn't. In the dialect of the Banda Islands they stress the last vowel of the last or penultimate word in a sing-song way that sounds quite cheerful. The tone at the end of an utterance sentence rises and then sinks. The word 'vowel' says it all; it derives from the Latin *vocalis* and means 'ringing or singing sound'. For example, in the phrase *terima kasi* [thank you] the tone of the 'a' in *kasi* rises and then falls towards the 'si'. When I tried to talk to the three cooks in their own dialect, they couldn't stop laughing. As early as 1876 Dutch linguists classified the Banda Island dialect as Banda Malay.

An Australian linguist explained to me that this sing-song Banda dialect shows great similarity with Portuguese. It is interesting that such idiosyncrasies have survived until now, considering that centuries have passed since the Portuguese traded on the Banda Islands. In Bahasa Indonesia there are nevertheless many words of Portuguese origin, such as::

English	Portuguese	Bahasa Indonesia
Shoe	*sepato*	*sepatu*
Table	*mesa*	*meja*
Butter	*mantaige*	*mentega*
Window	*janela*	*jendela*

During my stay I was unfortunately unable to find anyone who was an original inhabitant of the islands. I would have loved to talk to them. A bare 1,000 Bandanese succeeded in escaping the Dutch massacre in 1621 in their fishing boats. As I said in Chapter 6, their descendants now live only in two villages – Bandar-Eli[324] and Banda-Elat[325] on the island of Kei Besar, which is 300 kilometres from the Bandas. They are the only place where the Bandanese language, which differs significantly from the other languages in the region, survives.

The three cooks conjured up fantastic dishes every day, with lots of fresh fish, of course. The flavours used in Bandanese cooking are completely different from those in Bali or Java. While in Java and Bali chillis are used to spice and pep up dishes, on the Bandas they use pepper. On Java and Bali nutmeg is hardly ever used as a spice; on the Bandas it is found in every dish. There they cook with *santen*[326] quite a lot; here they use the milk of the kenari nut.[327] There are thousands of kenari nut trees here – they reach up to 40 metres high and act as a shade for the nutmeg trees. Kenari nuts or kenari flour are found in almost every Bandanese dish. Gado-Gado is a dish that is known all over Indonesia, served with peanut sauce; but on the Bandas it is served with kenari nut sauce. Other dishes too, like fried aubergines, are eaten with this almond sauce.

Illustration next page:
Ill. 16-4, Dilla, Abba's wife, is an excellent cook[328]

---

324 Aka Wadan El
325 Aka Wadan Elat
326 Thickened coconut milk
327 A kind of almond
328 With Abba's kind permission

Several times a week, the cooks prepared a dinner buffet of Bandanese delicacies. There was always a large grilled fish, usually tuna. There were dishes, which are among the best I have ever eaten in Indonesia. The guests, rich Bandanese and Western visitors, were seated at long tables. Even people who were staying in other hotels came for the good food and lively conversation.

Dilla, Abba's wife, has a degree in business administration, but she is also an excellent cook who is constantly developing new recipes for Bandanese delicacies.

Abba, a Muslim, still hasn't been to Mecca on the hajj. *If I did, I could no longer serve alcohol to my guests,* he says. Indeed, that would be a pity, since to my mind an Indonesian Bintang beer is the best accompaniment to Bandanese cooking.

Ill. 16-5
A delicacy conjured up by Dilla:
A kenari nut dip

Ill. 16-6
A small choice of dishes

Ill. 16-7
ditto

My favourite dish was a fish soup with tuna dumplings. Vita let me help her to make the soup, and she explained the recipe to me so that I could cook it myself later. On the Bandas, this soup is called *kuah iso*. As the national dish, it has to be served at every wedding.

Here is Vita's recipe:

Kuah Iso (Fish soup with tuna dumplings)
Ingredients and preparation:
- Grind 200 gr of kenari nuts (you can also use kemiri nuts, which are available all over Indonesia) in a food proccssor.
- Do the same with about 400 gr of tuna fillet.
- Mix the puréed tuna with the ground nuts, some finely chopped onion and celery leaves to a firm texture. Season with salt, pepper and nutmeg. To thin and bind the mixture add a little beaten egg. Allow the mixture to rest.
- Dice one potato and one carrot and boil in a good quantity of water.
- In a wok, slowly stir-fry about 10 finely chopped shallots, finely chopped ginger and garlic. Keep adding liquid from the vegetable broth and reduce.
- When the onions are translucent, add the vegetable broth with the potatoes and carrots. Season with nutmeg, salt and pepper.
- Allow the broth to come off the boil. Form the tuna mixture into little balls and add to the broth. Simmer for about 15 minutes.
- Finally, bring back to the boil and add roughly cut Chinese leaves, white cabbage and celery leaves.
- When the white cabbage is *al dente* the dish is ready.

Ill. 16-10
The Bandanese
national dish,
kuah iso

Ill. 16-11
Spices in the kit-
chen at the Cilu
Bintang Estate[329]

This is delicious: I enjoyed it very much in the Cilu Bintang Estate and have cooked it myself in Germany several times since. I brought the kenari nuts required back with me from the Bandas.

Bandanese cuisine uses a lot of fish, but apart from chicken there is hardly any meat. Pork is anyway absolutely taboo on the Muslim Bandas. There is an incredible profusion of fish in the Banda Sea around the islands. Even I, as an inexperienced angler, managed to catch several fish in a very short time in the sea near Gunung Api.

---

329 With Abba's kind permission

Rice has to be brought into the Banda Islands. Vegetables are difficult to grow in the unique local volcanic soil, and therefore vegetables like tomatoes and cabbage have to be shipped in from Ambon or Java. What do flourish on the islands are sweet potatoes, *singkong* [tapioca], bananas and avocados.

The hotel's name, Cilu Bintang Estate, does not come from Indonesia's very good Bintang beer – which is, even though we are among Muslims on the Bandas, served ice cold here. Cilu Bintang means 'radiant star' and is the name of a very important lady who plays a major role in Bandanese legend.

Ill. 16-12, The Bandanese Cilu Bintang[330]

330 With Abba's kind permission

The Cilu Bintang Estate is a treasure trove of antiques. In every hall there are old cannons from the colonial era, early navigational instruments or porcelain from the time the Dutch were here. Abba continues to trade in spices. There are sacks of nutmeg, cinnamon and cloves all around the place and their delightful aroma fills all the rooms. You find a symbol of the nutmeg everywhere, carved into the wood of chairbacks, tables – and even my bed.

Even today, when the farmers on the Bandas till their fields or scuba divers swim in the sea off the Bandas, they find treasures from the Dutch colonial period, such as coins, musket- or cannonballs or porcelain. Most of them take their finds to the island's museum or to Abba, who collects and preserves them. Staying in the Cilu Bintang Estate is like living in a museum – you can stay there day after day, and constantly find something new.

---

331 Ibid.

The walls are covered with old pictures, prints and photographs. And if you feel you haven't seen enough here, you can go to Abba's first, older and cheaper hotel, the Mutiara Guesthouse, which is close by. There are just as many precious antiques there too.

Ill. 16-20, The Cilu Bintang Estate with its long red roof, with Fort Nassau in the foreground[332]

Ill. 16-21, View of the Cilu Bintang Estate from Fort Belgica[333]

---

332 With Abba's kind permission
333 Taken with a telephoto lens

244

Ill. 16-22, The entrance to the Cilu Bintang Estate.[334] In the foreground a plan of Fort Belgica carved into the flagstones

It is remarkable to see how devoted Abba and his wife Dilla are to preserving the history of the Banda Islands. Building the replica of *perkenier* Pieter van den Broecke's villa is an outstanding achievement which cannot be overestimated.

Abba recreated the colonial villa in every detail – though the facilities conform to modern standards. Even so, within its walls you are transported back to the colonial past. But at least nowadays the local inhabitants – unlike the old days – are treated with respect and not as second-class human beings.

When I planned my trip to the Banda Islands, already aware of the difficulties involved in getting there, I didn't really expect to find accommodation that was any more than adequate. I was therefore all the more surprised when, thanks to Pak Umar, I found somewhere as luxurious as the Cilu Bintang Estate in Banda Neira. That made me want more, and I'm sure that I will visit the Bandas again at the end of 2021 for the third time.

---

334 With Abba's kind permission

---

335 With Abba's kind permission

Ill. 16-25, Detail of the exquisite oriental inlaid floor

Ill. 16-26, Viat – my room in the Cilu Bintang Estate.[336] In the foreground my break-fast table on the terrace.[337]

336 With Abba's kind permission
337 [Author's note: The pretty lady in the window on the left did not, unfortunate-ly, share the room with me. She was just the photographer's model.]

17. The Banda Islands today

Whenever I strolled along one of Banda Neira's two little main streets, my nose was constantly filled with a cloud of nutmeg, cloves or cinnamon. What an experience! The sulphurous steam that pours out of Gunung Api doesn't find its way this far down at the moment. But as the many centuries-old cannons – which you come across every step of the way here – suggest, you were more likely to smell gunpowder here in the past. There were bloody battles here between the Dutch and the native Bandanese, as well as the Dutch and the other Western colonial powers. A great deal of blood was shed.

The population of all the Banda Islands together is today about 14,000. Figures between 8,000 and 15,000 were suggested to me. The capital, Banda Neira, is a sleepy little village, which has visibly seen better days. Once elegant villas with massive pillars and imposing verandas catch your eye, as do the old cannons on display, reminders of Holland's brutal colonial rule. Everywhere on Banda Neira you still come across colonial architecture, which has largely been restored. The houses with their massive pillars are solidly built. Since they say that houses, like people, have faces, I get the impression that the faces of these houses express defiance to the unpredictability of the nearby volcano. As I was standing outside one particularly pretentious colonial building, pondering on the old name plate inscribed with the name Schelling, a Bandanese spoke to me. I shouldn't go into the building: though it had been cleared out, it was haunted and shadowy figures from the colonial past still lurked inside.

The Bandanese look after the old colonial buildings on Banda Neira; they are a tourist attraction and they are kept clean. On the other Banda Islands, the old Dutch colonial architecture seems to have been left to fall into ruin. The highlight of a walk around Banda Neira is the little *Rumah Budaya Banda Neira* museum. Des Alwi laid its foundation stone in what was formerly a colonist's villa. The building has a wide veranda with impressive pillars. The Museum's display rooms hold a collection of almost anything connected with the history of the Banda Islands. Coins, swords, muskets, cannons, old furniture and VOC porcelain. They have lots of old maps and paintings on show.

Illustrations next page:
Ill. 17-1, An old colonial building in the main street
Ill. 17.2, The somewhat dilapidated Societeit Harmonie building, formerly the Dutch clubhouse

---

338 Called *betjak* in Indonesia

Ill. 17-7, Street off the main street. The volcano Gunung Api in the background

A particularly striking painting depicts the Dutch massacre of the Banda-nese in 1621. Des Alwi and the citizens of Banda Neiras contributed the funds for the museum's first exhibitions.

Next to a collection of antique gramophones there are piles of old shellac records dating from the 1920s and 1930s with swing and other dance music, evidence of the high life that prevailed here in those days. It is admirable to see a museum here in Banda Neira devoted to preserving Bandanese history. Most of the people working there are volunteers.

The people here are extremely friendly. The first thing they ask me is where I come from, and when I say Germany, their faces brighten. I am greeted with friendly smiles wherever I walk in Banda Neira. After only three days everyone recognises me. They all want to chat with the *Orang Jerman,* the German, who speaks Bahasa Indonesia so well. When I go shopping, I don't have to haggle – I get the 'local' price straight away. I sense that I am respected everywhere. Because I'm so old? Because I speak the language so well? Or because I'm German? Perhaps a little bit of all of them.

I was surprised that people on these remote and lonely islands talk German at all. I've met many Bandanese – including young people – who speak a bit of German. All of them, old and young, know the names of the footballers in the German Bundesliga – which has been made possible by the Internet and television.

They are tickled pink to have an audience for the few German words or phrases they have learned in school. Yes, German is taught in the schools here! When I ask why the Germans are so liked and respected here, I always get the same answer:

You fought and conquered our worst enemies, the Dutch, our colonial rulers, and so you contributed to our finally being able to achieve our longed-for freedom and independence.

Ill. 17-8, Ships' bells found in the sea

Ill. 17-9, On the old sailing ships food was stored in these pots

When I remind these people of the atrocities that occurred in the Third Reich, the answer is always the same too: *All we care about is the end of colonial rule, and Germany helped us with that!*

On the Banda Islands there are elementary schools, and on Banda Neira there are also secondary schools. In addition to English, German is also taught. I wanted to meet the German teacher, Ibu Ayu, but it wasn't possible – she had just gone to Ambon for a few days.

It's not as easy as that for the Dutch. In Ambon I met a young couple from Holland in my hotel. They had travelled across Sumatra and met with hostility in Medan. To avoid further problems, they pretended to be German for the rest of their trip – and everything went smoothly.

I encountered people from other nations pretending to be German before, in the mid-1960s at the time of General Suharto's coup and the subsequent unrest. Germans had to show on Java their nationality by flying a flag or a pennant on their cars to avoid being harassed. Sales of German flags increased enormously as a result, because company representatives from other countries also used the German flags, so that soon they ceased to be effective.

Ill. 17-10, You see T-shirts with German logos everywhere. On young …
Ill. 17-11, … and old

Ill. 17-12, Street in Banda Neira

The roads on Banda Neira are narrow, and really only passable on a motor-cycle. During my nearly three weeks on the Bandas I only saw one car driving in the town of Banda Neira. It belonged to the Director of the islands' only bank. The police, the doctor and the little hospital were also said to have motor vehicles. There's nowhere you can really go by car, except in the village of Banda Neira and a few hundred metres around the town. No need to worry about traffic jams. On the other inhabited islands there are only motor bikes and no cars at all. For his Cilu Bintang Estate, Abba acquired a practical little motor tricycle with a large load space.[339]

Because of the forced settlement of slaves from mainly Islamic areas by the Dutch colonists, the population of the Bandas is predominantly Muslim. 95% are Muslims and only 5% – now probably even fewer – are Christian or belong to another religious community. Several times a day the loud-speakers on the minarets of the mosques blare out strongly Arabic sounding music and calls to prayer in every village on the islands. But when I walked through the village and listened to the music coming out through the open windows of the houses, the style of the music reminded very much of the *fado* I had encountered on the Cape Verde Islands.

339 See Ill. 15-2

Illustrations this side:

Ill. 17-13
Little coffee bars on the
side of the street

Ill. 17-14
The kiosks sell products
made in the Spice islands

Illustrations next side:

Ill. 17-15
This is a betjak, a bicycle
rickshaw, a common
means of transport

Ill. 17-16
Candied nutmeg peel, cin-
namon and nutmeg juice
are available everywhere

Ill. 17-17, The narrow lanes are only passable on foot

There is a new middle class on the Bandas. Many women are independent and run their own businesses. They are certain that this is the result of good education, and so they save to send their children to secondary school and university. On the other hand, an increasing number of Muslim women follow strict Islamic belief and cover their hair with the hijab. This seems very contradictory to me.

In January 1999, sectarian conflict between Christians and Muslims flared up in Ambon. Thousands of fanatical Islamists went to the Moluccas from Java to support their co-religionists against the Christians. The situation escalated. Even the mainly Muslim police and the military took part in the fighting. About 10,000 people, mostly Christians, were killed – just for being Christian. Several thousand non-Muslim men were forcibly circum-cised by fanatical Muslims using crude and insanitary methods. Many died from the resulting infection.

The conflict threatened to spill over to the Bandas. The Christians, who had lived there for generations, were evacuated. Des Alwi, himself a Mus-lim, organised an Indonesian naval vessel to bring the Bandanese Christians to safety in the Christian village of Suli on Ambon island. Very few of them returned to the Bandas.

Moslems on the Bandas told me the Christians had been taken to safety! In the city of Ambon, I spoke to Christians who had lived on the Bandas for generations. They claimed that they had been forced to leave the island by the Muslims. They had been deported. It all depends on where you're looking from! I was unable to find out if Christians had been harmed on the Bandas during the confrontations. No one, Moslem or Christian, wanted to talk to me about it. A veil of silence has fallen over the incident – even the minister of the only church in Banda Neira couldn't be persuaded to speak out. She simply said that before the incidents, her church in Banda Neira had always been full.

Although I'm not a churchgoer, I went to the services in the church on Banda Neira on Christmas Eve and Christmas Day. I counted the flock on both occasions: Twelve.[340] During the services, armed military police with machine pistols at the ready, patrolled around the church. One of the sol-diers was filming all the congregation. When I asked what it was for, I was told that it was for our security – for the security of the Christians. It seems that the situation is still tense – but no one wants to talk about it. There are many unanswered questions. Where did the Bandanese Christians end up? Were they all driven out? Or did they stay at home even when there was a Christmas service for fear of being attacked?

One thing did strike me: when the little bell on the church rings out for the service, the muezzin in the main mosque starts blaring out its amplified, multidirectional singsong. The little bell has little chance of being heard. Is it some sort of religious competition? Have the tensions between Muslims and Christians still not calmed down? Or are they just beginning? When I walked through villages on the island, I didn't sense anything of the kind. All the Bandanese were extremely polite and friendly with me, which is unprecedented, when you think what terrible times their ancestors suffered under Dutch – Christian – colonial rule.

---

340 I discovered from old documents that around 1850 there were still approxi-mately 1,500 Christians living on the Bandas, of whom 500 were Europeans.

Ill. 17-18, The old Dutch church in Banda Neira (dating from 1873)

Ill. 17-19, The thinly attended Christmas service

Ill. 17-20, Evidence of Dutch colonial rule carved into gravestones in the floor of the church.

Ill. 17-21, ibid.

Ill. 17-22, ibid.

Ill. 17-23, The VOC logo, „the symbol of Hate", as a Bandanese said to me

I then managed to find out from a Bandanese Muslim – who asked me not to name him – some details about the excesses of 1999. He told me that after the unrest broke out on Ambon, the Banda Islands were initially spared from religious conflict. However, on the night of the 19th to 20th of April 1999 young Muslim fanatics had murdered the family of a former Dutch plantation owner. Then any pretence of restraint was abandoned. A rowdy mob of Muslims thronged through the streets. The houses of the Christians and the mostly Christian Chinese were set aflame. Two days later, at the instigation of Des Alwi, the Christians were evacuated to the uninhabited island of Hatta and then to Ambon island. Now my interest was aroused, and I decided to try and find out what had happened to one of the descendants of a Dutch perkenier.

The Dutchman, who lived on Banda Besar, was Pongky van der Broecke. He was a descendant of the Pieter van den Broecke whose portrait hangs in the Banda Neira Museum and in the Mutiara Guesthouse.[341] Although all Dutch possessions were nationalised after Indonesian independence, Pongky's father was allowed to remain on Banda Besar. With his workers – who were all now state employees – he successfully farmed his plantation. Pongky van der Broecke was born there in 1956. His mother and grandmother were Muslims, and because of them he converted to Islam. Since he was a descendant of the Dutch colonists he was not accepted in Muslim society, even by moderate Muslims. In 1990 Pongky took over the farm from his father.

Now their Dutch past caught up with the family. When the mob stormed the house, Pongky's father, his wife and both the children who were there were murdered. The house was looted and set on fire. Pongky and one child survived the massacre, since they happened to be on Java at the time.

I wasn't able to find out anything about what happened to Pongky after that. Today there are only a few blackened stone walls where once their elegant colonial mansion stood.

My informant told me that nearly all the old colonial buildings in Banda Neira were burned down too. There is no trace of this today, nothing to remind us of the excesses of 20 years ago. The Christians didn't return to the Bandas after the evacuation and had to sell their lands and houses – often in prime locations – at prices far below their real value.

Today the Banda Islands are inhabited by the descendants of slaves brought in from Java, New Guinea, Timor, India and East Africa, as well as of condemned criminals from Macassar. They were all brought there by force by the Dutch colonial rulers. Europeans, too, have contributed to the gene pool here: first the Portuguese in their relations with the original native inhabitants, then the Dutch *perkeniers* and their descendants. Not forgetting the merchants from Arabia and China. You will find all skin colours from pale to dark, and raven black hair from smooth to curly. The Banda Islands are a human and cultural melting pot. And it is impossible to overlook a considerable proportion of people of Arabian descent. In 1936, during his exile, Sutan Sjahrir wrote home to his wife: *... Everyone here has their own history of their ancestral mixture, though there is always a touch of the Arabian beside other origins. ... The Arabs became Bandanese. Some of them still speak Arabic and there are even some who occasionally stroll around with a red fez on their heads ...*

---

341 See Chapter 16

When Somerset Maugham visited the Banda islands in the 1920s, he was struck not just by the sun-burned Dutchmen with their stout, listless wives, but also by the Arabs in particular. He writes:[342]

[There were] a number of Arabs, some in smart tarbouches[343] and neat suits of duck, others in white caps and sarongs; they were dark-skinned, with large shining eyes, and they had the Semitic look of the merchants of Tyre and Sidon[344]. There were Malays, Papuans and half-castes.

One result of this exotic mixture of several races is that there are extremely attractive women on all the islands – this struck me most of all on the furthermost Island of Run. Is this a faint trace of those Englishmen from the early expeditions who married native women and settled here permanently?

I tried to ask several people about their ancestry. Hardly any of them had any detailed knowledge. They might just about remember their grandparents. One exception to this is the families of Arabian descent – mostly quite well-off – who have detailed genealogies, some of which go back hundreds of years.It was only towards the end of my stay that I met a local inhabitant who knew a bit more. He had quite pale skin and there was obviously European blood in his veins. I spoke to him, and he told me proudly that his great-grandfather had been a Dutch official who had had four wives and countless children – he had no idea how many.

Banda Neira has a small hospital with a doctor. It is extremely clean, and I was able to chat to the friendly staff – I wanted my blood pressure taken. To the nurses' disappointment it was normal. They still had some beds free, they said, and would gladly have admitted me.

They cannot perform major operations here. Not even caesareans, which have become customary here in Indonesia. I was told that two or three mothers die every year because they can't have their babies by caesarean. Ambon is too far for emergencies. With the irregular shipping connections and the bad weather conditions, it can take up to two weeks to get there. The hospital doctor also regularly visits the neighbouring island, Banda Besar. On Pulau Ai and Pulau Run there are only a paramedic and a nurse. It is better to be healthy if you want to visit the Bandas.

Illustrations next page:
Ill. 17-24, People of the Banda Islands
Ill. 17-25, ibid.

---

342 W. Somerset Maugham, *The Narrow Corner*, p. 91
343 Another word for fez
344 In ancient times Tyre and Sidon were the most important Phoenician trading centres in the eastern Mediterranean

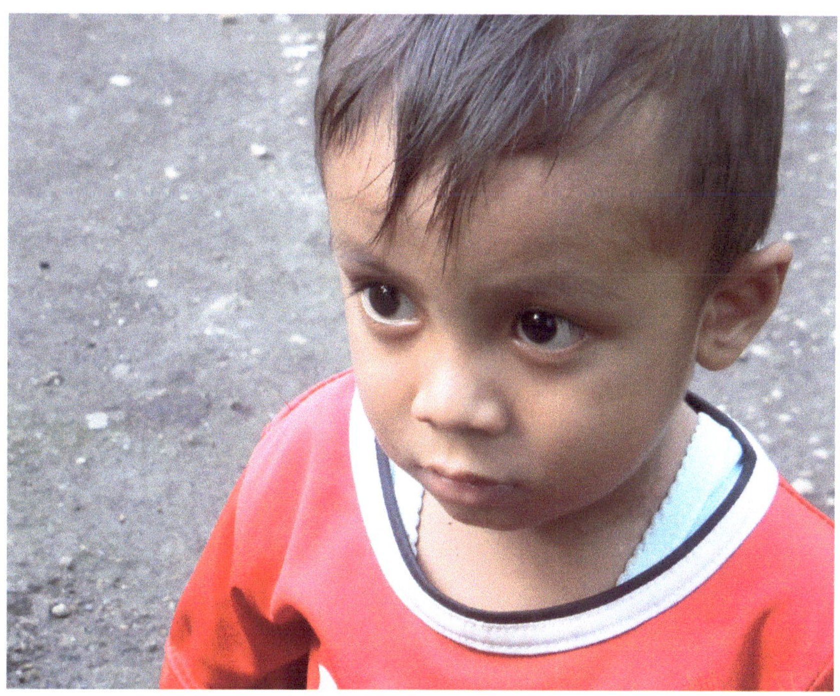

Ill. 17-26, A happy child

Ill. 17-27, ibid.

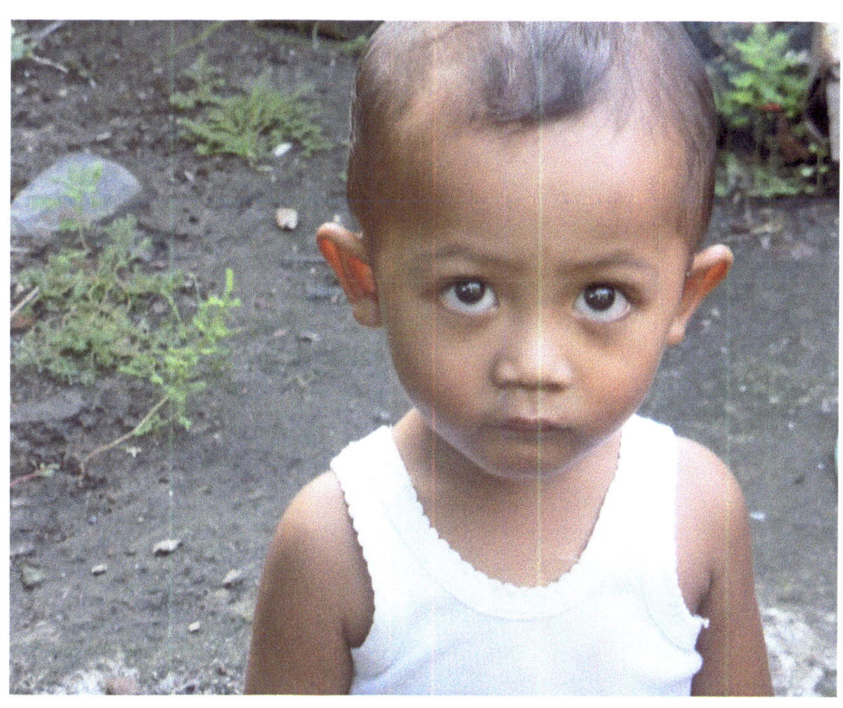

Ill. 17-29, ibid.

I always like visiting fish markets when I travel around the world – which obviously also includes the fish market in the port of Banda Neira. Nearly every day I went to see what the fishermen had landed. Tuna of all sizes, of course. In Ambon a smaller fish, a kind of herring, seems to be popular, and they ship them there by the box-load, packed in ice. Since the decline in nutmeg production, the fishing industry has become much more important.

A fisherman offered me a tuna fresh from the sea. It weighed about two kilograms, and he wanted the equivalent of 3 Euros for it! But what could I do with two kilograms of fish? There were always fresh tuna steaks in the Cilu Bintang Estate. Near the port, naked children were playing in the crystal-clear water and just a few metres offshore the fishermen in their broad-brimmed hats had cast their lines from their boats. It was a peaceful idyll.

Ill. 17-30 and Ill. 17-31
The fish market in Banda Neira

Ill. 17-32
A fisherman brings his
catch home

Ill. 17-33
Most vegetables are
imported from Ambon
or Java

Banda Neira is quite a compact town where you can get to all the sights in a few minutes on foot. When you saunter through the streets, you inevitably come across little restaurants, and next to them historical buildings with massive arcades. Rusty cannons line the streets. In the centre of town there are the houses where Mohammad Hatta and Sutan Sjahrir lived in exile. The buildings have been lovingly restored and opened to interested visitors. The fittings of the houses, from dining tables to typewriters, have been preserved in their original condition, and look as if the two national heroes had only moved out yesterday. It is remarkable how Indonesia values its more recent history: the Indonesians tend to regard their history as beginning only after the declaration of independence in 1945 and the subsequent bloody colonial war with the Dutch. A veil is thrown over their pre-independence history. They are still *malu* [ashamed] that their enormous territory in the Malay Archipelago allowed itself to be suppressed for 350 years by what was in comparison a European dwarf, Holland. The aggressors were simply better armed.

Many of the guesthouses are museums in themselves. One example is the Mutiara Guesthouse, which is also owned by Abba and was opened in 2007. It is more than sumptuously decorated with antique treasures from the colonial period. Old VOC porcelain plates are next to countless coins and muskets. Here, too, the portrait of Pieter van den Broecke, who has also been described in Chapter 16, hangs next to a large number of antique maps. As well as all these antiques, Abba has an extensive library of books about the Bandas here.

Fortunately, there is as yet no mass tourism on the Banda Islands, but they have already made preparations for a possible future stream of tourists. Cultural tours are very rare, in spite of the rich cultural offering here. The tourists are mainly young people who come to Banda Neira for the scuba diving. There are a few simple guesthouses on all the inhabited islands, and they are constantly frequented by divers who wish to see the beautiful banks of coral on the submarine cliffs. All the islands except Banda Neira also have beaches of fine white sand, which are almost always solitary and deserted. On Banda Neira there are a large number of acceptable guesthouses.

I have already written about Des Alwi, who was forced into exile by President Sukarno in Chapter 13. After the coup in 1965 when General, later President, Suharto, seized power, he returned home from Kuala Lumpur. As a freedom fighter, historian, writer and film maker he played a decisive role in the country now known as Indonesia. He was particularly active on Banda Neira, his birthplace, becoming a legendary figure who is still revered there. In Banda Neira he married Anna Marie Mambu, a granddaughter of the wealthy pearl fisherman and nutmeg farmer Said Baadilla. They had three children, who survived Des Alwi: two daughters, Mira and Tanya, and a son, Ramon Alwi. Des Alwi published several books and made a number of films, mostly documentaries: for example, he made one about Vice President Mohammad Hatta. Various business interests made him rich, and he invested his money in the Bandas.

Des Alwi returned to Banda Neira permanently in the early to mid-1970s. The Maulana Hotel, which he built in pseudo-colonial style in the 1980s, and which today exudes a morbid charm, is still owned by the family, as is the Baba Lagoon Hotel. Both hotels are right next to the sea near the port.

Des Alwi was an exemplary environmentalist. He would chase local fishermen in his speedboat if he heard that they were fishing with dynamite or carbide. If he heard a chainsaw anywhere, he'd get on his motorbike, even at the age of 80, and track down the miscreant in the woods. Des Alwi, the uncrowned 'King of the Banda Islands', died just before his 83rd birthday. He made an unparalleled contribution to the development of the island group.

This tradition of conservation is being continued by the family, as Des Alwi would have wanted. They have employed a German couple to run their diving centre[345] near the Baba Lagoon Hotel. Tuta is an experienced diving instructor and his wife Mareike has a doctorate in marine biology. She has spent several years observing various species of coral in order to monitor any changes as soon as they occur.

They are both founding members of the Verein Banda Sea e.V. [Banda Sea Association, Registered (Voluntary) Assocation] with its registered office in Bonn. The goal of the association is to restore the condition of marine and coastal environments in the Banda Sea and/or to ensure that they are protected and preserved.

In the 1990s there was practically no plastic on the Bandas, but now plastic has become a problem here too. Mareike, as a marine biologist, has declared war on plastic waste in the sea and initiated the collection of waste in Banda Neira. She has arranged for children on Banda Neira and other islands to be taught about the problems caused by plastic and to be aware of what they can do to help. We can only hope that her efforts are successful in the long term.

It's hard to believe that in the past world-famous celebrities were among Des Alwi's guests in this remote place. Diana, Princess of Wales, was a guest in the Maulana Hotel in 1994, and looked out over the narrow strait at Gunung Api volcano. In the foyer of the hotel there is a faded portrait of Prin-

---

345 Bluemotion Dive Center Banda

Ill. 17-34
In the Maulana
Hotel

Ill. 17-35
Here too a
solitary cannon
is aimed out
to sea

cess Diana with a signed dedication. The portrait, which she
dedicated to Des Alwi, is said
to have been painted during her
stay by an artist from Jakarta.

Ill. 17-36,
Portrait of Princess Diana

Also Mick Jagger, the British
rock-star and lead singer of the
Rolling Stones, and Sarah Fer-
guson, Prince Andrew's ex-wife,
enjoyed the solitude of the Banda Islands in the Maulana hotel.

What brought these famous
people to this isolated place?
Was it the remoteness of the
islands? Here they could walk
around unrecognised and without being harassed. You can
understand why Jacques Cou-

steau, who came to Banda Neira in his own ship, visited the Bandas. He
explored and filmed in the sea here, because the coral reefs around the
Bandas are among the most beautiful in the world, with an enormous profusion of marine creatures which have aroused enthusiasm since the time
of Rumphius, to whom I will return. But the others? Was there an element
of nostalgia involved? After all, the English were allied to the Bandanese
on Ai and Run for many years and – unlike the Dutch – were regarded as
friends by them.

Nowadays, Banda Neira has a little airport; a 12-seat Cessna occasionally
flies here from Ambon. There is no fixed timetable; you're very lucky if you
happen to catch a flight to Banda Neira. The runway stretches across the
whole width of the island and even had to be extended out to sea by means
of material dumped to form a causeway. Since there was nowhere flat on the
island that was long enough for a runway, it was laid out uphill. No matter
where the wind is blowing, they land in an uphill direction and take off
downhill. I haven't yet had the pleasure of landing here, but I hope – if I
should ever return – to get a flight next time. After all, I now know Umar,
the fixer on Ambon.

Ill. 17-37, The runway, but no aircraft. I tried to take off, but no luck.

Ill. 17-38, The narrow alleyways in the villages on Banda Neira

274

I explored the island of Banda Beira on the pillion of Saudara Iskandar's motorcycle taxi; most lanes were too narrow for a car. I also visited Saudara Iskandar's family in the village of Mangkobatu in the north of the island, and enjoyed a cinnamon tea under a nutmeg tree in his garden. On my tour, I was struck by the fact that outside the main township of Banda Neira[346] all the signs of the Dutch colonial past are mouldering away. I also noticed this on all the other Banda Islands. It was particularly apparent in the Dutch cemeteries. Some of them were even being used as rubbish dumps.

In my quest to find the name Van der Smissen, one of my Dutch ancestors[347], who traded with the Dutch East Indies – with spices in particular – I examined the gravestones of hundreds of Dutch people who were buried here between the 17th and 19th centuries. Van der Smissen was not among the names I found. There were old Dutch children's graves without any name on them everywhere. The chances of survival on the Bandas a few centuries ago were not particularly great. All the former Dutch cemeteries I visited were completely overgrown with weeds. There was often even a lonely grave in an untidy backyard.

Ill. 17-39, An overgrown Dutch cemetery

346 Both the island and the capital are called Banda Neira
347 Van der Smissen was the father-in-law of my great-great-great-great-uncle, the Mennonite Johann Wilhelm Mannhardt

275

Ill. 17-40
The gravestones
are often hard
to find

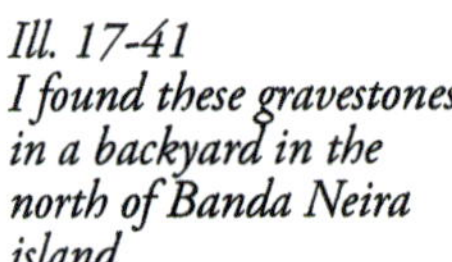

Ill. 17-41
I found these gravestones
in a backyard in the
north of Banda Neira
island

Ill. 17-42
Anonymous
children's
graves in a
rubbish tip in
Banda Neira

During my stay on Banda Neira I was lucky enough to see an unscheduled *Kora Kora* dragon-boat race. The races go back to an initiative of Des Alwi's: dragon boats from all the inhabited Banda Islands compete with one another. The narrow boats were about 25 metres long and painted in gaudy colours, one yellow, one blue and a third bright red. I discovered that all three boats were from Banda Neira Island and that the race was just for the amusement of the paddlers.

There were about 30 of them in each boat, naked from the waist up; there were also a captain, a helmsman, two men whose only job was to bail the water out of the boat and two musicians. One of the musicians was a drummer who beat the time and the other beat two little gongs, each with a different pitch. The paddlers timed the frequency of their strokes by the rhythm of the drum and the gongs, getting faster and faster, and then raised their paddles upright for a few seconds, letting the boat glide through the water and then starting all over again. The captain stood giving orders in the middle of the boat next to the central flagstaff. It was wonderful to watch the boats racing across the water with their fluttering banners. Boat races like this are found in New Zealand and all over the Pacific islands.

Ill. 17-43, The Kora Kora dragon boats: ready for the start

Ill. 17-44
Jolly diving inst-
ructor Nyello of the
Bluemotion Dive
Center in Banda
Neira gives the
orders

Ill. 17-45
I was invited to take
part in the paddling,
but declined with
thanks

The telephone and the Internet have arrived on the island of Banda Neira. There has only been electricity since the 1990s. There is even a photovoltaic solar farm on Banda Neira. I went there several times, but never met anybody. It was my impression that the facility was no longer – or not yet – working. Perhaps it is only for use in emergencies. It would have interested me to find out, since I was responsible for providing electricity to the villages on the island of Sumba in NTT[348] with equipment of precisely this type.[349] Unfortunately I couldn't find a single person to give me any sensible information.

Ill. 17-46
Photovoltaic solar farm for generating electricity on Banda Neira

I was surprised by the speed and stability of the Internet connection. They told me that a submarine glass-fibre connection had been laid between Ambon and Banda Neira. In the fields of telecommunications and Wi-Fi Indonesia is a world leader, and in many areas of digitisation is far ahead of Germany. But I am not sure if what they say about a glass fibre cable can be true. With those enormous depths of water? I have my doubts.

And on every street corner you can see (mainly) young people peering at their smartphones. In the old days the Bandanese were worried about survival, but today their only concern is: Where's the Wi-Fi connection? Where can I charge my smartphone? Have I missed something on Facebook? The Bandas have arrived in the 21st century!

While I was staying in the Cilu Bintang Estate, a Swabian couple, journalist and best-selling author Gunter Haug[350] and his wife Karin, were also pass-

348 NTT=Nusa Tenggara Timur, south east of Bali
349 See Horst H. Geerken, *A Gecko for Luck,* pp. 346 ff
350 https://www.gunter-haug.de/

ing through. We got on like a house on fire from the very beginning and had many an interesting conversation. On his return home to Stuttgart, Gunter wrote an article about me which appeared in the *Stuttgarter Zeitung* on the 31st of January 2019. You can read it in Chapter 25, Appendix I.

In my books I have written about the air of mystery that surrounds Indonesia's first President, Sukarno, even today.[351] Sukarno is still highly regarded and revered all over Indonesia. In his own lifetime, people swore that Sukarno could be in two places at once; when he was imprisoned by the Dutch, he could also be seen walking around openly on the streets. The villagers of Tampaksiring still regularly hear Sukarno's voice ringing out from his palace on Bali.

Or when the Bali Beach Hotel, built on his orders, burned down in January 1984, the only parts of the hotel that survived unharmed were the two rooms which had been permanently reserved for him and where he had often stayed. Or in 1963 when, shortly before Gunung Agung volcano erupted on Bali, he had all the people who lived near the volcano evacuated by the military, saving thousands of lives. 'Or' – there are so many stories which keep the Sukarno myth alive.

I was surprised to discover that Sukarno's magic has even reached the Bandas. In the town of Lonthoir on Banda Besar there is a mystic to whom he regularly appears. The mystic claims that he has regular encounters with him. He is convinced that Sukarno is still alive and living on Banda Besar. Sukarno is simply *moksa*, immortal! Perhaps Sukarno's 'second self' lives on Banda Besar, even though he never visited the Bandas. Unfortunately, much though I would have liked to meet him, I didn't manage to see the mystic of Banda Besar. Perhaps I'll be luckier next time.

The most impressive buildings on Banda Neira are still the historic Fort Nassau and the nearby, now renovated Fort Belgica on its hill. Fort Belgica is a favourite tourist attraction for the inhabitants of the Bandas or visitors from the Moluccas. I've never met a single foreign tourist in the forts. Since both forts are remarkable reminders of the Dutch colonial period on the Bandas, I will include a few of the photographs I took in 2018. The two forts – like all the streets and front gardens on the Bandas – make a very neat and tidy impression. Fort Belgica is regularly swept, and the garden is well looked after. Given that there are so few foreign tourists, and that funds are limited, this is admirable.

---

351 See Horst H. Geerken, *A Gecko for Luck,* pp. 171ff (especially 177 ff, 181f)

Ill. 17-47, In the foreground an old well, the exterior wall of Fort Nassau with the Cilu Bintang Estate in the background

Ill. 17-48, The courtyard of Fort Nassau with the entrance gate

Ill. 17-49, Fort Belgica on its hill

Ill. 17-50, The courtyard of Fort Belgica

282

Ill. 17-51, Gunung Api is always there

Ill. 17-52, Fort Belgica is only separated from the volcano by a narrow strait

Ill. 17-53, Schoolchildren always like foreigners to take their picture

Illustration next page:

Ill. 17-54, The island and town of Banda Neira with the main tourist attractions
Key to the map:

1. Petrol Station
2. Bluemotion Dive Center
3. Maulana Hotel
4. Harbour/ Pier
5. Chinese Temple
6. Fish Market
7. Traditional Market
8. Boats to the other islands
9. Bank Rakyat Indonesia/ ATM
10. The old church
11. Rumah Budaya Museum
12. Captain Christopher Cole's House
13. Mutiata Guesthouse
14. Fort Belgica
15. Cilu bintang Estate
16. Mayor's Office
17. Fort Nassau
18. Hospital
19. Post Office
20. Hatta's house
21. PELNI shipping line office
22. VOC Governor's Palace
23. Police
24. Dr Tjipto Mangoenkoesoemo's House
25. Aviastar airline office
26. Islamic cemetery
27. Army headquarters
28. Christian cemetery
29. Chinese cemetery
30. Airport
31. Malole Beach

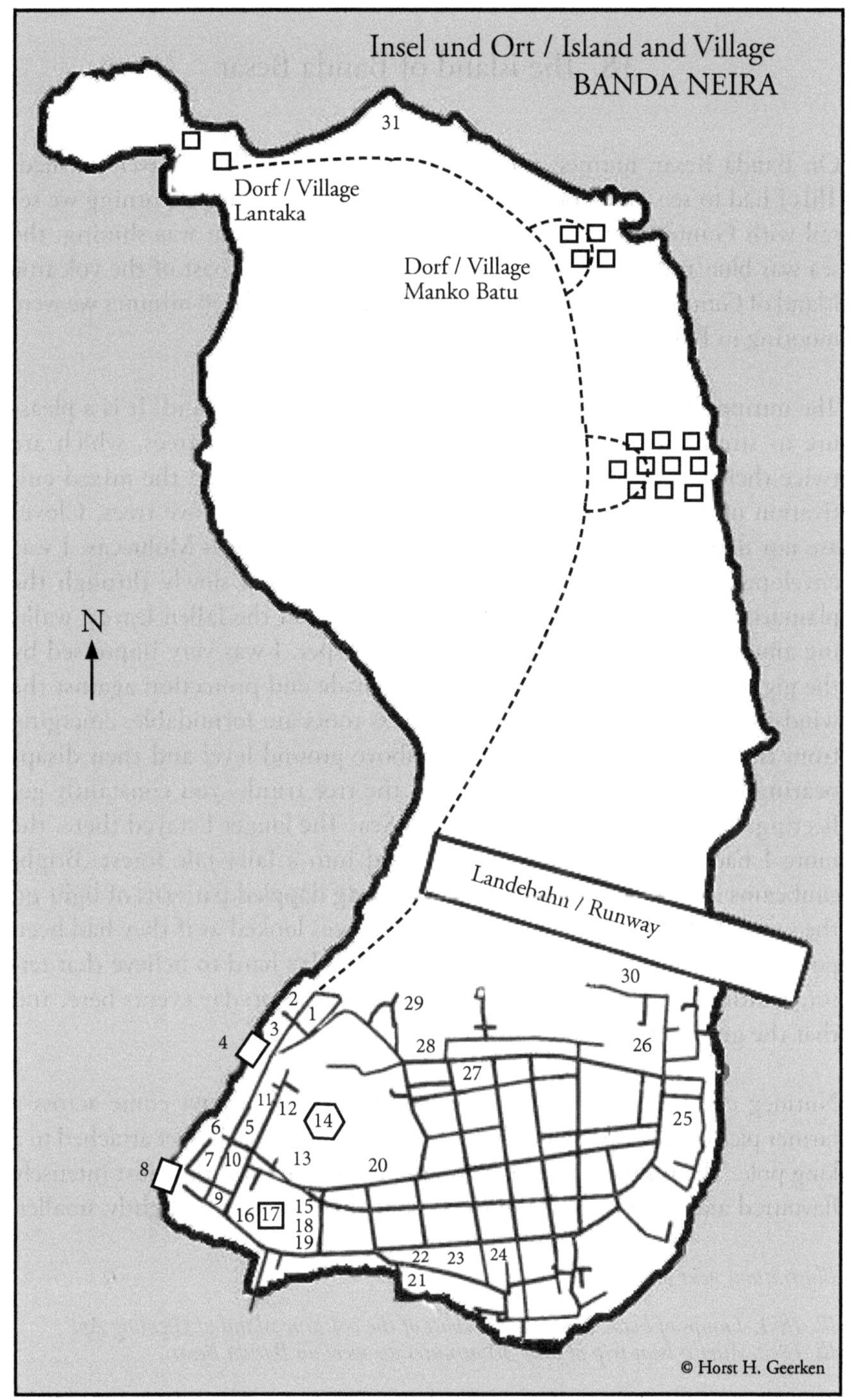

Insel und Ort / Island and Village
BANDA NEIRA
N
Dorf / Village
Lantaka
Dorf / Village
Manko Batu
Landebahn / Runway
© Horst H. Geerken
31
30
29
28
27
26
25
2
1
3
4
11
12
14
6
5
7
10
13
20
8
9
16
17
15
18
19
22
23
24
21

18. The island of Banda Besar

On Banda Besar, nutmeg and the kenari nut are still intensively farmed. This I had to see. Abba organised a boat, and the very next morning we set sail with Gunter und Karin, the two Swabians. The sun was shining, the sea was blue and calm. Lumps of black lava lined the coast of the volcanic island of Gunung Api. It was a short boat trip; after only 30 minutes we were mooring in Banda Besar.

The nutmeg plantations remind me of well-tended parkland. It is a pleasure to stroll beneath the nutmeg trees and the kenari trees, which are twice their height. The plantations are mostly devoted to the mixed cultivation of nutmeg, kenari, cinnamon and occasional clove trees. Cloves are not native here, but were an import from the North Moluccas. I was enveloped in a delicate, sweet aroma as I wandered slowly through the plantation. With the green, well-mown grass and the fallen leaves, walking among the trees is like treading on a carpet. I was very impressed by the gigantic kenari trees, which provide shade and protection against the wind for the nutmeg trees. Their buttress roots are formidable, emerging from the trunk two or three metres above ground level and then disappearing beneath the surface. Between the tree trunks you constantly get fleeting views of the blue of the Banda Sea. The longer I stayed there, the more I had the feeling of having strayed into a fairy-tale forest. Bright sunbeams shone between the leaves, creating dappled patterns of light on the ground. The lush green of the nutmeg trees looked as if they had been polished. Peaceful, delightful silence reigned. It's hard to believe that terror, murder and exploitation by the Dutch were everyday events here, and that the ground was soaked in blood.

Nutmeg can be harvested all year round. You will always come across a farmer picking the ripe, yellow fruit from the tree with a basket attached to a long pole. The nutmegs produced on the Bandas are still the most intensely flavoured and expensive in the world, but they are mostly slightly smaller.

Illustrations next page:

Ill. 18-1, Lumps of black lava line the coast of the volcanic island of Gunung Api.
Ill. 18-2, After a boat trip of only 30 minutes we were on Banda Besar.

Ill. 18-3
Brightly coloured
steps lead to the
upper part of the
village

Ill. 18-4
A nutmeg planta-
tion: a fairy-tale
forest

Next page:

Ill. 18-5
A break in the
plantation. Beside
me Karin, Gunter
Haug's wife

Ill. 18-6
The ripe fruits are
harvested from the
trees using a basket
attached to a long
pole

There is nowhere in the world that you can buy nutmegs that come exclusively from the Bandas – what you get is a mixture of nutmegs from several different areas.

The yellow nutmeg fruit reminds me, before it bursts open, of a large ripe apricot. All parts of the fruit are edible. A forest worker picked a ripe, open fruit off the tree for me. The peel was fleshy and tasted rather sweet, with a hint of nutmeg. The sweetened jam made from nutmeg peel that I was served at breakfast every day tasted better to me.

The forest worker was also collecting the nuts that had fallen from the kenari trees. The nuts, in their black shells, are a kind of almond, though rather milder tasting. They are extensively used in Bandanese cooking. I liked them very much and took lots of them home with me to Germany.

The way cinnamon is harvested is interesting. Cinnamon is the bark of the *kayu manis* tree, the tree with the 'sweet wood'. They remove a strip of bark and lay it in the sun to dry. The bark rolls up in the process. I tried the fresh bark, of course. It has a sweet and intense taste of cinnamon. The dried bark is then exported. In Europe it is then ground to make cinnamon powder and other products.

On this occasion I learned that nutmeg and other spices are still the Banda Islands' most important exports, ahead of fish. Nutmeg from the islands is exported exclusively to Europe. I bought a 1-kilogram sack of nutmeg from a producer: I was only charged 4 euros!

I naturally also visited Fort Hollandia which stands on a hill about fifty meters above sea level on Banda Besar. The fort, initially called Fort Lonthoir[352], was built with slave labour in 1624 – three years after Jan Pieterzoon van Coen's massacre. Soon afterwards, in 1743, it was destroyed by a powerful earthquake. Governor Francois van Boeckholtz ordered that it be rebuilt, since then the fort has lived through many earthquakes and volcanic eruptions, which means that it is now rather dilapidated and forlorn. But it has a wonderful view out across the sea to Gunung Api.

Everywhere, at the side of streets in the village, nutmegs and mace are laid out on raffia mats to dry in the sun. Though in the past there were big plantations farmed by the Dutch *perkeniers* and their slaves, today there are small peasant farmers who farm sections of a plantation and sell their fruit on their own account.

Illustration left page:

Ill. 18-7, At the foot of a kenari tree

352 Benteng Lonthoir

Ill. 18-8, Fort Hollandia is quite dilapidated

Ill. 18-9, From here there is a superb panoramic view over the sea to Gunung Api and of the lower part of the village

Ill. 18-10, Outside the houses and beside the paths there are nutmegs and …

Ill. 18-11, … mace lying in the sun to dry

19. A trip to Pulau Ai and Pulau Run

In December 2018 I made an effort to find a boat to take me to the islands of Ai and Run. The journey across is not without its dangers, since it is 20 kilometres of rough, open Banda Sea. The rainy season had begun, and the sea was becoming unpredictable. Storms meant that the seas were so high that there was no point in risking a crossing.

For several days I strolled around the port, assessing the boats tied up there and chatting to boat owners and fishermen. My final choice was a boat with three powerful outboard motors. It was a big wooden boat that was normally in service as a ferry between the islands. It was in good condition and Ibrahim the boatman seemed trustworthy. I negotiated with him, and we reached an agreement. As soon as the conditions at sea had calmed down, he would contact me. He'd need a mechanic and three other crewmen as well. In line with what had been recommended to me, I had gone for a wooden boat and not a fibreglass one: the fishermen told me that boats frequently capsized in sudden heavy seas when travelling between the islands. You could hang on to a wooden boat, but a fibreglass boat would sink immediately. I also checked that there were enough lifejackets on board – now nothing could go wrong.

It was a sunny morning, and the sky was blue; I was sitting at breakfast on the terrace outside my room. The view of Gunung Api was stunning as usual. At 8.15 AM my telephone rang. It was Ibrahim: the boat was ready, and the Banda Sea was relatively calm. We could sail! I should come down to the port. It was only five minutes on foot from the Cilu Bintang Estate. I wrapped up the rest of my breakfast. An omelette and toast and a big bottle of drinking water were my provisions for the trip.

The boat was ready at the pier, fuelled and with the whole crew on board. All I had to do was board, and we could leave. What a palaver – a captain and a crew of four just for me! It later turned out to be necessary, because we needed many hands. I chose a front row seat on the roof of the boat. The lookout boy was standing in front of me: his job was to watch for possible flotsam and later to guide the boat through the reefs.

We passed very close to Gunung Api. The volcanic island has a diameter of three kilometres. Now I could see the massive black lava streams reaching down to the sea on the other side of the mountain. The scars visible today were caused by the violent eruption in 1988.

Ill. 19-1
Front row seat in an
old tyre on the roof of
the boat

Ill. 19-2
Approaching Pulau
Ai. The lookout warns
us of shallows and
coral reefs

Ill. 19-3, There are deserted sandy beaches all round the island of Ai

Gunung Api is at the centre of a caldera that has mostly been flooded by the sea. If you consider that the volcano rises from the seabed 4,000 metres below and towers another 640 metres, you can see that this is quite some hill – and unbridled forces slumber within it.

We sailed for Ai first, reaching it after an hour. In the past sailing ships took at least a day for the journey even when the wind was favourable. So far, the sea had been relatively calm. Old chronicles tell us that when you approached the Banda Islands in a sailing ship you could smell the scent of the spices before seeing the islands. This is no longer the case: the exhaust fumes from the outboard motors fill the air.

Ai was Ibrahim's home island. We first visited the remains of Fort Re-venge, erected here by the English at the beginning of the 17th century and then taken by the Dutch in 1615/1616 against strong resistance from the English and the inhabitants of Ai. The Dutch extended the fort and re-named it Fort Revenge. The English nevertheless retained their economic and political influence on the island. Today Fort Revenge is just a ruin.

VOC General Governor Jan Pieterszoon van Coen created terrible havoc on Ai too. The whole population was killed or enslaved. They then brought slaves in to work on the plantations.

296

The other attractions of the island are the big nutmeg plantations under the tall kenari trees, the white, sandy beaches and best of all the still unspoilt coral reef all round the island with its wealth of marine and fish species. At its edge, the reef plunges down vertically for hundreds of metres. When I was snorkelling on the reef, I found it disturbing to move just a short distance from a depth of two metres of water and find myself looking down into the eerie unfathomable depths.

Ill. 19-4
The main street in the village of Ai

Ill. 19-5
The Main Gate of Fort Revenge

298

Rumphius[353] described the island of Ai as follows over 300 years ago:
The finest nutmeg groves are found on Poelo-Ay, which is an island about 2,000 paces long, but flat and covered everywhere with nutmeg trees ... they are so delightful to look at, and it is pleasurable to walk through them. They are so well tended that the whole island seems to be one continuous garden, which is bordered on the seaward side with little hillocks and wild bushes. ... There is a great shortage of fresh water on the island, but many townsfolk and garden-owners live there, who satisfy their needs from cisterns.

Not much has changed since Rumphius's time. There are still luxuriant, splendid, green nutmeg groves. The climate on Pulau Ai is not as humid as that on Banda Neira and Banda Besar. Because of its healthy climate the Dutch called the island *Oude mannen huis* [Old men's home]. Apart from the nutmeg trees there are very few other types of nut tree.

The island, whose population of roughly 1,000 lives on fishing and nutmeg farming, has only one village. We walked down the narrow streets through the village. Women were sitting on the verandas in front of their houses. They all gave me a friendly greeting. I had a feeling that I was bringing a little touch of variety into their monotonous lives. Throughout the village there were nutmegs drying in the tropical sun on woven mats beside the street.

Ibrahim told me that an Italian had lived on Ai for 22 years. He had married a local Muslim woman. Five years before, he had died in hospital in Ambon and been buried there. His widow still lived on Pulau Ai in a beautifully kept house right beside the beach. They are not so concerned about the properties of the old Dutch *perkeniers* here. Ibrahim showed me several old villas which were just being left to decay.

If the conditions allow it, there is a daily ferry from Ai to Banda Neira and Run. There is no fresh water on the island; they collect rainwater or ship water in from the other islands.

Ibrahim invited me to tea in his house, where I met his wife and his mother. We had to leave soon afterwards as dark clouds were gathering and the weather was getting worse. Ibrahim wanted to get to Run before the afternoon.

Illustrations left page:

Ill. 19-6, The Courtyard of Fort Revenge
Ill. 19-7, Dungeons in Fort Revenge

---

353 See Chapter 21

Ill. 19-8, Decaying old Dutch villa

Ill. 19-9, Village street on Ai

Ill. 19-10, Tea break with Ibrahim's wife and mother

Ill. 19-11, On we go! Gunung Api in the background

The journey was once more going to take a good hour. I settled down in comfort on the roof of the boat with an old tyre as a cushion. But as soon as we got out into the open sea, things became much less comfortable. The swell grew higher and higher and I had to hold on firmly on both sides to stop myself tumbling off the roof into the water. The boat began to pitch and toss in the high waves. It was getting too dangerous for me, and one of the crew helped me down into the lower part of the boat. The lookout was still standing forward on the roof, but now he had to hold tight to the mast so as not to fall overboard. The deck was continually swept with waves from the spray. Now the two other crewmen came into play. Every time the boat lurched a breaker would swamp the boat, and they both had to keep bailing the water out by hand so that the boat wouldn't fill up. It now became clear to me why Ibrahim needed such a big crew for just one single passenger.

Run is surrounded by a dangerous reef where countless ships have been wrecked. What a challenge it must have been in the old days for the mariners to navigate through the reefs without any charts and powered only by the wind. Even today, with charts and experienced navigators, it is often still impossible. Especially in the rainy season at the time of the West Monsoon, the island is frequently inaccessible for weeks: the wind blows from the west from October to March. In the dry season from April to October there is less wind, more sunshine, and it is a lot hotter.

The west wind was too strong and the swell was too high for us to be able to run in to the harbour on the west coast of Run. We had to anchor off the coral reef on the uninhabited lee side of the island. It was low tide, and the boat couldn't get any closer to the shore than about 100 metres – and I had to wade those 100 metres through knee-deep water over banks of coral. And what coral! Coral of all sizes gleaming in a host of colours, blue, reddish, green, yellow. Beautiful! Coral bleaching has not yet spread to these islands. I had to step very carefully on my way to the shore, checking where I could safely put my foot down. I naturally didn't want to damage any coral. My Bandanese companions were less careful. Jacques Cousteau, the pioneering marine explorer, came here with his boat Calypso and dived around the Banda Islands, including Run. The islands are still a divers' paradise.

After we got to the shore, my two companions led me to a narrow, barely discernible path which led through the jungle, over the crest of the island to the village on the other side. It went straight uphill, and the heat made the walk quite strenuous, because the hills here are up to 200 metres high.

Ill. 19-12, A stormy crossing

Ill. 19-13, They had to keep bailing water out of the boat

Ill. 19-14, On the left the headland of Run, on the right Nailakka

Ill. 19-15, On the lee side of the Island of Run

It looked as if very few people used the path, because it was overgrown in places. When the West Monsoon is blowing, the fishermen and other inhabitants of the island stay at home in their village and wait patiently – often for weeks – for the weather to improve.

The march through the jungle was hard work. Admittedly, the island is only two kilometres wide, but the path – because of the way it wound up the steep hill – was considerably longer. Previously the whole island was covered in nutmeg trees, but because of the destructive deforestation and removal of saplings by the Dutch and English in the past, I only saw the occasional isolated nutmeg or kenari tree. But they are now starting to replant the nutmeg groves – I saw many young trees which were not yet ready to fruit.

According to Wurffbain's[354] eyewitness account, Run – before the Dutch destroyed all the nutmeg trees – produced the finest, best and biggest nuts in the whole archipelago. After the trees were cut down, the island was said to be covered in nothing but scrub. The Dutch forbade any new settlements, but in spite of that a few fishermen lived on the coast in the 18th century. They were driven out by pirates in the 19th century, so that the island was uninhabited for a long time. In 1840 there were 20 people living there, who apparently drank only palm wine because of the poor quality of the water.[355]

Ill. 19-16, A narrow path leads through the jungle and over the hill to the village of Run

354 See Chapter 8
355 Dr O. Warburg, *Die Muskatnuss*, 1898, p. 153

Ill. 19-17
Fortunately I had one
of the crew to help me
because …

Ill. 19-18
… it was sometimes
impossible to see the
path

More and more trees grew because of the seeds spread by the island's pigeons, and now there are nutmeg plantations again. Arcadie and Eldorado are the biggest. Fortunately, the vegetation has recovered very quickly over time because of the tropical climate. The narrow path was often overgrown, and a way had to be hacked through. It obviously wasn't used much.

The climb up the hill and down into the village took an hour. The village of Run on the west coast finally came into sight. The sun was reflected in the metal roofs of several mosques. In the village they were starting to lay a concrete path for motorcycles which should eventually reach the east coast of the island. If I ever return, I hope the path will have been finished so that I can make the journey on a motorcycle taxi – or else that the sea is calm enough to be able to dock at the pier.

I strolled through the village, stopping here and there for a chat. More and more people gathered around me. In the monotony of their daily lives I was an attraction; a foreigner – and more than that, one who spoke their language – was something very much out of the ordinary. I found a simple little guesthouse: it was clean and quite acceptable. I decided that if I came back I would spend a few nights – in one of the remotest spots on the planet. I wouldn't starve; there was plenty of fish and other seafood.

Then I wanted to visit the tiny neighbouring island of Nailakka, which can even be reached on foot at low tide. I have already mentioned how historically important this little uninhabited island surrounded by coral reefs had been – even if it was only 200 metres in diameter. There had been a little English fort there, armed with three ship's cannons. The English used to withdraw there when threatened by a Dutch attack. There are no wells on Nailakka. The English only had rainwater to drink, and certainly could not have survived a siege for very long. Still, because of the abundance of fish in the waters around the island they would certainly not have gone hungry.

On this trip it wasn't possible to land on Nailakka because of the heavy seas. I was also warned that there were large snakes there, so I certainly didn't want to take any risks in this remote spot.

Run[356] is about three kilometres long and less than one kilometre wide. There are a bare 1,000 inhabitants, most of whom live in the village. There are no cars, as the roads are narrow and only suitable for the few motorcycles available her. It is very rare for a Western visitor to end up here. And certainly not in the rainy season.

---

356 For maps of Run see Chapter 5

Ill. 19-19, *The village and port of Run*
Ill. 19-20, *The pier where I had intended to dock*

Even for Indonesians, Run is the end of the world. Like all the Banda Islands, it is two time zones away from Jakarta. The electricity supply is limited to two hours in the evening, but almost every home still has satellite television.

The people are interesting. On all the Banda Islands I have frequently noticed an Arab element in the features, but it is particularly striking here. For some time now, the island has been connected to the telephone network and the Internet. In this respect Indonesia is very advanced, and in my opinion far ahead of Germany when it comes to Wi-Fi.

Apart from *singkong*[357] and sweet potatoes, hardly any vegetables grow here. The variety of fruit and vegetables on the market is limited. They are shipped in from Ambon and the other Banda Islands. Sometimes during the western monsoon season no boats are able to get to the island for weeks. Then the locals have to make do with whatever the island has to offer, but they can't live on nutmeg alone.

In 1649 the English built a small fortification, Fort Swan, on Run. It too was armed with three ship's cannons. But the fort was soon abandoned and fell into ruins. It was meant as protection against the Dutch. The English didn't otherwise need a fort to retreat to. They were, after all, friendly with the natives, who regarded them as their protectors.

There was supposed to have been a *rumah besi,* an iron house, built by the English. It is said to be in the south of the island and only accessible on foot. After my route march through the jungle, I didn't want to put myself through that. Anyway, I still had to get back over the mountain to the east coast where the boat was moored. I was told that it was a building made of iron with a common room and a bathroom. The English held their celebrations there. But why an iron house? For safety from Dutch attacks? I haven't seen it for myself.

I have my doubts about it anyway. Could a building made of iron survive several hundred years in the salty sea air? I don't think so! It would have corroded long ago. And, according to the descriptions the villagers gave me, all that's left is an iron framework with a roof. The Iron House is presumably a ruined trading post or storehouse, and the villagers have made up their own stories about it to add another attraction to the island's list.

However, one thing that gives me pause for thought is the fact that, according to the bills of lading which still survive, there was sheet lead and sheet iron on the ships that sailed from England on James Lancaster's expedition February 1601. For what purpose? It remains a puzzle.

357 Tapioca

Ibrahim insisted that we leave. He wanted to get back to Banda Neira as quickly as possible, because he was expecting a storm. Getting back to the boat was a little easier, since several hundred metres of the path up to the ridge from the village were already concreted.

The voyage back was stormy: my beloved red cap was blown overboard and vanished in the Banda Sea. I was glad when we finally moored in the port at Banda Neira. If I ever make the trip again, I'll make sure I have better weather!

Ill. 19-21, The return to Banda Neira

Illustrations next page:

Ill. 19-22, The island of Nailakka. At low tide it is possible – as you see – to walk across the beach and the reef to Run

Ill. 19-23, We are near Gunung Api again

20. The island of Ambon and the Amboyna[358] Massacre

Before travelling back to Bali I decided to spend a few days on the island of Ambon. I wanted to visit the old Dutch forts, Fort Victoria and Fort Amsterdam, and also to find information about the German naturalist and biologist Rumphius.

After I had been on the Banda Islands for two weeks and had collected a great deal of information, I went to the PELNI[359] office every day, to find out about a ship that would take me back to Ambon. The office was in a little hut about ten minutes' walk from the Cilu Bintang Estate. Even making an enquiry was a challenge, because at navel height in a glass window covered in advertisements and old timetables there were two small holes, through which you could talk to a lady who was invisible against the dark background inside. Tickets were also bought through these holes. To be understood, and to be able to understand what the lady inside was saying, I had to crouch down and bend my back at a right angle. At my age! A real challenge.

She told me that the PELNI liner *KM Pangrango* would dock in Banda Neira on the 30th of December. The next ship would not arrive in Banda Neira until two weeks later. That would be too late for me, and so I bought an economy class ticket for the *Pangrango* for only seven euros. Given my experiences on the overloaded and totally chaotic ship that brought me there, I would have preferred to fly. But unfortunately, although there was an airport, there were no flights! Not for several months! The runway is used by the local youth in the daytime as a playing field and a motorcycle racing track.

The *KM Pangrango* is a relatively small ship, a combination carrier for both freight and passengers, which entered service in 1995. It has only two dormitories and is designed to take about 500 passengers. It regularly sails the route through the Moluccas and makes deliveries to a number of small islands. About every three or four weeks it docks at Banda Neira, once on the way to Ambon, and once on the return voyage.

Illustrations next page:

Ill. 20-1, At the PELNI ticket office
Ill. 20-2, Buying a ticket exercises the back

---

358 Previously Amboyna, now Ambon
359 Pelayaran Nasional Indonesia, Indonesian State Shipping Line

LOKET PENJUALAN TIKET
BUKA
OPEN

Ill. 20-3, The runway on Banda Neira. Gunung Agung is always close

Ill. 20-4, The KM Pangrango ...

Ill. 20-5, ... at the pier in front of the Maulana Hotel

The ship docked at the quay in Banda Neira in the morning, so that it was possible for me to board early. It was just as filthy and run-down as the *KM Leuser*. I chatted to the ship's cook, and we agreed on a deal. He rented me his cabin for the night for 20 euros, as I had no desire to spend the night in a dormitory with several hundred other people. He also promised that the bed would be freshly made, and that he would provide me with food. At two o'clock I went on board, and found that everything was as he had promised. I was happy to have a clean bed and a cabin to myself.

But where were the passengers? The ship arrived empty, and now only two locals came on board. My fears that the ship would be overcrowded turned out – this time – to be groundless. The ship sailed at 4 o'clock in the afternoon on the dot.

After we cast off, I went up to the bridge. The friendly captain invited me to have a coffee and said that I could come up to the bridge any time I liked, day or night. Once we had left the narrow strait between Banda Neira and Gunung Api, we were accompanied by flying fish. They would break the surface of the water and fly away from the ship. I remained on the bridge until sunset. Twilight was very short, as it always is in the tropics. I walked round the ship and counted only seven passengers, all locals, of course. The dormitories were completely empty. What a difference from the outward voyage on the *KM Leuser*.

Ill. 20-6, The dormitories were completely empty

Ill. 20-7, My cabin, four bunks for just me

Ill. 20-8, On the bridge

Ill. 20-9, A last look at Banda Neira …

Ill. 20-10, … and then we sailed off – past volcanic rocks – into the wide Banda Sea.

Ill. 20-11, Gunung Api was the last thing to fade out of sight

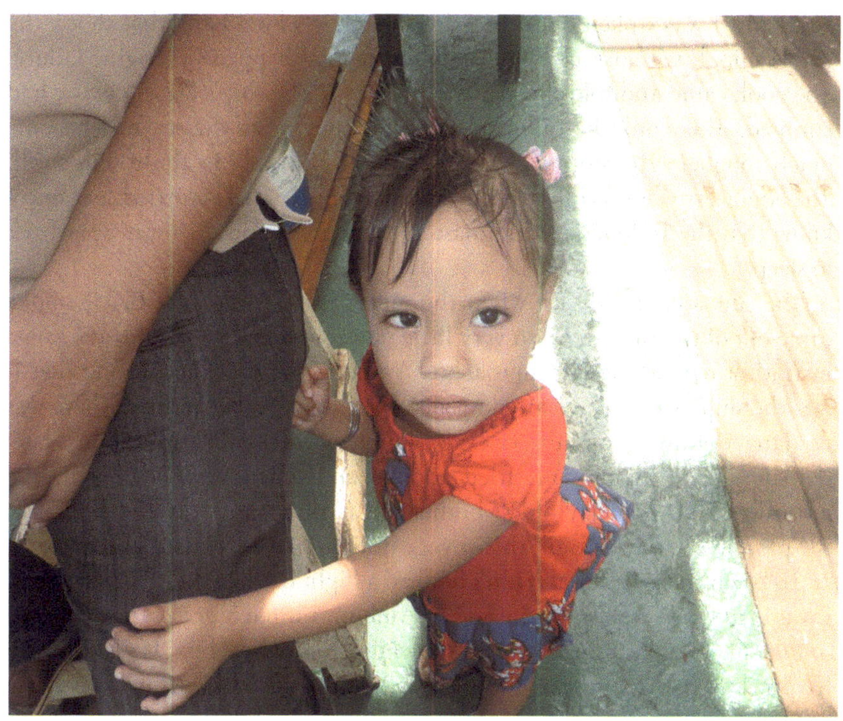

Ill. 20-12, A little boy gives the 'foreigner' a frightened look

The ship was not even 25 years old and already in terrible condition. It was not only filthy, it was also run-down. Rusty ironwork had simply been painted over, and the poor condition of the steel hawsers from which the lifeboats hung led me to the conclusion that the boats hadn't been moved for years. I just had to hope that there wouldn't be an emergency. On the ship's hull there were welded joints that had burst and not been repaired. It was a real floating death trap!

Soon afterwards I retired to my cabin. This was where the advantage of having the cook's cabin was revealed: I was served with mouth-watering fried rice, vegetables and fried chicken. I couldn't eat it all. Later the cook brought me a dessert of pudding[360] and fruit salad. The cook was a skinny, bustling man. Unusually skinny for a cook. He treated me like a son. Was I still hungry? More chicken? Do you need anything else? No, I just wanted to be left in peace! I went to bed early. The rocking of the ship quickly sent me to sleep.

---

360 [Translator's note: In Germany (and the USA) the word 'pudding' is used to describe a custard-like milk dessert]

Suddenly, I was woken out of my deep sleep by a loud bang that shook the whole ship. It was just after midnight. What had happened? Engine failure. The cook came and told me that the pistons in the ship's diesel engine had jammed. This could be quite amusing, I thought, as the sea had become much rougher. The ship was bobbing about aimlessly in the rough swell. The engineers were trying to repair the damage. I wasn't worried, because I know that the Indonesians are masters of improvisation. I soon went back to sleep.

The sun was already up when the motor rattled into life. Black smoke came out of the funnel. With very little power and at a speed of three knots instead of ten, we slowly approached Ambon. The captain told me that it was the ship's first voyage after a general overhaul of the engines! There was no danger of my going hungry even though we were over twelve hours late: the ship's cook brought me fried noodles and other delicacies during the morning. And the delay didn't bother me at all: what are twelve hours! In the past, in the days of sail, this voyage often took twelve days and more.

To be on the safe side, I hadn't booked a flight back to Bali. Nevertheless, I was glad when we finally docked in Ambon. I hired a *betjak*[361] at the port to take me to a pleasant hotel recommended to me by Abba. It was great to have a clean bathroom after the voyage. And the sun was setting once more.

In 1511 the Portuguese were the first Europeans to arrive in Ambon. In 1609 they were expelled by the Dutch. Ambon is 51 kilometres long and has a population of about 230,000. It is a much bigger island compared with Banda Neira. After being on the Banda Islands I was shocked to find so much rubbish and plastic waste in the canals in the city and on the beaches. Disgraceful!

I intended to visit Fort Victoria in the city of Ambon and Fort Amsterdam in the town of Hila at the northern end of the island. But my main aim was to find out more about the German naturalist and botanist Georg Eberhard Rumpf, who worked here his whole life and left his mark on the Spice Islands. As with the German painter and musician Walter Spies, whose name is familiar to every child on Bali though in Germany he's only known in specialist circles, so it is with Rumpf, who called himself Rumphius. His memory is honoured on the island of Ambon and the Ambonese still revere him. He's also known on the Banda Islands. To judge by his writings, he must have visited them several times. He classified several previously unknown species of fish found in the waters around the Bandas. But more about him in the next chapter.

361 Tricycle rickshaw

First I wanted to visit Fort Victoria in Ambon, where in the spring of 1623 the Dutch perpetrated a gruesome massacre of the English who lived in the town. It is the oldest fort on Ambon, and was built by the Portuguese in 1576. In 1580 it was fortified and extended by the building of four bastions. The Portuguese named it *El Forte de Nossa Senhora da Anunciada*. [The Fort of Our Lady of the Annunciation]. The native inhabitants called it *Kota Laha* .

Ill. 20-13, View of Ambon after an engraving from 1655[362]

Ill. 20-14, View of Ambon after a print from ca. 1725[363]

---

362 Public Domain, Wikipedia
363 Public Domain, Wikipedia

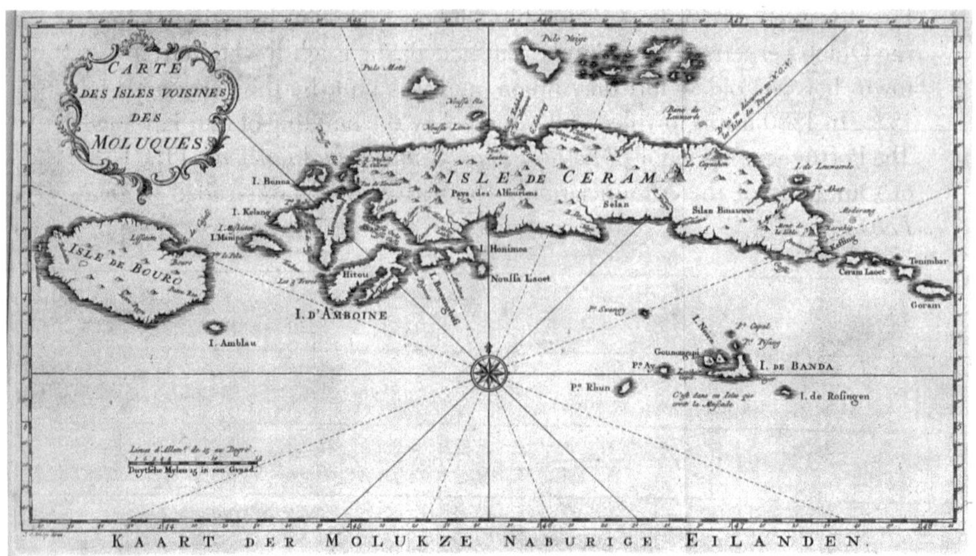

Ill. 20-15
Old map, 1753[364]

Ill. 20-16
Defeat of the Portuguese off Ambon, illustration from 1645[365]

When the Dutch took the fort on the 23rd of February 1605, they renamed it Fort Victoria. It became the VOC's administrative headquarters and in the years that followed, its defences were strengthened and enlarged. After devastating earthquakes in 1643, 1672, 1673 and others in later years, it was regularly renovated. Three extra bastions were added and the seawater moat around the fort was extended.

---

364 Atlas of Mutual Heritage and the Koninklijke Bibliotheek, Public Domain
365 Public Domain, Wikipedia

The worst damage the fort suffered was from the earthquake of 1898 and bombing raids by the US Air Force in the Second World War. The seaward parts of the fort are still well preserved. Its gate has been restored many times.

When I asked the friendly owner of my hotel where Fort Victoria was, and how far away, she immediately offered to accompany me there on foot. It is now a closely guarded military complex. I wanted to take a picture of the entrance gate, but was immediately prevented from doing so by two heavily armed soldiers. They explained, in a harsh military tone, that photography was absolutely forbidden in the vicinity of the fort, and if I continued to take pictures, they would confiscate my camera. There was no way I wanted to risk that, of course, though I ventured to take a photograph at hip level. We had to depart in a hurry. Such a pity – I would have liked to see the interior of the fort .

After the massacre on the Banda Islands, Governor General Jan Pieterszoon van Coen carried on to Ambon. He made it his headquarters, since Batavia had not yet been pacified. Shipping to the Banda Islands would be under surveillance from Fort Victoria. Its strongly fortified walls were right next to the port, and it had powerful, long-range cannons. It could house at least 200 Dutch soldiers, and over 400 mercenaries. Japanese executioners were billeted outside the fort. There were always some Dutch ships in the port near the fort to deter foreign rivals and native smugglers.

Ill. 20-17, Forbidden photograph of the entrance gate to Fort Victoria

Ill. 20-18
Entrance to Fort Victoria from the seaward side, 1899[366]

Ill. 20-19
One of Fort Victoria's Bastions, 1921[367]

There were over twenty Englishmen living on Ambon at the time, most of them in the town of Ambon, where the English factory was situated. Other factors[368] lived in the villages of Hitu and Larica. They received hardly any support from the English East India Company in London. Their trade in the cloves harvested on the island was going badly and they were little competition for the Dutch. The two nations were even starting to be on friendly terms with each other. When Fort Victoria was finally completed, the English were allowed to go in and out as they wished.

Nevertheless, Governor General Coen still regarded the English with great suspicion. Before he left Ambon to return to Holland, he ordered Herman van Speult, the Governor of Ambon, to take severe action against the English if there was the slightest suspicion.

366 Collectie Tropenmuseum Amsterdam, Free Wikipedia
367 Wikimedia Commons
368 company agents

324

The English had always been a thorn in Coen's flesh, and he wanted to be rid of them .

From the night of the 10th–11th of February 1623 onwards, the previously good relationship between the Dutch and the English took a sudden turn for the worse. A Japanese mercenary[369] was arrested on suspicion of spying on the fort. Since the Dutch had a fundamental distrust of the Japanese, they were always billeted outside the fort. For Governor van Speult this seemed like a good opportunity to be rid of the English on Ambon, which was the last bastion of the English on the Moluccas.

The Japanese insisted that he was innocent, but they tortured him with red hot iron until he made a 'confession'. The interrogators got him to say that he had been spying on the fort on behalf of the English, who were intending to capture the fort in a surprise attack. Other Japanese were then tortured until they too gave in to the prompting to confess. The English had no idea of these confessions, and went about their daily business as usual. They felt safe. How could they, with only 20 men, take the fort with its garrison of at least 200 armed Dutch soldiers? The only weapons they had were three swords and two muskets.

Under the pretence of holding a business meeting, Governor van Speult lured the head of the English factory, Towerson, as well as the English officers and merchants, into Fort Victoria. Without any kind of due process, they were all arrested, chained together and thrown into prison. Then the English too were tortured with unbelievable cruelty, until they too, unable to bear the torture any longer, made forced 'confessions' to the interrogators. The English warehouses were looted and all their private possessions confiscated.

In Fort Victoria the English were hoisted up against a wall with outstretched arms and legs. Their armpits were burned right down to the bone with red hot irons, their feet were held in a flame for so long that the fat that ran from the wounds put out the candles. They kept falling into the relief of unconsciousness. In the evening, the victims were thrown back into their cells without any medical attention. After only a few days the wounds were full of pus and fat maggots. But most of the men continued to insist that they were innocent.

Every morning Governor Speult and his torturers attended a Christian service on the chapel in the fort, and then returned to the torture. Next they applied the 'water torture'. A piece of sailcloth was tied around the victim's neck like a funnel, which was then filled with water until his mouth and

---

369 http://tei.it.ox.ac.uk/tcp/Texts-HTML/free/A27/A27176.html, according to this transcription of a later pamphlet of 1624 it was a Dutchman

nose were under water. The victim had to drink to be able to breathe. The torture was continued until water started pouring out of their eyes and ears. Those who were tortured like this became so bloated that they doubled their body weight. If they passed out, the sailcloth was removed, but only until they came round. And then the torture began again.

Ill. 20-20, How the English were tortured[370]

---

370 Etching ca. 1700, Wikipedia Public Domain

This inhuman form of torture is reminiscent of waterboarding, the torture authorised by US President George W. Bush and used regularly by the US secret service, the CIA, in Guantanamo and during the wars in Iraq and Afghanistan. In the 21th century! The US clandestine services have frequently hit the headlines for their brutal disregard of human rights in the use of violent torture. Anyone's resistance can be broken by waterboarding.

Since some of the Englishmen persisted in refusing to make the false confessions dictated to them, their toes were split. Later they even blew off parts of their bodies by means of gunpowder charges attached to their hands and feet. The Dutch acted with unimaginable brutality. This went on day after day for a whole week until the last Englishman signed a 'confession' that there had been a conspiracy aimed at the Dutch. After being tortured, most of the victims had to be carried back to their dungeons because they could no longer stand. All the English and a number of Japanese were now charged with conspiracy.

The English remained in prison for two days longer. Anyone who had hoped for mercy from the Dutch was bitterly disappointed. Towerson, the head of the English trading post, was sentenced to be beheaded and quartered. The other Englishmen who had been found guilty were simply beheaded, as were the Japanese. Only two Englishmen were released. Although everything the condemned men had written had been confiscated by the Dutch, some of their written protestations of innocence reached London.

371 Detail from an etching ca. 1700, Wikipedia Public Domain

The day of the executions was celebrated in Ambon like a festival, with drums and music. They were revelling in Holland's triumph over England. When the news of the massacre reached London there was universal outrage. The two nations were on the brink of war. Anti-Dutch sentiment worsened. Every day the public were showered with new broadsheets and pamphlets in which the atrocities committed by the Dutch were described in gruesome detail. The subject was hotly debated all over England.

Were these brutal Dutchmen human, let alone Christians from a civilised country? It's hard to believe. Anyone who reads the 1624 pamphlet *A True Relation of the Unjust, Cruel and Barbarous Proceedings against the English at Amboyna*, is likely to want to put it straight down because of the horror of the atrocities it describes.[372] The entire original text can be accessed on the University of Michigan's website.[373]

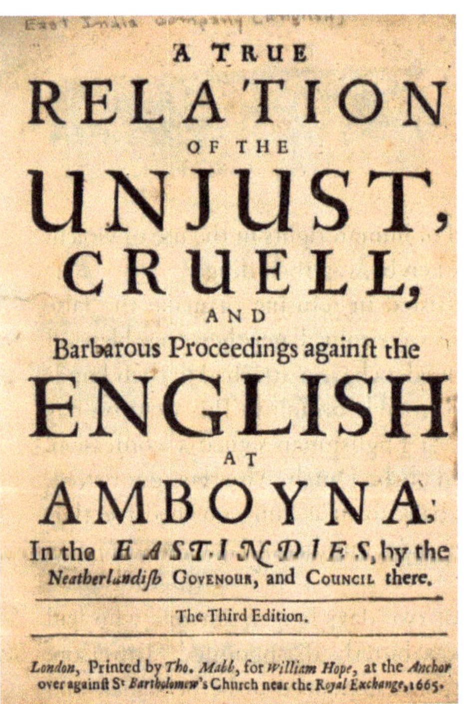

Ill. 20-22, The 1624 Pamphlet, 3rd edition

Ill. 20-23, A Page of the original Pamphlet

to the ENGLISH *at* AMBOYNA.

Towerſon falſly and wrongfully, onely through fear of Torment.

The five and twentieth of *February*, old ſtile, all the Priſoners, as well the *Engliſh*, as the *Portugal* and the *Iaponers*, were brought into the great Hall of the Caſtle, and there were ſolemnly Condemned, except *Iohn Powl*, *Ephraim Ramſey*, *Iohn Sadler*, and *Thomas Ladbrook*, formerly acquitted, as aforeſaid.

Captain *Towerſon* having been (during all his Impriſonment) kept a part from the reſt, ſo that none of them could come to ſpeak with him; writ much in his Chamber (as ſome of the *Dutch* report,) but all was ſuppreſſed, ſave only a Bill of debt, which one *Thomas Iohnſon*, a free Burgher got of him by favour of his Keepers for acknowledgement, that the *Engliſh* Company owed him a certain ſumm of money. In the end of this Bill he writ theſe words: *Firmed by the Firm of me Gabriel Towerſon, now appointed to dye, guiltleſs of any thing that can be juſtly laid to my Charge. God forgive them their Guilt, and receive me to his Mercy: Amen.* This Bill being brought to Maſter *Welden* the *Engliſh* Agent at *Banda*, he paid the money, and received in the acknowledgement,

William Griggs (who had before Accuſed Captain *Towerſon*) writ theſe words following in his Table-Book: *We, whoſe names are here ſpecified*; John Fecomont, *Merchant of* Loho, William Griggs *Merchant of* Larica, Abel Price, *Chyrurgion of* Amboyna, Robert Brown, *Taylor, which do here lye Priſoners in the Ship* Rotterdam, *being apprehended for Conſpiracy, for blowing up the Caſtle of* Amboyna: *We being judged to Death this fifth of* March, Anno 1622. *which we through Torment were conſtrained to ſpeak, that which he never meant, nor once imagined; the which we take upon our Deaths and Salvation: they Tortured us with that extreame Torment of Fire and Water, that Fleſh and Blood could not endure: and this we take upon our Deaths, that they have put us to Death guiltleſs of our Accuſation. So therefore we deſire, that they that ſhall underſtand this; that our Imployers may underſtand theſe Wrongs, and*

D   *that*

---

372 There are transcriptions of several of these pamphlets on the Internet
373 See: https://quod.lib.umich.edu/e/eebo/A21090.0001.001?rgn=main; view=fulltext

Ill. 20-24, A Page of the original Pamphlet

50 years after the massacre the subject was still a hot topic in England. In 1673 the poet and dramatist John Dryden published his play *Amboyna, or, The Cruelties of the Dutch to the English Merchants, A Tragedy*, a piece of anti-Dutch propaganda.

In 1625 the English East India Company commissioned the English artist Richard Greenbury to paint a massive depiction of the massacre in Ambon for their London headquarters. The Company also wanted portraits of Governor Speult and the main interrogator to be included. The details of the torture are said to have been depicted so graphically that the wife of one of the victims fainted when she saw it. Since the government did not want the flames of anti-Dutch resentment to be fanned still further, some of the scenes were toned down. Unfortunately I have not been able to discover if this painting still exists somewhere in England. Nor have I been able to find a reproduction of it anywhere on the Internet.

The tension between Holland and England intensified. The Dutch government set up a special commission to shed light on what had actually happened in the massacre. Governor van Speult was summoned to Amsterdam for questioning, but died before he got there.

After those who had been involved in the interrogation of and torture of the English had been questioned, it was clear that there was no proof of a conspiracy.

A commission in England came to the conclusion that the massacre had been orchestrated and instigated by the Dutch simply out of greed for profit by permanently driving the English out of the Spice Island region.

In Holland by contrast a special court came to a different conclusion, after months of deliberation: *The court saw no reason why the accused should be punished for something they had done in the conviction that they were acting for the good of the country.*[374]

Dutch justice was, then as now, applying double standards. As even the Dutch historian Lou de Jong writes in his standard work *Het Koninkrijk der Nederlanden in de Tweede Wereldoorlog* [The Kingdom of the Netherlands in the Second World War]: *War crimes were committed in Indonesia to a far greater extent that has so far been publicly acknowledged. Murder and mass murder, systematic terror, torture, rape, interning citizens in inhumane conditions, looting and destruction, barbaric executions were the order of the day.*[375]

---

374 Giles Milton, *Nathaniel's Nutmeg*, p. 366
375 Der Spiegel 4/1988

The same double standards were also applied by the Dutch justice system in the case of the sinking of the KPM[376] ship *Van Imhoff* in 1942[377] with over 400 German victims. The two Dutch captains, H. J. Hoeksema and M. L. Berveling should have been tried for breaches of the Geneva Convention and the international Search & Rescue Convention, but neither of them was ever called to account in Holland. A veil was cast over the crime.

It led to tension between the German and Dutch governments. But according to the Dutch courts there were no grounds for investigating any misdemeanours committed by the two captains. It was not until 2017 that any attempt was made to come to terms with the war crime in Holland, in a three-part TV series made with my co-operation, and that there was recognition on the part of the Dutch that a war crime had been committed.[378] In the Dutch press, too, this crime was discussed – after a delay of 75 years.[379]

But now, after that digression into modern history, let us return to the 17th century. After the Dutch denied any guilt for the massacre, the English fleet patrolled the Channel, threatening to capture any inward or outward bound Dutch shipping. England demanded appropriate compensation for the crimes committed against its citizens. And what was that compensation? The Island of Run was returned to the English!

But Run was now worthless. The Dutch had felled all the nutmeg trees to ensure that the island would be unproductive. They also wanted to avoid over-production, thus keeping the price of nutmeg as high as possible. The inhabitants of the islands were deprived of their source of income and were pauperised. But England now had a valuable asset: an island in the Bandas, which they were later able to exchange for Manhattan.[380]

In Chapter 25, Appendix IV, I have included the entries on Ambon in Volume 1 of the 1875 edition of the *Encyclopaedia Britannica*, which also mentions the massacre, and in Volume 1 of the 1888 edition of *Pierers Konversations-Lexikon*.

In Ambon, just like the Banda Islands, there was constant warfare between the European colonial powers. The first Portuguese settled on the Island of Ambon in 1512 and traded with the native population, but were expelled

376 Koninklijke Paketvaart Maatschappij
377 See *Hitler's Asian Adventure*, Chapter 15, pp. 160 ff
378 *De Ondergang van de Van Imhoff* was broadcast on Channel 2 on three successive Sundays in December 2017. The title of the English version is *The Doom of the Van Imhoff*
379 De Telegraaf, 2nd of December 2017
380 See Chapter 8, *The Island of Run exchanged for Manhattan*

by the Dutch in 1605. In 1615 the English conquered the island and built several trading posts, which were plundered and destroyed by the Dutch in the massacre of 1623. The 1888 edition of the *Encyclopaedia Britannica* suggests that the English received the sum of £300,000 as compensation for the atrocities committed, as well as a small island.[381] I could not find any documentary evidence for such a payment.

In 1796 Ambon was retaken by the English under Admiral Rainier, but returned to Holland soon afterwards, in 1802. In 1810 England once more occupied Ambon, but returned it to the Dutch again in 1814. Like the Banda Islands, Ambon has a chequered history. Lots of blood has been shed there – not just as a result of war between the European colonial powers. The soil of Ambon is drenched in the blood of hundreds of thousands of the native inhabitants, who only wanted self-determination.

From 1814 onwards until the end of the Second World War and the declaration of Indonesian independence on the 17th of August 1945 Ambon remained in Dutch hands. But the road to independence was long and arduous. The Dutch came with all their military might to reconquer their former colony and exploit it.[382] On the Moluccas, however, there were additional problems which, as we will see, were of religious origin.

Thanks to a stroke of luck, I was able to get some photographs of Fort Victoria in spite of the prohibitions. I was talking to an Ambonese, and he told me that he worked in the military administration and had open access to the fort. He said he was prepared to take some secret photographs for me. We went over to the fort, I gave him my camera and off he went. When he still wasn't back after an hour, I began to think I'd lost my camera with all my pictures of the Bandas – either stolen or confiscated! Had I been too trusting and gullible? But all my worries were groundless. My photographer returned, and told me with a beaming smile that our project had succeeded! So here are some secretly taken photographs that my foreign companion, whose name I won't give here, took for me inside the fort.

My photographer told me that inside the fort there were several memorial plaques from the days of the Dutch. He had taken pictures of a few particularly well-preserved plaques, especially the ones mentioning the foundation and expansion of the old Portuguese fort. He mentioned that the expansion of the fort had been planned and supervised by a German master builder, Hans Ernst von Wagner. His name was on many of the plaques, as was his profession of master builder. His name suggests that he was of German origin, but I could find no proof of this.

---

381 See Chapter 25, Appendix IV
382 See Horst H. Geerken, *A Gecko for Luck*, pp. 132ff

Ill. 20-25, The gateway – many times restored

Ill. 20-26, The outer wall of Fort Victoria

Ill. 20-27, A corner of the Fort

Ill. 20-28, Foundation plaque in Fort Victoria, anno 1770

Ill. 20-29
Memorial plaque, anno 1770

Ill. 2 0-30
Memorial plaque, anno 1771

But why is the old fort so strictly guarded that you can't even take a photograph of the entrance gate? Since the unrest in 1999 and 2000 there has been instability and tense calm. The current of tension between the two religious camps, Christian and Muslim, must be due to the region's history.

As a result of the Portuguese presence in the 16th and 17th century, the population of Ambon

was mainly Christian. That was of little concern to anyone, not the Dutch, who expelled the Portuguese, or the English who occupied Ambon in 1796 and expelled the Dutch.

In 1802 the English returned the Island of Ambon to the Dutch, though they reoccupied it from 1810 to 1814. After that, the island became a Dutch colony once more. In 1942, Japanese troops occupied Ambon. They too had no interest in missionary activity – it was wartime, after all!

The vast majority of the population of the Malay Archipelago, roughly 90%, is Muslim. This results from the Dutch colonialists' attitude to the native population, because they regarded themselves as possessing a superior religion and culture. To keep the natives down in their state of – ostensible – inferiority, they did their best to hinder any attempts by the Christian churches to convert them, since if the Indonesians were Christian, they might have to treat them as equals, at least in religion. This attitude seriously prejudiced their colonial interests. Christianity spread to the neighbouring islands, like Ceram, at the beginning of the 20th century. It was not the Dutch colonists, however, who were responsible for this, but Indonesian missionaries from Ambon.

When Indonesia's first President, Sukarno, proclaimed Indonesian independence on the 17th of August 1945, the first unrest broke out on the Moluccas. Holland wanted to make the young republic's nascent independence as difficult as possible. With support from The Hague, politicians on the Island of Ambon who favoured Holland founded an independent republic, the *Republik Maluku Selatan*[383] in April 1950. This state within a state was not recognised internationally. The Ambonese, who since their early conversion by the Portuguese had been very Christian and therefore felt themselves to be closer to the Dutch, had been on the side of the Dutch even in colonial times and also collaborated with them against Sukarno during the War of Independence. The majority of the native soldiers serving in the KNIL[384], the Dutch colonial army, came from Ambon. They were soldiers who were loyal to the Dutch; the mainly Muslim Indonesian army dismissively referred to them as *Belanda Hitam*.[385] In the colonial army they had always fought in the vanguard, even in the War of Independence against Sukarno's troops, which ended in December 1949.

It is therefore easy to understand Sukarno's aversion to the Ambonese. He was, of course, also determined to nip any attempt to secede from his nascent republic in the bud.

Sukarno sent Indonesian – Islamic – troops to Ambon and by November 1950 they had bloodily put down the Ambonese rebellion. It became a war between Muslims and Christians, and the fronts hardened .In Sukarno's eyes the Ambonese who served in the KNIL were scum, the tools of the Dutch, and his Islamic troops persecuted them mercilessly. Since the Christians in the Moluccas now feared for their lives, there was a mass evacuation. Tens of thousands fled to Holland to escape prosecution. Today there are still large

---

383 Republic of the South Moluccas
384 Koninklijk Nederlandsch Indisch Leger
385 Black Dutchmen

colonies of Ambonese families there, and an Ambonese government in exile, which is a major problem for the Dutch. They had promised the Ambonese their independence, but had not been able to keep their promise .It is sad to see the way the European colonial powers have created sources of unrest in Indonesia, in India and Pakistan, in the Near East and elsewhere which are still causing problems today.

The tension between Christians and Muslims in the Moluccas got worse from year to year. Another reason for this was an Indonesian government project to settle hundreds of thousands of Muslim Malays from Sulawesi and Java in the Moluccas. This altered the religious balance of the islands from a Christian to a Muslim majority, which resulted in conflict between the two religious groups and a situation close to civil war.

In 1999 serious violent conflict flared up again. Hundreds of houses were burned down .Mosques and churches went up in flames. Large areas of the city of Ambon were destroyed. The largely Islamic army sent from Java could – or would – not pacify the situation. There were even elements within the army who fought on the Muslim side against the Christians. There were soldiers who supplied the Muslims with weapons.

The Indonesian military played a catastrophic role, allowing thousands of members of the Islamist militia *Laskar Jihad* to travel from Java to the Moluccas without hindrance. This fundamentalist anti-Christian movement's leaders were trained by the *mujahadeen* in Afghanistan.

Terrible things happened during the unrest. On PELNI ships, for example, Christians – who were always in the minority – were simply thrown overboard into the sea. PELNI then changed its routes. There were now ships that only served islands with mainly Christian populations and others whose route served islands with mainly Muslim.

In April 1999 all the Christians on the Banda Islands were evacuated on a ship that Des Alwi managed to acquire from the navy through his connections with the Indonesian armed forces. At least, that's what they told me on the Bandas. In reports on the internet, they were said to have been expelled, and that's what they told me in Ambon. Whom should we believe? Those who fled have certainly not returned to the Bandas. In 2018, I only saw a handful of Christians at the Christmas Service in the church in Banda Neira. There were armed soldiers guarding the church for security.

I wanted to find out more about this, but, as you know, no one in Banda Neira was prepared to talk to me about what had happened. For example, I wanted to know how many Christians had been living on the islands at the time, and how many there were currently, where they lived, if any of them had been killed during the unrest and so on. But a veil of silence seems to have been cast over the events of that time.

The only person who would speak to me openly was Cornelis J. Böhm MSC, the last Christian minister still living on Ambon. According to him, between 9,000 and 10,000 people lost their lives on Ambon, most of them Christian. During my stay on the Bandas and Ambon there was a sense of tense calm, but there are many reasons why the conflict is still bubbling beneath the surface.

That was clearly the reason why the guards outside Fort Victoria reacted as they did when they saw me with my camera in my hand. Perhaps they thought I was a journalist – and journalists are *persona non grata* on Ambon at the moment .

I toured the island with Pak Umar. I was particularly interested in the town of Hila, which is about 35 kilometres from the city of Ambon in the north of the island. The first thing I visited in Hila was the oldest church in the Moluccas, *Geredja*[386] *Immanuel,* built by the Portuguese[387] in 1659. The first mosque in the Moluccas was not built until 200 years later. It is quite near the church.

In the 1999-2000 unrest, *Geredja Immanuel* was set on fire by Muslim fanatics and partly destroyed. All the windows and mural paintings were irreparably destroyed in the fire. In 2011 the church was rebuilt and restored – as far as possible – by the Indonesian government.

The old Fort Amsterdam is close to the church. Initially, it was a Portuguese trading post, and then the VOC transformed it into a defensive fort in 1637, renaming it Fort Amsterdam in 1656. The fort has three stories. The arsenal and the prison were on the ground floor. The external walls are about 52 metres by 52 long and the ground plan area of the main building is 16 metres by 16. The German biologist Rumphius lived and worked here from 1660 to 1670. In the next chapter I will write about him in more detail.

In 1991 the Fort was completely repaired and restored by the Indonesian government. From the top floor there is a lovely view of the Island of Ceram. *Geredja Immanuel* can also be seen from there.

From Hila we took the coast road back to Ambon city. After a very full day, I was glad to spend an enjoyable evening over a cold beer and a Chinese meal in a restaurant near the hotel.

---

386 17th-century spelling
387 Some sources say that it was the Dutch who built the church

Ill. 20-31, The oldest church in the Moluccas, Geredja Immanuel built in 1659

Ill. 20-32, The interior of the church, now simple and unadorned

Ill. 20-33, Fort Amsterdam in Hila

Ill. 20-34, The fort entrance

Ill. 20-35, Fort Amsterdam and the well[388]

Pak Umar acquired a plane ticket to Bali for me for the next day. First we went to see the sights of Ambon and the vicinity. I was shocked by the garbage and plastic waste in the city's canals. Even in the sea, if you wanted to go for a swim from one of the beaches near the city, you would have had to wade through all the plastic bottles and plastic bags floating in the water. I decided not to bother. What a difference from the ecologically aware Bandas!

In the centre of the city Pak Umar took me to Medan Pelita [literally 'Lamp Square'] to see the 34th World Peace Gong. The two-metre diameter gong was unveiled on the 22nd of November 2009 by President Susilo Bambang Yudhoyono. Previously, on the 31st of December 2002, the then President of Indonesia, Megawati Sukarnoputri, sounded the first note on the biggest Peace Gong in the world – with a diameter of five metres – in the *Cultural Village Kertalangu* near Denpasar on Bali.

388 Wikipedia, Public Domain

The origins of this movement go back to the destruction of Hiroshima by an American atom bomb. During the Second World War bells had been melted down to make guns. But on the 6th of August 1947, only the second anniversary of the bombing of Hiroshima, the first Peace Bell was hung and inaugurated. By now there are more than 200 World Peace Bells and World Peace Gongs, which are sounded every year on the 21st of September, World Peace Day.

The *Gong Perdamaian Dunia*, World Peace Gong, in Ambon, was erected as a monument warning against conflict between Christians and Muslims. The forced resignation of President Suharto, the devaluation of Indonesia's currency and the general economic crisis in South East Asia are said to have been the trigger for the civil war of 1999-2000. This symbol of peace is supposed to help achieve lasting reconciliation. Will it succeed? I have my doubts!

In his speech, Indonesian President Susilo Bambang Yudhoyono said: *Ambon's past racial conflict has suffered many casualties. But not anymore. Ambon has been transformed into a city of peace. The proof is the World Peace Gong Monument in Ambon...*

The Peace Gong was erected to remind the people of Maluku and the visitors of a fundamental need for peace and security. On the surface of the gong, national flags of all countries around the world and the symbols pertaining to religions, including Christianity, Islam, Judaism, Buddhism, Hinduism and others have been printed. Above all, there is also a symbol of Pancasila, the symbol of the nation of Indonesia. The World Peace Gong has been set up in the Maluku provincial city of Ambon instead of Indonesias capital city Jakarta, because peace and security has been restored in the province after a three-year sectarian violence.

I visited the market in Ambon with Pak Umar. The variety of fruit and vegetables on display was amazing.

I also visited the *Museum Siwalima* which is divided between several sites in Ambon. It was officially opened in March 1977. It's worth a visit! You could spend a whole day in the various different sections and always find something new.

Illustrations next page:

Ill. 20-36, The World Peace Gong, Gong Perdamaian Dunia, in Ambon
Ill. 20-37, Tropical fruit

Ill. 20-38, Durian, the smelly fruit that is popular all over Indonesia

Ill. 20-39, Vegetables and spices

344

Ill. 20-40, Fresh fish

When I went into the museum, I was welcomed by a senior museum official. They gave me a book and some other small things. I was more than surprised. Were they this generous to all their visitors? No. My visit took place on the 2nd of January and I was the first visitor in the new year.

Ill. 20-41, I was the Museum's first visitor in 2019

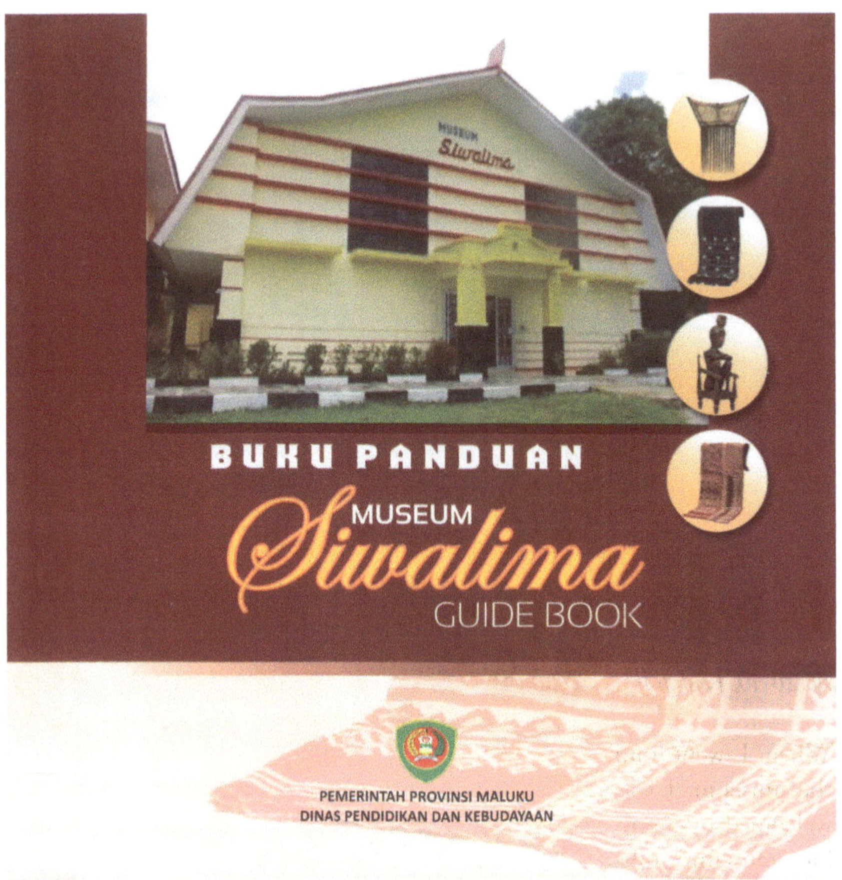

Ill. 20-42, The Museum catalogue

I was particularly interested in references to Georg Eberhard Rumphius and was surprised to come across him in almost every department. He was an all-round genius, as we will see in the next chapter.

21. Georg Eberhard Rumpf, known as Rumphius[389]

Everywhere I went in Ambon, I encountered Rumpf, a German whose latinised name was Rumphius. There was a Rumphius memorial stone, a Rumphius garden, a Rumphius Library, a *Kumunitas Rumphius Ambon* society, and in the *Siwalima* Museum in Ambon and Fort Amsterdam in Hila whole walls are covered in Rumphius' drawings. Nearly every child in Ambon knows him. I found him interesting and wanted to find out more about him, especially as he had carried out research on the Banda Islands.

Georg Eberhard Rumpf was born in No. 1, Rathausgasse, in Wölfersheim in Hessen in 1627[390], during the turmoil of the Thirty Years' War. He was a botanist, naturalist and administrator in the service of the Dutch colonial government. His grandmother was Dutch, which is why he grew up speaking both German and Dutch – he regarded them both as his mother tongues, and spoke both fluently.

On Ambon I had the honour of getting to know Pastor Cornelis J. Böhm. He is the last Dutch minister living in the Moluccas. He has researched the life of Rumpf for many decades, and is regarded as the leading expert on this extraordinary man. But before I say more about Rumpf, I will let Pastor Böhm speak.

This is a free translation of the lecture Pastor Böhm gave about Rumpf in Bahasa Indonesia in November 2018 at the 7th Borobudur Writers & Cultural Festival in Malang on the island of Java.[391]

Rumphius, a biologist who made a name for himself on the Island of Ambon

The name of Rumphius is still spoken of with great respect among biologists and scientists. Georg Eberhard Rumpf (alias Georg Everhardus Rumphius) was a German who was born in 1627 in Wölfersheim in Hessen, Germany. His father, August Rumpf was an engineer and businessman. His mother's maiden name was Elisabeth Keller. Her mother, Rumpf's grandmother, was Dutch,

---

389 1627-1702, latinised as Georgius Everhardus Rumphius
390 Sometimes also mentioned 1622
391 Used and published with the kind permission of Pastor Cornelis J. Böhm, STPAK St. Yohanes Penginjil Ambon, Jl. Pakatora Pohoh Mangga Kole, Poka – Rumahtiga, Ambon, issued on the 2nd of January 2019

which is the reason why Rumpf spoke fluent Dutch and also wrote many of his scientific works in the language. In his youth he had a good education at a Gymnasium[392]. In religion he was a strict Calvinist.

In 1645, at the age of 18, he was the victim of human trafficking. He was persuaded by false promises to join the army. When he was posted to Crete to help expel the Turks from the island, he left the army and applied to join the Dutch West Indies Company, an organisation like the VOC, but focussed on the West Indies and the Americas. Rumpf sailed for Brazil, where the Dutch and the Portuguese were competing for control of the region[393], on the ship De Swarte Raef[394]. But for some unknown reason the ship never reached its destination and Rumpf and all the other passengers had to disembark in Portugal, where Rumpf spent about three years. The Dutch academic W. Buijze published a monograph in 2002, which describes his stay in Portugal in detail. He writes that Rumpf was fascinated by the botany of Portugal. His main focus of attention was on plants of all kinds.

In 1649 he returned to Hanau in Germany to help his father with his business. Because he was fascinated by the stories told about the Moluccas and the cultivation of spices, he applied to the VOC in Amsterdam. On this occasion Rumpf changed the spelling of his name from Rumpf to Rumph so that it looked and sounded Dutch.

On the 26th of December 1652, now aged 25, he set sail for Batavia[395] on the Muijden. On the way the ship made an intermediate stop at the port of Harapan in southern Africa, where Rumphius made sketches of many plants which he found interesting. We can see that an interest in botany already played an important role in his life. He landed in Batavia in July 1653 and in January 1654 he finally reached Ambon. The journey from Amsterdam to Ambon took a whole year.

Illustrations next page:

Ill. 21-1, The Dutch settlement at Batavia, a drawing from 1665[396]
Ill. 21-2, Plan of Ambon in 1718[397]

---

392 [The German equivalent of a Grammar School]
393 Presumably Pastor Böhm is here referring to Surinam (then Dutch Guyana), which is north of today's Brazil
394 The Black Raven
395 Now Jakarta
396 Wiki Commons, Public Domain
397 Ibid.

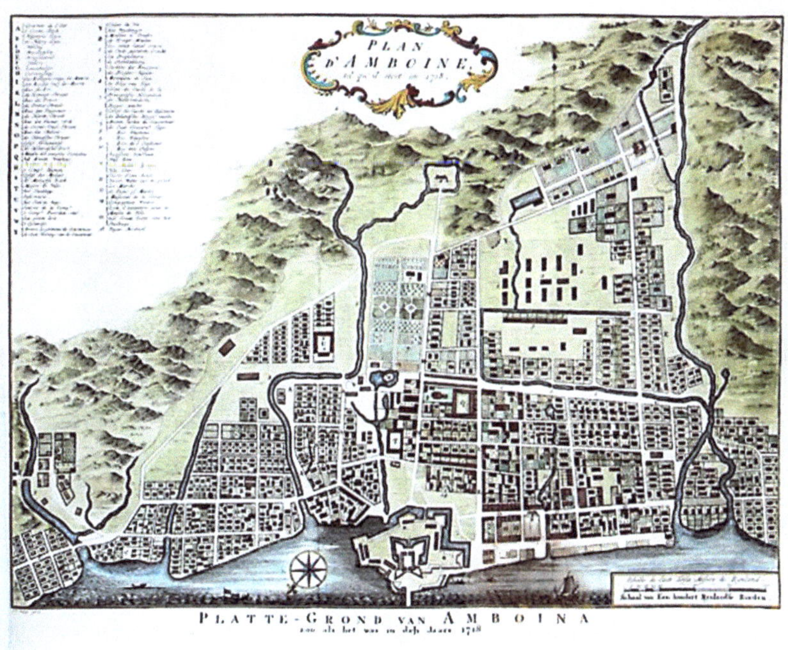

PLATTE-GROND VAN AMBOINA
soo als het was in deese Iaere 1718

The Island of Ambon

The Island of Ambon is relatively small. It was chosen by the VOC as the headquarters for its trade in the Moluccas because it was relatively easy to defend against attacks by its rivals from Portugal and England. The island is made up of two parts which are joined by a narrow strip of land near the village of Passo. The northern half of the island is called Jazirah Lei-Hitu and consists for the most part of thick forest. Most of the inhabitants of this area are Muslims. The main village is Hitu. One of the best-known inhabitants of this village was Rijali, who regularly rebelled against the VOC. The southern half is called Jazirah Lei-Timur. It is smaller, but more densely populated. Most of the inhabitants are Christians. There is an enchanting bay between the two halves of the island .

The first Westerners to arrive in Ambon were the Portuguese in 1512. In 1605, VOC troops captured the fort the Portuguese had built on Jazirah Lei-Timur – Nossa Senhora da Anunciada – and took control of the whole island. The fort was renamed Fort Victoria.

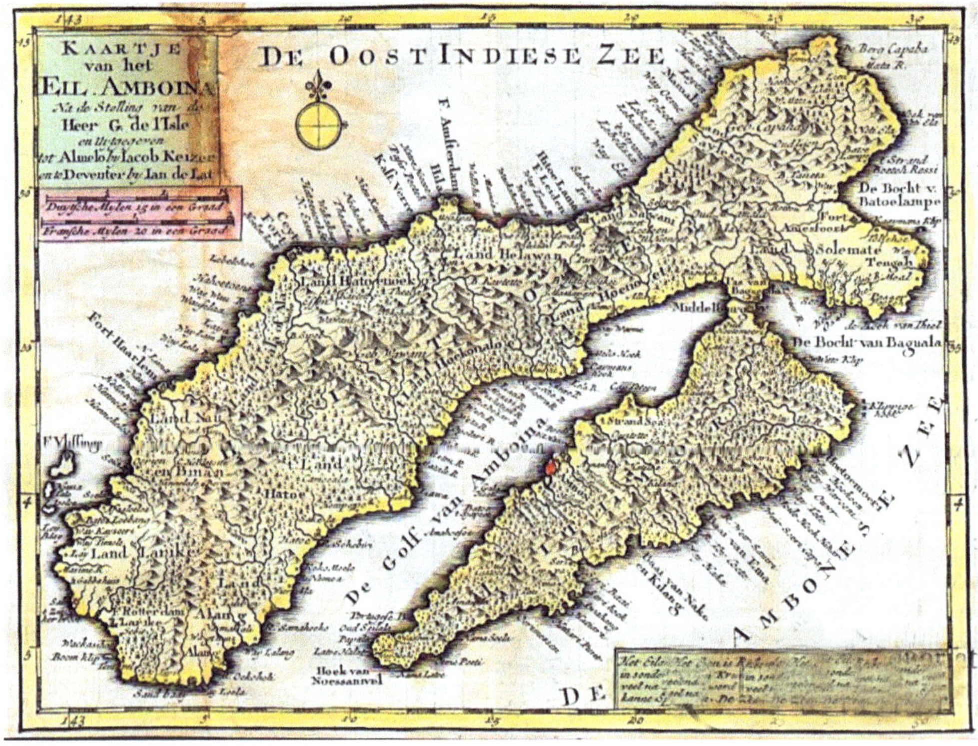

Ill. 21-3, The Island of Ambon

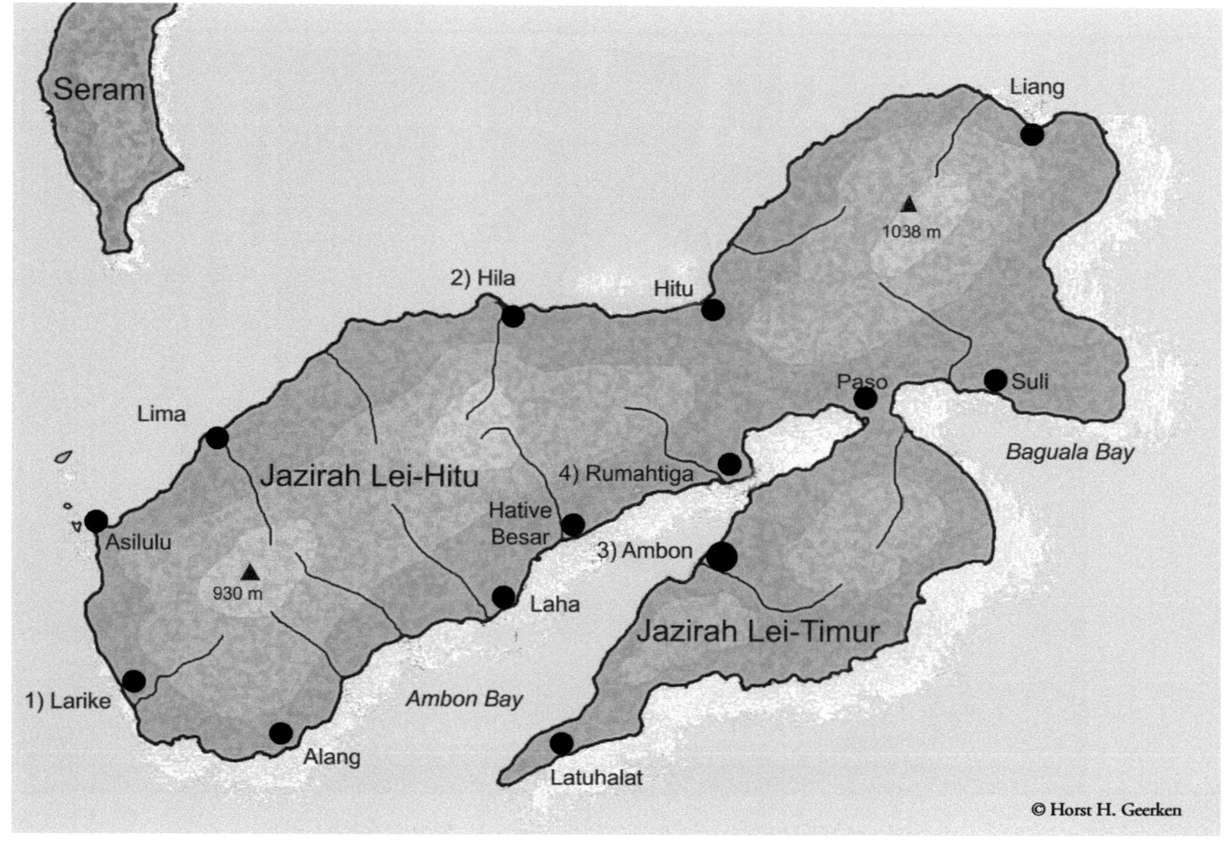

Ill. 21-4, The Island of Ambon

1) Rumphius was a merchant in the village of Larike
2) Rumphius carried out research in Hila from 1660 until 1670
3) Ambon was Rumphius' last home from 1670 until 1702
4) The Rumphius Garden is in Rumahtiga

Ill. 21-5, Georg Eberhard Rumphius at work. It is the only surviving portrait of him. It was made as an etching by his son Paul August between 1695 and 1696.[398]

398 Wikipedia, Public Domain

352

After his arrival on Ambon, Rumphius was involved in planning work. There was a suggestion that Fort Victoria should be moved to Laha, on the other side of the bay, but Rumphius argued that there would be many more cloves and nutmegs on Jazirah Lei-Timur than on the other half of the island. The plan of moving the fort was therefore abandoned.

The Rumphius Family

In Ambon Rumphius married a young lady by the name of Suzanna. We don't know when she was born, or even her maiden name. We only know that his wife was called Suzanna because he named a rare white orchid Flos Suzannae[399] in her memory. The couple named their first- born Paul August. Then followed two or three girls whose names we don't know. Unfortunately, his wife and the youngest girl were killed in an earthquake in 1674: they were crushed by a collapsing wall. He did not marry again until 1690 or 1691, this time to a widow named Isabella Ras. The only existing portrait of Rumphius was painted by his son, Paul August.

His second wife and the children helped him to gather and dry plants. The local community, old and young also helped with the work. He also gathered information from local healers about what plants had medicinal uses. He did actually discover that some plants can be used to heal diseases. Everyone around him was glad to help, as Rumphius treated the natives with consideration. He was always prepared to listen to their problems.

When Rumphius later moved to the city of Ambon, he continued to be closely involved in the welfare of the Ambonese people. All his life until shortly before he died he was a member of the political organisation Politieke Raad van Ambon [Political Council of Ambon]. He was also chairman of the Dewan Urusan Perkawinan dan Perkara Judicial Kecil[400] public authority.

Rumphius' Career

In 1655 Rumphius was involved in the 5th Ambonese War, which was fought mainly in the southern parts of the island of Ceram. The VOC troops were commanded by De Vlaming[401], a man who treated the native population with extreme cruelty. Rumphius could not accept the brutality and bloodshed committed by the Dutch and left the military, settling in the village of Larike as a merchant. At the same time, he was appointed to a new position in the VOC. Apparently they were very satisfied with his work, because soon afterwards he was entrusted with the supervision of the coastal waters off the village of Hila in

---

399 Pectelis susannae
400 Office for matrimonial issues and minor legal questions
401 Aka Vlamingh; for his punitive expeditions see Chapter 8

Jazirah Lei-Hitu, where Rumphius lived from 1660 onwards. He had a house built next to Fort Amsterdam. The fort occupied a strategically important position. It was restored in 1993. Outside the fort you can still see the well-shaft where Rumphius must surely have got his water.[402]

From the very beginning, Rumphius was fascinated by the extraordinary tropical flora and fauna in the island of Ambon, whose beauty delighted him. He was aware that this beauty had not yet been investigated scientifically and recorded in writing. He began to study all these previously unknown plants. With great enthusiasm he catalogued all the plants he could find on Ambon and classified them, a project whose systematic execution began in 1660. Fortunately, the Governor General in Batavia, Joan Maetsuycker, was a learned jurist who was interested in the sciences. He therefore gave Rumphius permission to devote his attention entirely to the flora and fauna of Ambon and the Banda Sea.

Rumphius was, however, aware that his knowledge of botany was limited, as he had not yet had an opportunity to educate himself in the fields of botany and biology. To do so, he needed books and instruments, such as a magnifying glass. He asked his friends in Holland to help him to acquire all these things. Fortunately, all the books and equipment he wanted arrived safely in Ambon. If he had ordered them via the VOC in Amsterdam, the cost would have been deducted from his pay. Over the course of time, Rumphius acquired many more books, so that he soon had an extensive library at his disposal. The languages of the books he used in his work were, apart from Latin, German and Dutch. He was also able to speak Malay, French, Spanish, Portuguese and Italian. Rumphius was a linguistic genius, but he had no English at all. As well as texts for his biological studies he collected books about all the states and regions of the world. Almost all his books had been printed in Antwerp in Belgium and Amsterdam. In 1687 there was unfortunately a major fire in Ambon, where Rumphius was living at the time, and most of his library was destroyed.

Fortunately, there was a Dutchman who had researched Rumphius' life in detail. He died several years before the fire. He wrote a book about all Rumphius' works and his library. It was a weighty tome with over 400 pages. It shows that Rumphius was in contact with many people, especially with biologists and scientists from other fields.

Rumphius never left the Moluccas again, and so never met any of his correspondents face to face. Correspondence by letters — and transported by sailing ship — naturally took a long time, but Rumphius was nevertheless a keen and regular letter writer. All his books and his correspondence contributed enormously to his long-term development into a famous professional biologist whose name is still

---

402 See Ill. 20-35

mentioned in professional circles. In 1681 he was even elected a member of the Leopoldina, the imperial Academia Naturae Curiosorum [Academy of Natural Scientists] in Vienna, Austria.

Until 1670 Rumphius lived and worked in Hila, in the north of the island of Ambon, where he was given a plot of land by the VOC as his own private property. The plot was near Fort Amsterdam. He welcomed the gift and immediately used the plot to make an 'experimental garden' where he grew various plant species for his research. The VOC allowed him the time and the opportunity to carry out his biological investigations. They even assigned a draughtsman, a secretary and several servants to him. Rumphius then began on the work of classifying his discoveries and naming them in Ambonese, Malay and Latin. He constantly encouraged his draughtsmen and secretaries to work conscientiously and rigorously. He was himself a good draughtsman.

Catastrophe after Catastrophe

In 1670, at the age of 43, Rumphius began to suffer from blurred vision. He had incurable glaucoma. It wasn't long before he was totally blind. He believed that his blindness was due to his exposure to intensive sunlight, as he hadn't done enough to protect himself against it. In his work looking for plants and marine life he had always been exposed to sunlight. He himself called his eye disease Suffosio or Cataracta Nigra. People regularly came to him bringing various plants as medication for his eyes, but all to no avail. By this time he had already collected many specimens, particularly of plants, snails and corals, which now had to be systematically classified. Fortunately, the VOC provided additional secretarial help and draughtsmen. Presumably the 17th-century Dutch were particularly talented at writing and drawing. One of the draughtsmen was his own son, Paul August. Because the secretaries had no Latin, all the works he had written in Latin were translated into Dutch.

Although he was now completely blind, he continued to pursue his investigation and classification of many plants and marine creatures with great diligence. His blindness did not prevent him from expanding his field of research to include all the species of crustacea in the waters around Ambon. He also listened to the native inhabitants' stories about the shellfish and then dictated his conclusions to his son or a secretary. Because he was so friendly, many Ambonese were glad to help him in his investigations. He examined his material by touching it with his fingers and his lips. He was also a good listener.

He moved from Hitu to the town of Ambon with his family. He was still generously supported by his employer, the VOC in Batavia, receiving a salary as well as support from secretaries and draughtsmen. For ten years, his wife and children also helped him with his work from dawn till dusk.

But then came another catastrophe. A major earthquake devastated Ambon on the 17th of February 1674, killing the people he loved the most, his wife and his youngest daughter, who had both been with him day and night, guiding his steps outside the house and making the wonders of Ambon accessible to him. The earthquake killed 2,322 inhabitants of Ambon. Rumphius nevertheless still managed to complete his manuscript entitled Sejarah dan Geografi Pulau Ambon[403]. After he presented the book to his superiors, it was kept under lock and key by the VOC in Batavia. They feared that it could be of use to their competitors. Later, after Rumphius' death, Francois Valentijn, a priest, discovered the book. He made minor alterations and published it under his own name.

On the 11th of January 1687 Rumphius met with yet another catastrophe: a large part of the town of Ambon was destroyed by a terrible fire. Many books in Rumphius' library and sketches he had made for his botanical books were lost in the flames, as were his collections of shells and also manuscripts and the drafts of new book projects, which he had been working on assiduously for 15 years. The VOC supported Rumphius in his efforts to replace all the documents and drawings that had been burned. Rumphius never gave up. His pleasant character had gained him many friends in Ambon, who helped him with this difficult task. They were there for him when he needed them.

His house was rebuilt, and he moved back in. It was a sturdy building that survived and could be visited until the 24th of August 1944.[404] Because the city of Ambon was occupied by Japanese forces during the Second World War, allied aircraft made bombing raid on it, in which Rumphius' house was destroyed.

---

403 *History and Geography of the Island of Ambon*
404 See Ill. 21-6

Rumphius' Scientific Publications

Rumphius spent a year working to produce a book which he gave the title Ambonese Historie, completing it in 1679. However, his superiors kept the manuscript locked away, since it contained too much information that might be of use to their English competitors. There were, nevertheless, a few copies circulating among Rumphius' friends, so that the book survived. Finally, after 231 years, the book was published in The Hague in 1910 .

Between 1724 and 1727 Francois Valentijn published a series of books about the Dutch East Indies in which he used a lot of material from Rumphius' manuscripts – though without mentioning his name .

In 1672 the VOC asked Rumphius to produce a map of the town of Ambon and the surrounding area. He completed it by 1678, to the complete satisfaction of the VOC. For strategic reasons, the maps and the accompanying descriptions were kept top secret. It was not until 323 years later – in 2001 – that the material was edited and published by a team led by W. Buijze. The work includes various maps, as well as many drawings and explanations.

In 1690 Rumphius' 12-volume masterpiece was completed. It was a massive work on which he had spent more than 20 years. The title he gave it was Herbarium Amboinense alias Het Amboinsche Kruidboek [The Ambonese Herbal]. He sent the book to VOC Governor General Johannes Camphuys in Batavia. It was not, however, sent to Holland until 1697, because the Governor General, himself an amateur astronomer, was delighted with the book and wished to study it himself. It contained 1,200 plant species and it took seven years for it to be copied; he then sent it to Europe. However, the Dutch ship carrying it was attacked and sunk by a French fleet – taking the original manuscript with it. Fortunately, there was still the copy that had been made in Batavia, which later safely reached Holland. There, Joannes Burmannus was commissioned to translate the work into Latin. It was a massive task, but Burmannus succeeded, and the book was published in two languages, Latin and Dutch. Translating and preparing the book for translation took 44 years, and it was finally printed and published in 1741, 1743 and 1747. The original 12 volumes had been compressed into six, though they were thicker. A seventh volume, entitled Auctuarium [Addenda] appeared in 1755. It contained several previously unknown plant species that Rumphius had classified before he died.

The delay in publication was mainly due to the VOC's excessive caution about competitors, though there was also doubt about whether the book would attract sufficient interest. An English edition was finally published by E. M. Beekman in 2011. Rumphius also collected information about the fauna in Ambon into a book, but the manuscript was lost with the ship that was carrying it to Europe; unfortunately, there was no copy of this one.

Since his arrival on Ambon Rumphius had made a habit of collecting and cataloguing all kinds of objects. His extensive collection included snails, seashells, corals, fossils, sea urchins, starfish, minerals, crystals, eggs, insects, meteorites and many other things. He even collected unusually shaped driftwood. In 1682 he sent all these 'curiosities' to Amsterdam in six large chests.

In 1699 his book D'Amboinese Rariteitkamer [The Ambonese Cabinet of Curiosities], in which all these objects were described, was ready for publication. He placed particular emphasis on the shellfish and crustacea found in the waters around Ambon. The book was authentic and was better received in Europe than its predecessors. This time Rumphius sent the manuscript directly to Holland, to his friend Dr Hendrik D'Acquet in Delft who published it in 1705. Sending his books through the VOC, as he had done previously, had not only led to delays: whole passages had also been deleted or altered by the VOC in their anxiety about English competition. Rumphius never published a single book himself. He died in 1782 in his house on Olifantstraat[405] in Ambon, a main street that is now called Jalan Pattimura[406].

Memorials

It is almost certain that Rumphius was buried beside his house on Olifantstraat. Apparently, there was a marble gravestone on the spot, but during the period of British control[407] this was destroyed in 1800. On the initiative of Governor General Godert van der Capellen a new monument was erected in the same place in the garden of Rumphius' house in Ambon in 1824.

Ill. 21-7, Dedication of the monument by Gov. General Godert van der Capellen, 1824[408]

Ill. 21-8, The Rumphius memorial

405 Elephant Street
406 Jalan Pattimura, named after an Indonesian freedom fighter executed by the Dutch in 1817.
407 1796-1803 and 1810-1817
408 Collectie Tropenmuseum Amsterdam

Ill. 21-9, Gov. General Cornelis Dirk de Graeff and Gov. van Sandick laying wreaths on the 1ˢᵗ of November 1927 to commemorate the 300ᵗʰ anniversary of Rumphius' birth[409]

In 1944 the monument was destroyed when the Allies bombed Ambon in the Second World War. On the initiative of Monseigneur Sol and W. Buijze, a replica of the monument was made and dedicated by the Governor of the Moluccas on the 22ⁿᵈ of April 1996. The monument is now on a site on the corner of Jalan Pattimura outside the Xaverius Gymnasium.

Ill. 21-10
Detail of the inscription

Ill. 21-11
New Rumphius Monument, 1996

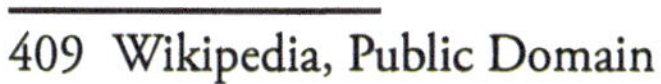

409 Wikipedia, Public Domain

The name of Rumphius lives on in Ambon; his memory is also perpetuated by the Rumphius Library, founded by the Dutch Bishop Andreas Sol[410], who later became an Indonesian citizen. During his time in office as Bishop of Ambon he displayed great interest in the history and culture of the Moluccas and collected books and articles with particular reference to the development of the Catholic Church in the region. His collection also extended to other areas of Indonesia. His collection grew to over 5,000 books, and in 1984 he founded the Rumphius Library. The pride and joy of the collections are original works by Rumphius and Valentijn. On the 11th of October 2012 Monseigneur Sol was awarded a decoration, the Nugrah Jasadarma Pustaloka, for his achievement in founding the library. This is the highest distinction awarded by the Indonesian National Library for services to the development of libraries. We are optimistic that one day a worthy successor to Sol will be found to maintain and further develop the library. The legacy of Georg Everhardus Rumphius, that extraordinary scientist and author, must be preserved. He is still honoured here as a 'Hero of the Moluccas'.

Recent Literature about G. E. Rumphius

- *W. Buijze, Leven en Werk van Georg Everhard Rumphius, The Hague 2006*
- *W. Buijze, Rumphius's reis naar Portugal, The Hague 2002*
- *W. Buijze, Georg Everhard Rumphius, Hidupnya dan Tugu, Ambon*
- *W. Buijze, Rumphius, Bibliothek op Ambon 1654-1702, The Hague 2004*
- *W. Buijze, Georg Everhard Rumphius, Een Duitse Botanicus in Dienst van de VOC, Magazin Indische Letteren, 22 (2007), pp. 98-133*
- *W. Buijze, Die Bibliothek von Rumphius auf Ambon, in der Reihe Bibliothek und Wissenschaft, pp. 151-163, published by Harrassowitz, Wiesbaden*

That was what Pastor Böhm had to say about Rumphius. In the Rumphius Library there are more than 700 books by and about Rumphius.

Rumphius was honoured in many other ways. For example, the Dutch national shipping line KPM[411] named one of their ships the SS Rumphius, which sailed the route between Holland and Java as well as between the islands in the Dutch East Indies.

After his arrival in Ambon in January 1654, Rumphius never left the Moluccas. His permanent home was the Island of Ambon, but he also visited the islands of Ternate and Tidore in the northern Moluccas.

---

410 1915-2016
411 Koninklijke Paketvaart Maatschappij

Ill. 21-12
The SS Rumphius, in 1929 in the Sunda Strait. In the background the small volcano Anak Krakatau [412]

Ill. 21-13
The SS Rumphius on a KPM brochure

According to Pastor Cornelis J. Böhm, the Rumphius expert, he visited the Banda Islands at least once, as is shown by his description of the flora and fauna of some of the islands.[413] Unfortunately, I have been unable to discover any documentary evidence to show how often he was on the Bandas, or how long he spent there.

In professional circles Rumphius is often referred to as the Blind Seer of Ambon, because of his ability, in spite of his blindness, to assemble and document his extensive collection of specimens from the plant and animal world with the help of his son. He was a master of observation and, after his blindness struck, of the sense of touch.

He was also called the Blind Poet of Ambon. This was because Rumphius spiced the systematic descriptions in D'Amboinsche Rariteit Kamer with anecdotes, or because as a scientist he introduced a touch of poetry into botany in the way he named the plants he was classifying. He continually had to find new Latin, German and Dutch names for them. When I leaf through Rumphius' works, I am frequently struck by names that could be the titles of a poem or a short story. For example, there are plant names like:
The Poet's Fern,
The Naked Tree,
The Blue Clitoris,

---

412 Collectie Tropenmuseum Amsterdam
413 See Chapter 19, Pulau Ai

The Nymph's Hair,
The Wild Drummer's Tree,
Saturn's Beard or
The Memory Plant.

The same is true for the animal world:
The Little Dreamhorn,
The Princess's Funeral,
The Double Venus Harp,
The Blue Sailor or
The Village Musicians.

Each of these names could be the title or the first line of a poem. But he did more than give the species poetic names. He also described their structure, form, colour and so on. For every plant, he described the structure of the roots, the arrangement of the leaves and possible uses, for example, for medical purposes. But there was always something romantic. He even described the Ambonese women's secret knowledge of herbs that act as an aphrodisiac or make the young man you desire do what you want.

Here are a few examples of Rumphius' work.

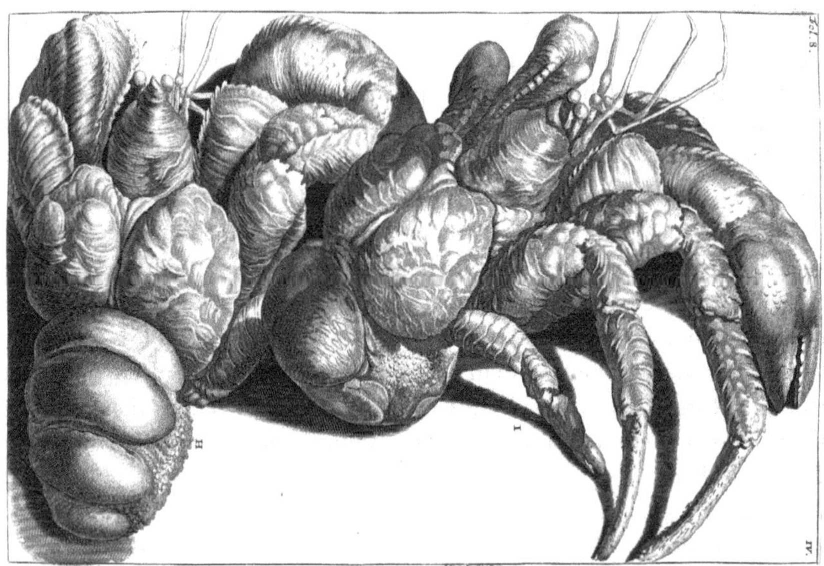

Ill. 21-14, The Coconut Crab

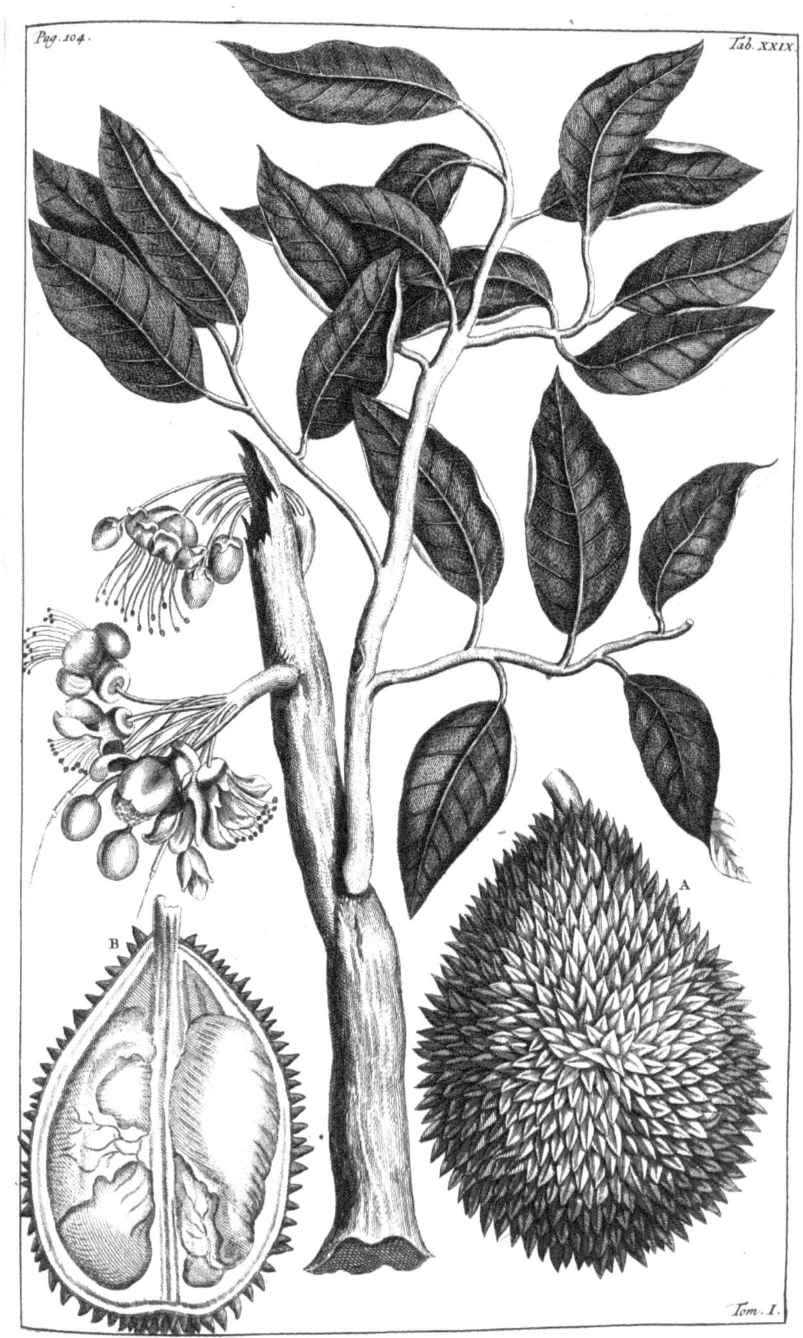

Ill. 21-15, Durian, the smelly fruit

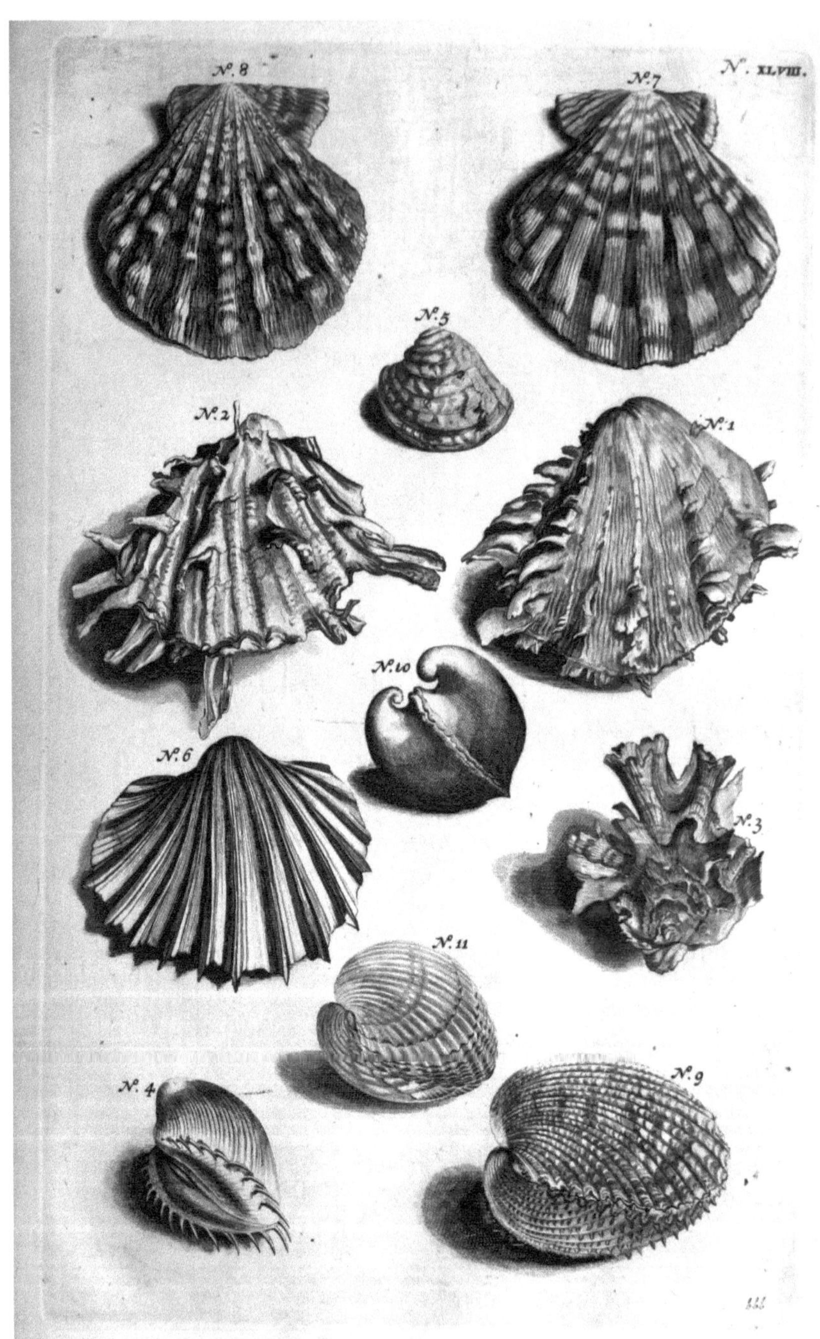

Ill. 21-16, Shellfish

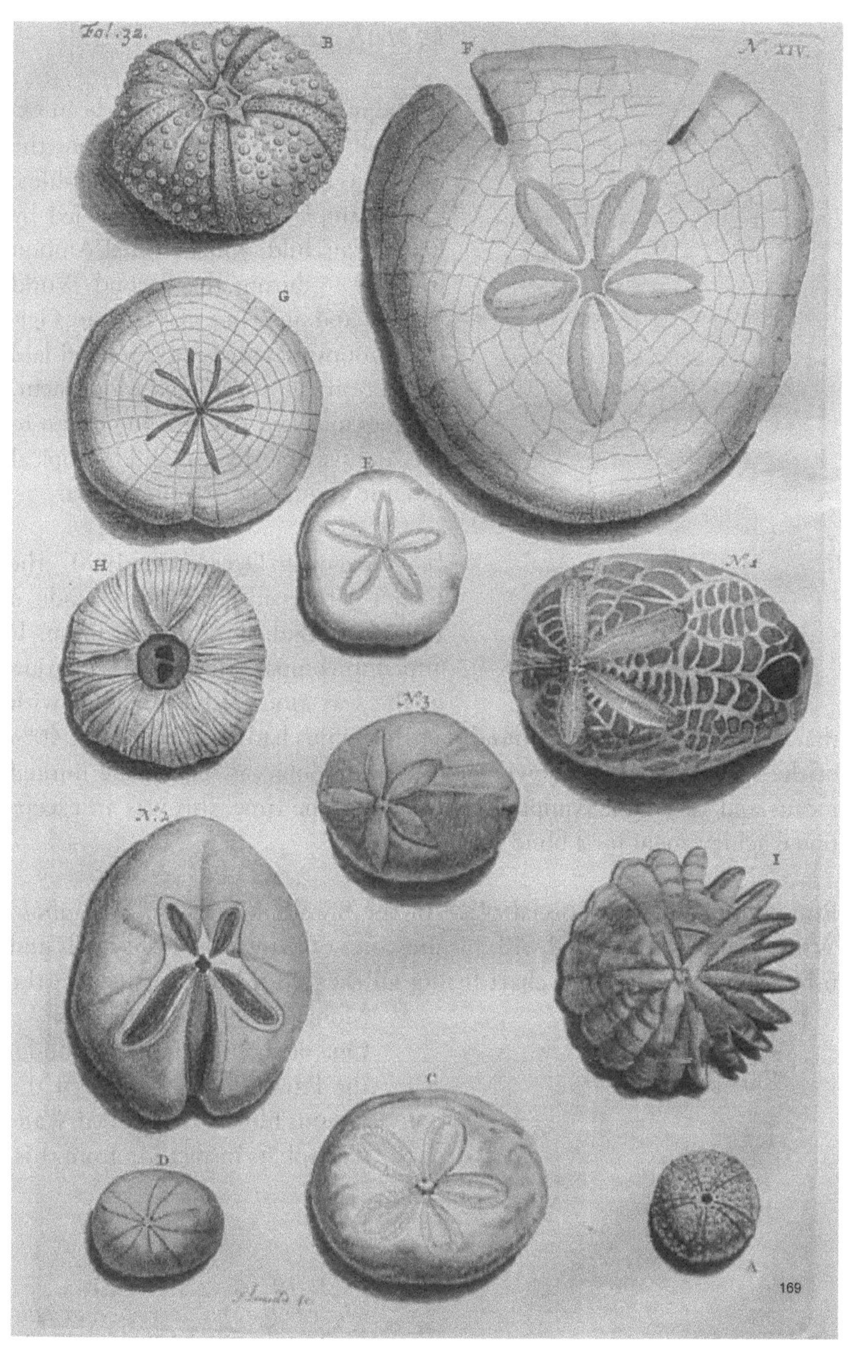

Ill. 21-17, Sea Urchin Skeletons

365

Ill. 21-18, Starfish

In the modern era, there have been expeditions which aimed to explore the Moluccas in the footsteps of Rumphius. One example is the expedition led by David Fairchild, which visited Ambon in 1940 – during the Second World War – and just one day before German troops marched into Holland laid flowers on the Rumphius Monument. Photographs and reports can be seen in the archives of the Fairchild Tropical Botanic Garden in Miami/Florida.

In November/December 1990 the Dutch University of Leiden made a Rumphius Biohistorical Expedition. It aimed to compare the current situation in the seas around the Moluccas with that of 300 years ago. They found that Rumphius had described about 40% of the species that are known today in the Moluccas. Given the limited means and very basic equipment available at the time, this was an exceptional achievement for a blind scientist.

Rumphius has a very special place in the Siwalima museum in Ambon. Whole walls are decorated with his drawings of plants, shellfish, snails and fish. There is a large wall chart listing all the 528 fish he classified in the Moluccas and the Banda Sea.

One of them is the Ikan Banda, the Banda fish. I wonder if the famous film 'A Fish Called Wanda' took its inspiration from this.

Ill. 21-19
Chart in the Siwalima museum with the names of 528 fish which Rumphius classified in Ambon and the Banda Islands.

The walls in Fort Amsterdam in Hila are also decorated with copies of Rumphius' drawings. Unfortunately, my camera's battery ran out inside the fort, so that there is only one picture .

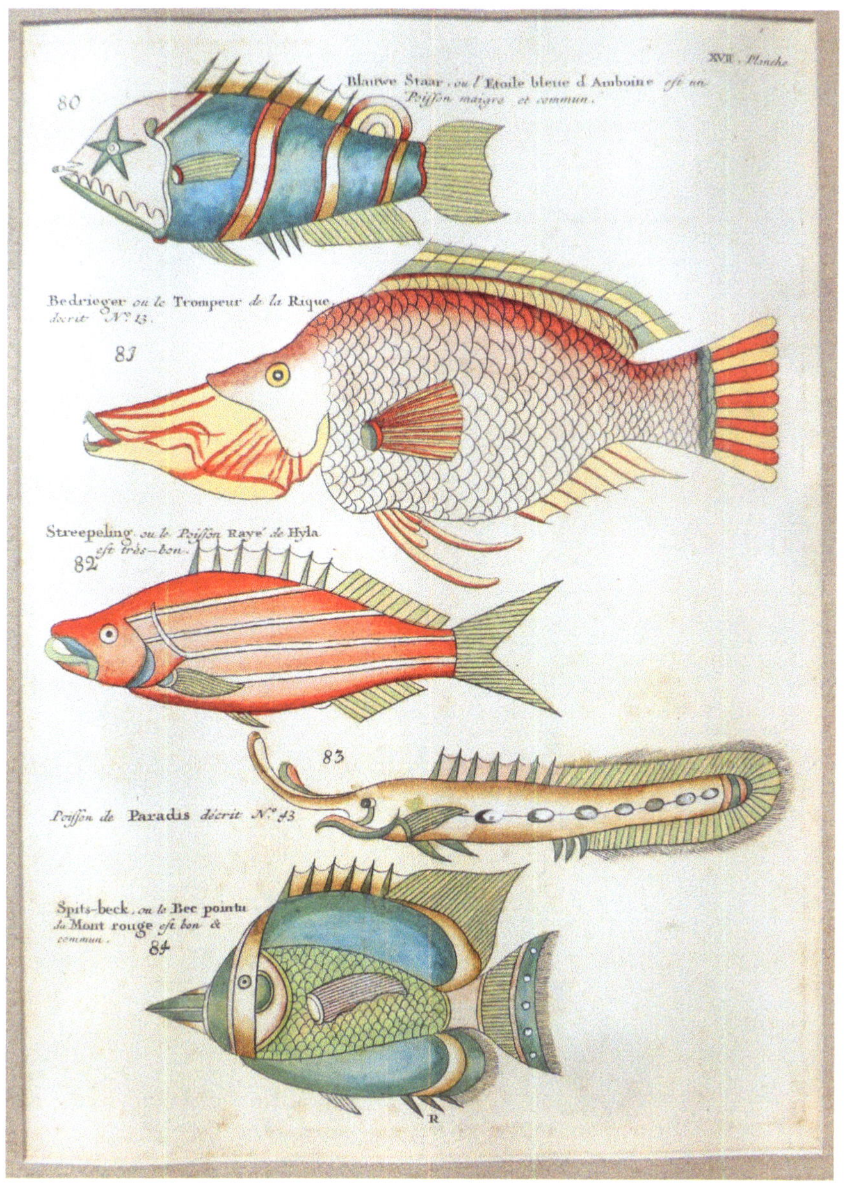

Ill. 21-20, Exotic fish in Fort Amsterdam

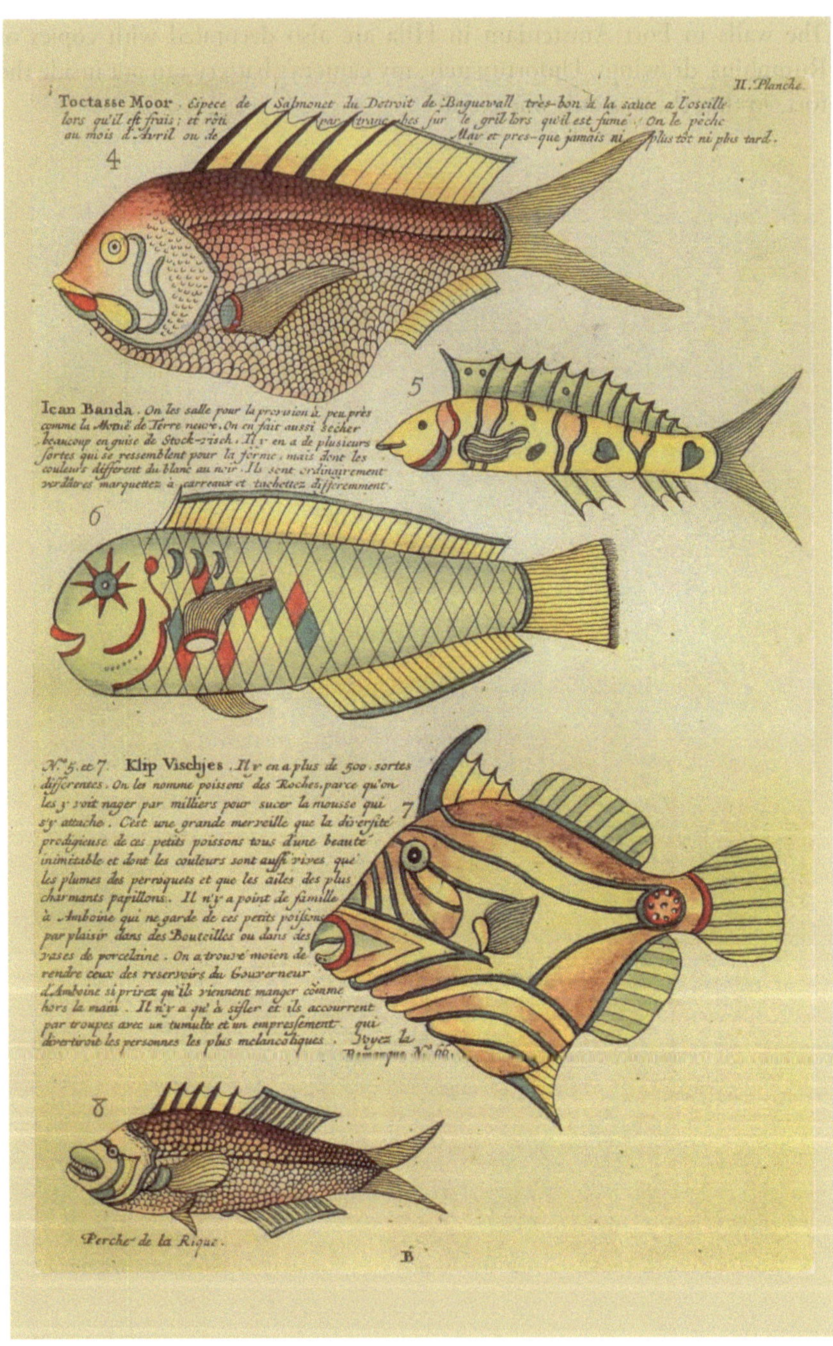

Ill. 21-21, A picture including the Ikan Banda, the Banda fish (number 5)

Ill. 21-22, The nutmeg by Rumphius

Here is also a Kebun Rumphius, a Rumphius Garden in Ambon. It is in the Poka-Rumahtiga district near the Protestant St Yohanes Church. Rumphius experimented with saplings of various types of trees here. Apart from the well, whose water he used to water his saplings, and the garden's name, there is nothing else to see which might remind us of him.

The Tropenmuseum [Tropical Museum] in Amsterdam[414] is located in a magnificent old building. They have a permanent exhibition about Rumphius. They even have a waxwork of him investigating something by touch. I would recommend the museum to anyone who is interested in the history of the colonial period or slavery. However, I could not find anything connected with the Dutch massacre of the Bandanese, or the Amboyna massacre .There is also a permanent exhibition about Rumphius – and another waxwork – in the Boerhaave Museum in Leiden.

Ill. 21-23 Rumphius waxwork in the Tropen-museum in Amsterdam[415]

---

414 https://www.tropenmuseum.nl/
415 Tropenmuseum Amsterdam, Photograph: Ester Helena Arens

In the archives and museums in Holland there is an abundance of documents and material which, if studied, would surely fill a large number of books. There seems to be serious renewed interest in Rumphius. Cologne University also has a group – Indisch-Nederlandse Letterkunde – which is investigating Rumphius' life and work. Even in distant Singapore homage was paid to Rumphius in the context of the Singapore Garden Festival in 2008 with a waxwork and an exhibition of his work.

In Georg Eberhard Rumpf's birthplace, Wölfersheim in Hessen, there is a memorial plaque to this extraordinary, admirable German scientist.

Rumphius' works are still regarded as of great value to science. The renowned doctor, zoologist, philosopher, artist and writer Ernst Heinrich Philipp August Haeckel[416], who spent five months exploring the Malay Archipelago in 1901[417] recognised Rumphius' contribution in the following words: Georg Everhard Rumphius, who meticulously observed the lives, habitat and forms of the coral polyps in the Malay Archipelago, was one of the first naturalists to recognise that these zoophytes were actually animals.

Ill. 21-24
Rumphius Memorial in Wölfersheim

---

416 1834-1919

417 Haeckel, Ernst, *Aus Insulinde: Malayische Reisebriefe* [From Insulinde: Malay Travel Notes], 1901

22. Recipes

As early as the 14th-century *buoch von guoter speise*[418] [Book of good food/dishes] we find mention of *ingeber vnd kümel vnd muschat bluomen vnd negelin* [ginger and cumin and mace and cloves]. These spices were, however, reserved for the nobility and the wealthy. Nutmeg and mace were an expensive delicacy. In 1511, at Duke Ulrich of Württemberg's wedding, and in 1575, at that of Ludwig of Württemberg, mace and nutmeg were used in the dishes that were served at the wedding feasts. In 1526 a *suppe mit ganzem ingber, muskatenblumen und zibeben*[419] was served at a feast held by the Elector of Saxony at the Imperial Diet in Speyer.

After the Europeans discovered the sea route to the Spice Islands, spices grew in importance and began to be used by the middle classes as well, for seasoning vegetables, preserves and baked goods. The ordinary citizen could now afford nutmeg and it is now mentioned in all the cookery books of the period. In the 19th century nutmeg and mace were used with increasing frequency. In the 1805 *Preußisches Kochbuch* [Prussian Cookery Book] one of the two spices is found in almost every soup, every fish dish, for poultry and pies, in sauces and even in *Glühwein*[420]. Interestingly enough, galangal[421] is also found in almost every old cookery book – as a medicinal plant as well. It is nowadays used in almost every dish in Asian cuisine, though it has completely vanished from European cookery.

Nowadays nutmeg is rather out of fashion. Mace is still mainly used in Great Britain; on the continent they prefer nutmeg. On the Banda Islands I could taste mace in almost every dish.

I remember that my mother always seasoned her Swabian *Spätzle* with a pinch of mace ground in a mortar. Where had my mother got the spice from? In the years around the Second World War, it was practically unknown in Germany and not available anywhere. Presumably, she brought it back from visits to our Dutch relatives in Amsterdam, since it was well-known there. Or is it a further clue that my mother's Dutch relatives did actually have some link to the Banda Islands?

418　Consulted at: uni-giessen.de/fbz/fb05/germanistik/absprache/sprachverwendung/gloning/tx/bvgs.htm
419　Soup with whole ginger, mace and raisins or currants
420　A mulled wine, served hot with spices
421　A member of the ginger family

In my mother's cookery book I found the following list of ingredients for

Spätzle (it's the recipe I always use myself):
*   500 gr. flour
*   ½ cup wheat semolina
*   6-7 eggs
*   water as necessary
*   1 pinch of salt
*   1 pinch of ground mace or nutmeg

The dough is 'beaten' until it threads. After I got to know mace on the Bandas and brought some home with me, I decided to try this dish with mace – previously I had always used nutmeg. The *Spätzle* tasted more delicate with mace than with nutmeg. No wonder mace is known on the Bandas as 'nutmeg's up-market sister'. *Spätzle* taste best when they are scraped off a wooden board.

My mother also used mace in quince compote, mashed potato, casseroles, potato dumplings, *Maultaschen*[422], fish, and yeast buns and apple pie. Although my mother used mace almost every day when I was young, I had completely forgotten it. It was only when I visited the Bandas that I remembered this precious spice.

Another old recipe of my mother's is for *Weckklöße* [bread dumplings] with nutmeg. She said it was an old wartime recipe she had got from her father, who had worked in the kitchen of the officers' mess during his military service.

Bread Dumplings
Ingredients and preparation:
*   10 stale rolls or dry white bread cut into small cubes. Remove a handful of the cubes and soak the rest in about 150 ml of hot milk.
*   1-2 onions finely chopped. Fry at low temperature in plenty of butter until transparent.
*   Add the onions to the steeped bread, and then add 1 cup of wheat semolina and an egg. Season with salt, pepper, fresh parsley and half a teaspoon of ground nutmeg.
*   Mix thoroughly and allow to rest for 30 minutes.
*   Fry the remaining cubes of bread with garlic in butter until crisp.
*   Mould dumplings about 2 inches in diameter by hand, placing a few of the fried bread cubes in the middle of each of them.

---

422 Swabian 'ravioli'

Allow to simmer in plenty of salted water for about 30 minutes. The water must not boil! I wish *bon appetit* to anyone who makes these delicious dumplings .

I have already mentioned *Kuah Iso,* a fish soup with tuna dumplings in Chapter 16, and included the recipe.

Another Bandanese dish served in the Cilu Bintang Estate is *Tuna Rujak.* I could not deprive my readers of this delicious dish, and fortunately the kitchen at the Cilu Bintang Estate gave me the recipe:

Tuna Bumbu Rujak (serves 4)

Ingredients:

* 500 gr tuna fillet (the tuna must be very fresh, as it is eaten raw – no problem on the Bandas!)
* 7 shallots (or an equivalent quantity of red onion)
* 5 cloves of garlic
* 10 large long chilis (not hot)
* 1 cm ginger
* 1 cm galangal root (should be available in Asian shops)
* 1 cup of kenari nuts (if unavailable, almonds or Indonesian kemiri nuts)
* 3 tablespoons coconut oil
* 5 tablespoons sweet soy sauce
* 1-2 teaspoons white vinegar or lemon juice
* 3-4 tablespoons tamarind sauce, or 1 of tamarind paste
* 300 ml. water
* 1 stick cinnamon (2 inches)
* 6 cloves
* 1 nutmeg (cut in half)
* Some shrimp paste
* ½ teaspoon sea salt
* 1 tablespoon palm sugar (or brown sugar)

Preparation:

1. Finely chop the shallots and garlic. Chill.
2. Grind chilis, shrimp paste, ginger, galangal and salt to a fine paste in a mortar
3. Finely chop the tuna and add to the paste
4. Grind the kenari nuts, cinnamon, cloves and nutmeg to a coarse powder in a mixer and add to the paste, together with the sugar.

5. Now add the shallots, garlic, vinegar or lemon juice, tamarind, soy sauce and water as necessary, and mix thoroughly.
6. Chill for 1-2 hours and serve cold with rice or white bread.

Tuna Rujak reminded me a little of ceviche, a raw fish dish served all over South America, though the spice mixture is different. If fresh tuna – or another fresh salt-water fish – is available, *Tuna Rujak* makes an excellent starter. Instead of rice it can also be served with white bread.

Ill. 22-1
Tuna Bumbu Rujak[423] as it is served at the Cilu Bintang Estate (if desired you can also add a few thin slices of raw tuna as shown in the picture – but only freshly caught tuna)

Ill. 22-2
Sup Labu pumpkin soup[424]

---

423 With Abba's kind permission
424 Ibid.

Another typical Banda Island dish is pumpkin soup. This is how it is prepared in the Cilu Bintang Estate:

Sup Labu (serves 4)
Ingredients:
- 1 kg. pumpkin
- ½ litre water
- ½ teaspoon ground nutmeg
- 1-2 pieces of chopped mace
- ½ teaspoon ground white pepper
- ½ teaspoon ground cinnamon
- 1 teaspoon salt
- chopped celery leaves

Preparation:
1. Peel the pumpkin, remove the seeds and cut into ½ to ¾ inch cubes
2. Boil for at least 20 minutes in water, or until the pumpkin is soft
3. Process the pumpkin to a pulp in a mixer
4. Add the spices and gently simmer for another ten minutes
5. Garnish with the celery leaves and serve

As you see, Bandanese cooking does not use the hot chilis or the sambal[425] that are used on Java or Bali. Coconut, too, which is present in most Balinese and Javanese dishes, is very seldom used here. On the other hand, almost every dish includes nutmeg, mace, cinnamon, kenari nuts and pepper. *Sup Labu* is very simple and quick to prepare. All my guests who have tasted it have enjoyed it.

Indonesian light Bintang beer is, of course, the perfect accompaniment to all these Bandanese dishes. If you prefer tea, then I can warmly recommend Bandanese cinnamon tea.

Teh Kayu Manis/Cinnamon Tea[426]
Ingredients:
- 1 cinnamon stick
- 1 teaspoon black tea
- 1 litre water
- Sugar as required
-

---

425 Spicy sauce
426 Indonesisian: Teh Kayu Manis

Preparation:

1. Slowly warm up the cinnamon stick in the water. Allow to simmer gently for 5 minutes, then remove from the heat
2. Allow to rest and brew for 15 minutes
3. Bring back to the boil and add the black tea
4. Allow to rest for 3 minutes
5. Pour into the cups using a sieve

This tea can be drunk hot or cold. It is one of the Cilu Bintang Estate's specialities.

Ill. 22-3, Cinnamon tea

23. Back to Bali

At five o'clock on the dot the next morning, Pak Umar picked me up at my hotel. It was called Clean & Comfort Homestay and did its name proud, even if its location was not particularly good. Pak Umar took me to the airport. I promised him I'd return in December. Next time it would be easier, since I knew him. I flew back to Bali via Macassar, this time without turbulence. Here on Bali life is less exciting .

It had been an interesting trip; I collected many new impressions. It's always impressive to see how many different cultures and histories the 'Land of the 17,000 Islands' has to offer. Where history is concerned, the Banda archipelago has a great deal to offer.

In Bali I immediately began committing my impressions to paper while they were still fresh. Back in Germany I worked hard on sorting out the various strands of information and reducing them to book form. I am determined to visit the Banda Islands once more this December no matter how difficult it is to get there. Although I have seen a great deal of Indonesia's island world over the past 55 years, I found this group of islands particularly fascinating.
I will do all I can to have this book about the Bandas out in published form in time for my trip in 2021. It would be a unique occasion to launch the new book on the Bandas themselves.

24. Epilogue

I have described many past events in my books – always from the Indonesian point of view. And it is the same with this book. My information is to a very large extent based on conversations with Indonesians, and Indonesian archives. The Indonesians often see the events I describe from a different perspective from their former colonial rulers. In Holland many of the atrocities committed against the native population, from the 1621 massacre to the terrible colonial war from 1945 to December 1949, are officially concealed or glossed over, but the Indonesians have not forgotten the awful things that were done to them. Here on the Banda Islands I sensed this very clearly in the case of older people. I was particularly amazed when an educated Bandanese said to me, *This is a symbol of Hate!* as he pointed to the VOC emblem carved into the stone floor of the little church in Banda Neira.

The Indonesians spoke to me about the atrocities without pulling any punches and without their normal inborn polite reticence, in a way they would never do to a Dutch person. The Indonesian perspective is totally different from that of the Dutch, and the deeper the level of trust in the relationship, the clearer it becomes that for the Indonesians there was very little that was good and much that was bad in the colonial period, which lasted almost 350 years.

I am continually surprised when I meet young Dutch people in Indonesia. Most of them have no idea of the crimes their ancestors committed against the Indonesians. When they come to Bali, they land at Ngurah Rai airport, and have no idea that Colonel I Gusti Ngurah Rai was a Balinese freedom fighter who, together with his fellow fighters, was slaughtered by Dutch troops 15 months **after** (!) the Indonesian declaration of independence. The subject of the atrocities committed during the colonial era, the genocide of the Bandanese and other war crimes are simply ignored in Holland. Young people hear nothing about them at school. The dark side of colonialism is taboo. Only a few countries have dealt with their past crimes. The Dutch still have this before them – like the recognition of Indonesia's independence on the 17th of August 1945!

When I ask people on the Banda Islands what the first thing that comes into their minds about their former trading partners and colonial rulers is, they answer that, where the Portuguese are concerned, there are many words of Portuguese origin in Bahasa Indonesia. As for the English, their first answer is that the English came to the Banda Islands with friendly intentions. And then, many of them are aware of the exchange of Run for Manhattan. The only thing they connected with the Dutch was the massacre of the Bandanese. Even children in the second and third years of school, with whom I played football on Banda Besar, were aware of the genocide.

So far only occasional travellers visit the Banda islands, and they are mostly more interested in diving than culture; the coral reefs are uniquely beautiful and still pristine. Even the stream of lava that flowed down into the sea in the eruption of Gunung Api in 1988 is now once more overgrown with corals. The sea is still healthy here! But how many visitors can a healthy nature preservation scheme take? Because getting there is so difficult, tourism today is – fortunately – very limited.

We have ultimately one man to thank for the fact that the tiny Island of Run became so valuable that it could be exchanged for the far larger area of New York. It was Nathaniel Courthope, who stood up to all the hostility and attacks of the Dutch as he held out heroically on Run for years – and paid for his heroism with his life. When I looked into his name in England, I discovered that Nathaniel Courthope is today forgotten. What did this hero look like? I couldn't find a single picture of him. Nathaniel Courthope's influence on history is as little known in England today as is the extraordinary scientific work of the biologist Georg Eberhard Rumpf, known as Rumphius, in Germany.

So far the Banda Islands are still an unspoilt paradise. But for how much longer? A cruise ship, the German ship *Albatros*, has made a first visit. And another German cruise ship, the grand old lady *Artania*, also recently docked in Banda Neira. In Germany the ship is well-known because of the television series *Verrückt nach Meer* [Mad about the Sea], and an episode about the Bandas has already been broadcast. If this catches on, paradise is finished. Like so many others. The Banda Islands are one of the last paradises in the world. Is this the beginning of the end of paradise?

On the last evening before my departure I was once more reminded that in the shadow of Gunung Api we live dangerously. The mountain rumbled again deep in its interior and the earth shook slightly for a few seconds. I had the feeling that the volcano wanted to say goodbye to me.

As I left the Banda Islands I was overcome by sadness. The islands have a magic and magnetic attraction for me, and I will – if this book is finished and God wills it – try to come back here again. I greet the islands with

Sampai berjumpa lagi!

Until we meet again!

I: Article by Gunter Haug in the **Stuttgarter Zeitung**, 31st of January 2019

24 REPORTAGE

Das Gold der Bandas

Abenteuer Der 85-jährige Stuttgarter Horst Geerken erforscht die Geschichte der legendären Inselgruppe. *Von Gunter Haug*

Grüß Gott, i bin dr Horscht!" Der ältere Mann in dem gelben Poloshirt streckt lächelnd seine Hand zum Gruß entgegen. „Wo genau kommsch denn du her?" Eigentlich ist das ja kein ungewöhnlicher Gesprächsauftakt zwischen zwei Schwaben. Doch an diesem Ort, beinah am Ende der Welt, klingt das grottenbreite Schwäbisch doch komisch.

Horst Geerken lebt zurzeit auf einer exotischen indonesischen Insel, die heute so gut wie niemand mehr kennt, noch nicht einmal die Indonesier selbst. Das liegt an der versteckten Lage der vulkanischen Banda Inseln unterhalb des Äquators, im hintersten Winkel der gleichnamigen Bandasee, irgendwo zwischen den Molukken und der Nordküste von Australien.

Die Anreise ist schwierig und langwierig. Auch wenn Banda Neira, die Hauptinsel von knapp zwei Handvoll ähnlich winziger Eilande, sogar einen sogenannten Flughafen mit geteerter Landepiste aufweist, ist das mit dem stressfreien Hierherkommen so eine Sache. Denn ob eine der kleinen zweimotorigen Propellermaschinen von Ambon aus, einer Provinzhauptstadt auf den Molukken, die Bandas heute oder morgen anfliegen wird, das ist tagtäglich genauso unsicher zu beantworten, wie die Frage, ob der Insel-Vulkan Gunung Api (der „Feuerberg") demnächst wieder ausbricht oder seit der letzten Eruption im Mai 1988 endgültig zur Ruhe gekommen ist, nachdem er in den 400 Jahren zuvor seine Lava 20 Mal turmhoch in den Tropenhimmel schleuderte. Weder das eine noch das andere ist sicher. Wobei es eher wahrscheinlich ist, dass die Maschine der regionalen „Susi Air" den Boden nicht verlässt.

Verrostete Schiffsungeheuer

Und deshalb bleibt Reisenden, die unbedingt die legendenumwobenen Gewürzinseln besuchen wollen, nichts anderes übrig, als von Ambon aus ein Ticket der staatlichen indonesischen Fährgesellschaft Pelni zu buchen. Das ist zwar spottbillig, aber jedem, der seinen Nerven schon eine Überfahrt mit den beeindruckend verrosteten, hoffnungslos überbuchten Schiffsungeheuern namens „Pangrango" und „Leusser" zugemutet hat, sträuben sich in Erinnerung an die neun- bis zwölfstündige Passage die Nackenhaare. Und an die Rückfahrt mit einem dieser grauslichen Seelenverkäufer mag man lieber gar nicht denken.

Horst Geerken beherrscht, wie sich bald herausstellt, nicht nur ein wunderschönes Schwäbisch und Hochdeutsch, sondern auch Englisch, Hoch-Indonesisch, dazu die eine oder andere indonesische Regionalsprache. Zudem verfügt er über einen respektablen Grundwortschatz an Japanisch und Malayisch. Das alles gewürzt mit seinem unschlagbaren schwäbischen Slang.

Er wirkt wie Mitte 60, ist in Wahrheit jedoch bereits 85 Jahre alt. Während einem hier bei gut 35 Grad im Schatten und gefühlten 100 Prozent Luftfeuchtigkeit der Schweiß in wahren Sturzbächen herunter strömt, bleibt Geerken immer cool.

Der gebürtige Stuttgarter absolvierte in den USA sein Ingenieursstudium und lebte von 1963 bis 1981 als Resident von Telefunken in Jakarta. In diesen Pionierjahren war er genauso am Flughafenbau auf Bali beteiligt wie beim Errichten eines 100 Kilowatt Kurzwellensenders, dem größten in Indonesien, sowie am Bau einer Wasserversor-

Horst Geerken lebt zurzeit auf der Hauptinsel Banda Neira. Schon früher war die heimische Muskatnuss das wertvollste Handelsgut, auch heute noch ist sie der größte Schatz der Einwohner und wird auf den Märkten in allen möglichen Variationen verkauft.

Fotos: Gunter Haug

gung auf der Insel Sumba, deren Pumpen er mangels Stromnetz mit einer 35 Kilowatt-Solaranlage betrieben hat.

Im Alter von 48 Jahren konnte er sich dann „zur Ruhe setzen", wie er sagt, um fortan die Hälfte des Jahres in Deutschland und die anderen sechs Monate in Ubud auf Bali zu leben. Seitdem schreibt er Bücher über die Liebe seines Lebens: Bücher über Indonesien, die selbstredend auch auf Indonesisch erscheinen. Über die Geschichte, die Kultur, die Landschaften und die Menschen dieses riesigen Archipels mit seinen mehr als 17 500 Inseln, der sich vom Norden Sumatras über 5000 Kilometer bis nach Neuguinea erstreckt. Höchstwahrscheinlich hat niemand so viele Bücher über Indonesien geschrieben wie Horst Geerken. Und er schreibt fleißig weiter. Natürlich hat er längst alle Winkel Indonesiens bereist, früher geschäftlich, später aus Neugierde und aus Begeisterung.

Nur die Bandas kannte er bis vor kurzem noch nicht. Vor zwei Jahren nahm er schon mal einen Anlauf, wartete aber in Ambon vergeblich auf ein Flugzeug, und ein Schiff lief wegen der stürmischen See nicht aus. So musste er nach zwei Wochen Wartezeit unverrichteter Dinge wieder abreisen.

Jetzt ist er doch noch auf den Inseln gelandet. „Es hat es mich schon immer hierher gezogen, denn die Bandas mitsamt ihrer tragischen Historie waren einst weltberühmt. Über die wollte ich schon immer schreiben", sagt er. Geerken recherchiert emsig die Geschichte der einst legenden-

umwobenen Inseln, von denen es heißt, dass schon Christoph Kolumbus bei seiner Entdeckung Amerikas in Wahrheit zur Suche nach den Bandas aufgebrochen sei, die er freilich ebenso wenig gefunden hat, wie Ferdinand Magellan und viele weitere europäische Seefahrer.

Ihnen allen ging es darum, den einzigen Ort auf dieser Erdenscheibe zu finden, an dem die sündhaft teuren Muskatnüsse wuchsen, mit denen arabische Kaufleute einen florierenden Handel trieben. Erst im Jahr 1512 gelang es schließlich dem Entdecker Alfonso de Albuquerque, diese Eilande aufzuspüren und nunmehr eine für Portugal höchst einträgliche Geschäftsbeziehung mit den Einheimischen zu beginnen, die sich „Orang Kaya" – „die glücklichen Menschen" – nannten.

Der erbitterte Kampf um die Nuss

Dieses Glück endete freilich jäh, als europäische Ärzte plötzlich behaupteten, Muskatnuss sei ein sehr wirksames Heilmittel gegen die Pest. Die ohnehin schon hohen Preise für das Gewürz schossen durch die Decke. Gewinne von bis zu 60 000 Prozent waren an der Tagesordnung. Die Muskatnuss wurde wertvoller als Gold.

Und so begann ein erbitterter Kampf um die Nuss, den schließlich die Holländer für sich entscheiden konnten, indem sie nicht nur die Engländer und die Portugiesen von den Bandas vertrieben, sondern auch das gesamte Volk der Orang Kaya, etwa 8000 Menschen, ermordeten. Nur die

Nachfahren der einstigen Sklaven, die von der Niederländischen Ostindienkompanie anstelle der ausgerotteten Orang Kaya hierher verschleppt wurden, bewahren die Erinnerung an die grausame Geschichte und sorgen dafür, dass sie zumindest auf den Bandas noch jedes Schulkind kennt.

Auch Horst Geerken will in seinem Buch die Geschichte der Muskatnuss und der einstmals glücklichen Menschen für die Nachwelt erhalten. Natürlich wird dabei auch erwähnt, dass eine andere Banda, die Insel Rhun, eine ganz besondere Rolle in der Weltgeschichte spielte. Die drei Kilometer lange und ein Kilometer breite, westlichste Bandainsel war lange zwischen Holland und England umstritten, bis man sich im Jahr 1667 im „Frieden von Breda" darauf verständigte, die Gebietsansprüche der Engländer an Rhun mit einem Stückchen Land in Nordamerika zu kompensieren. Das Ländchen der Holländer hieß Manhattan, ein unscheinbares Eiland an der Mündung des Hudson River. Damals angesichts der enormen Weltmarktpreise für die Muskatnuss ein guter Tausch.

Seitdem es jedoch den Franzosen Ende des 18. Jahrhunderts gelang, Muskatnusssetzlinge herauszuschmuggeln und die circa zehn Meter hohen Bäume in anderen tropischen Gebieten zu kultivieren, war das Monopol dahin, und die Gewinne der Händler sanken ins Bodenlose.

Bis heute wird das wirtschaftliche Leben auf den Bandas neben dem Fischfang und dem Anbau von Gewürznelken von der Muskatnuss dominiert: Es ist ihr größter Schatz, den die Nachfahren der einstigen Sklaven auf ihren Plantagen sorgsam hüten. Sei es die als „Macis" besonders teuer gehandelte „Muskatblüte", bei der es sich in Wahrheit um die schwarz-rote Haut handelt, die den Kern umhüllt. Sei es die Nuss als solche. Oder aber der Muskatnusssaft und die Muskatmarmelade, die von der pfirsichartigen Schale gewonnen werden.

Das Müllproblem

Ein staunenswertes Stückchen Welt irgendwo im Nirgendwo. „Wenn sie hier jetzt noch das Plastikproblem in den Griff bekommen, dann wäre eine Reise auf die Bandas wie ein Ausflug ins Paradies", sagt Horst Geerken. „Aber der allgegenwärtige Plastikmüll ist ja in ganz Indonesien ein riesiges Thema. Ich glaube fast, darüber werde ich demnächst auch einmal ein Buch schreiben müssen."

In den nächsten Tagen wird der schwäbische Abenteurer für einen Kurzstopp zuhause in Bali auf der berüchtigten Pelni-Fähre in einer auf verschlungenen Wegen für umgerechnet 20 Euro gemieteten extra Kajüte mit eigenem Bett zurückschippern.

Beim letzten Mal tat es mitten in der Bandasee „einen Mordsschlag", dann drang nur noch dicker schwarzer Qualm aus dem Schornstein: Maschinenschaden. Das bringt Horst Geerken nicht aus der Ruhe. Schon gar nicht, wenn ihn der Smutje, während das Schiff stundenlang auf dem Ozean dümpelt, „beschtens bekocht".

The Gold of the Bandas

Adventure: 85-year-old Stuttgarter Horst Geerken researches the history of the legendary archipelago. By Gunter Haug

"Grüß Gott, i bin dr Horscht."[427] The elderly man in the yellow polo-shirt smiles and reaches out to shake hands. 'Where exactly are you from', this is actually not an unusual beginning to a conversation between two Swabians. But here, at the end of the world, the broad Swabian accent does sound a bit funny.

At the moment, Horst Geerken is living on an exotic Indonesian island that hardly anyone knows about today, not even the Indonesians themselves. That is because of the secluded location of the volcanic Banda Islands, below the Equator in the furthest corner of the Banda Sea, somewhere between the Moluccas and the north coast of Australia.

Getting there is difficult and tiresome. Even though Banda Neira, the main island in this handful of equally tiny islands, has what they call an airport with a tarmac runway, getting here without stress is quite a business. Because the question of whether one of the two little propeller-driven planes is going to fly to the Bandas from Ambon, capital of one of the Moluccan provinces, today or tomorrow, is an everyday question that is as difficult to answer as the question of whether the volcanic island of Gunung Api (Fire Mountain) will erupt again soon, or whether it has finally calmed down after its latest eruption in May 1988: in the last 400 years it has spewed its lava high into the sky on at least 20 occasions. There is no certain answer to either question. Though it is usually more likely that the plane run by Susi Air, the local airline, won't leave the ground.

Rusty floating death-trap

And so travellers who are determined to visit the legendary Spice Islands are left with no other choice but to book a ticket from Ambon on the Indonesian state shipping line PELNI. Admittedly, it is dirt-cheap, but anyone who has dared to submit their nerves to a crossing on one of the impressively rusty, hopelessly over-booked floating death-traps *Pangrango* or *Leusser* will surely find their hair standing on end at the memory of the nine- to twelve-hour voyage. And a return trip on one of these floating rust-buckets is something you'd rather not contemplate.

---

427 [Swabian dialect: Grüß Gott (literally may God greet/bless you) is used for Hello. So: "Hello, I'm Horst!"]

Not only does Horst Geerken speak Swabian and Standard German, as I've already said, he also speaks fluent English and Bahasa Indonesia, as well as several Indonesian regional dialects. He has a basic grasp of Japanese and Malay too. And everything is spiced with his inimitable Swabian slang.

He looks as if he were in his mid-sixties, but is actually 85. As the sweat pours down us in this climate with its 35 degrees in the shade and 100% humidity (at least, that's what it feels like), Horst always remains cool.

Born in Stuttgart, he graduated in engineering in the United States and lived in Jakarta from 1963 to 1981 as Telefunken's resident engineer. In those pioneer years he was involved in the building of the airport on Bali, putting up a 100-kw short-wave transmitter, the biggest in all Indonesia, and installing a water-treatment plant on the island of Sumba: as there was no electricity on the island, the pumps had to be powered by a 35-kw solar system.

At the age of 48 he was able to 'take his well-earned rest', as he says, and since then has spent half the year in Germany and the other six months living in Ubud on Bali. And since then he has been writing books about the love of his life: books about Indonesia, which are naturally also published in Indonesian. Books about the history, culture, landscape and the people of this gigantic archipelago of more than 17,000 islands, which stretches over 5,000 kilometres from northern Sumatra to New Guinea. It's very likely that no one has written as many books about Indonesia as Horst Geerken. And he keeps on writing! And of course he has long since visited every corner of Indonesia, initially in the course of his work and later out of curiosity and enthusiasm.

Until very recently the Bandas were the only place he wasn't familiar with. He tried to get there two years ago, but after waiting in vain for two weeks for a flight (the ships weren't sailing because of stormy weather) he had to give up.

But he did eventually manage to get to the islands. 'I've always been drawn here, since the Bandas and their tragic history were once world famous. I've always wanted to write about it,' he said. Geerken is busy researching the history of the once-fabled islands: they say even Christopher Columbus, though he discovered America, actually set out with the intention of reaching the Bandas, a quest in which he was as unsuccessful as Ferdinand Magellan and many other European explorers.

They all had the goal of finding the one place on earth where the nutmeg, that ferociously expensive spice traded extremely profitably by Arabian merchants, grew. It wasn't until 1512 that the explorer Alfonso de Albuquerque succeeded in tracking these islands down and starting a very lucrative commercial link between Portugal and the native inhabitants, who were known as *orang kaya* –the fortunate ones.

The Bitter Battle for the Nut

This good fortune came to an abrupt end when European doctors suddenly claimed that nutmeg was an effective remedy for the plague. The price of nutmeg – already high – rocketed through the ceiling. Profits of up to 60,000% were common. Nutmeg was more valuable than gold.

And so, there began a bitter struggle to gain control of the nutmeg, which was won by the Dutch, not only by expelling the English and the Portuguese from the Bandas, but by murdering the entire *orang kaya* population, some 8,000 in number. Now it is only the descendants of the slaves who were once brought here by the Netherlands East India Company to replace the exterminated *orang kaya* who preserve the memory of this gruesome history and make sure that at least every schoolchild on the Bandas knows about it.

Horst Geerken also wishes to preserve the story of the nutmeg and those once so happy people for posterity in his book. He also, of course, points out the fact that one of the Bandas, the Island of Run, played a very special role in world history. This westernmost Banda island, three kilometres long by one kilometre wide, was for a long time a bone of contention between Holland and England, until they reached an agreement in the Treaty of Breda in 1667: the English claims on Run would be compensated with a piece of land in north America. This Dutch owned land was called Manhattan, a nondescript island at the mouth of the Hudson River. Given the exorbitant price of nutmeg at the time, it was a fair exchange.

However, at the end of the 18th century, when the French succeeded in smuggling out nutmeg saplings and cultivating the 30-metre trees in other tropical regions, that was the end of the monopoly and the price sank through the floor.

Even now, although there is a fishing industry and cloves are also farmed, the economic life of the Bandas is still dominated by the nutmeg: it is their most precious treasure, carefully guarded by the descendants of the former slaves on their plantations. It is produced in the form of mace, the expensive 'flower' of the nutmeg, which is actually the blackish-red aril which surrounds the kernel; the nut itself; or nutmeg juice and nutmeg jam, which are made from the peach-like outer peel.

The Waste Problem

An amazing part of the world at the back of beyond. 'If they manage to control the waste problem here, a journey to the Bandas would be like a visit to paradise,' says Horst Geerken. 'But everywhere in Indonesia the problem of plastic waste all over the place is a major topic. I almost think I'll have to write a book about it very soon.'

In the next couple of days, the Swabian adventurer is sailing to Bali for a short stop on his way to Germany. He will be sailing on the infamous PELNI ferry in a cabin he managed to acquire 'under the counter' for the equivalent of 20 Euros.

On the way out, there was a 'terrific bang' in the middle of the Banda Sea, and thick black smoke poured out of the funnel: engine failure. That doesn't faze Horst Geerken. Especially not if the ship's cook keeps producing superb food as the ship drifts on the ocean.

Picture caption at page 383:
At the moment, Horst Geerken is living on the main island, Banda Neira. Even in the past the native nutmeg was their most valuable commodity, and today it is the locals' greatest treasure, and is sold on the markets in all possible forms.

II: A Description of the Banda Islands, by Albert S. Bickmore, M.A.

ADDITIONAL NOTICES.

(Printed by order of Council.)

1. *A Description of the Banda Islands.* By ALBERT S. BICKMORE, M.A.

ON the 5th January, 1865, I sailed from Boston for Batavia, with the hope of being able to reach the Moluccas, and re-collect the shells figured in Rumphius' 'Rariteit Kamer.' On the 1st of May I arrived at Batavia, where I was honoured, by his Excellency the Governor-General of the Netherlands India, with an order to all the officers in the Dutch possessions in the East to receive me kindly and aid me in every possible manner. Thence I proceeded along the north coast of Java to Macassar, the capital of Celebes, and thence southward through Sapi Strait between Sumbawa and Flores, and eastward to Kupang, at the southern end of Timur. From Kupang I passed northward along the western shore of Timur, and crossing the Banda Sea arrived at Amboina, the capital of the Spice Islands, or Moluccas.

Here, thanks to the privileges secured to me by the order of the Governor-General, and to the kind assistance offered me by every official, in three months I accomplished all, and even more than I had dared to plan, and was prepared to visit some other part of the Archipelago, and turn my attention to some other branch of natural history.

During all the time I had been gathering, arranging, and packing my collections, Mr. Arriens, the governor of those islands, had frequently honoured me with a visit. He now called again, this time to give me a pleasant surprise. He had a fine steam yacht of 300 or 400 tons. It was necessary that he should go to Banda, and he took it for granted that I would accompany him; and when we returned, the yacht would take me through a large part of the Archipelago north of Amboina,—a royal programme.

On the 7th of September we steamed down the magnificent bay of Amboina for Banda. Our company consisted of the Governor, who was on a tour of inspection, myself, and an "officer of justice" and lieutenant, with a detachment of soldiers, who had in custody a native of Java, that was sentenced to be hung as soon as we should reach our destined port.

The worst of the rainy season along the south coast of Ceram was now over, and the evening was cool, clear, and delightful. Early the next morning Banda, or more properly the Bandas, were in full view. They are ten in number; the largest, Lontar, or Great Banda, is a crescent-shaped island, about six miles long and a mile-and-a-half wide in its broadest parts. Its eastern horn curves towards the north, and the other points to the west. In a prolongation of the former lie Pulo Pisang, "Banana Island," and Pulo Kapal, "Ship Island." The first is only about two-thirds of a mile long and half as wide, and the last is merely a high rock, resembling the poop of a ship, hence its name. Within the circle of which these islands form an arc, lie three other islands. The highest and most remarkable is the Gunong Api,* or "Burning Mountain," apparently attaining a very considerable elevation, because its sides rise so abruptly up from the sea. Between the Gunong Api

---

* This Gunong Api must not be confounded with another similar volcano, of the same name, north of Wetta, and still another near the western end of Sumbawa, at the northern entrance of Sapi Strait.

and the northern end of Lontar lies Banda Neira, about two miles long and less than a mile broad. North-east of the latter is a small rock called Pulo Krakka, or "Women's Island." The centre of the circle of which Lontar is an arc, falls in Sun Strait, a narrow passage separating Gunong Api from Banda Neira. The diameter of this circle is about six miles. Without this another concentric circle may be drawn, which will pass through Pulo Ai (Wai), "Water Island," on the west, and Rosengain on the south-west; and outside of this a third concentric circle, which will pass through Pulo Swangi, "Sorcery," or "Spirit Island" on the north-west, Pulo Run (Rung), "Chamber Island," on the west, and the reef of Rosengain on the south-west. The total area of the whole group is only 17·6 geographical square miles.

The first European who reached these beautiful and long-sought islands was d'Abreu, a Portuguese; but he cannot properly be called their discoverer, for the Arabs and Chinese, and probably the Hindus, had been trading here for years before his arrival, and De Barros informs us that "d'Abreu (while on his way from Malacca) touched at Gresik, in the eastern part of Java, to procure Javanese and Malay pilots, who had made this voyage." Barros further adds:* "every year there repair to Sutatam (Lontar) Javanese and Malays to load cloves, nutmegs, and mace, for this place being in the latitudes most easily navigated, and where ships are most safe, and as the cloves of the Moluccas are brought to it by vessels of the country, it is not necessary to go to the latter in search of them. In the *five* islands now named—Lontar, Rosengain, Ai, Run, and Neira—grow all the nutmegs consumed in every part of the world. A proof of the correctness of Barros' statements is seen in the names of the different islands mentioned above, for they are all of Malay or Javanese origin. The aboriginal population at that time is given at 15,000, which, if correct, would have made this group far more densely peopled than any other island or number of islands in the whole archipelago at the present day.

Our fast yacht rapidly brought us nearer over the quiet, glassy sea. This is Pulo Ai on our right. It is only from 300 to 400 feet high, and, as we see from the low cliffs on its shores, is mostly composed of coral rock. This is also said to be the case with the other islands outside of the first circle, and we notice that they are all comparatiely low.

We now change our course to east, and steam up under the high, steep Gunong Api. On its n.n.w. side, about one-fourth of the distance from its summit down to the sea, there is a deep wide gulf, out of which rise thick, opaque clouds of white gas, that now, in the still clear air, are seen rolling grandly upward in one gigantic expanding column to the sky. On the top, also, thin clouds occasionally gather, and then slowly float away like cumuli, dissolving in the pure ether. These cloud masses are chiefly composed of steam and sulphurous acid gas, and, as they pour out, indicate what an active laboratory there is within the bowels of this volcano.

The western horn of crescent-shaped Lontar is before us. Its shore is composed of a series of nearly perpendicular crags, 200 or 300 feet high; but on the north side the luxurious vegetation of these tropical islands does not allow these rocks to remain naked, and from their horizontal crevices and upper edges hang down thick wide sheets of a bright green unfading verdure. The western entrance to the harbour, through which we are now passing, is between the abrupt magnificent coast of Lontar on the right, and the high, overhanging peak of Gunong Api on the left, and, as we advance, these separate and open to our view the steep lofty wall that forms Lontar's northern shore. This is completely covered with one dense matted mass of vegetation, out of which rise the erect columnar trunks of palms, from whose crests, as

---

* *Vide* "Barros" in Crawfurd's complete and accurate work, 'Dictionary of the Indian Islands.'

from sheaves, long feathery leaves hang over, and slowly and gracefully oscillate to and fro in the slight air which we can just perceive fanning our faces. Now Banda Neira is in full view. It is composed of hills, which gradually descend to the shore of this little bay. On the top of one near us is Fort Belgica, in form a regular pentagon. At the corners are bastions surmounted by small circular towers, so that the whole exactly resembles an old feudal castle. Its walls are white and almost dazzling in the bright sunlight, and beneath is a broad neatly clipped glacis, forming a beautiful, green, descending lawn.

Below this defence is Fort Nassau, which was built by the Dutch when they first arrived in 1609, only two years before the foundations of Belgica were laid, and both fortifications have existed, much as they are now, for more than two centuries and a half. To the right and left of this fort extends the chief village, Neira, with rows of pretty shade-trees on the bund, or front street bordering the bay. Its population is about 2000, and that of the whole group between 6000 and 9000.

In the roads were a number of praus from Ceram; odd-shaped vessels, high at the stern and low at the bow, and, instead of a single mast, a tall tripod, which can be hoisted or lowered at pleasure. They were all poorly built, and it seemed a wonder that such awkward boats could live any time in a rough sea. A number of Bugis traders were also at anchor near by. They are mostly hermaphrodite schooners, carrying a square-sail or foresail, a fore-topsail, and a fore-royal, and evidently designed like the praus to sail only before the wind. They visit the eastern end of Ceram and the western and south-western parts of New Guinea, the Arru group, and all the thousand other islands between Banda, Timur, and Australia. When the mail steamer that took me to Amboina touched here, a merchant of this place, who joined us, brought on board four large living specimens of the *Paradisea apoda*, or Great Bird of Paradise, which he had purchased a short time before from one of these traders, and was taking with him to Europe.* They were all very sprightly and in superb condition, and their colours had a bright, living hue, incomparably richer than the most magnificent specimens I have ever seen in any museum.

At our main truck a small flag slowly unfolds, and displays to those on shore a red ball. This indicates that the Governor is on board, and soon a boat comes off to take us to the village; but as business is not very pressing, as is usually the case here in the East, we prefer to conform to the established custom in these hot lands, and quietly enjoy a siesta instead of obliging our good friends on shore to come out in full dress and parade in the scorching sunshine.

Our first excursion was to the western end of the opposite island, Lontar, —the Malay name of the Palmyra palm, *Borassus flabelliformis*, whose leaves were used to write upon over all the archipelago before the introduction of paper by the Arabs or Chinese; and in some places even at the present time. Lontar, as already noticed, has the form of a crescent. Its inner side is a steep wall, bordered at the base with a narrow band of low land.

On its outer side, from the crest of the wall many radiating ridges descend to the sea, its south-western shore is a series of little points separated by small bays. The whole island is merely one continuous forest of nutmeg and *canari*-trees. The nutmeg-tree, *Myristica moschata*, belongs to the order *Myristicaceæ*. A foot above the ground the trunk is from 6 to 10 inches in diameter. It branches somewhat like the laurel, and its topmost sprays are frequently 50 feet high. It is diœcious, that is, the pistils and the stamens are borne on different trees, and of course some trees never bear fruit. The fruit, or *drupe*, before it is fully ripe, in size and form very closely resembles a

---

* I afterwards learned that two of them were still living when he reached France.

peach that has not yet been tinged with red; but this exterior is only a thick fleshy rind (*epicarp*) which soon opens into two equal parts; and within is seen a spherical, black, polished nut, surrounded by a finely branching aril—the " mace "—of a bright vermilion. In this condition it is probably by far the most beautiful fruit in the whole vegetable kingdom. It is now picked by means of a small basket fastened to the end of a long bamboo. The outer part being removed, the mace is carefully taken off and dried on shallow bamboo baskets in the sun. During this drying process its bright colouring changes to a dull yellow. It is now ready to be packed in casks and sent to market.

The black, shining part seen between the ramifications of the vermilion mace is really a shell, and the nutmeg is within. As soon as the mace is removed, these black nuts are taken to a room and spread on shallow trays of open basket-work. A slow fire is then made beneath them, and here they remain for three months. By the end of this time, the nutmeg has shrunk so much that it will rattle in its black shell. The shells are now broken, and the nutmegs sorted and packed in large carefully-made casks of *jati*-wood, and a brand is placed on the head, giving the year the fruit was gathered and the name of the plantation or " park " where it grew.

From Neira a large cutter took us swiftly over the bay to Selam,—a small village containing the ruins of the old capital occupied by the Portuguese during the sixteenth and early part of the seventeenth centuries, while their rights remained undisputed by the Dutch. This western end of Lontar is about 400 feet high, and is composed of coral rock of very recent date. Walking eastward we next came to a conglomerate containing angular fragments of lava. This was succeeded on the shore of the bay by a fine-grained, compact lava, somewhat stratified, and this again by trachytic and basaltic lavas. Indeed nearly this whole island is composed of such eruptive rocks, and Lontar may be regarded as merely a part of one immense crater about 6 miles in diameter, if it were circular, though it may have been more nearly elliptical. Pulo Pisang and Pulo Kapal, already noticed as falling in this circle, are two other fragments of the old crater walls—all the rest have disappeared beneath the sea. Here then, is another, enormous crater, greater even than that seen among the Zeugger Mountains on the eastern end of Java, whose minor and major axes severally measure *three miles and a half* and *four miles and a half*, and whose floor of naked sand is well named by the Malays " the Sandy Sea." Banda Neira represents the extinct craters rising in that Sandy Sea, and Gunong Api has a complete analogue in the still active Bromó. The enclosed bay, where vessels now anchor in 8 or 9 fathoms, is the bottom of this old crater, and, like that in the Zeugger Mountains, is composed of volcanic sand.

The radiating ridges on the outer side of Lontar represent the similar ridges on the sides of every volcano that is not building up its cone by frequent eruptions at its summit.

Lastly, the islands crossed by the second and third circles are so many cones on the flanks of this great volcano. True, those parts of some of them now above the sea are largely composed of coral rocks, like the west end of Lontar; but undoubtedly the polyps began to build their massive walls on the shores of islands of lava rock. They are doing this at the present moment. Every island in the group is now belted with a fringing reef, except at a few places where the shore is a perpendicular precipice, and the water of great depth. The western entrance through which we came to the roads is already quite closed up by a broad reef of living, growing coral.

A stroll through these beautiful groves, particularly at such a time, would be one of the richest pleasures a traveller could enjoy. All the nutmeg-trees were loaded down with fruit, which is chiefly gathered during this month, September, and again in June, though some is obtained from time to time throughout the year. It seemed surprising to me that the trees could be so loaded with fruit season after season; but the official reports show that, contrary to what has been true of the clove, there has been but little variation in the annual yield of the nutmeg for the last thirty years.

An average crop for the last twenty years has been about 580,000 Amsterdam lbs. of nuts, and 137,000 lbs. of mace. The whole number of trees on Lontar, Neira, and Ai, the only three islands where they are cultivated, is in round numbers 450,000, of which only two-thirds bear fruit. As the Governor remarked to me while I was wondering at the abundance of fruit on every side, it is indeed strange that the income from all this produce does not equal the expenses of the Government in this residency. For this cause the Government proposes to give up the monopoly. Beneath these trees is spread a carpet of green grass, while high above them the gigantic canari-trees stretch out their gnarled arms and shield the valuable trees entrusted to their care from the strong winds which strive in vain to make them cast off their precious fruit before it is ripe. Such good service do the tall canaris render in this way that they are planted everywhere, and when the island is seen from a distance their tops quite hide the nutmeg-trees from view. The roots of this tree are remarkable. They spring off from the trunk above the ground in great vertical sheets, which are frequently 4 feet broad where they leave the tree. These wind back and forth for some distance before they disappear beneath the earth, so that the lower part of one of these old trees might well be fancied to be a huge bundle of enormous snakes struggling to free themselves from the Titanic hands that held them firmly for ever. As we leisurely passed along the crest of Lontar, with a thick foliage over our heads that effectually shut out the direct rays of the sun, we occasionally caught distant glimpses of the blue sea breaking into white, sparkling surf on the black rocks, far, far beneath us.

Soon we came to the "Look-out," known here, however, by the Malay name Drang datang, "the People Come;" for it is a peculiarity of that language, instead of naming a place like this *subjectively*, as we do, that is, from one's own action, to name it *objectively*, that is from the result of that action. This is placed on the edge of the interior wall, and is about 600 feet above the sea. From this point most of the Bandas can be distinctly seen in a single glance; and this view is undoubtedly one of the finest among all the isles of the sea. Before us was Banda Neira, with Neira, its pretty village, and left of this the dark, smoking volcano, and beyond both, on the right, Banana Island, where the lepers live in solitary banishment, and still further seaward Ship Rock, with the swell chafing its abrupt sides, while on our right in the distance were Pulo Ai and Pulo Run. All these rose out of the blue sea, which was only ruffled here and there by light breezes, or flecked by shadows of white fleecy clouds that slowly crossed the sky.

The next day we again went over to Lontar, and walked westward along the narrow band of low land between the base of the old crater-wall and the bay, visiting a number of the residences of the "Perkenniers," or "Park-keepers." Each of these consists of a rectangular area of about a quarter of an acre, enclosed by a high wall. The side next the sea is formed by the proprietor's house, and on the other three sides of the great open yard are rows of store-houses, and the houses of the natives who work on that plantation. Near the place at which we landed was a small area where all the mace is *white*, when the fruit is ripe, instead of red. From the west end of the island we followed most of the distance round its outer shore, and then crossed to our landing.

The Governor having finished his inspecting duties, now proposed that we try to reach the top of Gunong Api. There was only one man—a native—who had ever been to the top, and "knew the way;" though, to judge from a distance, one part of the mountain was just as dangerous as every other. He was engaged as our guide, and some ten others, whose duty it was to carry our lunch and a good supply of water in long bamboos. Early the next morning the coolies were ready. From the west end of the village we crossed the narrow "Strait of the Sun" to the foot of the mountain. Some coolies who had preceded us had cleared a path up the steep declivity, but soon our only road was one of the many narrow tracks, where large masses of rocks and sand, which had loosened from some place high up the mountain, had shot down in a series of small land-slides, ploughing up the low shrubbery during its thundering descent. As long as we climbed among the shrubbery, although it was very difficult and tiring, it was not particularly dangerous until we came out on to the naked sides of the mountain; for this great elevation is not covered with vegetation more than two-thirds of the distance from its base to its summit. This lack of vegetation is caused by the frequent and wide land-slides, and by the great quantity of sulphur brought up to its top by sublimation, and washed down its sides by the heavy rains. Here we were obliged to crawl up on all fours among small, rough, black rocks of porous lava, and here all spread out until our party formed a horizontal line on the mountain side; so that when one man loosened the rocks, as every one was constantly doing, these might not come down and carry away some other man beneath him.

Our ascent now became slow and difficult; but we kept on, though sometimes the top of the mountain seemed as far off as the stars, until we were within about 300 feet of the summit. Here we came to a horizontal band of loose, angular fragments of lava from two to six inches in diameter. The mountain here rose at least at an angle of 35°, and to us, in either looking up or down, it seemed almost perpendicular. This band of stones was about 200 feet wide, and so loose that, when one was touched, frequently half-a-dozen would go rattling down the mountain. I had got about half-way across this dangerous place, when the stones on which my feet were placed *gave way!* This of course threw all my weight on my hands, when at once the rocks which I was holding with the clenched grasp of death also gave way, and I began to slide downward. The natives on either side of me now gave a loud shout, but not one dared to seize me, for fear that I should carry him down the mountain with me. Among these loose rocks a few ferns grew up and spread out their leaves to the sunlight. As I felt myself going down I chanced to roll toward my right side and notice one particularly, and quick as a flash of light the thought crossed my mind that my only hope was to seize *that fern.* This I did with my right hand, burying my elbow among the loose stones with the same motion; and that, thanks to a kind Providence, was sufficient to stop me, otherwise in less than a minute, probably in thirty or forty seconds, I should have been dashed to pieces on the rough rocks beneath me. The whole certainly occurred in a less space of time than it takes to read two lines on this page. I found myself safe, drew a long breath of relief, thanked God it was well with me, and, kicking away the loose stones with my heels, turned round, and kept on climbing. Above this band of loose stones the surface of the mountain was covered with a kind of crust formed chiefly of sulphur washed down by the rains. These rains had also formed many small grooves, and we made better progress here by crawling in these small gullies. At this moment the natives above us suddenly gave a loud cry, and I supposed of course that some one had lost his footing, and was going down to instant death. "Look out! Look out! Great rocks are coming!" and the next instant several small blocks and one great flake of lava two feet in diameter bounded by us with the speed of lightning. "Here is another!" It is coming straight for us, and it will take out one of our number to a certainty, I thought. I had stood up in the front of battle when shot and shell were flying and men were falling, but now to see the danger coming, and to feel that I was perfectly helpless, did, I must confess, make me quiver, and I crouched in the groove where I was climbing with the hope that it might bound over me; and that instant a fragment of lava about a foot square leaped up from the side of the mountain and flew directly over the head of a coolie a few feet on my right, clearing him by not more than five or six inches. I then supposed that the mountain was suffering another eruption, and that in a moment we should all be shaken down its almost vertical sides; but soon the rocks ceased coming down and we continued our ascent, and in a few moments stood on the rim of the crater.

The mystery in regard to the source of the falling rocks was now solved. One of our number had reached the summit before the rest of us, and with the aid of a native had been tumbling off rocks, for the sport of seeing them bound down the mountain, having stupidly forgotten that we all had to wind part-way round the mountain before we could get up on the edge of the summit, and not being able to lean over far enough to see that we were just beneath him.

The whole mountain is merely one great cone of small angular blocks of trachytic lava and black volcanic sand. The crater at its top is merely a conical cavity in this mass. The form of the summit is nearly elliptical, and is approximately given in the accompanying plan and section.

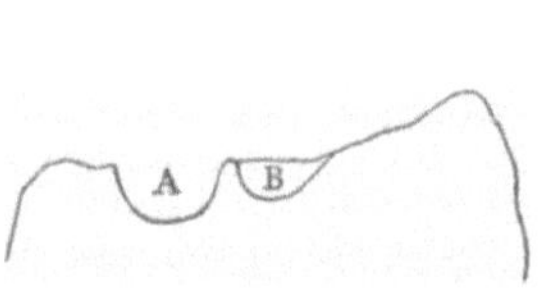
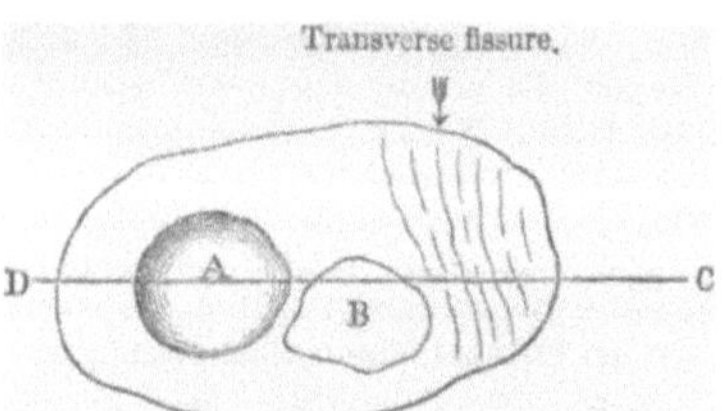

Vertical section along the line C D,
i.e., North-west and South-east.

Plan of the area on the summit of the Gunong Api
of Banda.
A, "the summit" crater. B, "old" crater.

The depth of the crater is about 80 feet. Its diameter we roughly estimated at from 100 to 150 yards. The area at the top is about 300 yards long, by 200 wide. This is composed of heaps of small lava-blocks, which are whitened on the exterior, and in many places quite encrusted with sulphur. Through these heaps of stones steam and sulphurous acid gas are continually rising, and we soon hurried round to the windward side to escape their suffocating fumes. In a number of these places we were glad to run, to prevent the shoes from being scorched on our feet by the hot rocks.

On the western side of the crater the rim is largely composed of sand, and in one place rises 120 feet higher than on the opposite eastern side. The top, therefore, partly opens out toward the east, and from some of the higher parts of Lontar one can see most of the area on the summit of this truncated cone. In this western part were many fissures, out of which rose sheets and jets of gas. When we had come to the highest point we looked over the north-west side down into the great crater, now active, one-fourth of the distance from the summit down to the sea. Dense volumes of steam and other gases were rolling up, and only now and then could we distinguish the edges of the deep, yawning abyss beneath us. Here we rested and lunched, enjoying meanwhile a magnificent view over the whole of the Banda group, when the suffocating gases were not blown into our faces. Again we continued round the northern side, and came down into an old crater, where we found a large rock with the word 'Etna,' the name of a Dutch warship, cut on one of its sides; and our Captain spent some time carving 'Telegraph,' the name of our yacht, beneath it. Great quantities of sulphur were seen here, more, the Governor said, than he had seen on any mountain in Java; for the great abundance of sulphur they yield is one of the chief characteristics of the volcanoes in this archipelago.

It was now time to descend. We called our guide, but he did not know where we ought to go, everything appeared so different when we looked down, from what it did when we looked upward. I chose a place where the vegetation was nearest the top, and asked him if I could go down there, to which of course he answered Yes, as most people do when they do not know what to say, and must give some reply. I had brought up with me a long stick or kind of alpen-stock, curved at one end, and with this I reached down and broke places for my heels in the crust that covered the sand and small stones. For hundreds of feet beneath me the descent seemed perpendicular, but I slowly worked my way downward for more than a hundred feet, and had begun to congratulate myself on the good progress I was making—soon, I thought, I shall be down *there*, where I can lay hold of that bush and feel that the worst is past—when suddenly I was startled by a shout from my companions who were a short distance on my left. "Stop! Don't go a step further, but climb up just as you went down." I now looked round for the first time, and found to my surprise and alarm that I was on a tongue of land between two deep long holes or fissures, where great land-slides had recently occurred. I had kept my attention so fixed on the bush before me that I had never thought of looking to the right or left, generally a good rule in such perilous places.

To go on was simply impossible, so I turned round, climbed up again and passed round the head of one of these frightful holes. If at any time the crust had been weak and had broken beneath my heels, no earthly power could have saved me from instant death. As I broke place after place for my feet with the staff, I thought of Professor Tyndall's dangerous ascent and descent of Monte Rosa.

At last I joined my companions, who had found the way we had come up; and, after some slips and sprains and considerable bruising, we all reached the bottom and were glad to be off the volcano, and reaching Banda Neira, feel ourselves on *terra firma* once more.

For a few days I could scarcely walk or use my arms; but that lameness soon passed away—not so with the impressions made on my mind by the perils I had so narrowly escaped, and even now, when suddenly aroused from sleep, for a moment the past becomes the present, and I am once more on the tongue of land with a deep gulf on either hand, or I am saving myself again by grasping *that fern*.

The first European who reached the summit, so far as I am aware, was Professor Reinwardt in 1821; the second was M. S. Müller in 1828, and from that time till the 13th of September, 1865, when we ascended it, only one party had attempted this difficult undertaking, and that party was from the steamer *Etna*, whose name we had found on a large rock in the old crater.

The height of this volcano we found to be 707·5 mètres, 2321 feet. Its spreading base occupies less space, 2 miles square. In size, therefore, it is insignificant compared to the gigantic mountains on Lombok, Java, and Sumatra; but when we consider the great amount of suffering, and the immense destruction of property that have been caused by its repeated eruptions, it becomes one of the most important volcanos in the archipelago.

From Valentyn and later writers we learn that eruptions have occurred in the following years :—1586, 1598, 1609, 1615, 1632, 1690, 1696, 1712, 1765, 1775, 1778, 1820, and 1824.

That of 1615 occurred in March, just as the Governor-General, Gerard Reynst, arrived from Java with a large fleet to complete the war of extermination that the Dutch had been waging with the aborigines for nearly twenty years. For some time previous to 1820, many people lived on the lower flanks of Gunong Api, and had succeeded in forming large groves, or, as the Dutch prefer to name them, "parks" of nutmeg-trees. On the 11th of June of that year, just before 12 o'clock, in an instant without the slightest warning, an eruption began which was so violent that all the people at once fled to the shore and crossed in boats to Banda Neira. Out of the summit rose perpendicularly up a great mass of ashes, sand, and stones, heated until they gave out light like living coals. The latter hailed down on every side, and as the accounts say, "set fire to the woods and soon changed the whole mountain into one great cone of flame." This happened unfortunately during the western monsoon, and so great a quantity of sand and ashes were brought over to Banda Neira, that the branches of the nutmeg-trees were loaded down until they broke beneath its weight, and all the parks on the island were totally destroyed. Even the water became undrinkable from the light ashes that filled the air and settled in every crevice. This eruption continued incessantly for *thirteen* days, and did not wholly cease at the end of six weeks.

During this convulsion the mountain was apparently split through in a N.N.W. and S.S.E. direction. The large, active crater, which we saw beneath us on the north-west side of the mountain, from the spot where we lunched, was formed at that time, and another was reported higher up between the new crater and the older one on the top of the mountain. A stream of lava poured down the western side into a small bay and built up a tongue of land 180 feet long. This fluid rock heated the sea within a radius of more than half a mile, and nearer the shore eggs were cooked in it. This lava stream is the more remarkable, because it is a great characteristic of the volcanos throughout the archipelago, that, instead of pouring out fluid rock, they only eject hot stones, sand, and ashes, or mud—that is, water mingled with sand and ashes,—such materials as are thrown up in those volcanos where the eruptive force is known to have attained its maximum and to be becoming weaker and weaker.

On the 22nd of April, 1824, while Governor-General Van der Capellen was entering the roads an eruption commenced, just as had happened 209 years before, on the arrival of Governor-General Reynst. A great quantity of ashes again rose upward from its summit, accompanied by clouds of "black smoke," in which lightnings darted, while such a heavy thundering rolled forth that it completely drowned the salute from the forts on Neira, in celebration of the Governor's arrival. This was followed by a second eruption, succeeded by a rest of fourteen days, when the volcano again seemed to have regained its strength, and once more ashes and glowing stones were hurled into the air, and fell in showers on all sides.

But the people of Banda have suffered quite as much from earthquakes as from eruptions, though the latter are usually attended by slight shocks. Heavy earthquakes, without eruptions, have occurred in 1629, 1683, 1710, 1767, 1816, and 1852.

Almost the first objects that attract one's attention on landing at the village are the ruins of those houses that were destroyed by the last of these fearful phenomena. Many houses had their walls levelled to the ground, but others, that were built with especial care, suffered little injury. These walls are made of coral-rock or bricks. They are two or three feet thick, and covered with layers of plaster. At short distances along their outer side, sloping buttresses are placed against them, so that most of the houses in Banda look more like fortifications than private residences. The first warning that any one had of the coming destruction was that the water suddenly began to stream out of the enclosed bay, and this continued until the war brig *Haai*, which was at anchor in 8 or 9 fathoms touched the *bottom*. Then came in a great wave from the ocean that rose at least to a height of 25 or 30 feet over the low western part of the village, which is separated from Gunong Api by the narrow Sun Strait. Praus lying near this shore were swept up against Fort Nassau, which was so completely engulfed, that it was stated to me that one of these native boats was carried over the walls of the fort, and remained inside when the sea had receded to its usual level. The part of the village over which the flood swept contained many small houses, and nearly every one of them was carried away.

This rapid outpouring of the water from this enclosed bay, or old crater, was probably caused either by the elevation of the bottom at that spot, or else by a sinking of the floor of the sea outside, so that this water was drained off into some depression that had suddenly been found. We have no reason to suppose that there was any great commotion in the sea outside, and certainly there was no high wave or bore, or it would also have risen on the shores of the neighbouring islands. There are three entrances or straits which lead from these roads out to the open sea. Two of these are wide, and one is narrow. When the whole top of the volcano, that is Neira, Gunong Api, Lontar, and the area they enclose, was raised for a moment, the water streamed out through these straits, causing very strong currents, but as the land again instantly sank to its former level, the water poured in, and the streams of the two wider straits meeting and uniting, rolled on towards the inner end of the narrow passage. Here they all met, and piling up spread out over the adjoining low village, causing great destruction of life. At the Resident's house, a few hundred yards east of Fort Nassau, the water only rose some ten or fifteen feet above high-water level, and farther east still less. The cause assigned above, therefore, though the principal one, may not have been sufficient in itself to have made the sea rise so high over the south-western part of Neira and the opposite part of Gunong Api, and I suspect that an additional cause was that the land there sank for a moment below its proper level.

Valentyn thus describes another less destructive earthquake wave :—" In the year 1629, there was a great earthquake, and half an hour afterward a flood, which was very great, and came in calm weather. The sea between Neira and Selan (on the western end of Lontar) rose up like a high mountain, and struck on the right side of Fort Nassau, where the water rose nine feet higher than in common spring-floods. Several houses near the sea were broken into pieces and washed away, and the ship *Brill* lying near by, was whirled round three times." In this case, the facts that the water did not pour out of the roads into the sea, and that the " flood " did not come until half an hour after the shock had occurred, indicated that this wave had its origin elsewhere, and there is no need of supposing, as in the case of 1852, that any part of the group was elevated or depressed. However, all these events are but as yesterday, when we look back into the past history of this ancient volcano, for if we can judge by analogy, taking the great crater this day existing among the Zeugger Mountains as our guide, we see in our mind's eye an immense volcanic mountain before us. From its high crater, during the lapse of time, poured out successive overflows of lava, which solidified into the trachyte of Lontar. Then came a period when stones and sand were thrown up, which has not wholly ceased at the present day. During one of its mighty throes, its western half disappeared beneath the sea, if the process of subsidence had gone on so far at that time.

Slowly it sinks, until it is at least 400 feet lower than at the present time, for we found a bank of coral rock on the western end of Lontar at that height. The outer islands are now wholly submerged. This period of subsidence is then followed by one of upheaval, but not till the slow-building coral-polyps have made great reefs, which now become white chalky cliffs, and after many years attain their present elevation above the sea. A tropical vegetation meanwhile by degrees spreads downwards, closely pursuing the retreating sea, and the islands are exactly what we see them to be at the present day.

In 1846, Mr. Jukes announced, as the result of his observations in the southern part of this archipelago, that the whole line of islands eastward from the Strait of Sunda, to and including Timur, had been elevated within a recent period. On the latter island my observations, I now find, are quite identical with his. From Kolff we learn that elevated reefs are found among the islands eastward from the northern end of Timur, and here they occur again in the Bandas. Eastward of this point, and south-east from Goram, are the Matabello Islands, which, according to Mr. Wallace, are only coral reefs raised 300 or 400 feet.

North-west from the Bandas we come to Amboina. The most recent coral rock which I observed on that island was about 500 feet above the present sea-level. At that elevation many valves of the gigantic *Tridacna gigas* were found considerably decomposed, but always in pairs, as if they had once been partially surrounded with soft coral rock, which, wasting away, had allowed the valves to fall apart. Governor Arriens, who had carefully studied these recent coral reefs, gave me the important fact that he had followed them upward to a height of 800 feet, but not higher, and that at that elevation they seemed to suddenly disappear. At Wahai, on the north coast of Ceram, I found many recent corals, about 50 feet above high-water level, and also at Kayéli Bay, on the north side of Burn, at an elevation of 100 feet. The natives here assured me that the same kind of "white stone," coral rocks, was found among the hills; and I have no doubt that it will be found in the mountainous parts of all the other Moluccas, as high up as Governor Arriens has already observed it at Amboina. A member of the Commission sent by the Dutch Government to examine the coasts of New Guinea, informed me that at the back of Dorey, on the north coast, at the mouth of Geelondk Bay, there are hills of very late formations, and that he found there a recent shell at a considerable elevation, 100 or 200 feet. From this point westward, as far at least as the northern end of Celebes, all the islands are probably rising.

Thus we find over all this wide area a repetition of the subsidence followed by an upheaval already noticed on Banda. Indeed, there is every indication that all the eastern part, if not the whole, of the archipelago is now rising, and thus we have before us the grand spectacle of a great continent forming itself at the present time.

"RUMPHIUS"

Biolog ternama di pulau Ambon (1627 – 1702)

Nama "Rumphius" harum di kalangan orang biolog / botanis dan di kalangan ilmuwan di Indonesia.

Georg Eberhard Rumpf (alias Georg Everhardus Rumphius) adalah seorang berbangsa Jerman, yang lahir pada tahun 1627 di desa Wölfersheim, wilayah Hessen, negeri Jerman. Ayahnya, August Rumpf, adalah seorang insinyur dan kontraktor, sedangkan ibunya, Elisabeth Keller, adalah seorang keturunan Belanda (ibunya orang Belanda). Hal itu barangkali menyebabkan bahwa kemudian hari ternyata Rumphius berbahasa Belanda dengan lancar dan juga menulis karya-karyanya dengan memakai bahasa Belanda.

Sejak kecil ia menekuni pendidikan formal yang memadai dengan mengikuti sekolah *gymnasium*. Agamanya protestan-kalvinis; agama itu dihayatinya dengan sangat serius.

Dalam tahun 1645, *waktu berumur 18 tahun, ia menjadi korban "human trafficking": orang membujuk dia menjadi tentara untuk mengusir orang Turki dari P. Kreta. Ternyata ia ditipu. Melarikan diri ke "West-Indische Compagnie" (sebuah* perusahaan Belanda yang sejenis dengan VOC, tetapi berfokus pada Amerika, yang

1

IV: Entries in the 1875 Encyclopaedia Britannica and 1888 Pierer's Konversationslexicon

AMBOYNA, one of the Moluccas or Spice Islands, belonging to the Dutch, lying south-west of Ceram, in 3° 41′ S. lat. and 128° 10′ E. long. It is 32 miles in length, with an area of about 280 square miles, and is of very irregular figure, being almost divided into two. The south eastern and smaller portion (called Leitimor) is united to the northern (known as Hitoe) by a neck of land about a mile broad. The island is mountainous, but is for the most part fertile and well-watered. Large tracts are covered with rich tropical forests, which embrace a great variety of trees, although ordinary building timber is scarce. The climate is comparatively pleasant and healthy; the average temperature is 80° Fahr., rarely sinking below 72°. The rainfall, however, after the eastern monsoons, is very heavy, and the island is liable to violent hurricanes and earthquakes. Amboyna produces most of the common tropical fruits and vegetables, including the sago-palm, bread-fruit, cocoa-nut, sugar-cane, maize, coffee, pepper, and cotton. Cloves, however, form its chief product, and the only one that is of any real commercial importance. The Dutch have done much to foster the cultivation of this article in the island, and at one time prohibited the rearing of the clove-tree in all the other islands subject to their rule, in order to secure the monopoly to Amboyna. Each tree yields annually from 2 to 5 ℔ of cloves, and sometimes even more; while the total annual quantity produced probably averages about 500,000 ℔. The animal kingdom is poorly represented. Indigenous mammals are feeble in species as well as few in number; birds are more abundant, but of no greater variety. The entomology of the island is, however, very rich, particularly among the *Lepidoptera.* The aborigines of Amboyna are a race called Horaforas, but Malays constitute the main body of the population; there are also Chinese, Dutch, and a few Portuguese. The Malays in most points resemble those of Java. They are naturally lazy and effeminate, but when properly trained make good soldiers. The inhabitants are mostly Christians or Mahometans. Amboyna is the chief island of the Dutch residence of the Moluccas, which comprises, in addition, the islands of Boeroe, Amblauw, Ceram, Manipa, Kilang, Bonoe, Haroekoe, Honimoa or Saparoa, Noesa-laut, and Hila. The Portuguese were the first European nation to visit Amboyna (1512). They established a factory there in 1521, but did not obtain peaceable possession of it till 1580, and were dispossessed by the Dutch in 1605 About the year 1615 the British formed a settlement in the island, at Cambello, which they retained until 1623, when it was destroyed by the Dutch, and frightful tortures inflicted on the unfortunate persons connected with it. In 1654, after many fruitless negotiations, Cromwell compelled the United Provinces to give the sum of £300,000, together with a small island, as compensation to the descendants of those who suffered in the "Amboyna massacre." In 1796 the British, under Admiral Rainier, captured Amboyna, but restored it to the Dutch at the peace of Amiens in 1802. It was recaptured by the British in 1810, but once more restored to the Dutch in 1814. Population, about 50,000. See MOLUCCAS.

Amboïnen Inselgruppe im Ind. Ozean, den mittleren Teil der Molukken bildend. Die Insel **Amboina** umfaßt 530 qkm, 58 000 Ew., meist Christen. Gesundes Klima, reichl. Bewässerung, üppige Vegetation (große Wälder), Heimat der Gewürznelken u. des Amboinaholzes. Die gleichnam. Hauptstadt (16 000 Ew.) ist Sitz der niederländ. Residentschaft der Molukken (der Resident wohnt in Batu-Gadjah), hat einen treffl. Hafen (seit 1854 Freihafen). Ceram (Sirang), größte Insel der Gruppe, 18 060 qkm, ist schwach bevölkert. In ihrem wenig erforschten, gebirgigen Innern hausen die wilden Alfuren, die als die Urbewohner der Molukken gelten. Buru hat einen großen See im Innern. Außer diesen verschiedene kleinere Inseln. Die A. wurden 1564 von den Portugiesen besetzt, die sie 1607 an die Holländer verloren. Gleichzeitig suchte die Engl.-ostind. Kompanie sich dort festzusetzen, was zu langwierigen Kämpfen Anlaß gab. 1796 kam A. in brit. Besitz, im Frieden v. Amiens 1801 an die Holländer; 1810—1814 waren abermals die Engländer Herren der Insel; durch den Pariser Vertrag von 1814 wieder die Holländer.

[Amboinas. Archipelago in the Indian Ocean, forming the central part of the Moluccas. The island of **Amboina** has an area of 530 square km, 58,000 inhabitants, mostly Christians. Healthy climate, rich water resources, lush vegetation (large forests), home of the clove and Amboina wood. The capital town of the same name (16,000 inhabitants) is the seat of the Dutch Residency of the Amboinas (the Resident lives in Batu-Gadjah), has an excellent harbour (freeport since 1854). **Ceram** (Sirang) largest island of the group, 18060 square km, thinly populated. In its mountainous interior, which has been little explored, live the savage Alfurs, who are thought to be the original inhabitants of the Moluccas. **Buru** has a large lake in the interior. Apart from these, several smaller islands. In 1564 the Amboinas were occupied by the Portuguese, who lost them to the Dutch in 1607. At the same time, the English East India Company attempted to establish itself there, which led to long drawn-out hostilities. In 1796 the Amboina came into the possession of the British, returning to the Dutch with the Peace of Amiens in 1801. 1810-1814 the British were once more masters of the islands; the Treaty of Paris, 1814, returned them to the Dutch.]

V: Entry in 1889 Pierer's Konversationslexikon, Vl. 2, p. 378

Banda 1) (Banda Islands) A Dutch Island group, East Indies, southern group of the Moluccas, 44 sq km, volcanic with frequent earthquakes, steep, mountainous, previously unhealthy, now a sanatorium; 6 small and 4 large islands: the biggest (Lontor, 16 km long, 3.5 km wide) with Fort Hollandia; Neira (7.4 km long, 3.7 km wide) with the capital and freeport Banda Neira and the active volcano Gunung Api (530 m), often with fearsome eruptions. Main product: the nutmeg tree, for a long time restricted to the Bandas by the Dutch. About 6,000 inhabitants, Malays and Papuans and people of mixed race between the two. The Bandas are part of the Dutch Residency of Amboina; discovered in 1512 by the Portuguese; occupied by the Dutch, seized from the English in 1796 and 1810 but returned in 1801 and 1814.

26. Bibliography

Alwi, Des, *Friends and Exiles. A Memoir of the Nutmeg Islands and the Indonesian National Movement*, 2008

Bokemeyer, Heinrich, *Die Molukken: Geschichte und quellenmäßige Darstellung der Eroberung und Verwaltung der ostindischen Gewürzinseln durch die Niederländer*, Leipzig 1888

Buijze, W., *Georg Everhard Rumphius*, Hidupnya dan Tugu, Ambon

Burnet, Ian, *Spice Islands*, 2011

Burnet, Ian, *East Indies, The 200 Year Struggle Between the Portuguese Crown, the Dutch East India Company and the English East India Company for Supremacy in the Eastern Seas*, 2013

Crab, Petrus van der, *De Moluksche Eilanden*, 1861

Dash, Mike, *Batavia's Graveyard*, 2002

Day, Clive, *The Dutch in Java*, 1904

Deventer, M.L. van, *Geschiedenis der Nederlandsers op Java*, 1886

Drake-Brockman, Henrietta, *The Reports of Francisco Pelsaert*, 1956

Drake-Brockman, Henrietta, *The Wicked and the Fair*, 1957

Drake-Brockman, Henrietta, *Voyage to Disaster*, 1963

Drake-Brockmann, Henrietta, *The Report of Fransisco Pelsaert, Early Days: Journal and Proceedings*, WA Historical Society, Perth, 1956

Edwards, Hugh, *Islands of Angry Ghosts*, 1996

Elsner, Dr. Fritz, *Die Praxis des Chemikers*, 1895

Ennen, Leonard, *Geschichte der Stadt Köln*, 1863

Forrest, John, *Report on a Visit to the Abrolhos Islands*, Western Australian State Archives, 1879

Frik, Christoff, *Ost-Indianische Reisebeschreibung, Java, Ceylon, Bali*, 1692

Geerken, Horst H., *Der Ruf des Geckos*, 2009

Geerken, Horst H., *Hitlers Griff nach Asien 1*, 2015

Geerken, Horst H., *Hitlers Griff nach Asien 2*, 2015

Gelder, Roelof van, *Het Oost-Indisch Aventuur. Duitsers in dienst van de VOC (1600-1800)*, 1997

Gordon, Maurice Bear, *Naval and Maritime Medicine during the American Revolution*, 1978

Gründer, Horst, *Geschichte der deutschen Kolonien*, 2004

Haeckel, Ernst, *Aus Insulinde – Malayische Reisebriefe*, 1901

Hake, Claire, *Mein geteiltes Herz*, 2011

Hanna, Dr. Willard A., *Banda. A Journey through Indonesia's fabled Islands of Fire and Spice*, 1997

Hanna, Dr. Willard A., *Indonesia Banda: Colonialism and its after-math in the Nutmeg Islands*, Philadelphia: Institute for the Study of Human Issues, 1978

Hantzsch, Viktor, *Wurffbain, Johann Siegmund*, Allgemeine Deutsche Biographie 44, 1898

Heuken SJ, Adolf, *... dahin, wo der Pfeffer wächst. Vierhundert Jahre Deutsche auf den Inseln Indonesiens*, 2010

The Jakarta Post, 13. November 2010, *Des Alwi, the boy from Banda*

Kirsch, Peter, *Die Reise nach Batavia*, 1994

L'Honoré, S.P., *Reisebeschreibungen von deutschen Beamten und Kriegsleuten im Dienst der Niederländischen West- und Ost-Indischen Kompanien 1602-1797*, 1930

Loth, Vincent C., *Pioneers and perkeniers: The Banda Islands in the 17th century*, 1995

Maughan, W. Somerset, *Der schmale Winkel*, 1982, 2007

Merwin, W.S., *The blind Seer of Ambon*, 2005

Milton, Giles, *Muskatnuß und Musketen*, 2002

Milton, Giles, *Nathaniel's Nutmeg*, 1999

Olivier, Johannes, *Reizen in dem Molukkschen Archipel naar Makassar in 1824*, 1827, 1834

Otheniel, Hermes, *Simeon Seth*, 2013

Oxley, Thomas, *Banda Nutmeg Plantations*, Journal: Indonesian Archipel, 1856

Oxley, Thomas, *Statistic of Nutmeg*, 1856

Oxley, Thomas, *The Banda Nutmeg Plantations*, 1856

Reid, Anthony, *Introduction: Slavery and bondage in Southeast Asian history in slavery, bondage and dependency in Southeast Asia*, Univerity of Queensland Press, 1983

Richthofen, Ferdinand von, *Über den Seeverkehr nach und von China im Altertum und Mittelalter*, 1876

Rose, H.-D., *Die Arbeit deutscher Ärzte im Dienste der Niederländisch-Ostindischen Kompagnie (1602–1797), dargestellt am Beispiel des Ulmer Wundarztes Christoph Frick*, 1982

Rumphius, Georg Eberhard, *Herbar amboinense*, 1741

Rumphius, Georgius Everhardus, *De Ambonse Histoire*, 2 volumes, 1910

Seemann. Dr. Heinrich, *Von Goethe bis Emil Nolde*, 1996

Siebert, Rüdiger, *Tod auf Mactan*, 1982

Siebert, Rüdiger, *Deutsche Spuren in Indonesien*, 2002

Sjahrir, Sutan, *Out of Exile*, 1949

Tantri, K'tut, *Aufruhr im Paradies*, 1961

Toussaint-Samat, Maguelonne, *A History of Food*, 2009

Turner, Jack, *Spice*, 2001

Valentijn, Francois, *Beschrijv. van Boomen, Planten etc. en Zaaken van Amboina in Oud en Nieuw Ost-Ind.*, 1726

Vincent, William, *Commerce and navigation of the Ancients in the Indian Ocean*, 1805

Vogel, Johann Wilhelm, *Beschreibung von Java und Sumatra 1678-1687*, 1704

Warburg, Dr. O., *Die Muskatnuss: Ihre Geschichte, Botanik, Kultur, Handel und Verwertung, sowie ihre Verfälschungen und Surrogate. Zugleich ein Beitrag zur Kulturgeschichte der Banda Inseln*, Leipzig 1897

Weil, Andrew T., *The use of nutmeg as a psychotropic agent*. UNOCD Unites Nations Office of Drugs and Crime Bulletin, 1.1.1966

Weiss, E. A., *Spice Crops*, 2002

Winn, Phillip, *Slavery and cultural creativity in the Banda Islands*, Journal of Southeast Asian Studies, 42(3), © The National University of Singapore, 2010 (Online-Version: http://www.academia.edu/368084/Slavery_and_cultural_creativity_in_the_Banda_Islands)

Wurffbain, Johann Sigmund, *14jährige Reisebeschreibung, Oostindian Kriegs- und Oberkaufmanndienst*, 1646 (Online Version: https://www.deutsche-biographie.de/pnd124881947.html#adbcontent)

27. Archives Consulted

ANRI, Arsip Nasional Republik Indonesia, Jakarta (National Archives of Indonesia)
Archiv of Abba Rizal Bahalwan, Banda Neira, Banda Islands
Artis Bibliothek, Amsterdam
British Library, London (Nationalbibliothek des Vereinigten Königreichs)
Deutsches Historisches Museum, Berlin
Deutsches Marinemuseum, Wilhelmshafen
Geraldton Museum, Western Australia
Koninklijke Bibliotheek, The Hague
Museum Siwalima, Ambon, Indonesia
Nationaal Archif, The Hague
The National Archives, Kew, Richmond, Surrey
National Maritime Museum, Sydney, Australia
National Museum of the Royal Navy, Portsmouth
PNRI, Perpustakaan National Republik Indonesia (National Library), Jakarta
Rumah Budaya Banda Neira, the Banda Neira Museum
Shipwrecks Museum in Fremantle, Western Australia
Tropenmuseum, Amsterdam
Western Australian Museum, Perth

28. Index of Names

Aaron of Alexandria 22
Abba, *see* Bahalwan, Rizal Abba
Abdul Rahman, Tengku 205
Abreu, Antonio de 53
Acosta, Christobal 24
Albius, Edmond 150
Albuquerque, Alfonso de 53, 387
Alexander VI 44
Alfonso V 4
Alwi, Des 5, 190, 197, 200-204, 206, 208, 248, 252, 259, 262, 270-272, 277, 337, 349
Alwi, Lili 201
Alwi, Mimi 201
Alwi, Mira 271
Alwi, Ramon 271
Alwi, Tanya 271
Arnold, Christoph 120, 125f.
Assagaff, Said 135
Ayu, Ibu 254
Azevedo, Miranda de 55, 70
Baadilla, Ali 201
Baadilla, family 18, 200f.
Baadilla, Said 200, 271
Bahalwan, Rizal Abba 2, 7, 10, 13, 240-242, 246f., 249-256, 265, 281, 298, 332, 388
Ball, George 83
Barewitz, Ernst Christoph 217
Barros, de 32
Bastiansz, Gysbert 169, 182
Bastiansz, Judith 169, 179
Beekman, E. M. 357
Beresford, Bruce 189
Bergel, Hendrik van 79
Berveling, M. L. 331

Bickmore, Albert S. 219, 389
Boeckholtz, Francois van 291
Böhm, Cornelius J., MSC 7, 338, 347f., 359-361
Both, Pieter 122, 164
Bräker, Annette 229
Brandes, Dr. 102
Brassavola, Antonius Musa 32
Brito, de, Captain 55
Broecke, Pieter van den 18, 233f., 245, 262f., 270
Broecke, Pongky van den 262f.
Brouwere, Henderik 164
Buchheim, Martin von 47
Buijze, W. 348, 357f., 360
Burckhardt, Christian 125
Burmannus, Joannes 357
Bush, George W. 180, 327
Cabral, Pedro Alvares 50
Camphuys, Johannes 357
Camões, Luis Vaz de 60
Capellen, Godert van der 163, 224, 358
Chancellor, Richard 63
Charles I, King of England 129
Charles V 56, 60
Claes, Wybrecht 179
Cocks, Richard 91
Coen, Jan Pieterszoon 5, 79, 87-90, 92-94, 97-103, 107, 109-111, 156, 167, 178, 182, 291, 296, 323-325, 335f.
Cole, Christopher 156, 159-162, 197, 284
Colthurst, Kapitän 76f.
Columbus, Christopher 9, 43, 56, 67

29. Subject Index
(The names of ships are written in Italics)

414

Other books by the same author in German

Horst H. Geerken
Der Ruf des Geckos. 18 erlebnisreiche Jahre in Indonesien
436 Pages, Paperback, Norderstedt 2009, € 24,90

Horst H. Geerken
Missbrauchte Kindheit. Geboren im Jahr von Hitlers Machtergreifung
240 Pages, Norderstedt 2011, € 16,90

Horst H. Geerken
Hitlers Griff nach Asien. Eine Dokumentation, Band 1
380 Pages, Paperback, Norderstedt 2015, € 27,95

Horst H. Geerken
Hitlers Griff nach Asien. Eine Dokumentation, Band 2
432 Pages, Paperback, Norderstedt 2015, € 27,95

Horst H. Geerken
Hitlers Griff nach Asien. Eine Dokumentation, Band 3
436 Pages, Paperback, Norderstedt 2020, € 27,95

Horst H. Geerken
Hitlers Griff nach Asien. Eine Dokumentation, Band 4
348 Pages, Paperback, Norderstedt 2020, € 30,99

Horst H. Geerken
Erinnerung an Annette. Der letzte Weg einer außergewöhnlichen und tapferen Frau
148 Pages, Paperback, Norderstedt 2015, € 14,99

Horst H. Geerken
Annettes letzte Reise. Die ungewöhnliche Reise einer außergewöhnlichen Frau
80 Pages, Paperback, Norderstedt 2016, € 9,95

Horst H. Geerken
Die Ahnen. Eine Familiengeschichte in Wort und Bild. Geerken/Gerken – Thiel – Mannhardt – Schenk
516 Pages, Hardcover, Norderstedt 2018, € 98,99

Horst H. Geerken
Eine Balinesin in Deutschland und ein Deutscher auf Bali
183 Pages, Paperback, Norderstedt 2019, € 17,99

Horst H. Geerken
Das Gold der Bandas: Die Geschichte der Muskatnuss.
436 Pages, Paperback, Norderstedt 2020, € 29,90

Annette Bräker, Horst H. Geerken
Indonesien Gestern und Heute. Reiseberichte der anderen Art
316 Pages, Paperback, Norderstedt 2016, € 19,95

Annette Bräker, Horst H. Geerken
Der Karakorum-Highway und das Hunzatal, 1998: Geschichte, Kultur und Erlebnisse
244 Pages, Paperback, Norderstedt 2016, € 19,95

Piet Jonasson (Hrsg. Horst H. Geerken)
Die Tote am Blutturm. Schatten über dem Schützenfest
192 Pages, Paperback, Norderstedt 2010, € 11,90

Piet Jonasson (Hrsg. Horst H. Geerken)
Glaube? Sitte? Heimat? Pecunia non olet!
256 Pages, Paperback, Norderstedt 2013, € 14,95

Other books by the same author in English

Horst H. Geerken
A Gecko for Luck. 18 years in Indonesia
392 Pages, Paperback, Norderstedt 2010, € 24,95

Horst H. Geerken
A Magic Gecko. CIA's Role Behind the Fall of Soekarno
360 Pages, Paperback, Jakarta 2011, ISBN 978-979-709-554-3, IRP 150.000,00

Horst H. Geerken
Hitler's Asian Adventure
572 Pages, Paperback, Norderstedt 2015, € 27,95

Horst H. Geerken
My Ancestors. A Family History in Words and Pictures. Geerken/Gerken – Thiel – Mannhardt – Schenk
508 Pages, Paperback, Norderstedt 2020, € 75,99;
Hardcover: € 92,99

Annette Bräker, Horst H Geerken
The Karakoram Highway and the Hunza Valley, 1998: History, Culture, Experiences
232 Pages, Paperback, Norderstedt 2017, € 19,95

Annette Bräker, Horst H. Geerken
Indonesia Then and Now. A Different Kind of Travel Book
300 Pages, Paperback, Norderstedt 2018, € 19,95

Other Books by the same author in Bahasa Indonesia

Horst H. Geerken
A Magic Gecko. Peran CIA di Balik Jatuhnya Soekarno
498 Pages, Paperback, Jakarta 2011, ISBN 978-979-709-555-0, IRP 85 000,00

Horst H. Geerken
Jejak Hitler di Indonesia
402 Pages, Paperback, Jakarta 2017, ISBN 978-602-412-175-4, IRP 119 000,00

Horst H. Geerken
Indonesia Then and Now. A Different Kind of Travel Book
A version in Bahasa Indonesia is in progress, expected release date: 2021

All these books in German and English can be bought from the publisher under www.bod.de/buchshop/catalogsearch/result/?q=Horst+H.+Geerken, at book-shops or from more than 1000 online shops like www.amazon.de

Books published in Indonesien can only be bought there in all GRAMEDIA bookshops or at the publisher, www.buku.kompas.com or www.gramedia.com

A BukitCinta Book

Deksel van doofpot met Dodenschip
(The Death Ship Cover Up)
Report on the three-part TV documentary *De Ondergang van de Van Imhoff* [The Sinking of the Van Imhoff], filmed with my collaboration and making use of Chapters 5 and 16 of my book *Hitlers Griff nach Asien* [Hitler's Asian Adventure], Volume 1.

   De Telegraaf, Amsterdam, 2nd of December 2017

The documentary was broadcast on the Dutch television NPO 2 on the 10th, 17th and 24th of December 2017, attracting an audience of about 500 000 for each episode.

   A number of excerpts from this documentary are available on www.youtube.com.

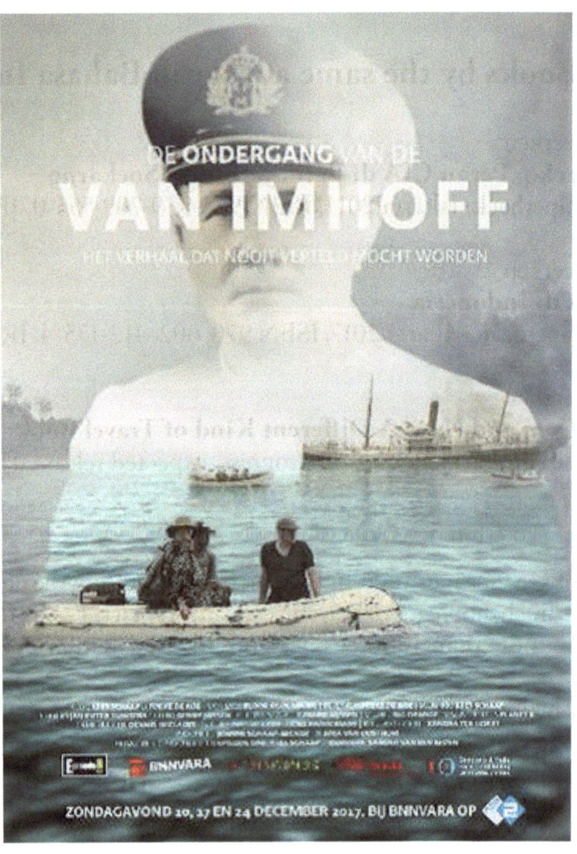